D1162726

Organizational Culture

We dedicate this monograph to our colleagues as a contribution to the ongoing efforts of organizational scholars:

- to further the spirit of diversity in the work that is done in our field;

- to provide bridges among theoretical, empirical, and historical perspectives in our field;

- to establish links between and among generations of organizational scientists; and

- to focus work grounded in fields and disciplines different than those of traditional organizational science on phenomena of mutual interest and concern.

Organizational Culture

Peter J. Frost
Larry F. Moore
Meryl Reis Louis
Craig C. Lundberg
Joanne Martin

SAGE PUBLICATIONS
Beverly Hills   London   New Delhi

For information address:

SAGE Publications, Inc.
275 South Beverly Drive
Beverly Hills, California 90212

SAGE Publications India Pvt. Ltd.
M-32 Market
Greater Kailash I
New Delhi 110 048 India

SAGE Publications Ltd
28 Banner Street
London EC1Y 8QE
England

Printed in the United States of America

Library of Congress Cataloging in Publication Data

Main entry under title:

Organizational culture.

   Bibliography: p.
   1. Organizational behavior--Addresses, essays, lectures.
2. Corporate culture--Addresses, essays, lectures.
3. Organizational change--Addresses, essays, lectures.
4. Quality of work life--Addresses, essays, lectures.
I. Frost, Peter J.
HD58.7.0736 1985   302.3'5   85-2172
ISBN 0-8039-2459-3
ISBN 0-8039-2460-7 (pbk.)

FIRST PRINTING

Contents

Prologue

Every time I go to Canada, I am struck by how well the cities work, and how young and vital even the old ones seem. Toronto, Montreal, and Quebec are all exciting places to visit. Then the Culture Conference brought me to Vancouver in April for the first time in twenty years. And, once again, I was taken by surprise by another clean, livable, civilized, varied, and delightful Canadian city that seemed alive, energetic, and still possessed of much potential. Maybe it was the country itself, or the wide-open western vitality of Vancouver, or the cool, promising sunshine and early flowers of spring, or the lively energy of the University of British Columbia campus, but something in the context of the conference felt young and energetic and beautiful to me.

We began by gathering around a huge wood sculpture of the "birth of the raven" in the Anthropology Museum. The raven was a kind of logo for the conference, and the old myths about its birth somehow anchored the potential all about us to the museum's past. The place was stunning, a building of great scale in which tall old totem poles could rise to their giddy heights without fear of roofs. The English sense of history and form seemed to rest lightly upon British Columbia, and the mix of many peoples was there to see on campus. Birth, and youth, and spring; respectful acknowledgment of the past; the potential suggested by the present; and the almost shy understatement of polite and welcoming faculty—all provided happy circumstance for the conference.

Of course, the conference was largely peopled by men and women younger than I. I was taken by their talent, edginess, ambition, charm, brashness, and gifts. I felt like a sour old fud suggesting that the idea of "culture" was too often being used as a way to repackage old stuff as if it were new. I was informed that, unlike soaps with NEW printed on their boxes, culture can suggest a deeper grasp of old understandings as well as a developing grasp of deeper patterns below the levels of prior familiarity. If the label "culture" helps encourage such new depths, get off knocking it. So I thought, what the hell, let's ride the hopefulness.

And what an up-and-down ride it was! At the end, Karl Weick said in effect, "Let's give culture a chance and see what comes of it," which, of course, is what most of us did during the conference, and I for one am glad I did. Some of the reasons are to be found in what follows in this volume.

Other reasons are related to my way of experiencing conferences. I hold them as picture frames in which a small number of people come more clearly into view. And I really enjoyed getting to know better more of the "young" in the field of organizational behavior. They are an engaging lot, perhaps as neurotic as their elders, but more forceful and instrumental earlier in their careers. They seem much more realistic and less romantic about their *jobs* and *occupation* than we were. We seemed more concerned with our *vocation* and *mission* from the late 50s to the early 70s. I still think any professional worth his or her salt can identify with all four of the words italicized here, but it is probably this generation's task to reach for the larger meanings, while we who preceded them frequently had to confront the more concrete realities in order to grow.

Peter Frost, Larry Moore, and their UBC cohorts did a truly outstanding piece of work setting up and pulling off this conference, and the present volume clearly results from more of the same care and effort. I thank them for everything, but especially for renewing in me an affection for springtimes. When I was a young professor, I made a collage once, all pink and yellow and white, with a vibrant green used to write the words "The green in me grows toward you." In Vancouver, I felt many others saying that in their own ways, and I came away refreshed. Perhaps a bit of that can still be found in what follows.

—Anthony G. Athos

Acknowledgments

This book could not have been prepared without the generous contributions of a great number of very dedicated and talented persons; it is truly a group effort. Members of the Research Group for the Study of Organizational Life (Merle Ace, Richard Barth, Peter Frost, Jill Graham, Tom Knight, David McPhillips, Vance Mitchell, Larry Moore, Craig Pinder, Ralph Stablein, Mark Thompson, Anil Verma, and Gordon [Skip] Walter) generated many of the initial ideas and plans that led to the Conference on Organizational Culture and the Meaning of Life in the Workplace, where most of the authors in this book made presentations. From the inception of this project Peter A. Lusztig, Dean of the Faculty of Commerce and Business Administration, University of British Columbia, provided his enthusiastic encouragement.

Financially, the project received support from several organizations, including the Social Sciences and Humanities Research Council of Canada, the Faculty of Commerce and Business Administration and the Alumni Association of the University of British Columbia, the School of Business Administration of the University of Southern California, the Industrial Relations Management Association, the Mark Anthony Group, Canadian Pacific Airlines, and McDonald's Restaurants of Canada Ltd.

Excellent administrative and word-processing assistance was provided by Rano Sihota, Lori Thomas and staff, Gail Robertson, Shari Altman, and Judi Wolch. Thea Vakil rendered special assistance in compiling references. The staff at Sage Publications supplied liaison, editorial assistance, and production services.

Finally, we are indebted to the authors who wrote the chapters contained herein.

1

AN ALLEGORICAL VIEW OF ORGANIZATIONAL CULTURE

Peter J. Frost
Larry F. Moore
University of British Columbia

Meryl Reis Louis
Boston University

Craig C. Lundberg
University of Southern California

Joanne Martin
Stanford University

Several spirit birds were flying together, returning from an extensive trip to investigate the cultures of human organizations. The birds had been flying for a long time and, as they were weary, they stopped to rest on a large rock. In the group were a raven, an owl, a wren, an eagle, a stork, a pelican, and a phoenix. In popular folklore, each of these birds is associated with distinctive qualities. The raven is a restless, raucous fellow who is creative and crafty, eager to deceive and play tricks in order to get his own way. To the owl have been attributed powers of introspection, deliberation, and wisdom—a creature more given to thinking than to action. Wrens, by contrast, flit from place to place, poking into crevices for what might be hidden there. While the wren is a fussy bird who concentrates on the bits and pieces of her immediate surroundings, the eagle glides along far above the surface, with a keen eye for perspective and the broad picture. Eagles can stay aloft longer and fly much farther than almost any other bird, but they can also dive from great heights in order to grasp in their talons any small object that interests them or whets their appetite. Of course, this speed and decisiveness sometimes results in the eagle missing some of the interesting and valuable material that is noticed only by those who stay longer on the ground. The stork, however, travels neither far nor often. He likes to develop his home, build his nest in one place, and preside over his territory. The pelican, who possesses a large pouch, is thought to be a sustainer of life. A nurturer, she sometimes pierces her own breast to feed her young. Finally, the phoenix is a miraculous bird fabled to rise in youthful freshness from its own ashes.

Though tired, the birds were excited as they perched there on the rock, and all were chattering at once. Each bird was attempting to describe the cultural experiences it had had during its travels, for each had found the cultural aspects of human organization particularly fascinating. The raven cocked his head at this rather useless cacophony and decided that somehow sense-making must occur—you can't have a conference if everyone talks at once. He picked up a large stick. The others, being somewhat wary of the unpredictable ways of their companion and afraid that he might hit them with his stick, immediately stopped talking.

The raven stepped forward and offered a ground rule: "We all have important things to say, and we can learn much from one another. We all have different perspectives and interests and talents that can be shared, but we cannot all talk at once. I have in my claw a stick. Let us agree to give this stick special power, so that when the stick is held by one of us, the others will listen. That way, we can all think about what is being said—and, eventually, as the stick is passed around, we will all be able to share our adventures." The raven handed the talking stick to his friend the owl, who began relating his experiences. Deep in thought and somewhat perplexed as usual, Owl raised the fundamental question of why organizational culture was attracting so much attention.

By way of answering his own question, Owl described three sets of problems that necessitate investigating organizations and their milieu from a cultural perspective. "In my travels," said Owl, "I paid rather close attention to a number of economic problems plaguing North America. Productivity has declined over the past several years, while economic models and assumptions, although increasingly sophisticated, often seem to provide varying conclusions and thus contrary advice. Increasingly, it appears that economic theories of the firm are naive and incomplete. The real cause of economic malaise seems to lie deep within the culture of the organization, and perhaps within the society itself. For example, I observed strong interest in attempting to understand the cultural variables operating in Japan that serve to make its organizations very competitive and highly productive—consider the Japanese automobile and electronics industries. Do cultural phenomena hold the key to better economic understanding?

"A second area of concern," continued Owl, "centers on a number of social forces that are increasingly being felt by organizations but that are not well understood. For example, there seems to be a growing tendency for people to insist on deriving more from work than simply a paycheck. Work can be viewed as a setting in which people can experience a sense of community. The search for community is widespread and a fundamental part of human experience. Thus the expectation that the workplace be designed to function as a community is a legitimate and important concern of organizational designers—one that traditional emphasis on the division of labor, as well as increased specialization and reliance on rules, has largely ignored.

"I noticed other shifts in values and social perspectives. More and more, the concept of success is being redefined. For many, success no longer means material success. Rather, success is interpreted in quality of life terms. Thus workers are less willing to trade off personal considerations for some vaguely specified organizational end. Middle managers are not as responsive when they are ordered to transfer to another location as they once might have been. It is also being recognized that workers bring outside issues to work with them. Personal concerns such as managing a dual-career family can impinge strongly on performance and satisfaction, so that narrow role definitions no longer capture current organizational demands. At the same time, quality of life expectations may have profound implications for understanding and managing facets of the organization's cultural domain. These include indicators of status such as the size and decor of offices, rituals and ceremonies such as promotion and retirement parties, signs of community such as dress codes, and so forth.

"My third observation," said Owl, "has to do with some problems and opportunities within the field of organizational behavior. There is widespread dissatisfaction with the knowledge scholars have gained about how organizations should be structured and designed, how managers should behave, and how organizations should be evaluated in terms of effectiveness. Research designs and methods commonly used in studies of organizations (based on questionnaire-survey techniques) have been largely inappropriate for the study of many of the variables that show promise in exploring deep meaning. Furthermore, the explanatory power of most of our correlational based designs is very low.

"Scholars have also been disappointed to note that organization theory developed in Western settings does not apply well to organizations interacting in different cultural settings. The point here is that organizations as open systems are influenced by and in turn influence their cultural milieu. What works in one cultural setting may not work in another—and we need to know why.

"On the positive side, organizational scholars are increasingly recognizing the limitations in the epistemological bases of traditional approaches to the study of organizations. They are becoming more aware of alternative ways of originating and examining knowledge about organizations. For example, they have begun to study social processes in addition to social structures, using qualitative methods of observation and analysis in addition to quantitative methods, and they are using inductive methods along with the more traditional deductive ones. Adopting a cultural perspective may lead to an important epistemological synthesis wherein a much richer set of organizational variables is studied using a deeper theoretical frame of reference and a broader range of acceptable methods of analysis.

"In my travels, I sensed a growing degree of willingness among scholars from an astonishing range of disciplines—from folklore to biology—to be tolerant of one another's points of view in attempting to understand organizational phenomena. Conferences are being held, proceedings are being published, newsletters are being circulated, cross-disciplinary teams of researchers are being formed. There is excitement, energy, and creativity in the intellectual atmosphere.

"Finally," said Owl, "there is some evidence that organizational practitioners are becoming more aware of the importance of understanding and enhancing the cultural life of an organization. One study of a group of high-performance companies in North America indicated that paying attention to organizational culture is an important ingredient in organizational success. This means that research and consulting opportunities in North American organizations may be much improved as managers seek to learn more about their organizations through a cultural perspective. More and better research may soon be possible."

The eagle, who had become restless, feeling the need to climb back into the heavens, grasped the stick from Owl's outstretched claw and talked energetically about her views on the matter. "I too found much ferment and excitement in the human organizations I observed during my flights," said Eagle. "I heard and saw an image that can best be expressed in the terms of organizational culture. It stood out above all the other images that appeared on the ground. But when I tried to hear and see more, no matter how hard I strained my ears and eyes, I found it impossible to discern any audible or visual patterns. There seemed to be a certain amount of chaos that swirled around the image of organizational culture that I had detected. It had ragged edges that seemed to have diverse threads woven through it (always interesting for those among us looking for new material with which to build or renew our nests).

"I was both frustrated and stimulated by all this," said Eagle, "and so I decided to swoop down in a few places to find out what was going on." Eagle had a way of speaking and gesturing that was quite dramatic; she was almost majestic in her movements, and she had clearly caught the other birds' attention with her commentary.

There was an air of expectancy among the birds as Eagle continued. "What I found," she said, "was a great deal of excitement among managers, academics, and consultants. Many had discovered that organizations have cultures . . . " ("*Rediscovered* cultures would be more accurate," said the phoenix under his breath.) Eagle noted the phoenix's movement, paused, and then continued: "and that an organization's culture has to do with shared assumptions, priorities, meanings, and values—with patterns of beliefs among people in organizations. Some people see such a culture as emerging to solve problems posed by situations that people encounter in organizational settings; others see a culture as the ways in which people cope with experience. Some talk of it as social "glue." Those who express a sensitivity to the idea of organizational culture say that what it does is sensitize people to the softer, less tangible, more subtle aspects of organizational life. Talking about organizational culture seems to mean talking about the importance for people of symbolism—of rituals, myths, stories, and legends—and about the interpretation of events, ideas, and experiences that are influenced and shaped by the groups within which they live. This approach draws people's attention to artifacts in organizations and the meanings attached to them, and to an awareness of history, of the past in organizations having a bearing on the present and the future in those organizations."

The other birds found themselves excited by this speech. "I like all this interest in meaning and interpretation," said Owl. He thought of how all this had to do with the observation of situations, identifying what was important to others in that situation, reflecting, and making wise pronouncements on the subject.

"We are creating some organizational culture of our own, with this great adventure of ours, with this talk and our use of this stick as a symbol of our process, aren't we?" observed Wren, proud of himself and his ability to note the detail of their situation and its connection to the discussion at hand.

"I'm delighted that there is some concern with the past, with history," said Phoenix. "Perhaps they will now be drawn to look at patterns and cycles of change and the fall and rise of organizations. It seems to me that knowing something about organizational culture would be useful in this regard."

Eagle continued, "I am intrigued with how organizational culture provides a context to talk about socializing all those people who join and move about in organizations. Helping people make their way in life is so important. Perhaps it will also give us a way to talk about the meaning of life as it takes place in organizations," she added, "although it may take a while for that idea to catch hold, since there is so much concern for performance, for results in organizations. People may not see that the myth of rationality and the shared emphasis on outcomes can blind people to the need to attend to processes that humanize organizations."

Ideas and reactions were beginning to flow in several directions, but no one was listening to anyone else, so Raven spoke up. "I'm pleased that this is proving so exciting for all of us, but we do need to press on. Let me remind you of our rule, that only the bird with the stick has the right to speak. Please continue, Eagle, if you have more to say. It seems to me you talked of chaos, ragged edges, and threads, but all you have told us so far suggests agreement, order, and harmony."

"That is correct," said Eagle. "There are many ideas about organizational culture that seem to be shared by those who call themselves 'organizational scientists.' However, even in this community there are important differences and even disagreements. For example, some see the term 'organizational culture' as a metaphor—organizations are like cultures—and they try to understand the attributes of culture that might be relevant to organizations in terms of a symbolic process. Others see organizational culture as a thing, an objective entity that can be examined in terms of variables (independent and dependent) and linked to other things such as performance, satisfaction, and organizational effectiveness. There is disagreement as to where the organizational culture originates, whether the unconscious mind plays a role, whether there is a single organizational culture or many cultures, whether an organization's culture or cultures can be managed, whether organizations have cultures or are places to study cultures, whether and how organizational cultures can be studied and whether they should be studied at all.

"As I swooped into different places where I heard or saw activity concerned with organizational culture, I noticed that not everyone there was an organizational scientist. In fact, there really is only a small segment of this breed who are looking at this idea. I heard and observed managers, anthropologists, newspaper reporters, writers of popular literature, sports fans, politicians, biologists, artists, and theologians all using the term 'culture,' sometimes with respect to organizations and sometimes not.

"I heard one astute person at a conference on the topic of organizational culture make the observation that culture has a different meaning for each person who uses it, that perhaps we need about a dozen words for it, just as the Eskimos have for the word 'snow.' After I had made a few sorties down from the sky and had achieved some sense of the organizational culture idea, I noticed something else as I circled up high and reflected on my experiences," said Eagle. "I noticed that organizational cultures seemed embedded in larger cultures, sometimes similar, sometimes different from them, and I feel sure that this embeddedness has meaning and implications for both organizations and wider cultures. I suspect that it will be an area of concern to some of the people who work in and who study organizations. Also, from a great height, the broader cultural context I am talking about became the only thing I could see with any clarity, and work organizations themselves became only a speck on the ground, even to my sharp eyes. I am sure, however, that even when people look at the very broad cultures of societies and other systems, they will find implications for organizations and for refining the concept of organizational culture."

Eagle had spoken for some time now and was getting tired. "That's about all I have to say," she said. "It seems to me, taking a broad perspective, that there is something that people are finding of value when they talk about organizational culture, that it is an emerging idea and brings into focus many issues about organizations that might otherwise be neglected, overlooked, or misunderstood. However, it seems there is a lot more that we need to know before a pattern can be established, and before we can tell just what benefit to our knowledge about organizations this idea will bring."

There was a murmur of appreciation among the birds for Eagle's contribution. "Who wishes to speak next?" asked Raven, taking the stick offered to him by Eagle.

"I do," said Wren after a moment's silence. "As you all know, I like to play around with the specifics of things, and it seems to me that while Eagle has very nicely given us something of the big picture on what seems to be highly visible in human organizations at present, there are some things I have been wondering about." Wren took a breath and then continued, "I heard the phrase 'organizations as culture-bearing milieus' used by one learned scholar, and on listening carefully I discovered that this meant that organizations may be settings through which shared understandings may emerge. This intrigued me, so I flitted about in and around a variety of organizations and observed that they do indeed have properties that make them potential bearers of culture. For example, people in organizations convene regularly over time—the same old faces (and some new ones) come together to talk and do things together over and over again. The way organizations are structured means that people are, in varying degrees, dependent on one another to get things done, both for themselves and for the organization. They are places that provide opportunities for people to find others with whom they can pursue social experiences. They are settings in which people work, with and through purposes, interests, and expectations that create and reflect constellations of interests. These serve to focus people on some issues and away from others.

"As I poked away in organizations trying to get a handle on cultures, I found that there are a number of important empirical issues facing people who want to study organizations and their cultures. Owl seemed confident that people were becoming more willing to harness qualitative as well as quantitative methodology. I would agree, but as I listened to people who study organizational culture argue and struggle with the concept, it seemed to me that they have a long way to go before they will have gained important empirical ground in understanding what organizational culture is and how it unfolds. Researchers need to examine both the content and context of organizational culture issues and to pay attention to both theory and method as they unravel their research findings." This was quite enough for Wren; he made a little bow and handed the stick to Stork, who had moved quickly to Wren's side.

"Well done, Wren," said Stork. "Why don't you rest for a while?

"I'd like to endorse some of the things Wren has told us about contexts and culture-bearing milieus," said Stork, "but I find that all the flowery generalizations and conceptual leaps that come from a perspective far above the ground such as that of Eagle, and even the patterns that are discovered by flitting about, sampling organizations here and there as Wren does (and some humans do), tell us little or nothing about organizational cultures. I think it may not be possible to generalize about these cultures—certainly not based on what is now known about them. I believe, based on what I have seen in my travels (which admittedly have not been very far-flung), that if people are to study organizations properly and meaningfully, they will need to stay in one place on the ground and peck away at one culture until they know what's true. In fact," said Stork, drawing himself up to his full height and striding about on his great long legs, "they will need to peck at the surface hard enough to get beneath it, if they are to discover the fundamental assumptions that people in a culture hold, often so tacitly that even those who are in and of the culture are not consciously aware of them. When, and only when, students of organizational culture have looked at culture in this way will they know something substantive about the subject." Stork ended with a quick fluttering of wings, handed the stick to Raven, and settled back onto one leg, satisfied that he had stirred up the discussion a bit and pleased with what he had said.

There was a moment of tension, with some milling about in the group. No one seemed to know quite what to say next. Raven was about to call for a new speaker, when Pelican intervened. "Quite a speech! Quite a speech, Stork! You certainly spoke with conviction," she began. "I shall be brief, and I hope you will find useful what I describe of my experiences. I want to talk about how I felt about what I saw rather than just relate the generalities or specifics," Pelican continued, "though with no insinuation that what we have heard before was unhelpful. I observed that there was a real concern among some people, members of organizations as well as researchers, for helping to create meaningful experiences at work. For some it was a concern with the question of what the meaning of life in organizations might be; for others it was a sense that there was little, or insufficient, meaning to life in organizations and that we really ought to do something about this. You all know that I feel very strongly about this latter concern—that it is very important. It seems to me that an idea such as organizational culture might be very appropriate as a vehicle for exploring and understanding life at work, and for making it more humane, more meaningful. It has stirred some real optimism in me. Perhaps humans will amount to something after all. However, after listening to many of the people who study organizations talk about what they do and how they are rewarded in their own organizational cultures, I am not sure that something as basic or challenging as grappling with the 'meaning of life' will attract attention and energy from the very scholars who could provide an important contribution to this matter. We shall have to see.

"I feel that there is one other set of issues that ought to be attended to when studying organizational cultures, and on these, I am more sanguine. This set of issues has to do with ethics. Should researchers go in and study organizational cultures? Are they perhaps meddling where they have no right? Does making members of a group or an organization aware of their culture help or hinder them in their day-to-day existence? Are we playing with fire? Do we unleash events and forces that we have no right to deal with unless we are around to wrestle with the consequences? Do we know how to deal with the consequences? On one of my stops, I heard members of a particular culture say that anthropologists had ruined their world, had meddled, and were no longer welcome as investigators or observers. Is this pertinent to organizational scientists, I wonder?" The other birds thought about this as Pelican paused, but said nothing.

She continued: "Should people try to manage culture, and if so, to what end? I supppose managers, administrators, and others try to do this as part of their jobs," she said, "so perhaps it's a question of the depth of involvement, of intervention. People ought to be looking at guidelines that deal with limits and boundaries. Anyway, I find it all very stimulating, if a little frightening. There is no doubt in my mind that thinking about organizations in terms of cultures brings alive issues of meaning, ethics, and the quality of life in interesting and provocative ways."

Pelican's emotional involvement in the experiences she described affected each of the birds in the circle. There was a long pause. Raven thought the meeting might be over. Testing this idea, he asked, "Does anyone else have anything to say? Phoenix, perhaps you would like a turn with the stick?"

Phoenix took the stick. "I was thinking that perhaps it had all been said, and then I thought about the whole issue of rises and falls, of endings and renewals. It seems to me, reflecting on my own travels, on what has been said here today, and on the history of the study of organizational culture, that we are dealing with the regeneration of an earlier mode of conceptualizing organizational phenomena. Cultural elements such as beliefs, sentiments, collective conscience, anomie, social symbolism, and systems of common values were investigated many years ago using not only traditional logics—experimental approaches— but also methods that relied heavily on subjective interpretation. Using these concepts, several scholars studied and wrote about organizations, but then the approach died of neglect—it was abandoned. My hunch is that this occurred for reasons other than the utility of the idea. Perhaps the very shift in the culture, in the sharing of values of organizational scientists themselves, was part of its demise. It became a way of thinking that was no longer considered useful for making sense of organizational problems and dilemmas.

"I am delighted that the idea is once again alive, and that it seems healthy. I am always happy to see people, things, and ideas revitalized. But I believe that scholars who wish to nurture this field of inquiry need to maintain a healthy sense of discipline about the way they conduct their work. It needs to be rigorous, in the best sense of the term, as well as relevant. People need to ask and explore questions about what the study of organizational culture might contribute to an understanding of organizational life, and of how organizations might be made more humane and productive. What are the actual benefits of such work on organizational culture, I wonder? What hazards and pitfalls must be overcome to do good work? What misgivings need to be surfaced about the study of organizational culture for it to be pursued intelligently and openly?" Pelican, who had first raised the ethical issue, nodded vigorously in agreement. "I think these are important questions to add to those already raised" said Phoenix. "My concluding thought is that the future of the concept of organizational culture is going to rest on how well these questions are answered."

"Thank you, Phoenix" said Raven. He took the stick and looked around the circle of friends. "I'm pleased with the way this meeting has turned out. I think each of you has had interesting experiences and has brought to our forum some intriguing ideas and insights regarding organizational culture.

"Many of the ideas and observations that keep cropping up in your reports are unique to your own particular perspectives and experiences. It is interesting to me that as each of you covered ground and said or echoed things that others were saying, the image of organizational culture changed a little. It reminds me of what I experience when I pick up or move an abalone shell. The beautiful, polished interior, with its mother-of-pearl surface, gives off a variety of colors and images, so that each time I handle the same shell, I come to see something new in it. It sounds to me as if that is what has happened here today as we have talked about organizational culture, and it is perhaps the way it will always be with this complex and intriguing subject.

"As I see it, the road ahead for organizational culture will be worth our observation. I think that as you travel abroad this next year and gather impressions for when we meet again, you should keep an eye on organizational cultures. Look for them on the highways and byways of life in human organizations. Examine blind alleys. Watch for the unexpected curves, for potholes, for washouts. Let us see whether we can discern, in time, the development of useful maps of the terrain. Let that be our charge. Until then, I shall keep the talking stick safe."

The discussion over, the birds flew on their way, stimulated and enriched by sharing their ideas and experiences. They promised to meet again in the same place at the end of another year of travel and adventure.

THE CONTENT OF THE BOOK

In April 1984, Vancouver, B.C., *was* spring. To be sure, snow still capped the surrounding mountains, but in the city, lawns and trees were green and everywhere flowers punctuated the vistas. Gentle breezes filled sails in the bay and carried the pungence of spring. Nowhere was the change of seasons more dramatic and beautiful than on the University of British Columbia campus.

Participants at the conference on Organizational Culture and the Meaning of Life in the Workplace gathered one morning in the Museum of Anthropology. Greetings were made under the towering totems and beside the canoes and other ritual artifacts of the Pacific Northwest coast people. At a signal from the conference coordinators, all assembled around a handcarved, human-sized raven, where officials welcomed the participants. The raven, a local symbol of wisdom and playfulness, was to be the focal symbol of the conference. In fact, as participants filed into the first session, raven medallions were placed around each person's neck. The meeting began in earnest when one of the coordinators held up the conference "talking stick" and explained its function in story form.

Like the individual birds in the spirit group, each conference participant brought along a different perspective on organizational culture. Many of those perspectives—those ideas, experiences, and observations—are reported in the chapters that follow. The organization of the book has its roots in the Culture Conference, but its structure represents the results of our reflections on what constituted a meaningful whole on the subject. Many of the chapters in this book extend and elaborate on ideas expressed in conference papers, while some chapters represent approaches and ideas that were not presented at the conference. In many respects, the book goes beyond the work of the conference. It is a next step in the development of the study of organizational culture.

The theme of perspectives on organizational culture is emphasized in Part I of the book. Authors here grapple with issues that are fundamental to our quest for meaningful views of organizational culture. Included in these chapters are concerns about what is meant by "organizational culture," why we study it, how we know when we have organizational culture within our investigative sights, how many cultures an organization can bear, whether culture is a paradigm for inquiry, and whether culture has anything to do with the meaning of life in the workplace and/or with organizational effectiveness. Meryl Reis Louis introduces and provides an overview to the chapters in this section.

In Part II of the book, we explore the question uppermost in the minds of many people who are attracted to the concept of organizational culture: Can it be managed? The authors of the chapters in this section provide interesting answers to this question, suggesting some of the complexities that accompany any attempt to manage or change organizational culture. Joanne Martin describes in her introduction to this section some of the commonalities and differences among the various positions taken on this question.

In Part III, we confront a different managerial question—how to perform and manage organizational culture research—and the ethical question of whether organizational cultures should be studied. Inquiry into organizational culture involves probing at levels of organizational functioning that are close to the core of the values and identities of the members of a culture. Are conventional research strategies and methods adequate for culture research? What is likely to impede such inquiry? Should we intrude? Do we disrupt existing patterns of organizational life? Is the gain in knowledge at too high a price—to members or researchers? Craig Lundberg introduces and grounds the chapters that grapple with considerations of how organizational culture should be researched.

Part IV of the book adds new lenses to our camera as we lift our heads to examine the terrain, the broader context within which organizational cultures exist. Some authors in this section address the question of how organizational culture is influenced by and has an impact on the immediate environment. What changes and adjustments ought we be alerted to as we consider immediate external forces and processes in an existing organizational culture? Other authors pay attention to the broad cultural systems within which organizations operate. These authors are primarily interested in macro issues that have to do with cultures of countries, or of whole disciplines. While they are cognizant of the fact that organizations exist within such contexts and often mirror or translate what goes on in their contexts, these authors do not address themselves specifically to events and processes at the organizational level. Larry Moore introduces and frames with his commentary the chapters of this section.

The final section of the book contains a single chapter that one might call a reflective piece. The author addresses very insightfully the significance and the usefulness of corporate culture in a fitting capstone to the issues and ideas reviewed earlier in the book. Peter Frost provides a brief introduction to this section.

PART I

PERSPECTIVES ON ORGANIZATIONAL CULTURE

MERYL REIS LOUIS

Concern with workplace cultures—with informal organizations and work-group norms—is not new. In 1939, Chester Barnard noted that informal organization was essential to the successful functioning of formal organizations. Codes of conduct, as he referred to them, arose and ensured commitment, identity, coherence, and a sense of community. Somewhat earlier, Elton Mayo and his colleagues had documented elaborate, differentiated, and compelling systems of norms and symbols that had emerged among members of two cliques—individuals who were part of the same organizational unit and who worked in close proximity.

Recognition of the prevalence and potency of workplace culture is not restricted to business scholars and social scientists. Most anyone entering an unfamiliar work setting knows the feeling of being an outsider; one sometimes feels as though one had just arrived in a foreign country. Real wisdom in such situations means recognizing that the unspoken is more powerful than what can be conveyed through speaking. One gradually gains a sense of the feel, the smell, the personality of a workplace, a way of working, or a kind of work—though it may be difficult to translate all of this into words that an outsider could grasp.

This indigenous feel of a place and its caste has been studied in the past by organizational scientists under a variety of labels. Thus the notion of organizational culture has a rich heritage. The phenomenon has been considered as the character of an organization, its climate, ideology, and image. It encompasses notions of informal organization, norms, and emergent systems.

What distinguishes the current formulation—as culture—is its basis in anthropology. The quest here is not for the strictly psychological or sociological components of the phenomenon, as was the case in the past. Rather, the uniquely integrative and phenomenological core of the subject, in which the interweaving of individuals into a community takes place, has finally become the subject of investigation among organizational scientists. So too has the conceptually slippery notion of meaning—its ontological status, emergence, and function. Thus the notion of meaning and the phenomenon of community bind together the disparate perspectives represented by current scholars of culture, including the authors of chapters in this book.

The theoretical chapters in the first section of the book set the stage for the more pragmatic studies to follow. The first group explicitly discusses the issue sof meaning and community. All three chapters consider different ways of thinking about culture and trace how such differences are reflected in the understandings produced by any one perspective.

In the first chapter, John Van Maanen and Stephen Barley identify four clusters of variables relevant for appreciating any particular culture. They use the clusters to help us shift our perspective from considering culture in general to considering culture in work settings, and focuses on the group rather than the organization as the context of culture. At this point, sources of subcultural formation are examined. The questions of how and why subcultures proliferate in work settings are richly illustrated. The reader is offered a perspective at once semiotic, cognitive, and interactional.

In the second chapter, Linda Smircich asks whether the concept of culture can serve as a paradigm for understanding organizations and ourselves. She acknowledges the multiple concepts of culture while drawing our attention to the ways in which an interest in culture signals a fundamental shift—even a paradigm shift—in understanding organizational life. Smircich is not content to let us reduce the notion to one more variable in a static model of life at work. Rather, she illustrates what the use of culture as an analytic lens can reveal about organizational life and identifies the pedagogical implications of such a perspective.

In the final chapter of this section, I attempt to outline a range of issues that investigators of workplace cultures, whether researchers or practitioners ought to consider explicitly. Matters of definition, source and boundary, and conceptual focus are discussed in terms of theoretical and pragmatic bases; interpretive practices and sampling strategies are also examined. Properties of organizational settings as culture-bearing milieus, a notion borrowed by Wren in our prologue, are set out in more detail.

In all, these three chapters offer cautions and reveal promises associated with applying the notion of culture to understanding organizational life. Issues of community and meaning figure largely in each of these studies. We are concerned, and our concerns focus on the too simple use of a notion, on the unexamined application of an approach. We would urge our colleagues to consider carefully premises of any perspective, and we hope that these chapters will help them in doing so.

All the same, we are hopeful. We read the current interest in organizational culture as a sign of great potential, since fundamental understanding may thus be enhanced We are at last in possession of an integrative lens, one that is essentially phenomenological.

Of course, more than understanding is at stake. The views of work life revealed through this lens throw into relief possibilities of other, perhaps better scenarios of life at work. The same descriptions that cultural perspectives contribute carry with them questions of *pre*scription. What should be the role of work? How might individuals contribute and receive . . . ? Toward what ends ought efforts to be organized (for example, would output be a moot point if community were achieved)? Thus the promise in terms of culture is one of both understanding and improvement, or potentiation. Let us proceed, then, in recognition of the inherent hazards and promises to consider some altenative perspectives on organizational culture.

2

CULTURAL ORGANIZATION
Fragments of a Theory

John Van Maanen
Massachusetts Institute of Technology

Stephen R. Barley
Cornell University

The phrase "organizational culture" pivots on the linguistic device of juxtaposition: placing two lexemes side by side to create a thought or perception signified by neither alone. Juxtaposition derives the recombinatory power of metaphor, the semantic tool by which language turns attention to novel conceptions (Richards, 1936; Black, 1962).[1] Aside from the pleasures of word play, metaphorically juxtaposing unconnected semantic entities sometimes stimulates solutions to previously intractable problems and, on occasion, leads to advances in the natural and social sciences (Brown, 1977; Boyd, 1979; Morgan, 1980). Schon (1979) calls such metaphors "generative" because they allow one to reframe phenomena to apprehend the familiar from an unfamiliar and perhaps productive vantage point.

The generative potential of the trope, organizational culture, resides in its ability to direct researchers to interstices within organizational theory. The notion that organizations have cultures is an attractive heuristic proposition, especially when explanations derived from individual-based psychology or structural sociology prove limiting. Culture implies that human behavior is partially prescribed by a collectively created and sustained way of life that cannot be personality based

Authors' Note: An earlier version of this chapter was presented at the annual meeting of the Academy of Management in Dallas, Texas, during August 1983 as part of a symposium entitled "Many in One: Organizations as Multicultural Entities." Partial support for the writing of this document was provided by a grant from the Office of Naval Research under contract N00014-80-C-0905; NR 170-911.

because it is shared by diverse individuals. Neither can a way of life be derived solely from structure, since members of separate collectives themselves occupy equivalent positions in a structural matrix. Rather, culture points to an analysis mediating between deterministic and volunteeristic models of behavior in organizations.

Like all tropes, organizational culture promises insight by bartering away other conceptual opportunities. Attributing culture to a collective not only presumes that members share common bonds, but also that commonalities are identified by contrasting one collective with another. In Weber's (1968: 42-43) terms, culture presumes "consciousness of kind" as well as "consciousness of difference." Accordingly, the phrase "organizational culture" suggests that organizations bear unitary and unique cultures.

Such a stance, however, is difficult to justify empirically. Moreover, culture's utility as a heuristic concept may be lost when the organizational level of analysis is employed. Work organizations are indeed marked by social practices that can be said to be "cultural," but these practices may not span the organization as a whole. In this sense, culture is itself organized within work settings. How this process operates is the central problem we address in this essay.

CULTURAL ORGANIZATION

Our notion of cultural organization is rooted in both anthropology and sociology. Anthropologists emphasize the close description of relatively small, remote, and self-contained societies.[2] Descriptive details are organized as ethnographies wherein the presence of culture is displayed by the identification and elaboration of such matters as the language, child-rearing practices, totems, taboos, signifying codes, work and leisure interests, standards of behavior (and characteristic deviance), social classification systems, and jural procedures shared by members of the studied society. From the description of these various domains, the analyst infers the pattern(s) said to simultaneously knit the society into an integrated whole and to differentiate it from others. Whether a group's practices are found to be similar to our own or spectacularly alien, culture is cast as an all-embracing and largely taken-for-granted way of life shared by those who make up the society.

These bases of collective action, however, shift in both form and function when fragmented, mobile, and highly industrialized societies are contrasted to tiny, preliterate societies located in remote and sparsely populated regions of the world. Lost are the predictability, simplicity, and apparent social order of less complicated societies where all members know what other members should do. In place of a single "design for living," industrial societies offer members many such designs. Anthropologists have noted that distinct enclaves exist within the boundaries of simpler societies, but it has been sociologists, with their concern for contemporary societies, who have most fully developed the notion of cultures within a culture (see, for example, Becker, 1982; Peterson, 1979; Fine, 1979; Schwartz, 1972; Arnold, 1970).

Unitary culture is primarily an anthropological idea, while the notion of subcultures is predominately sociological. Nevertheless, a reading of the two literatures suggests that similar social processes underwrite the rise of cultures and subcultures alike. In crude relief, culture can be understood as a set of solutions devised by a group of people to meet specific problems posed by the situations they face in common.[3] Social innovation is, then, not so much a matter of individual accomplishment as it is a matter of changing group standards. Cultural manifestations therefore evolve over time as members of a group confront similar problems and, in attempting to cope with these problems, devise and employ strategies that are remembered and passed on to new members. Within such a framework, form initially follows function, but function seems often to give way to form.[4] This notion of culture as a living, historical product of group problem solving allows an approach to cultural study that is applicable to any group, be it a society, a neighborhood, a family, a dance band, or an organization and its segments.

THEORETICAL FRAGMENTS

Four interconnected domains of analysis are involved in our accounting for the genesis, maintenance, and transmission of culture. The first domain concerns the ecological context in which a group is embedded. All collectives occupy physical territory and a material world, persist in (and sometimes across) particular time periods, and exist within a social context that includes other groups of people. Thus, a group's position can be mapped along physical, temporal, and social coordinates. Although the topographies are themselves multidimensional and intercorrelated, together they suggest the major types of problems a group is likely to face. A group's ecological context is therefore, theoretically, the primary catalyst for a culture's genesis.

To specify an ecological context, the attributes of the group's physical setting, the pertinent historical forces, and most importantly the expectations, demands, and social organization of those who surround the group and who lay claims on the group's conduct must be identified. Hypotheses can then be derived about the routine as well as the dramatic problems that the group must confront and manage in order to survive. In short, the problematic situations that culture addresses are not capricious or randomly generated, but rather reflect both past and current nooks in the social and material world.

Ecological problems, however, are not in and of themselves sufficient conditions for the formation of culture. A culture's genesis also depends on a second set of conditions that we refer to as "differential interaction." Given a particular ecological context, patterns of inter-action emerge between persons who may or may not be members of the group to which one wishes to attribute a culture. These interactions can be visualized sociometrically as a network of exchanges and com-munication links between people. Only when the ratio of intragroup ties to extragroup ties is high will a common frame of reference regarding ecologically based problems be likely to develop among the members of a collective. One may even argue that unless differential interaction can be demonstrated, there is little reason to consider a collection of individuals a group.

Ecological context and differential interaction are both structural substrates in reference to the collective understandings that develop among members of a group. This is the pivotal third domain in our model of cultural development. Any social world consists of a collection of signs that are essentially devoid of meaning until they are noticed and interpreted by members of a collective.[5] Interpretations of objects, events, and activities are, for this reason, the quintessential content of any culture. Only when members of a group assign similar meanings to facets of their situation can collectives devise, through interaction, unique responses to problems that later take on trappings of rule, ritual, and value.

As sociocultural variables, ecological context, differential inter-action, and collective understandings are conceptually independent of individual actors and can be examined, and perhaps patterned analyt-ically, without recourse to individual behavior and belief. Indeed, individuals may be unaware that they have a culture unless it is pointed out to them. Even those collective understandings which typify an unusually self-conscious group are independent in the sense that when people move into the group they will find others on the scene who have already defined the situations that group members face. If newcomers are to interact successfully in the setting, thus becoming members of good standing, these preexisting definitions have to be learned and respected (Van Maanen, 1979).

Nevertheless, since a group has no mind of its own in which to store interpretations and solutions to problems, a culture cannot be divorced from the people who carry it. The fourth domain of analysis, the reproductive and adaptive capacity, therefore centers on the individual members who make up the group to which a culture is attributed. While a group is necessary to invent and sustain culture, culture can be carried only by individuals. Cultural patterns of behavior and interpretation cease to exist unless they are repeatedly enacted as people respond to occurrences in their daily lives. Similarly, cultures endure only to the degree that their content is transmitted from one generation to the next. Finally, since cultures are not static, some allowance must be made for the ability of interacting individuals to elaborate a culture's content by devising innovative interpretations and strategies of action.

Interacting members of a group selectively attend to their environment, experiment with different frames of reference, and constantly alter, usually in small ways, the collective understandings with which they work. Culture is about people doing things together in both old and new ways. Altered perspectives may subsequently lead to new interaction patterns and, hence, influence the group's position relative to other groups. A complete developmental model must therefore have a social psychological and process component if the individual's attachment to and support of the group's collective understandings are to be explained.[6] This seems particularly important in contemporary societies where individuals are members of many groups, each more or less in competition for a person's attention and commitment.

Several clarifications are now in order. First, the model is both structuralist and interactionist in intent. Theories that posit the overriding importance of structure for the collective understandings held by members of a group discount the potential autonomy of cultures created through interaction and interpretation. Mechanically linking structure to meaning denies the active, ongoing, and always problematic character of interaction, as well as the conflict and ambiguity that attend any sense-making process. On the other hand, theories that treat meaning as pure social construction jump into the middle of the culture-building process and fail to appreciate the fact that people's actions and interactions are shaped by matters often beyond their control and outside their immediate present. In everyday life, actors are always the marks as well as the shills of a social order. It is in this sense that culture mediates between structural and individual realms.

One should also keep in mind that culture's contents are symbolic and ideational. They are carried in the form of norms, rules, and codes that people use to interpret and evaluate their own behavior as well as the behavior of others. Thus the culture of a society and the culture of a group within a society are neither qualitatively nor quantitatively different, even though the collective understandings that define the two cultures may be quite distinct. A subculture should also not be considered smaller than the culture of a society, even though the subgroup is much smaller numerically than its encompassing collective. Neither is it possible to claim that some cultures are necessarily better than others, or that one culture is stronger or weaker than another. All that can be said is that cultural understandings differ in respects that can be enumerated, and that these differences lead to differences in behavior. In terms of form and function, all cultures are constructed in similar ways and serve sense-making ends.

CULTURES IN WORK ORGANIZATIONS

To examine how culture emerges in work organizations, the four analytic domains identified above can be given specific focus. The ecological context of a work setting refers primarily to the ways in which workplace activities are structured: who does what, when, and where. An organization's internal topography usually cleaves, both formally and informally, around products, materials, tasks, technologies, and shifts. More often than not, these cleavages are reinforced by territorial segregation so that social mappings become spatially encoded (Miller, 1959). Historical forces also shape the ecological context of a work organization. Current practice reflects not only the weight of a firm's past policies and strategies but also the dynamics of regulation, competition, and market structure that mark the organization's external environment during particular eras. As to social demography, workplaces are populated by specific types of actors who have interests in and expectations for each other's behavior: workers, staff, managers, suppliers, customers, and so forth.

Out of this ecological context arise the many routine problems that members of an organization face. Some of these problems exist by design and are hence tied to the formal purposes of the organization.

Others come about incidentally as unintended consequences of the organizing process. Coupled to these organizational problems are work roles, each involving a particular bundle of tasks and a particular status relative to other roles in the organization.

The structuring of an organization into work roles in turn influences patterns of interaction found in the organization. Differential interaction among an organization's membership may reflect physical proximity, the sharing of common tasks or status, dependencies in the workflow, demands made by some members on others, and even accidents of history. While the reasons for sustained interaction among an organization's members vary, to the degree that some members interact more frequently with others who share similar problems, this is where the seeds of organizational subcultures are sewn.

As a subgroup's members interact over time and address problems cooperatively, collective understandings form to support concerted action. These perspectives are likely to pertain not only to the nature of the work and to the solution of task-related problems, but also to the nature of the organization and to the individual's position within it. Collective understandings may therefore shade conceptions of self as well as opinions of others and, in essence, provide an interpretive system that actors can use to make sense of ongoing events and activities. To the degree that a group's interpretive system provides distinctive motives within the organization, members may begin to perform for reasons that are incomprehensible to outsiders and in ways that are incongruent with formal decree.

Although our theoretical perspective suggests that organizations harbor subcultures, it does not preclude the possibility of a homogeneous organizational culture, a situation where all members of an organization subscribe to the same normative order and where the normative order can be distinguished only by contrast to other organizations. Indeed, the framework specifies explicit conditions under which single cultures are likely to form. Unitary organizational cultures evolve when all members of an organization face roughly the same problems, when everyone communicates with almost everyone else, and when each member adopts a common set of understandings for enacting proper and consensually approved behavior. Subcultural contrasts could, of course, still be made on the basis of individual attributes such as age, gender, or race, but such distinctions would have greater relevance for what people do outside rather than inside the organization.

Such homogeneity may in fact be approximated in some organizations in certain periods of their history. The founding phases of organizations, for example, seem to produce social systems marked by little internal or subcultural differentiation (Schein, 1983b; Martin et al., 1984). Organizations that manage to remain small and local may also maintain dense social ties and a unitary normative system. Larger organizations, when facing a severe crisis, can approximate the unicultural case if the membership turns only to collective understandings held by all to inform immediate action—a situation that seems unlikely unless subgroups establish communicative ties before a crisis ensues (Krackhart and Stern, 1984). Finally, as a result of common socialization experienced by members of professionalized occupations, organizations such as medical and legal practices that are populated by the similarly trained frequently sport distinct and pervasive cultures.

More commonly, organizations intentionally differentiate their members by assigning them relatively insulated roles and position-specific niches. When these niches are occupied by people facing similar problems, who have both opportunities and motives for interaction, organizational subcultures are born. We shall define an organizational subculture as a subset of an organization's members who interact regularly with one another, identify themselves as a distinct group within the organization, share a set of problems commonly defined to be the problems of all, and routinely take action on the basis of collective understandings unique to the group.

Subcultures can be pictorially represented as Venn diagrams by drawing small circles that cluster and overlap as the collective understandings of one group approximate those of another. The degree to which smaller circles coalesce onto a larger, hypothetical one determines the analytical and empirical justification for talk of an "organizational culture." The less such circles overlap (the more spread out and mutually exclusive they appear), the greater the cultural diversity. Organizational culture is therefore understood as a shadowlike entity carried by subcultures and defined as the intersection of subcultural interpretive systems. From this perspective, organizational culture is a rendering across subcultures of what is common among them. If there is much overlap and tight clustering, subcultures can be said to take part in an organizational culture. But if the area of intersection is small, attributions of a unitary culture become tenuous.

We now take up more concrete matters by examining several social processes that appear to sire organizational subcultures. Six spurs to subcultural formation will be discussed. Our purpose is not to be exhaustive as to the sources of subculture, but rather to illustrate precisely what we mean by our title phrase, "cultural organization."

THE SEEDS OF
ORGANIZATIONAL SUBCULTURES

Segmentation

The idea that cultural processes are crucial to the dynamics of organizational life has a long and venerable history. For example, Selznick (1949), Gouldner (1954), Blau (1955), and Dalton (1959) all express interest in how interpretations, values, and elaborate behavioral rituals shape the manner in which organizations perform. From their close analysis emerged portraits of organizations beset by conflicts of interests played out between subgroups possessing alternative ideologies and interpretive systems. Cultural processes, at least as they were depicted in these early field studies, were forces that segmented organizations.[7] Even in the more pragmatic and managerially focused writings of Lawrence and Lorsch (1967), cultural understandings such as performance timeframes and forms of social relations among organizational units were seen to contrast, both empirically and normatively. Culture, as invented by various groups of an organization, was found to be a differentiating, rather than an integrating, mechanism.

In his discussion of the "dysfunctions of bureaucracy," Merton (1957: 201) ties subcultural formation and ensuing provincialism to the very processess that sire bureaucracy:

> Functionaries have the sense of a common destiny for all those who work together. They share the same interests, especially since there is relatively little competition in so far as promotion is in terms of seniority. In-group aggression is thus minimized and this arrangement is therefore conceived to be positively functional for the bureaucracy. However, the *esprit de corps* and informal social organization which typically develops in such situations often leads the personnel to defend their entrenched interests rather than to assist their clientele and elected higher officials.

That subcultures and the problems they pose are by-products of bureaucratization, a process intended to make organizations more efficient and effective, is the essential irony of Merton's analysis. In a more general vein, numerous theorists have written that the elaboration of organizational forms in both industry and government is premised on the notion of "technical rationality."[8] Technical rationality refers to the conviction that tasks are most effectively (and economically) performed when executed in line with the canons of scientific and technological models of action, and when entrusted to experts trained to execute tasks parsimoniously. The belief that benefits are reaped from the rationalization of work justifies a host of familiar organizing strategies; including functionalization, specialization, automation, professionalization, standardization, and specification.

By and large, these strategies seek the imputed benefits of efficiency and productivity by segmenting the work force. But in so doing, each promotes subcultural possibilities. The large organizational niches created by functionalization foster domain-specific identities that distinguish employees by the area of the organization to which they are attached. Specialization narrows the population of employees who can be said to do the same type of work and hence differentiates sectors within functional areas. Professionalization brings together employees with occupational identities and ideologies that set them apart from other employees (Van Maanen and Barley, 1984).[9] Automation creates groups of employees devoted to specific machines, while specification and standardization deskill employees and concomitantly increase the probability of differentiation by proximity and shared working conditions.

To the extent that segmentation is accepted as natural and appropriate, differentially interacting role clusters emerge. As each develops its own language, norms, time horizons, and perspectives on the organization's mission, subcultural proliferation should be expected. Moreover, as members of segmented groups come to possess and express a "consciousness of difference" in their everyday interaction, they are likely to hold that only they can adequately control work performed on their own turf.[10] Consequently, as an outgrowth of the expanding tendency to rationalize work, managers must increasingly rely on "coercive authority"(such as the power to reward and punish) to control the centripetal tendencies of the work force rather than on whatever "cultural authority"(such as the power to define and lead) they might otherwise claim as fellow members of a common work culture (Starr, 1983). Perhaps because managers have slowly begun to realize that they have let "cultural authority" slip through their fingers, the notion of "organizational culture" has attained a faddish appeal in the business literature.

Importation

Organizations do not always spin off subcultures as a matter of gradual and routine segmentation. Acquisitions and mergers are obvious examples where the creation of subcultures is sudden and swift. Of course, tasks, roles, and interaction patterns often change with such expansions so that old loyalties vanish and new patterns of commitment and obligation appear as merged and acquired groups reposition themselves vis-à-vis others. But to the degree that an acquisition or merger leaves intact the previous order with its more or less established intergroup structure, new subcultures will be simply added to the now enlarged organization, a process that appears similar to colonization. The power of the colonized to maintain a separate sense of identity within a more heterogeneous environment may actually be bolstered, since a background of foreign normative orders is likely to enhance consciousness of difference.

Aside from acquisitions and mergers, subcultural variation spreads as groups with occupationally specific cultures are added to organizational charts. Williamson's (1975, 1981) notion of transaction costs provides one rationale for this form of subcultural importation. In skeletal form, Williamson suggests that organizations alter their structure when the cost and uncertainty of engaging in an exchange relation with groups outside the organization's boundaries outstrip the cost of providing the desired resource internally. In the case of services rendered by a particular occupational group, structural inclusion becomes more likely when such services are seen as having potential to evolve into an "organizationally specific asset." Among other things, the term refers to the idea that an occupation's members are more likely to cast their loyalty with the organization than the occupation, especially if they work inside an organization and derive their salaries solely from the organization's largess.

The current growth of in-house legal staffs in large corporations is an example of such an importation process. Chayes et al. (1983: 85-87) argue that not only can an internal legal staff save a corporation impressive sums of money in legal fees (Xerox is said to have reduced its annual legal expenses by $21 million), but also certain forms of legal work can rapidly become organizationally specific assets:

> Effective anticipatory law requires a degree of involvement and knowledge of the corporations's business rarely found outside the company.... Lawyers who lack business appreciation tend to err on the side of caution.

They feel responsible when a suit is brought, but don't when productivity declines, market shares decrease, or profits dwindle.

Another view of the importation process is provided by institutionalization theorists who argue that organizations may adopt certain specialists as a matter of structural mimicry (Meyer and Rowan, 1977; Dimaggio and Powell, 1983). When organizations employ uncertain technologies, have diverse goals, and suffer from ambiguous feedback on relative performance, managers may become attentive to what similar organizations are up to. If it appears that other organizations are bringing in members of specific occupations or hiring people with distinctive attributes, then managers in attending organizations will move to import similar personnel. Although the motives that support such action are undoubtedly multiple, for some organizations at least, one motive seems to be simply the desire to signal to clients and competitors that this organization is also modern, progressive, and up-to-date (Tolbert and Zucker, 1983). Ritualistic modeling, for example, appears to explain the spread of school psychologists and school health professionals, at least among California school districts.

Occupational groups can also be foisted on an organization by outside agencies. Organizations may even welcome mandated importation and the possible creation of a new subculture within its boundaries. Police agencies are, for example, called upon periodically to take part in state and federal crime programs such as those designed to curb drug traffic. Often, these programs include funds and legal provisions that encourage police departments to expand existing narcotics operations or to institute new ones. Since the creation or strengthening of the narcotics bureau entails higher levels of funding and manpower, police agencies are typically eager to accept the governmental mandate, especially when there are few constraints attached to the funding. Other governmental interventions may be more grudgingly accepted by organizations. Although equal employment, occupational safety, and environmental legislation may require organizations to import new occupational groups, these initiatives are often resented by private and public organizations alike. As is apparently the case with new EEO offices, positions may be created that then remain isolated and marginal, with little if any potential for spawning viable subcultures.

Technological Innovation

Technological advancement in work organizations is often portrayed as a process that progressively robs members of various occupations of their expertise by embodying a worker's manual and cognitive skills in the design of machinery (Braverman, 1974; Noble, 1979; Haug, 1975, 1977; Wallace and Kallenberg, 1982). Evidence supporting the pertinence of this view in certain industries, organizations, and occupations is simply too strong to dispute. It would be an empirical and ideological mistake, however, to claim that all technical advancement separates conception from execution or deskills and alienates workers. Moreover, technological innovation need not be equated with automation, nor need automation itself be understood as unilaterally alienating (Blauner, 1964; Shepard, 1971; Hull et al., 1982). Whereas certain types of technological change, particularly incremental innovations that simplify existing technologies, may lead to the demise of organizational and occupational subcultures, other technical advances may actually empower old subcultures or create new ones. In this regard, the spread of computerized medical imaging technologies is instructive.[11]

Until the late 1960s, the work of radiology departments in community hospitals consisted primarily of the production and interpretation of radiographs (X-rays) and fluoroscopic studies such as the barium enema and the barium swallow. Except for slight gradations in personal skill, few differentiations were made among either the radiologists or the technologists who staffed the radiology departments. However, with the advent of nuclear medicine, the invention of the gamma camera, and the use of computers to capture, transform, and display images, a new family of technologies has gained importance in diagnostic imaging. During the 1970s, two computer-based technologies, ultrasound and CT-scanning, gained widespread acceptance and use. Both created new systems of diagnostic signs, expanded the number of anatomical systems that could be imaged, and enlarged the range of diseases that could be diagnosed visually. To operate these technologies and to interpret their relatively esoteric output, both radiologists and technologists were forced to acquire new skills.

CT-scanning, ultrasound, and nuclear medicine also generated new occupational subcultures within radiology departments, particularly among technologists. For instance, as selected X-ray technologists were trained in the computerized modalities, they adapted new labels and new occupational identities as "sonographers," "nuclear medicine techs," or "CT techs." Not only did the members of these groups cease to call themselves "X-ray technologists," but they also began to view X-ray work pejoratively. As one might expect, X-ray technologists often returned the negative opinions of their work in kind.

When compared to X-ray technologists in a given hospital, sonographers, nuclear medicine technologists, and CT techs are considerably more autonomous, have greater prestige, and are more likely to interact regularly with radiologists and other physicians in their day-to-day work. Moreover, since the technologies' operation requires one to understand and use images cybernetically, and since most radiologists are initially unskilled in interpreting images produced by a new modality, some technologists may initially know more about the technology and its images than the average radiologist (not to mention the average referring physician). While a radiologist or a referring physician would never ask an X-ray technologist to read a film, such requests are routinely made of sonographers and CT techs. As if to institutionalize their recently acquired status, sonographers, in particular, are currently in the process of developing their own restrictive occupational associations and certification processes.

Ideological Differentiation

Technological innovation, importation, and segmentation sire structural shifts that alter interactional opportunities which, in turn, spawn the contrasting interpretive systems that characterize organizational subcultures. This process may also occur in reverse, as when shifting interactional patterns within a subculture lead to eventual structural differentiation. Subcultures may arise within subcultures when members develop competing ideologies regarding, for example, the nature of the work, the choice of appropriate techniques, the correct stance toward outsiders, or the best way to treat particular clients. Moreover, many people in an organization may remain unaware of a development until it has proceeded well along its path.

Schisms in academic departments and research institutes frequently begin when members start to distinguish themselves on the basis of differing paradigms. Although one or more competing paradigms may arrive with the employment of new members, new paradigms can also emerge out of sequences of events within a department that terminate in the formation of a splinter group. To the extent that the new group is able to train graduate students or market its paradigm to academics at other institutions, a "school" or, in our terms, a subculture, grows (Crane, 1972). Occasionally, antagonism between proponents of competing paradigms becomes so intense that members of the two camps cease to communicate and become, for all practical purposes, two subcultures delimited mainly by their scorn for one another.

Sometimes rifts within subcultures can be traced to implicit faults in the very ideology that initially served to set the subculture off from others around it. In his research on the Israeli probation system, Kunda

(1983) argues that the doctrine of "authoritative treatment" secures for probation officers a place among the other occupational groups that have an interest in shaping the moral career of juvenile delinquents in Jerusalem. While the criminal justice system wields authority and the psychiatric community offers treatment, only the probation officer fuses authority and treatment into a unique program of rehabilitation. Within probation work itself, however, several camps are to be found, each with its own interpretation of what "authoritative treatment" means in practice. Some probation officers underscore the authoritarian side of the doctrine and emphasize the quasi-police functions of their office. Others take treatment as their primary function and, hence, regard therapy as their most critical chore. In the absence of clear-cut criteria for effective performance, time itself seems to be the crucial determinant of whether or not the schism will produce separate subcultures.[12]

Contracultural Movements

Closely aligned with ideological differentiation is a process of subcultural formation that we label "contracultural movements." Whereas ideological differentiation occurs primarily when the members of a group reposition themselves relative to other members of the same group, contracultural movements draw members from many subgroups and develop on the grounds that all accepted organizational subcultures treat their members dismally or subscribe to wrongheaded ideas. Indeed, most organizational subcultures develop collective understandings that by and large accept the group's organizational position and do not conflict overtly with the organization's presumed mission. While subcultures imply an internal political economy, subcultural disputes are usually played out over particular issues so that no single subculture is likely to be overwhelmingly at odds with the remainder of the organization. By joining a typical organizational subculture, a member does not risk losing his or her status or offending others in the organization. In a contracultural movement, however, behavior that is explicitly forbidden or viewed as improper by most outsiders is sanctioned within the group. Gaining status within a contracultural movement is therefore accompanied by a loss of status outside the group and a forfeiture of others' respect.

Nonconformity is the price of membership in a contracultural movement. Furthermore, the collective understandings carried by individual parties to the movement promote visibility, since they center on the relations that members have with outsiders. Thus contracultural movements gain momentum as previously ungrouped organizational members begin to share a sense of stigma. Such stigmatization, when it is seen as pervasive, may eventually become a mark of membership in a deviant subculture. It is important to recognize that the norms of a contraculture can only be understood by reference to the relationships members maintain with their surrounding audiences. As a pure type, a subculture does not require such intensive analysis of intergroup relations, since the collective understandings that signify membership stem primarily from interactions with each other, not from interactions with outsiders. Such is not the case for a contracultural movement whose members most frequently interact with outsiders.

Perceived or real deprivation is the most prominent sentiment in a contraculture. If people cannot achieve the rewards valued by others in the organization, they will discount and deny the importance of such rewards. Blocked ambitions, poor training, inadequate rewards, impersonal management, inadequate resources or equipment, and unrealistic performance standards are all conditions that encourage contracultural movements and the rituals of resistance that define them.[13] Kanter's (1977) description of immobile office workers provides a good illustration of how such situations bolster a contracultural movement. Thwarted in their desire to achieve higher status and increased responsibility in the organization, "stuck" office workers retaliated by blocking the efforts of others. Negativism, malicious behavior, and nonutilitarian values were rewarded within the group of "stucks," especially when the targets of such posturing were outsiders. "Working to rule," as expressed by factory operatives, is another example, as is Ditton's (1977) splendid telling of the "fiddle" as worked by bread-truck drivers in London.

Career Filters

Incentive schemes to link the personal ambitions of employees to the espoused goals of the employing firm sometimes unwittingly promote subcultures. In particular, as people move toward the higher ranks of an organization's hierarchy, it becomes more difficult to know what others consider to be desirable performance. In doubt about what is expected and therefore somewhat fearful about standing out in the crowd, newly appointed upper-level managers sometimes play it safe by emulating perspectives and behaviors already prevalent among their newfound colleagues. Thus conformity can gradually displace individual achievement as managers climb higher in the organization.

Kanter's (1977) memorable phrase, "homosexual reproduction," captures elements of just such a process. She uses the phrase to describe how the like-minded and the like-skilled come together to form timid managerial enclaves or subcultures within organizations. The conformity among high-level managers that Kanter depicts rivals that of the hypothetical "organization man" made sport of by business commentator W. H. Whyte (1956) almost thirty years ago. But conformity's utility as a substitute for performance appraisal is not limited to those who reach arenas of power by climbing institutionalized career ladders. Hammer and Stern's (1984) study of labor representation on corporate boards suggests that workers often fail to champion the cause of labor after they become board members precisely because they adopt the perspective of the board on the good of the larger corporation in lieu of an alternate schema for determining how board members should act.

In a more analytic vein, March (1980) argues that the accuracy of performance evaluations in organizations varies inversely with the rank being evaluated. The higher one moves in an organization, the more problematic and, hence, ambiguous the performance appraisal. "The joint result," writes March (1980: 21) "is . . . the noise level in evaluation approaches the variance in the pool of managers." In effect, promotions may represent successive filters that screen managerial applicants at each level on roughly indentical attributes. Since each filter reduces the pool, attributional variance is continually reduced.

Progressive screening seems to increase the basis for cooperation and effective interaction among those at the top of an organization at the price of conformity to accepted points of view. Perhaps the formation of diverse subcultures within hierarchical ranks is therefore possible only at the lower levels of organizations. At the upper levels one would expect to find a solid and pervasive managerial subculture. It fact, what is so glibly called the organizational culture by many observers of the business scene may simply be the collective understandings that define the subculture of the carefully chosen few. We would expect such understandings to trickle down the hierarchy with at least as much difficulty as other perspectives trickle up.

CULTURAL CLASHES IN ORGANIZATIONS

Over the course of this essay, we have sought to elaborate and illustrate a theoretical rationale for the presence and proliferation of subcultures in organizations. Our reading of organizational dynamics implies that structural ironies and normative tensions between groups are facts of life in most organizations, and that these facts are suspiciously tinged by telltale hues of cultural processes. Many discussions have portrayed culture in organizations as a force for organizationwide solidarity. While we do not deny that normative unity is a distinct empirical possibility, our perspective on cultural organization intimates that cultures are just as likely, if not more likely, to act as centripetal forces that encourage the disintegration of that very unity for which commentators occasionally pine. Whereas proponents of organizational culture sometimes argue that modern corporations suffer from a lack of culture, we submit that organizations often get more culture than they bargained for. From the perspective we have elaborated, the study of cultural organization is therefore closely bound to the study of organizational conflict. To inquire about cultural organization is to inquire about the processes that transform organizations into veiled political economies.

Because subcultures are scattered throughout an organization, members of one subculture are often inattentive to, if not ignorant of, other subcultures. This is not to say that the members of two subcultures are likely to be unaware of each other as persons, but only that they may not recognize the subcultural differences that divide them until the realization is triggered by unexpected events. While intergroup squabbles in organizations are not uncommon, such conflicts tend to center on situations specific to the resolution of current issues and role definitions. Subcultural formation plants seeds of potential conflict, but the potential usually remains dormant until activated by a specific course of events (Becker and Geer, 1960). In other words, points of contention between the members of different subcultures can undulate mutely for long periods of time beneath the surface of day-to-day activities without openly disrupting relationships.

A good example of the latent nature of much cultural conflict in organizations is provided by Bailyn (1983). She shows how various groups of scientists, engineers, and managers, as well as those more or less uncommitted members of a high-status industrial research organization are able to handle what she calls the "inner contradictions of technical careers" without undue organizational disruption. The working out process is not without its serious human and organizational costs, but subcultural battles between scientists, engineers, and managers are, by and large, subtly and ambivalently carried on beneath the veneer of everyday life. Distinct occupational viewpoints only come to light around situationally specific issues that force the members of the laboratory to confront their different values regarding research.

Barley's (1984) study of two radiology departments during the year that each began to operate its first body scanner offers another example of latent subcultural collision. Prior to the arrival of the body scanners, technologists in both hospitals made clear occupational distinctions among themselves. Some X-ray technologists even resented the sonographers and the "specials" techs, not simply because their pay was higher, but because theirs was not "dirty work," and because radiologists accorded the latter groups higher prestige. However, before the arrival of the scanners, conflict between the various technologists remained mute, since all technologists were required to pull duty assignments in the main department.

Once the body scanners arrived, the specials techs (for different reasons in the two hospitals) were assigned less frequently to the main department, and the CT techs were absolved of X-ray responsibilities. Moreover, the scanner operations began to preoccupy the radiologists' attention, and the technologists perceived that the radiologists were no longer interested in the older technologies. As a result of these events, the boundaries between the various technological subunits quickly solidified and subcultural identities became apparent. X-ray techs began to complain more frequently about their work, while sonographers and specials techs deplored the privileged treatment given CT techs and began to protest loudly about being assigned to X-ray. CT techs began to derogate X-ray work as well as the lofty attitudes of the sonographers and specials techs, who in turn concluded that CT work was mere "button-pushing." Seemingly the only common ground was that members of each technological subculture blamed the "bosses" and the radiologists for the perceived inequities of their respective situations, and each therefore began to press hard their individual claims with whomever would listen. In response, administrators haphazardly attempted to respond to subcultural pressures; but since honoring one group's claims involved affronting another, administration actions only amplified the conflict.

Once latent tensions between organizational subcultures are activated, the character and outcome of the ensuing conflict depends on a host of variables, including the political clout that a group can muster, the number of opportunities to exercise such clout, and the conditions that shape each group's position vis-à-vis others in the organization.[14] To underline the importance of subcultures for understanding organizational actions, and to note why subcultures may or may not control their own density, we now briefly consider several such variables. To anchor our discussion, we draw on the above-mentioned dispute in the two radiology departments.

One dimension along which organizational subcultures vary is the degree to which their boundaries extend beyond or are confined within a particular organization. For subcultures surrounding occupations, this is a crucial matter. All else being equal, members of organizationally dispersed occupational subcultures who have skills currently in demand are more apt to obtain favorable resolutions of conflict. Dispersed subcultures provide members with career opportunities outside the confines of a single organization (Van Maanen and Barley, 1984). For example, all technologists in radiology departments are relatively mobile, but at the time of Barley's (1984) study, CT techs had the strongest local job market. Since trained CT techs were scarce, the radiology departments could ill afford to alienate their CT techs for fear of losing them to other hospitals.

Another dimension of apparent importance concerns the prominence of a particular subculture within an organization. Such prominence may have several sources. Centrality in an organization's work flow correlates with a subgroup's power, since groups in key positions are able to regulate the overall quality and quantity of work produced by the organization (Hickson et al., 1971; Crozier, 1964). Members of a subculture may also gain prominence to the degree that they are seen by others as irreplaceable. Such a perception may be fostered either because the members have gained valuable organization-specific knowledge, or because certain types of work are held in high regard by others for what are essentially symbolic reasons. In our example, CT techs enjoyed a measure of prominence beyond that bestowed by a favorable labor market because the machines they operated were new, expensive, and required high usage rates as a way of justifying their purchase by the hospital. They also gained status because CT technology was still surrounded by an aura of mystery.

Finally, members of a subculture approach not only their work, but also those who witness their work, in mannered ways. Subcultures provide members with a characteristic style (Hebdige, 1979). For example, Schon (1983) argues that city planners have viewed themselves differently over the years: as "policy analysts," "designers," "advocates," "regulators," "administrators," and "mediators." Each stance involves a qualitatively different relationship with managers, engineers, architects, developers, and other groups. Matters such as a planner's loyalty to an employer, conflict with other subgroups, and the amount of control planners seek over their work depend on the role frames that they have enacted in particular areas.

In the two radiology departments, CT techs held quite different understandings of their roles. In one hospital, the techs viewed themselves as "employees," while in the other hospital the technologists saw themselves as "experts." In the first setting, the CT techs often refused to accept full responsibility for an examination and would usually check with a radiologist before dismissing a patient or processing images. These technologists lamented the absence of standard operating procedures on which they might rely when in doubt. At the second hospital, attempts to establish procedures or to require the technologists to consult with radiologists before making routine operational decisions were met with great resistance. Here, the CT techs were bound to each other, not to the larger department. The "employee" technologists, however, oriented themselves on these matters to the department as a matter of course. Yet, as might be expected, the "employee" orientation gained technologists little autonomy, while the "experts" often managed to keep administrators at bay and to operate the scanner without a radiologist being present.

COMMENT

Louis (1983) proposes that organizations be viewed as "culture-bearing milieus." Over the course of this essay, we have raised another question: How many cultures can an organization bear? The answer, we think, is many. There are sound theoretical reasons to expect multiple subcultures within organizations, and we have suggested a number of places where such subcultures may be found. Yet the formation of a subculture provides no guarantee that the life of a subculture will be a long one, or that its members will have much voice in the organization, either individually or collectively. What is likely, however, is that if we wish to discover where the cultural action lies in organizational life, we will probably have to discard some of our tacit (and not so tacit) presumptions about organizational (high) culture and move to the group level of analysis. It is here where the people discover, create, and use culture, and it is against this background that they judge the organization of which they are a part.

NOTES

1. To see clearly that "organizational culture" is a metaphor, one need only transform the phrase into the syntax of a simile: "Organizations are like cultures." In the

transformation, none of the phrase's pragmatic import is lost, although the simile's syntax may hinder the perception of referential naming by making explicit the hypotheticality of the comparison.

2. In the 1940s and 1950s a handful of anthropologists turned their attention to the study of industrial organizations and founded a journal, *Human Organization*. But over the years, those who started this work became estranged from academic anthropology, and interest in the study of organizations waned among anthropologists. Recently, there has been a revival of interest in the study of complex organizations among certain anthropoligists. These individuals have formed a loose association to further their efforts: NESSTO (Network for the Ethnographic Study of Science, Technology, and Organizations). Representative of the work by this group of anthropologists is Wynn's (1976) study of office workers.

3. The notion that cultures are historical records of a collective's response to problems posed by its environment is most clearly found in the work of those anthropologists considered to be structural-functionalists (especially Radcliffe-Brown, 1952) and in the cultural materialism of Harris (1981). As Schein (1985) points out, although functionalist thought draws criticism because it is rarely possible to document whether societal cultures actually arose in response to problems, one can more easily reconstruct and even observe the historical evolution of organizations. Hence the hypothesis that cultures evolve in response to problems is testable in the study of organizations. Our own stance takes problem solving as a force that generates cultural understandings, but our notion of culture itself (collective understandings) is more akin to those proposed by symbolic (Leach, 1976; Douglas, 1975; Geertz, 1973) and cognitive anthropologists (Frake, 1961; Conklin, 1955; Goodenough, 1981; Tyler, 1969).

4. It is this point that clearly separates our notions from the ideas of functionalism. From the a strict functionalist standpoint, social and cultural forms never lose their "functionality," since their purpose is viewed in relation to hypothesized social goals rather than in terms of historical elaboration.

5. This is essentially a semiotic perspective on the symbolic nature of culture. The theory of semiotics is far too complicated to detail in a footnote, and the task of explicating in text would take us too far afield from our main line of discussion. The interested reader should consult Barthes (1967), Hawkes (1977), McCannell and McCannell (1982), and especially Eco (1976) for discussions of semiotic theory. General and detailed statements on studying organizations from a semiotic perspective are to be found in Manning (1979) and Barley (1983), respectively.

6. Schein (1985) takes these matters much further than we do here and points to the crucial matters of group dynamics as a way of understanding cultural processes. The importance of intragroup processes is obvious since significant cultural variations are visible among groups with very similar socioeconomic backgrounds, current situations, and social histories (Schwartz and Merten, 1968; Fine and Kleinman, 1979). A marvelous example of the relevance of group dynamics to cultural studies is given in Orthe's (1963) woefully neglected study of differing student subcultures at the Harvard Business School.

7. Silverman's (1970) "social action" framework draws on just these studies for examining organizations as complex, conflictual "systems of meaning."

8. The structural elaboration of organizations in line with "technical rationality" is well argued elsewhere (Chandler, 1962; Blau and Scott, 1962; Mintzberg, 1979; Edwards, 1979; Miles, 1980b). Our discussion draws liberally from this literature. The Weberian doctrine of "technical rationality" has also been studied by Schon (1983).

9. Some may be surprised to find professionalization listed among the practices usually associated with bureaucratic forms of organization. Although professionalization

has been frequently portrayed as hostile to bureaucratic control, current arguments (both empirical and theoretical) suggest that professionalization is but one form of market control (see Larson, 1977, 1979; Benson, 1973; Montagna, 1968; Goldner and Ritti, 1967). Nor is there much evidence to suggest that professions themselves are particularly distressed when working in highly bureaucratized settings (Bailyn, 1980).

10. This process is a thematic matter in another paper that we regard as the flip side of this one (Van Maanen and Barley, 1984). Instead of organizational cultures and subcultures, there we examine occupational ones. How to bring these two analytic domains together is the wave we are currently riding. (It is a bone cruncher on a deserted sea.)

11. This and the following references to radiology are drawn from Barley's (1984) field study of radiology departments in two community hospitals.

12. Small groups will usually find it more difficult to fragment than large ones since, in small groups, people must see others frequently. A front of "getting along" is usually maintained even if people detest one another. In this regard, we are perhaps treating Kunda's (1983) careful work a little too casually, because the probation office he studied was a small one and the groups we have labeled subcultures were really just emerging. The contrasting views on probation work existed in this office, but there were only a few officers who clearly fell in one camp or the other. Most probation workers operated in the gray area between the poles and used authoritative or therapeutic orientations in strategic rather than committed ways. Were the organization to experience rapid growth, one or the other orientation might give way, or full-bodied subcultures might develop that were routinely antagonistic to one another. As Kunda suggests, the instrumental value of an internally contradictory ideology may continue to serve probation workers quite well and, at the same time, allow the office to remain flexible in its dealings with other groups who might threaten whatever autonomy probation officers have thus far managed to carve out.

13. There are, of course, ironies associated with contracultural movements. Foremost among them is the fact that by engaging in ritual resistance, the expectations of the dominant groups are confirmed. Thus when workers peg production at low levels, managers regard it as just another instance of worker laziness or recalcitrance. Willis (1977) provides a tidy analysis of this sort of process when he asks the question: "Why do working class kids get working class jobs?"

14. Benson (1973) is a good source on these matters. In particular, he suggests that internal organizational changes of the sort that threaten the current distribution of pay, prestige, authority, and autonomy trigger conflict and thus bring subcultures and subcultural identities out of the closet. During such periods, the relative power of these groups is on display, often in raw form.

3

IS THE CONCEPT OF CULTURE A PARADIGM FOR UNDERSTANDING ORGANIZATIONS AND OURSELVES?

Linda Smircich
University of Massachusetts

* * * * * * * * * * * * * * *THE GALAXY TODAY* * * * * * * * * * * * * *

Archaeology Dig Uncovers Meaning of Corporate Forms

Positive Proof That "Organization" Is *The* Paradigm
Of Ancient Culture

Planet Earth (UPI)—A major discovery was revealed today (April 1, 3084 AD) by Richard L.S.B. Leakey XII, leader of the Archaeology expedition on the ancient Planet Earth. Leakey, who has been conducting research on the site known as "Wall Street" for the last 20 years, believes he has at last unlocked the key to understanding the way of life in what is referred to as "Western Civilization" of the time period 1870-2000 AD.

The Leakey expedition has been searching among the leftovers of life at that time and has recovered an astonishing number of "computer printouts," "Xerox machines," "organization charts," and "dress for success" books. But these mere artifacts did not provide Leakey with sufficient evidence to confirm his hypothesis about that time period.

In an interview, Leakey said, "In order for us to make sense of the physical findings we needed to uncover a mode of thought, some symbolic connection, between the artifacts. And today we've found it."

Leakey was referring to a remarkably well-preserved copy of a book by Robert Denhardt, called *In the Shadow of Organization*, published in 1981.

Denhardt's commentary on this civilization called it "an age of organization." He characterized society as dominated by an organizational ethic which "offers itself as a way of life for persons in our society."

Leakey was visibly excited as he told reporters, "This book was all I needed to confirm my own theory. These people were crazy for organization. They valued discipline, order, regulation, and obedience much more than independence, expressiveness, and creativity. They were always looking for efficiency. They wanted to control everything. They had a fetish for 'managing.' They managed stress, time, relationships, emotions, but mostly they managed their careers.

"They were somewhat more civilized than the even more ancient Aztecs. Their sacrifices were bloodless and were conducted on symbolic ladders of success, instead of stone altars."

Leakey went on to say, "I'd concluded on my own that these people had a fairly impoverished existence, and this book validates my findings. In the 1980s, organization was the meaning of life. I'll be publishing my findings in *Administrative Arts Quarterly*, and I will argue conclusively that organization was *the* paradigm of this culture!"

* * * * * * * * * * * * * * * * * * * *

Is Culture a Paradigm for Understanding
Organizations and Ourselves?

Academic Gives Typical Hedging Answer:
Says Culture "Could Be" a Paradigm

Vancouver, BC (UPI)—Linda Smircich addressed an elite collection of people concerned about organizational life today (April 1, 1984) and wrestled with the question, "What is the relationship between organization and culture?"

Before going out to make her presentation, she was overheard saying, "I really don't have much to say. Organizations are cultural phenomena and need to be understood in those terms. Of course, I think that means a radical reorientation in how we think about organizations and how we think about ourselves and what we are doing. I'm not too sure about how this will go over. I'm only just learning it for myself."

The gist of Smircich's argument was that the concept of culture could be a paradigm for inquiry, depending on what the inquirer was concerned about. If it was the meaning of life in the workplace—yes. If it was improving organizational effectiveness—no.

Reaction to Smircich's presentation was mixed. Some snatches of conversation overheard at the coffee break included: "More academic navel gazing"; "irrelevant"; "provocative"; "subversive"; "too personal for my tastes"; "So what else is new?"; and "She's talking in a whole new language for understanding organizations."

The conference continued for another two days. To this reporter's surprise and regret, there appeared to be very little discussion of the meaning of life in the workplace.

****

For the organizational culture conference, I was asked to address the following question: What is the relationship between organization and culture? One quite plausible answer comes from the standpoint of a future archaeologist who studies the artifacts of our lives and calls ours "a culture of organization." From that perspective it is clear that the Western world has elevated organization and management to the status of cultural values. A trip to a bookstore quickly reveals our fascination with organizations and careers, and our preoccupation with managing them. We understand and make sense of our lives with reference to the concepts of organization and management. These concepts are filters through which we experience our lives and know ourselves. It is possible, of course, to answer the same question in other ways. In this essay I want to develop the argument that culture *could be* a paradigm for understanding organizations and ourselves.

"Paradigm" is a grand word, signifying a cluster of basic assumptions that form a world view, a way of filtering knowledge and experience. "Culture" is also a grand word. I wish I could link the two, present a bold claim, and argue it elegantly, for *the concept of culture is bringing forth a new way of understanding organizational life.*

In good conscience, I cannot yet make such a proclamation. There are two reasons: First, it is misleading to talk about *the* concept of culture. There is no single view of culture that has gripped anthropologists and that guides their work. Instead, there are multiple conceptions of culture (see Smircich, 1983a). The term "culture" is powerfully evocative, but it does not come from anthropology as an intact structural package ready to serve as a paradigmatic foundation on which to build the analysis of organizations.

The second reason I cannot boldly proclaim that culture signals a revolution in understanding organizational life is that organizational analysts, like other social scientists, are rooted in their paradigmatic positions. When a "new" idea or word comes to our attention, we see it from the standpoint of our own position. If we incorporate it into our

world view, we do so in a way that allows integration with our way of
ordering the conceptual universe. Thus many people are making culture
their own. They are incorporating it into their organizations-as-systems
models and adding it to the contingency theories of structure, leadership, and strategy. This direction may have some invigorating effects on
our discipline, and it is certainly financially rewarding for some, but it
does not represent a new paradigm for understanding organizational
life.

I believe that culture could be associated with a dramatic redirection
for our field—a paradigm shift—if it were accompanied by a major
reorientation in how we see both organizations and ourselves. Those of
us who study organizational life could join others in the social sciences
in what Geertz (1983) calls the "rise of the interpretive turn." We could
understand organizations as social constructions, symbolically constituted and reproduced through interaction. Our attention would then
shift to the realms of meaning and interpretation, and we would see that
we have much in common with disciplines in the humanities such as
history, rhetoric, literature, and literary criticism.

The point of view I am putting forward here is that organizational
analysis inspired by a symbolic conception of culture represents a
fundamentally different mode of understanding organizations in
general, as well as specific organizations and our work in them. To know
organizations in terms of their symbolic nature implies a dramatically
different form and purpose for organizational research and teaching. It
also means a different way of understanding ourselves.

BEHIND ORGANIZATIONAL CULTURE

Many students of organizational life are indeed inspired by the idea
of culture. The idea has launched an industry (we have corporate culture
conferences and consultants, culture audits, and culture-gap surveys)
and revived discussions of values and assumptions. Culture encourages
us to speak about something more than technical processes, and it
allows us to put some soul, as well as a little mystery, back into our
subject matter.

Usually the term "culture" describes an attribute or quality internal to
a group. We refer to an organizational culture or subculture. In this
sense culture is a possession—a fairly stable set of taken-for-granted
assumptions, shared beliefs, meanings, and values that form a kind of
backdrop for action. A consistent message coming from many people
writing about organizational culture is that managers need to be aware

of their group's or organization's culture because it will make a difference.

Culture has become an important element in the managerial equation. As applied to organizations, it extends rationality into interpersonal domains. The rational manager needs to take culture into account.

In my view, this development of the idea of culture does not go far enough. To proceed only in terms of organizational culture misses the full significance of culture as an idea for understanding and analyzing organizations. We turned to the idea of culture for a fresh slant on organizational life, for something different. But for the most part, we're not getting it.

One of the benefits of the culture idea is that it raises our consciousness of implicit assumptions that explain why we do things. This applies as much to those of us who study organizations as to those organization members at Hewlett-Packard, IBM, or AT&T.

Behind the way we develop the idea of culture is a particular set of assumptions that legitimates our actions as inquirers/scholars. I will elaborate this point with the aid of Table 3.1, which shows a rough typology for thinking about the various assumptions that different social scientists make about human beings and their world (Morgan and Smircich, 1980).

Behind the concern with organizational culture and implicit in the writing about it, there stands a familiar mode of thinking, represented in Table 3.1 under the heading, "Reality as a Concrete Process." This mode of thought conceptualizes the social world as an evolving process, concrete in nature. In this world human beings are adaptive agents, responding to forces in the environment. Organizational analysis based on these assumptions draws on a systems theory framework to articulate patterns of contingent relationships among collections of variables that figure in organizational survival.

Academics and management consultants are interested in specifying relationships among abstracted concepts such as culture, leadership, structure, and strategy so that they will add up in some way to organizational effectiveness. This mode of thought suggests a social engineering or social physics approach to organizational life, an approach evident in the kinds of research questions pursued and the kinds of articles written by many of us.

I see patterns in the "culture" literature that stem from this mode of thinking. The first pattern is exemplified by two papers appearing in *Organizational Dynamics* in 1984, "Compensation, Culture, and Motivation: A Systems Perspective" by Larry Cummings and "The

TABLE 3.1   Assumptions About Ontology and Human Nature

SUBJECTIVE APPROACHES ◄───

	Reality as a Projection of Human Imagination	Reality as a Social Construction	Reality as Symbolic Discourse
CORE ONTOLOGICAL ASSUMPTIONS	The social world and what passes as "reality" is a projection of individual consciousness; it is an act of creative imagination and of dubious intersubjective status. This extreme position, commonly known as solipsism, asserts that there may be nothing outside oneself: one's mind is one's world. Certain transcendental approaches to phenomenology assert a reality in consciousness, the manifestation of a phenomenal world, but not necessarily accessible to understanding in the course of everyday affairs. Reality in this sense is masked by those human processes which judge and interpret the phenomenon in consciousness prior to a full understanding of the structure of meaning it expresses. Thus the nature of the phenomenal world may be accessible to the human being only through consciously phenomenological modes of insight.	The social world is a continuous process, created afresh in each encounter of everyday life as individuals impose themselves on their world to establish a realm of meaningful definition. They do so through the medium of language, labels, actions, and routines, which constitute symbolic modes of being in the world. Social reality is embedded in the nature and use of these modes of symbolic action. The realm of social affairs thus has no concrete status of any kind; it is a symbolic construction. Symbolic modes of being in the world, such as through the use of language, may result in the development of shared, but multiple realities, the status of which is fleeting, confined only to those moments in which they are actively constructed and sustained.	The social world is a pattern of symbolic relationships and meanings sustained through a process of human action and interaction. Although a certain degree of continuity is preserved through the operation of rule-like activities that define a particular social milieu, the pattern is always open to reaffirmation or change through the interpretations and actions of individual members. The fundamental character of the social world is embedded in the network of subjective meanings that sustain the rule-like actions that lend it enduring form. Reality rests not in the rule or in rule-following, but in the system of meaningful action that renders itself to an external observer as rule-like.
	Humans as Transcendental Beings	Humans Create Their Realities	Humans as Social Actors
ASSUMPTIONS ABOUT HUMAN NATURE	Humans are viewed as intentional beings, directing their psychic energy and experience in ways that constitute the world in a meaningful, intentional form. There are realms of reality, constituted through different kinds of founding acts, stemming from a form of transcendental consciousness. Human beings shape the world within the realm of their own immediate experience.	Human beings create their realities in the most fundamental ways, in an attempt to make their world intelligible to themselves and to others. They are not simply actors interpreting their situations in meaningful ways, for there are no situations other than those which individuals bring into being through their own creative activity. Individuals may work together to create a shared reality, but that reality is still a subjective construction capable of disappearing the moment its members cease to sustain it as such. Reality appears as real to individuals because of human acts of conscious or unwitting collusion.	Human beings are social actors interpreting their milieu and orienting their actions in ways that are meaningful to them. In this process they utilize language, labels, routines for impression management, and other modes of culturally specific action. In so doing they contribute to the enactment of a reality; human beings live in a world of symbolic significance, interpreting and enacting a meaningful relationship with that world. Humans are actors with the capacity to interpret, modify, and sometimes create the scripts that they play upon life's stage.
SOME EXAMPLES OF RESEARCH	Phenomenology	Ethnomethodology	Social Action Theory

Performance Measurement and Reward System: Critical to Strategic Management" by Paul Stonich. Both of these authors discuss organizational culture and the need for a match between internal organizational components, such as reward systems, and external issues such as strategy. These papers are derivative of that by Schwartz and Davis (1981), "Matching Corporate Culture and Business Strategy." Common to these three papers and to many others is a concern with organizational design. They enumerate organizational "building blocks" and discuss the appropriate way to arrange them to achieve environmental

OBJECTIVE APPROACHES →

Reality as a Contextual Field of Information	Reality as a Concrete Process	Reality as a Concrete Structure
The social world is a field of ever-changing form and activity based on the transmission of information. The form of activity that prevails at any one given time reflects a pattern of "difference" sustained by a particular kind of information exchange. Some forms of activity are more stable than others, reflecting an evolved pattern of learning based on principles of negative feedback. The nature of relationships within the field is probabilistic; a change in the appropriate pattern and balance within any sphere will reverberate throughout the whole, initiating patterns of adjustment and readjustment capable of changing the whole in fundamental ways. Relationships are relative rather than fixed and real.	The social world is an evolving process, concrete in nature, but ever-changing in detailed form. Everything interacts with everything else and it is extremely difficult to find determinate causal relationships between constituent processes. At best, the world expresses itself in terms of general and contingent relationships between its more stable and clear-cut elements. The situation is fluid and creates opportunities for those with appropriate ability to mold and exploit relationships in accordance with their interests. The world is in part what one makes of it: a struggle between various influences, each attempting to move toward achievement of desired ends.	The social world is a hard, concrete, real thing "out there," which affects everyone in one way or another. It can be thought of as a structure composed of a network of determinate relationships between constituent parts. Reality is to be found in the concrete behavior and relationships between these parts. It is an objective phenomenon that lends itself to accurate observation and measurement. Any aspect of the world that does not manifest itself in some form of observable activity or behavior must be regarded as being of questionable status. Reality by definition is that which is external and real. The social world is as concrete and real as the natural world.

Humans as Information Processors	Humans as Adaptive Agents	Humans as Responding Mechanisms
Human beings are engaged in a continual process of interaction and exchange with their context — receiving, interpreting, and acting on the information received, and in so doing creating a new pattern of information that effects changes in the field as a whole. Relationships between individual and context are constantly modified as a result of this exchange; the individual is but an element of a changing whole. The crucial relationship between individual and context is reflected in the pattern of learning and mutual adjustment that has evolved. Where this is well developed, the field of relationships is harmonious; where adjustment is low, the field is unstable and subject to unpredictable and discontinuous patterns of change.	Human beings exist in an interactive relationship with their world. They influence and are influenced by their context or environment. The process of exchange that operates here is essentially a competitive one, the individual seeking to interpret and exploit the environment to satisfy important needs, and hence survive. Relationships between individuals and environment express a pattern of activity necessary for survival and well-being of the individual.	Human beings are a product of the external forces in the environment to which they are exposed. Stimuli in their environment condition them to behave and respond to events in predictable and determinate ways. A network of causal relationships links all important aspects of behavior to context. Though human perception may influence this process to some degree, people always respond to situations in a lawful (i.e., rule-governed) manner.
Cybernetics	Open Systems Theory	Behaviorism Social Learning Theory

SOURCE: From G. Morgan and L. Smircich, "The case for qualitative research," *Academy of Management Review* 5 (October 1980), pp. 491-500. © 1980 by the Academy of Management. Reprinted by permission.

fit and internal consistency, a long-standing interest in organizational literature. "Culture" here is a somewhat new term introduced into an old problem.

The second pattern is represented by papers that seek to offer ways to diagnose organizational culture, either to help an individual manager negotiate his or her way through an organizational maze or to provide assistance in the accomplishment of organizational change. Examples include works by Boje et al. (1982) on myths, Wilkins (1983a) on the culture audit, Sathe (1983) on corporate culture and managerial action, and Tichy (1982b) on culture and strategy. Recent conferences on managing corporate culture are part of this pattern of discourse. In this view, culture exists as an organizational variable that should be diagnosed or read prior to taking action.

Patterns such as these in the literature demonstrate one way to "do" culture. We can use culture to frame questions of organizational and personal effectiveness, but there is nothing new or dramatically different about this orientation to our subject matter. Old models have merely been opened up to accommodate new vocabularies. The research questions are coming from the same problematic that the field of organizational behavior has had for the last thirty years.

Behind this way of "doing" culture is a familiar mode of thought that aims at achieving predictability and control. Behind this work there is also a sincere desire to be helpful and relevant to practitioners, especially managers.

One striking aspect of this orientation to scholarly research is the degree to which authors have identified with the subjects of their studies. As a field we have taken on managers' problems and defined them as our own. Despite a rhetoric of objectivity in conducting research, the problems we select for study and the issues we identify as important are largely those that come to us from the concerns of the managerial class. For the most part, we uncritically adopt the values, purposes, and language of top managers. It is as if an anthropologist were to arrive at a South Seas island and proceed to launch investigations designed to help the high priests overcome bad kharma (Smircich and Stubbart, 1983).

Why do we do this? I think it stems from our own need to feel useful and valuable, our own need to contribute to something beyond ourselves—to give our work lives meaning. It comes from our sense of what we as professionals are about and the sense of tradition that this is how our work is done. It also comes out of our understanding that this is what our journals will publish, this is what reviewers feel comfortable with, and this is the way to achieve success in a business school environment.

I would like to suggest that there are other ways to "do" culture, ways that imply a different orientation to our subject matter and a different way of understanding what we are about. These are represented in the table under the headings "Reality as Symbolic Discourse" and "Reality as a Social Construction."

Why should we adopt a different way of doing culture, especially if it may challenge our self-conceptions and identities as professionals? The conference on organizational culture provided one reason by addressing culture and the meaning of life at work. In the first approach to culture there is actually little discussion about the meaning of life in the workplace. If we proceed to examine culture differently, meaning becomes the central question.

A DIFFERENT VISION OF CULTURE AND ORGANIZATION

Interpretive anthropologists and sociologists speak about culture as webs of meaning, organized in terms of symbols and representations (Berger and Luckmann, 1966; Cohen, 1976; Geertz, 1983; Hallowell, 1955; Schutz, 1967). They see human beings as makers of meaning, creating their social worlds through symbols. To study culture means to study social significance—how things, events, and interactions come to be meaningful. Studying culture means studying "world making."

Anthropologists have learned that there are many different ways of making a world. There are different ways of arranging personal relationships, and different ways of arranging such human expressions as work, play, and art. Anthropologists have been devoted to describing these worlds. I will give just one example from an anthropological study of social organization and then discuss its implications for those of us who are interested in organizational life.

The example comes from Walter Miller's study of the central Algonkian Indian tribes of the western Great Lakes region (Miller, 1965). When Europeans encountered the central Algonkians around 1650, they proclaimed that the Indians had an absence of authority. The Europeans saw no leadership and no visible forms of government. They also noticed that any comment that carried the appearance of a command was instantly rejected with scorn. The Indians seemed to be too independent to be controlled.

These Europeans were used to a society with highly centralized authority, which was assigned to position holders. They were used to distinguishing between people on the basis of assigned authority with such terms as master-servant, student-teacher, leader-follower, officer-enlisted man, coach-team member, foreman-worker, pastor-parishioner, and parent-child. To Europeans at that time and to many of us today, this ordering of relationships seems natural. The vertical authority relationship is a fundamental aspect of European society; the functioning of our organized institutions depends on this kind of ordering.

As Miller points out, however, to a member of seventeenth-century Algonkian society such authority would be oppressive and intolerable. The Algonkians did have coordinated collective action in the political, economic, military, and religious spheres, but this collective action was based on such a different conception of authority that the Europeans saw *no* authority. In Algonkian society "each individual participating in organized activity related himself directly to the body of procedural rules governing that activity. He was free to select and execute appropriate modes of action: his access to procedural rules was not mediated through another person who transmitted these rules to him" (Miller, 1965: 774).

Miller (1965: 768) observes that in the European cultural tradition, authority or power is conceptually equated with height or elevation. It originates in some elevated locus and passes down to lower levels:

> This metaphorical way of thinking about authority is closely tied in with European religious conceptions, many of which utilize the notion that power originates in a supernatural being or group of beings located in the heavens, or some elevated location. The equation of authority with altitude is firmly built into European linguistic systems; e.g., the terms *superior, inferior*, and *super*ordinate and *sub*ordinate.

By contrast, the central Algonkian religion places its deities at the four corners of the universe, and on the same plane as humans. It is possible for an individual to possess some power from a "manitu" (a kind of generalized essence of supernatural power), but such power is never possessed permanently. It is always temporary, the result of ongoing interactions between individuals.

In the European cultural tradition, authority is reified (pictured as a liquidlike substance). "We speak of the 'flow' of authority, of 'going through channels,' of the 'fountainhead' of authority. As a substance, authority can be quantified, and thus we speak of a great deal of authority, little authority, no authority" (Miller, 1965: 678).

To the central Algonkian, power is universally available and unlimited; it is everywhere and equally available to all. "Power is not hierarchical; since its possession is temporary and contingent, fixed and varying amounts of power are not distributed among a group of beings arranged in a stable hierarchy. The control of power is dangerous; powerful beings are to be feared, not adored or admired" (Miller, 1965: 771).

The central Algonkians' different conception of power and authority meant that they organized collective activity very differently from the

Europeans. In fact, their organization of village life, with its consensus decision making, facilitative leadership, and individually interpreted normative modes of social control, was very similar to the organization of many autonomous work groups in industry today.

So what of this example? We find that the central Algonkians practiced a highly refined version of consensus management in 1650. Anthropology can in fact provide many wonderfully rich examples of different modes of social organization. But what I take away from this example, and from my reading of anthropology literature, is not so much the content of the "story," although I find the content fascinating. Rather, the lesson I find here has to do with the form of analysis that many anthropologists employ in their studies of groups.

When interpretive anthropologists study cultural phenomena such as the potlatch, food preparation practices, marriage rituals, religion, or authority patterns, they regard them as symbolic expressions within a pattern of wider significance. When the eminent anthropologist Marshall Sahlins defined cultures as meaningful orders of persons and things, he framed the analyst's task as the discovery of that meaningful ordering and the processes that sustain it (Sahlins, 1976). Thus, for Miller to make sense of two systems of authority—two modes of organizing collective action—he had to examine not only "organization" but also the cosmology and metaphorical conventions underlying language and action.

This is a wider and deeper form of analysis than we typically encounter in organizational behavior. Miller's research argues that we cannot know how authority and social organization work without knowing the world that serves as its context.

Miller's work, and the work of other interpretive anthropologists (e.g., Geertz, Sahlins, and Cohen) demonstrates that we who study organizations can do our work differently. Instead of researching organizational culture, we can engage in cultural analysis of organizational life.

ORGANIZATIONAL ANALYSTS AS ORGANIZATIONAL ANTHROPOLOGISTS

Those of us who study organizational life are concerned with a special kind of human action: that which forms, reproduces, and is constrained by processes of organizing. We tend to locate our inquiry within a fairly narrow time frame, from the Industrial Revolution, with special emphasis on the later period, and to focus to a large degree on the modern corporate form. For us to see organizations in cultural terms is to understand them as symbolically constituted and sustained within a wider pattern of significance. Just as the anthropologist's task is interpreting, decoding, and deconstructing whole systems of meaning for particular groups, our task can be seen as interpreting, decoding, and deconstructing the meaning of organization in the modern age. Just as studying culture for the anthropologist means studying world making, studying organizations can mean studying "organization making."

Can organizational analysts become organizational anthropologists? Can we stand back from organizations and see them differently? Can we see organizations not only as places where we gather to get work done, but as symbolic expressions, as displays of meaning as well as representations of the search for meaning? Can we, as researchers, enter the organizational world not to provide the answers but to raise the questions about how organizational life is being made? Can we restore a sense of wonder, awe, skepticism, incredulity, and passion about the phenomenon of organization? Can we learn to ask first, and most importantly, "What is going on?" rather than jump in and attempt to change it?

To do cultural analysis of organizational life means the following:

(1) We realize that organizations are representations of our humanity, like music or art; they can be known through acts of appreciation.
(2) We realize that organizations are symbolically constituted worlds, like novels or poems; they can be known through acts of critical reading and interpretation.
(3) We realize that organizations are symbolic forms, like religion and folklore; they are displays of the meaning of life.

To think about organizations in this way represents a dramatic departure from our usual pragmatic stance. It represents different directions for our work as researchers, teachers, and organization members. The following sections contain my thinking on the implications of understanding organizational life in cultural terms.

IMPLICATIONS: A RESEARCHER'S PERSPECTIVE

Cultural Analysis of Organizational Life: Researching Organizational Life as Symbolic Construction

Focus on symbols, not culture. Culture does not exist separately from people in interaction. People hold culture in their heads, but we cannot really know what is in their heads. All we can see or know are representations or symbols. Abner Cohen, in *Two-Dimensional Man* (1976), argues that the term "culture" is too wide in its connotations to be useful for studies of specific groupings engaged in organized activity. The term "symbol" is preferable to "culture" because "symbol" refers to phenomena that are objective and collective, and thus observable and verifiable. He writes: "Symbols are objects, acts, concepts, or linguistic formations that stand ambiguously for a multiplicity of disparate meanings, evoke sentiments and emotions, and impel [people] to action" (p. 23).

Research from this perspective would center on the symbols that make organizational life possible. What are the words, ideas, and constructs that impel, legitimate, coordinate, and realize organized activity in specific settings? How do they accomplish the task? Whose interests are they serving?

Dialectical, not linear form of analysis. Cultural analysis can be conducted through the two concepts of symbol and power, as social organization is constituted by the symbolic order and the power order. These two dimensions are interdependent and function dialectically in the manifestation of social forms and social arrangements. Cohen (1976) argues that organized life can be known through reference to "symbolist man" and "political man"—hence the title of his book.

Emergence of a feminist critique. The unconscious (I presume) sexism of Cohen's labels should encourage us to examine the degree to which the production of knowledge about organizational life is permeated by gender bias. Just as a Marxist perspective on culture calls for analysis and critique of the underlying class basis of the production of knowledge and the prevailing social order, so a feminist perspective on culture calls for analysis and critique of the underlying gender basis of the production of knowledge and the prevailing social order (Firestone, 1971). Thus an important and necessary aspect of a cultural paradigm for organizational analysis is the addition of a feminist voice to the discussion on organizational life.

Inclusion of psychodynamic dimensions. The analysis of organizational life as symbolic construction will draw on other models for understanding human activity besides that of the "rational-economic" person. The First Cornell Conference on Psychodynamics in Organizational Behavior in October 1983 is testimony to interest in this direction. In fact, psychodynamic theories are increasingly relevant because they address unconscious motivation and offer frameworks for understanding symbolism and meaning.

Metaphors of theater, drama, text. Symbolic forms and symbolic action are essentially dramatistic (Cohen, 1976; Geertz, 1973). They involve the totality of the person, including cognitions, feelings, and sensations (Cohen, 1976). The dominant metaphors of organizational behavior—machine (with its input-output imagery) and organism (with its needs imagery)—are inadequate for capturing the holism of human experiencing. Metaphors drawn from cultural domains such as drama, theater, and text will be developed more fully.

Purpose. When we research organization making—an important phenomenon in the modern age—our inquiry raises to consciousness that which is often below awareness. Consciousness raising has political implications because it reveals symbols and the interests they serve.

> Symbols are essential for the development and maintenance of social order. To do their job efficiently, their social functions must remain largely unconscious and unintended by the actors. Once these functions become known to the actors, the symbols lose a great deal of their efficacy. This is one of the reasons why students of society are often so "revolutionary." But against this, it can be argued that the symbols of society are manipulated by interest groups for their own benefits and that unless we understand the nature of the symbols and of the ways in which they are manipulated, we shall be exploited without our knowledge [Cohen, 1976; 8].

Calling research political may be objectionable to those steeped in a vision of a neutral social science. But once we understand our world as symbolically constructed, we recognize that researchers, as much as those we research, are creators and manipulators of symbols. We too are "world makers" by our actions of researching, publishing, teaching, and consulting. As teachers of courses on management and organizational behavior, in executive development programs and as consultants, we are very much engaged in the process of creating that which we later go out and research. We are already co-producers of the world of organization. Thus we are not engaged in a neutral activity. Quite to the contrary, we are striving to be influential and to contribute to the world beyond ourselves.

We have to ask, then, what the ethical consequences of our actions are. We may comfort ourselves by saying, "Well, who reads such-and-such journal, anyway?" but that is not very comforting in a time when books on managing are at the top of the *New York Times* best-seller list. Ultimately, we have to turn our research questions back on ourselves.

IMPLICATIONS: A TEACHER'S PERSPECTIVE

Cultural Analysis of Organizational Life: Teaching Organizational Life as a Symbolic Construction

Emphasis on making organization. Judging by most organizational behavior textbooks, our courses present the organizational world as a given. Our courses are oriented toward helping students fit in and play their roles as organization members. Unfortunately, this orientation is incomplete. It stresses "reading" organizations and orienting action to the outside world. But organizational life is "written" as much as it is read; that is, by our actions we are writing or creating organizational life. When we recognize organizational life as a symbolic construction, we pay more attention to how it is that our actions make organization. Instead of offering courses that reproduce the culture of organization and management, our courses would then study the culture of organization and management as we produce it.

Teach less how things are and more how they get to be. Our courses should have more emphasis on process. They should address the question of how organizational life is accomplished. Rather than accepting organization as the natural order, they should emphasize the culturally constituted nature of organizational life.

Ourselves as subjects. On the first day of my undergraduate organizational behavior class, our topic is, "How did we happen to get here?" By an amazing array of social conventions and background assumptions, thirty or so individuals with diverse life histories and interests show up at the same location to begin a performance entitled "Managerial Behavior." How is it that we know what to do? Might we perhaps do it differently this time? This approach begins to put forward the vision of organizations as social constructions. What makes such a course an organizational behavior course and not a sociology course is that it is always centered on the problem of organizing.

The skill of self-reflection. This orientation to teaching organizational life has as its aim the cultivation of a dual focus of attention—to have students learn that by their actions they are making the world of organization, and to help them reflect on the world that they have made.

One exercise for doing this is the familiar "survival problem," but done a different way. Groups of five or six students are videotaped as they do the consensus decision-making part of the exercise. When they are done, they do not receive the expert's ranking, because the purpose here is not to teach that group decision making can be "better" than individual decision making. Instead, when the group decision task is completed, the students receive an assignment to study their videotape and make a presentation to the rest of the class (several weeks later) on how their group arrived at its list. How did they move from individual to group? The emphasis here is on the students' behavior and how they achieved organization.

There have been some stunning moments of personal insight as a result of doing the exercise this way, as in the case where a group of four young women reported how they gave over all the power in their group to the young man because they assumed he knew about the wilderness. He, on the other hand, reported that he resented being placed in the position of having all the answers. This group's presentation gave us lots of data for discussing how our behavior reproduces traditional sex-role patterns even though we may claim that we are liberated women and men.

Self-conscious instructors. Authority is a central issue in organizational life. To facilitate learning about authority, the instructor needs to be open and self-reflective about his or her own actions. In this regard the teacher is as much of a learner as the students.

An emotional climate. What are the conditions under which learning about ourselves as makers of organization can take place? I have found Edward Hall's comments to his fellow anthropologists very relevant:

> I think some antropologists gave the field a bad name because they thought of their tribes as resources to be exploited. They didn't like the people they studied very much. Now my view is that unless you feel love, have a real emotional attachment, understanding and learning will never happen. I know that's weird for a social scientist to say, because in our tradition it is assumed that love interferes with science, with truth. But without love, you get stereotyping: cold, intellectual appraisal [Tavris, 1983: 15].

I remember the first time I felt love for my class. I had unconsciously "let my guard down" and was swept with feelings of joy and appreciation at what we were doing together. I was also afraid!

IMPLICATIONS:
AN ORGANIZATION MEMBER'S PERSPECTIVE

Living Organizational Life

We're responsible for enlightened action. Although it is much easier to blame problems on others—the administration, the legislature, the students—ultimately we are responsible for making organizational life the way it is. We need to be self-conscious about what we are doing so that organizational action is enlightened action—but how?

I don't have all the answers to that question, but I think it has something to do with deliberately exploiting, or at least prizing, multiple realities instead of treating different realities or different interpretations as "communications problems." This is difficult, because individuals tend to want to be with people who think the way they do, and dealing with differences can be painful. But since we all come to problem-solving situations from a particular place in time and space, and from a discipline, our knowledge is always limited and fragmented. Somehow organizational practices need to encompass and embrace diversity in order to reintegrate knowledge.

This is not the same as participative management, which has taken on the aura of a motivational tool. Rather, what is needed are purposeful attempts to construct or reconstitute knowledge so that events, situations, and problems are confronted or engaged from multiple points of view. Decision-making and problem-solving activities thus become acts of consciousness raising designed to reconstruct holistic knowledge in order to facilitate enlightened action.

This suggestion is not new; others have talked about reframing and multiparadigm observation (for example, the work of Eric Trist and Gareth Morgan applies these ideas to organizational and interorganizational problem solving). What would be new with the inspiration of a cultural paradigm is a different orientation or attitude toward the process of managing. In a time when the idea of a common vision is so popular, I think it is necessary to entertain the possibility of managing *for* multiple realities, instead of managing *in spite of* multiple realities.

What this approach has meant for me on a personal level is much more reading outside the (artificial) boundaries of my discipline into such areas as literary theory and feminist theory, more frequent engagement with colleagues from physics, philosophy, sociology, and communications studies, and renewed interest in dialogues with managers and consultants—all in an effort to explore different ways of seeing.

Jacques Barzun has pointed out the origins of the word "culture" in the activity of cultivation. What I am suggesting here is that we seek to cultivate ourselves and our organizations.

No conclusions. In our organizations, we are continually engaged in the process of "culturing" (I apologize for the awkwardness of the term)—that is, producing and reproducing social reality in ways that are liberating, inhibiting, puzzling, boring, or exciting. Drawing conclusions about experience is always arbitrary, depending upon what one chooses to bracket and pay attention to.

In the same way, although these symbols are fixed upon these pages in an apparently stable way, the reader's interpretation of them and my interpretation of them are in no way fixed and stable. Our thinking is evolving. When I read these pages a year from now, they will no doubt mean different things to me. Thus this chapter represents one version of me in my process of cultivation, but its meaning to others depends on the ways they bracket and pay attention. There are no authoritative conclusions, just the confrontation of our multiple interpretations.

4

AN INVESTIGATOR'S GUIDE TO WORKPLACE CULTURE

Meryl Reis Louis

Boston University

The purpose of this chapter is to identify fundamental issues to consider in researching cultures in work settings. The chapter represents a compendium of stumbling blocks, common assumptions, and/or habits of mind and action that I have observed to be characteristic of much work on organizational culture. Rather than present it as a critique, it is framed as a guide; common assumptions are traced back to relevant choice points and alternatives.

The discussion is organized around four sets of issues:

(1) *Definition and purpose:* What is meant by organizational culture and toward what end is one studying culture?
(2) *Experiential boundaries:* Where is culture being examined, and how does one establish the source and extent of a culture's reach?
(3) *Conceptual focus:* What about culture is under investigation, and how does one bound a study and relate it to studies of similar and different facets of culture?
(4) *Sampling and interpretation:* Which interpretive levels are relevant in a study, and where does one look and how does one probe to access workplace cultures?

Author's Note: Support during the development of ideas presented in this chapter was provided by the Foundation Research Program at the Naval Postgraduate School and by the Chief of Naval Research, Psychological Sciences Division, Office of Naval Research, under contract N00014-80-C-09-05: NR170-911. I wish to acknowledge the especially helpful comments of Stan Davis, Joanne Martin, Ed Schein, Mike Tushman, and John Van Maanen on an earlier version of this chapter.

DEFINITION AND PURPOSE

Components of a Definition

What is culture? The *American Heritage Dictionary* (1976: 321) defines culture as

> the totality of socially transmitted behavior patterns, arts, beliefs, institutions, and all other products of human work and thought characteristic of a community or population; a style of social and artistic expression peculiar to a society or class.

What, then, is organizational culture? Sociologists Howard Becker and Blanche Geer (1970: 134) describe it as follows:

> Any social group, to the extent that it is a distinctive unit, will have to some degree a culture differing from that of other groups, a somewhat different set of common understandings around which action is organized, and these differences will find expression in a language whose nuances are peculiar to that group. Members of churches speak differently from members of tavern groups; more importantly, members of any particular church or tavern group have cultures, and languages in which they are expressed, which differ somewhat from those of other groups of the same general type.

A group's culture can be characterized as follows:

> A set of understandings or *meanings shared* by a group of people. The meanings are largely *tacit* among members, are clearly *relevant* to the particular group, and are *distinctive* to the group. Meanings are *passed on* to new group members [Louis, 1980a].

Three basic components of culture can be isolated from these definitions. First, there is content: the totality of socially transmitted behavior patterns, a style of social and artistic expression, a set of common understandings. Second, there is a group: a community or population, a society or class, a unit. Third, there is a relationship between the content and the group: content characteristic of the group, content peculiar to the group, or content differing from that of other groups.

The discussion in this chapter highlights the importance for research and practice of specifying cultural boundaries—the second and third definitional components of culture. It does not focus on cultural contents per se (the first component of culture), on which others have focused (Schein, 1985; Martin, 1982b). Specifically, the second part of the chapter discusses experiential boundaries, alternative sites at which cultures may emerge within organizational settings, and means of establishing their perimeters. The third section discusses alternative conceptual boundaries or focuses of study within the overall domain of organizational culture.

Anthropologists have long differed over the first component, the content. In fact, more than thirty years ago Kroeber and Kluckhohn (1952) identified 164 meanings of the term "culture" that had been used in anthropology. Most of the meanings dealt with nuances of the content component. The other two components of the definition did not figure significantly among anthropologists' concerns. But why not? Should they figure more heavily among the concerns of organizational practitioners and researchers than they did for anthropologists?

An anthropologist studying a primitive tribe in a remote geographic region could be fairly certain of which group had been studied, and that the particular content of the culture identified was peculiar to that group. The historic as well as geographic isolation that often characterized the group under study alleviated the need for explicit efforts to establish the group's boundaries or to demonstrate that the culture described was peculiar to the group. Although organizational researchers and practitioners tend to follow suit, the consequences may be dysfunctional. Quite simply, the qualities of geographic and historic isolation are unlikely to characterize groups in modern work settings. Hence we cannot assume that in identifying the cultural content to be found in an organization, we have also identified the bounds of the group to which any bit of content is peculiar.

Another clarification of terms is needed—that is, the relationship between organization and culture. In this chapter, organizations are treated as settings that *may* foster the development of cultures. As such, organizations are referred to as "culture-bearing milieus" because, among other properties, they convene regularly and provide opportunities for affiliation out of which may come sets of shared understandings that are relevant and distinctive to some group (Louis, 1980a).

Alternative Purposes

Beyond clarifying one's definition of culture and appreciating the immediate relevance of its three components, one needs to be clear about which of two broad purposes is being pursued. Is one seeking knowledge of culture (generically speaking) through the study of specific settings? Or is one seeking knowledge of a specific setting (to understand it, to function in it, to improve it) through the study of culture?

When knowledge of a specific setting is the object or end purpose, the practitioner's basic efforts vis-à-vis culture are directed toward identifying whether and, if so, what distinctive culture is to be found in any particular arena within the larger organizational setting. For instance, identifying "what it is like" in the Pet Products Team as compared with other teams in the Research Department of Alpha Corporation may be the objective. More basically, the practitioner seeks to know whether "what it is like" is somehow related to culture. That is the fundamental starting place for those pursuing this purpose. One theme of this chapter is the need to be clear about which particular arena or setting is under study. Toward that end, alternative experiential contexts or points of inquiry are examined.

When knowledge of culture is the object or end purpose, it is important to compare a number of settings, sifting until what is common across settings vis-à-vis some aspect of culture emerges with clarity. Thus another theme of this chapter is the need to be clear about the aspect of culture under study. Toward that end, alternative conceptual/analytic contexts or points of inquiry are examined.

The action perspectives associated with the two purposes differ significantly. Each requires vastly different "eyes and ears" of the practitioner. Specifically, efforts to understand culture in the generic sense require comparative analysis to see and hear what is common across settings, while efforts to understand culture as a means to understanding the setting require the detection of what is unique to this one setting.

EXPERIENTIAL BOUNDARIES

Much ado has been made about corporate culture by organizational scientists and managers in government and industry. A premise underlying much of this interest is that an organization is possessed of a single culture, one that is pervasive throughout the organization. My purpose in this section is to challenge this premise and trace the implications of an alternative view for the study of cultures in work settings.

That it is inappropriate to assume one culture per organization may be seen in the following illustrations. Recall the so-called output restriction norms associated with the Bank Wiring Room documented in Elton Mayo's Hawthorne Studies (Roethlisberger and Dickson, 1939). What had impact were the shared meanings that evolved and emerged from among the workers in Clique A and in Clique B as they worked together on a regular basis, in face-to-face contact. These meanings were more potent than the threat of job loss or the lure of additional pay proscribed in the formal procedures prohibiting job sharing and specifying piece-rate incentives for individual output levels beyond standard.

A second illustration is contained in the coal mine situation described by Trist and Bamforth (1951). Before the longwall method was introduced, a work-group culture had emerged among people in the mines with tasks that were interconnected. This culture served the company's interests as a by-product of serving the interests of the group's members. Physical safety, family support, and task scheduling were among the functions served through and by the emergent work-group cultures. In each of these cases, the cultures that had an impact on the workers were contained within the larger organization, but in neither case could it be said that the effective culture was that of the organization at large—that is, an organizational culture. Although culture was not the primary analytic category invoked by the authors of the Hawthorne studies or the coal mine studies, both sets of studies provide useful fodder for secondary analysis employing a cultural lens.

What errors are associated with the assumption that an organization has a culture? Several can be identified. For instance, if one assumes that an organization has a culture, then it should not matter where one looks to find it or who one chooses as informants from among the organization's members. In relying on this premise, one might develop a description of the organization's culture from talking with key executives and assume that their descriptions apply throughout the organization. Or one might gather information from several hierarchical levels, geographic regions, and/or product divisions and combine the information from the various subsettings, rather than treat each as a potential site of distinct culture.

Another error associated with the "organizational culture" assumption is that of attributing to the organization whatever cultural content is detected within the setting. This occurs, for example, when a researcher discovers that employees at, say, AVCO Bank of Anytown are "cautious" and thus concludes that a fundamental characteristic of AVCO's culture is caution. What the researcher in such a situation has failed to consider is the possibility that he or she has in fact picked up on a characteristic of Anytown's culture rather than one belonging to the banking industry. The repercussions are obvious when one imagines using the researcher's description of such an "organizational culture" as a basis for action or intervention. Changes made at AVCO Bank with the aim of transforming "caution" into "risk-taking" are unlikely to succeed in the long term. In this case, the caution of the banking industry culture and/or the Anytown culture would act as an inertial force undermining the change effort within AVCO Bank. Along the way, the action-taker has lost the benefits of working with those aspects of culture that specifically reflect the setting. Thus it can be seen that little action leverage comes from having identified any and all culture to be found within a setting.

Finally, actions may also be undermined by overlooking the relationships among various cultures internal to an organization. For example, consider the case of the proverbial tensions between sales and production groups. We would expect to find that each group's culture reinforces a somewhat negative orientation toward the other group. If we wished to reduce these tensions, mandating "harmony" and imposing integrating structures would be unlikely to succeed without giving some attention to subcultural reinforcers of historic tensions.

It should be clear that it is both erroneous and costly to assume that (1) an organization has only one culture, and/or (2) whatever culture is detected within an organization is necessarily a determining force in the culture of that organization. How, then, should one proceed? Where might cultures be located and how might they be untangled and sourced?

Sites of Culture

There are several sites at which a culture may develop within a single organization. Alternative sites of culture internal to an organizational setting are referred to here as intraorganizational loci of culture. For instance, recall the Bank Wiring Room in which different sets of shared understandings developed around each of two cliques. In addition, strands of culture commonly found within an organization may reflect cultures from elsewhere, from beyond the organizational boundaries. For example, there are industry cultures, referred to here as "transorganizational loci" of culture.

The term "locus of culture" rather than "unit of analysis" was chosen to reflect that there may or may not be an indigenous culture at any particular site. The term "locus" is used to signal that the specific site in question is *potentially* a site of distinctive culture; that the presence of cultural phenomena in or at the site, as well as the determination of specific aspects of culture distinctive to the site, are matters to examine rather than to assume. Whether it is important to isolate culture that is either experientially distinctive and/or descriptively unique (Martin, Sitkin, et al., 1983) depends on the purposes at hand. Any efforts to change and/or manage culture, for instance, necessarily entail the isolation of distinctive cultures.

What, then are alternative intraorganizational sites or loci of culture? Where might cultures develop within work settings? Culture may develop around the top of an organization. There may be a "for-our-eyes-only" culture encompassing the secrets that have emerged among a ruling elite. There may also be a "for-public-consumption" culture at the top, one deliberately designed by the ruling elite to be passed down through the organization. Finally, an emergent yet more public culture may also emanate from the top of the organization. It is this last variant that is usually referred to as the "corporate" culture.

A second experiential context or locus in which culture may develop is a vertical slice of the organization, such as a division. The medical products division of Avery Instruments, for example, may have developed a culture that is somewhat different from that of the overall organization or another division. A third locus of culture is the horizontal slice, such as a particular type of job or hierarchical level. For example, loan officers at Crocker Bank or systems engineers at IBM may have developed a set of shared understandings. Fourth, a particular unit such as a department may manifest a characteristic culture, as in the Management Department at the ABC Business School.

The (top of the) organization, vertical and horizontal slices, and other formal unit designations (such as department) all represent typical sites in and through which cultures may develop. Some relevant properties of organizations, and of these sites in particular as "culture-bearing milieus," are: They are regularly convening settings, they impose structural interdependencies among people performing tasks, they provide opportunities for affiliation, and they constitute constellations of interest or purposes. As such, they serve as breeding grounds, if you will, for the emergence of local shared meanings. Thus any site characterized by such properties could be considered a culture-bearing milieu or a locus of culture. A fifth and final intraorganizational locus of culture is any group, regardless of whether members come from the same or different formal organizational units. The people who get together for bridge at lunch on Thursdays may develop a culture, for example, despite the fact that members span several departments and hierarchical levels.

Transorganizational loci of culture constitute "feeder" cultures, streams of culture flowing into organizations. An ethnic group within an organization may serve as a locus with a highly elaborated culture. For example, light industry in south central Los Angeles may manifest a Chicano culture spanning several departments, divisions, and even corporate bounds.

In addition, industry may provide a substantial portion of the culture manifested within an organizational setting. For instance, commercial banks may have a strong common culture across individual banking organizations. A final transorganizational locus of culture is an occupation or profession. The legal department at Exxon, or the tool and die makers across departments at Ford Motor Company, are illustrations.

With so many different experiential sites around which cultures may emerge, it is very easy to pick up on culture in a setting. The idea of a cultural blank slate in modern work organizations is meaningless. The problem of determining post hoc whose culture has been described is analogous to the problem of naming factors generated in a factor analysis. The next section takes up this problem, fleshing out a set of questions for establishing cultural boundaries, for determining the reach of a culture in a work setting.

Penetration of a Culture

Beyond recognizing the multiplicity of cultures possible within an organization, one needs to assess the penetration of any one culture. Through the issues of penetration, the subtasks of establishing the boundaries of a culture can be identified. Sociological, psychological, and historical aspects of penetration need to be examined in diagnosing cultures in organizations. In sociological terms, penetration translates into pervasiveness, extensiveness, or the reaching through space of a culture. For example, how far down into the organization does the corporate level culture extend? Are top-level prescriptions about developing subordinates manifested among first line supervisors? These are the kinds of queries that can be used to establish the pervasiveness of a culture.

Psychological penetration refers to the consistency or homogeneity in interpretation of shared meanings among individuals in the group whose culture has been isolated. Is there significant variation among group members' translations of shared understandings? Around what issues is there most (and least) variance in interpretation? Through questions like these, the homogeneity of a culture can be empirically investigated.[1]

In general, the results of such an investigation can indicate how tight a hold over members the culture maintains, and how narrow the interpretive bandwidth that can be tolerated. More specifically, within-culture variance can provide clues to central themes and orientations of the locale. What does it mean if there are wide differences, for instance, among Digitech's technical representatives in "acceptable" career aspirations and negligible differences in "acceptable" means of pursuing one's aspirations? What might it mean if the reverse were the case? The interpretation of such differences falls out of the analysis when the investigator thinks to notice and follow up on this issue.

How does homogeneity differ from pervasiveness? What is the relationship between them? When concerned about pervasiveness, the questioner asks: Does the motto, "We try harder" (for purposes of illustration, considered to be an aspect of Avis culture), have special meaning for maintenance personnel as well as for sales personnel? Given that the answer is "yes," that it *is* pervasive, then homogeneity becomes the focus. When concerned about homogeneity, the questioner asks: What is the meaning of the motto for Avis's maintenance personnel and sales personnel? And how different are the meanings among and between maintenance and sales personnel? Interpretations among maintenance personnel may be very loose, or they may be tight but with an anticustomer or antisales cast to them, or they may mirror quite closely the interpretations given by sales personnel. Whether and how a motto can be used as a rallying point or integrator across sales and maintenance functions ten years after its introduction depends in part on both its pervasiveness and the homogeneity of its interpretations.

Historical penetration calls attention to the stability over time of a set of shared understandings. "For how long has this practice been the status quo?" is the kind of query by means of which stability as an empirical concern can be pursued. Stability indicates the degree of entrenchment or embeddedness of understandings. As such, it is an important clue to inertia or a potential resistance to change.

The usefulness of applying the ideas in this section can be seen in the following example. Take again the case of AVCO Bank. Assume that the aim is to shift from "caution" to "risk-taking" as a basic response at AVCO Bank. It would be a mistake to assume either that caution is an AVCO-wide issue, or that it is merely an AVCO issue. In terms of penetration, looking up, down, and out may reveal pockets of caution within AVCO and support for caution within AVCO from the industry culture. Caution may be prevalent among those boundary-spanning units that interface with industry institutions. And these units may be particularly powerful ones within AVCO, so that they set the tone for interactions with other units in the bank. Such an analysis of cultural penetration reveals leverage points toward which change efforts are most appropriately directed.

A final aspect of penetration bears consideration. In the past, the term "subculture" has been used to indicate relations among contemporaneous cultures. A finer-grained analysis can be achieved by attending to the direction and target, or orientation, or subcultures. We might hypothesize that, like individuals, groups and their cultures may orient toward, against, or away from other groups and their cultures (Horney, 1945). "Toward, against, and away from" indicate the direction of a culture vis-à-vis some target. The direction could be negative, or it could be positive or enhancing of the target group; for instance, in a division culture that supports the goals of the overall organization. Or the direction could be neutral, in which case the culture might be inwardly rather than outwardly oriented. The culture that emerged among the workers in the coal mines (Trist and Bamforth, 1951) could be characterized as neutral, whereas in Hawthorne Electric's Bank Wiring Room, two somewhat negatively directed cultures targeted at the other clique developed in the room.

Of what benefit is this finer-grained analysis? What is the advantage of knowing the direction and target of subcultures? Such detail provides a better basis for action. With knowledge of directions and targets, managers can dedicate resources to the trouble spots, or the dysfunctional cultures. The manager can likewise avoid frittering away resources on benign cultures or mistakenly disrupting positive or enhancing cultures.

Imagine having a cultural Geiger counter. This instrument would signal when we are at the center of one locus of culture and when we are moving out of range. We would pick up different loci on different channels of the Geiger counter, switching channels to assess overlaps and nestings of loci. We would have a "meta" switch to shift our range gauge from detecting sociological penetration (pervasiveness) to detecting historical penetration (stability) or psychological penetration (homogeneity). Such an instrument is what we need for work with cultures in organizational settings. In its absence as a physical fact, investigators might choose to retain the metaphor as a reminder of the issues to address in order to establish the boundaries of a culture and/or to identify the group whose culture one has detected.

CONCEPTUAL FOCUS:
THERE'S MORE THAN ONE WAY
TO SLICE A CULTURE

Current efforts to understand organizational culture are analogous to the Sufi story of the blind men's efforts to decipher the elephant. Many are interested; some pursue one end of the beast, others pursue another. For instance, some are concerned with the origins of workplace culture, others with stories as evidence of that culture. Most proceed as if the single focus pursued were the sum total and the definitive focus.

Almost no one has discussed the possibility that the beast is larger than any one focus. As a result, differing approaches are rejected rather than reconciled through appreciation of the differences among the issues they address.

The student of culture who is without a framework for subdividing and bounding the topic assumes the burden of comprehensiveness—an awesome burden in the case of workplace culture. The issues are too vast, the subject too complex, and the territory too extensive for any one investigator or investigation to do it justice overall. What is needed is a conceptual framework through which the larger culture in work settings can be brought into view. Such a framework is needed to facilitate identifying and bounding the focus of any particular investigation of culture, relating one study to a larger context, building on past works, and collecting and interrelating information from various studies. Toward that end, I will describe one possible framework of conceptual/analytic facets or foci of culture.

The foci are organized into natural, purposeful, and reflective levels. Grouped at the natural level are aspects of culture typically pursued in traditional descriptive or sociological field work. Thus the structural/functional analysis of workplace cultures can be organized into such concerns as: Where does "it" come from (origins)? What does "it" lead to (outcomes/effects)? and What does "it" look like (manifestations/evidence)? In contrast, a focus on culture from a purposeful level of analysis concerns issues of management, of doing something with, to, and/or about the culture. Finally, the reflective level encompasses efforts to establish the nature and characteristics of culture, as well as the debate over appropriate philosophic assumptions, constituencies, and aims. Any single study can and usually does encompass more than one focus, and most studies, at least implicitly, encompass the purposeful focus. That is, studies of the origins or functions of culture are grounded in a concern for making improvements.

Focus 1: Origins of Workplace Cultures

Within a focus on origins, the concern is with antecedent conditions and historical emergence processes (Chandler, 1962; Pettigrew, 1979). An appreciation of typical origins can enhance practitioners' efforts. Nascent cultures can be judiciously nurtured by those who know where to look, as well as when and how to seed them. An appreciation of origins can also ground action planning and allow anticipation of natural drifts and developments in cultures over time.

The origins of both designed cultures, such as official corporate cultures, and emergent or informal workgroup cultures are of interest here. Concern with origins leads one to examine, for example, the developmental role of such conditions as membership stability, membership restrictions, members' perceptions of the relative youth and size of the unit, the permeability of unit boundaries, extraorganizational ties among members, task interdependence among members, and the idiosyncracies of key people. In terms of research agenda, one might examine start-up operations in new versus well-established organizations, trace the processes and conditions in which cultures proliferate in work settings, or distinguish the preconditions of supportive versus subvertive subcultures.

Focus: 2 Manifestations of Workplace Cultures

The term "manifestation" refers to the evidence or demonstration of the existence of something, or the form in which something is revealed. Artifacts as products fall within the general category of manifestations. The manifestations given most attention to date are symbols. So far, sagas, stories, legends, myths, and other linguistic symbols have been subjects of much interest (Martin, 1982b; Dandridge et al., 1980; Clarke, 1970). Some work has been done on types of humor and metaphors used in work settings, all of which fall within the category of manifestations of culture. Physical symbols such as office furnishings, layout, and building architecture have symbolic potential as manifestations of workplace cultures. In *The Soul of a New Machine* (1981), Tracy Kidder's description of Data General's corporate office building, for instance ("Building 14A/B looks like a fort, with narrow windows, an American flag out front, a dish antenna on a latticed tower, and TV cameras mounted and turning on corners of the roof . . . designed, not by an architect, but by themselves"), leaves no doubt that its subject is a manifestation of top-level corporate culture.

In addition to physical and linguistic symbols, workplace cultures are manifested in the experiences of group members. Shared understandings show up in the ways in which individuals "negotiate" their daily lives in the work setting, in the sense of navigating through and orienting to a setting—what is actually noticed and responded to, the markers by which a landscape is taken in and traversed. Negotiating also occurs in the sense of bargaining with others when there is conflict or doubt—the rationales, warrants, and claims that are invoked and considered legitimate for conducting and settling disputes in a specific setting. The particular direction and extent to which individuals' daily negotiations reflect any one group culture depend on the situation. The simplest general illustration is the case of the newcomer negotiating the new setting badly as a result of relying on shared understandings from an old setting.

Focus 3: Outcomes of Workplace Culture

A variety of outcomes, effects, and functions of workplace cultures have been documented. In the Bank Wiring Room, for example, group output was restricted, affecting organizational output. Additionally, individuals gained some sense of participation or membership. The Trist and Bamforth (1951) coal mine studies documented some positive effects of culture at both individual and organizational levels: Work was getting done on a team-managed basis; the safety of the workers was facilitated; the meaningfulness of going to work each day was enhanced, if not generated, through the group culture; and families of members were taken care of.

In terms of overall functions, workplace cultures have been shown to affect workers' commitment to and identification with the group and organization, as well as their sense of involvement with their work assignments (Etzioni, 1961). The need for control systems and design parameters serving continuity functions is affected by the existence of cultures in work settings (Louis, 1980a; Ouchi, 1981). The current volumes on Japanese management techniques deal most fundamentally with issues of the effects of workplace cultures on the commitment and productivity of workers, as well as the lack of a need for structural controls to induce desired attitudes and behavior when strong cultures are operative. Finally, the socialization of new members is facilitated by work group cultures (Louis, 1980b).

Focus 4: Management of Workplace Cultures

Encompassed here are issues of cultural control and the change, design, and management of cultures. At this point, the active design and creation of culture is to be distinguished from its more passive or unguided emergence and evolution. Until now, it has been customary to think of activity designing culture at only the topmost levels of organizations. It was assumed that such designed cultures would be pervasive throughout an organization. The collapse of that assumption, coupled with a growing recognition of the potential for a multiplicity of emergent group cultures within an organizational setting has opened the way for experiments in designed or guided subcultures. It has also raised issues about how feasible it is to alter the culture of an organizational unit and what is involved in doing so—namely, the means of revitalizing cultures and of harnessing subcultures to larger corporate aims and cultures.

Clearly, these challenges differ depending on whether the situation is a start-up of a new unit or an overall organization, or an ongoing unit in need of reorientation. In the latter case, members' acceptance of the past and of some current critical need for change will probably be necessary before a shift in culture can be accomplished. Additionally, "planting" a culture in either the start-up or the reorientation situation seems to require a key person with a vision and the capacity to get others to subscribe to it. In fact, recent work on characteristics that distinguish leaders from managers singles out just this capacity to create and communicate a lucid and compelling vision which subordinates internalize (Bennis, 1985).

A final note with respect to the issue of change and culture: There is solid documentation that overlooking organizational culture has impeded efforts to change organizational functioning (Beer, 1980; Mirvis and Berg, 1977). Examination of past failures in organizational development efforts point to the role of culture as a critical force to be considered in effecting change. So, although the aim may not be to change a culture per se, practitioners intending to introduce change in various aspects of organizational functioning are well advised to anticipate fallout due to potential conflicts between the proposed change and the existing culture.

Focus 5: Approaches to Workplace Cultures

The final focus is on approach, in the sense of understanding the nature of a culture. An approach is identified as a separate focus in an effort to raise it from the level of assumption to a more explicit level, one subject to investigation.

Several questions capture the range of differences in approaches to workplace cultures. For instance, what constitutes the essence of a culture? For some, it is the basic assumptions underlying the group's values (Schein, 1985). For others, it is the group's norms (Kilmann and Saxton, 1982). Another question of approach is captured as: Are workplace cultures characterizable according to universal themes, or are contents best considered to be group-specific? For instance, Schein (1985) classifies organizational cultures along four universal themes borrowed from anthropology. In contrast, Kilmann and Saxton (1982) identify group-specific content themes, without presuming that one set of themes will tap the essential content of any and all other groups' cultures. The first approach is not inherently better than the other. The test is the extent to which an approach yields a description of culture that identifies what is distinctive to a group and that indicates the group to which it is distinctive.

Assumptions

The framework of conceptual/analytic facets of culture can be useful for surfacing assumptions embedded in the logic and conduct of inquiries on culture. For instance, a typical argument is structured in the following terms:

(1) Culture is associated with critical outcomes (e.g., level of worker commitment).
(2) Characteristics of culture in terms of one conceptual focus (e.g., manifestations, origins, content) account for significant variance in critical outcomes.
(3) Outcomes can be altered by altering characteristics associated with one conceptual focus.

The problem arises when links of the argument remain implicit and/or are taken as premises. Effort is often expended to understand one conceptual focus, without commensurate effort being given to support other links in the argument. Even when each link is investigated, other assumptions may underlie the argument and undermine it.

The assumption of linearity or symmetry refers to the habit of assuming that if, for instance, a strong culture is associated with high performance, then a weak culture is associated with low performance.

The assumption of implementation refers to the presumption that one can deliberately change key conditions, and that changes thus made will result in foreseeable outcomes. It is a view that "you can get from here to there," encompassing appreciation of both the means and the ends. Ouchi's *Theory Z* (1981) and Peters and Waterman's *In Search of Excellence* (1982), as well as the practical implications they suggest, rely on this assumption.

The assumption of "all else being equal" refers to the practice of generalizing a relationship that holds in one context (e.g., one industry setting or organizations at one stage of development) into other contexts without testing for the effect of context on the relationship. For instance, whether the finding that strong cultures are associated with high performance in young high-tech firms applies in mature financial institutions or smokestack industries is an empirical question.

Finally, the assumption of correspondence links back directly to the section on experiential boundaries. It refers to the dubious habit of assuming that findings from an inquiry conducted at one locus of culture (e.g., a work group or department) are applicable elsewhere (e.g., at the corporate level). It differs from the previous assumption ("all else being equal") in highlighting the potential structural differences among loci (workgroup versus corporate level) rather than differences in manifestation within a single categorical form (Industry A versus Industry B). For example, Schein's (1985) assumption that time orientation and man-nature relationships are similarly compelling as content themes at corporate and workgroup levels illustrates this assumption of correspondence.

INTERPRETATION AND SAMPLING

The traditional research issues of interpretation and sampling take on special significance when the subject under investigation is workplace cultures.

Levels of Interpretation

Interpretation is a fundamental issue in studying culture in work settings. Interpretive processes are fundamental to both the phenomena under study and the process of studying those phenomena. Cultural phenomena are generated through interpretive processes. These processes, as well as the cultural manifestations enacted through them, are likely focuses of study (Louis, 1981a). In addition to interpretation being characteristic of the phenomena under study, and thus a likely subject of study, interpretive processes are also part of the research act. Figure 4.1 identifies six prototypic levels of interpreting the primary experience of an actor in a situation. Each level represents a way in which interpretation can enter into the process of researching cultural phenomena. In the figure, levels of interpretation are arranged in order of physical psychological distance from the organizationally situated

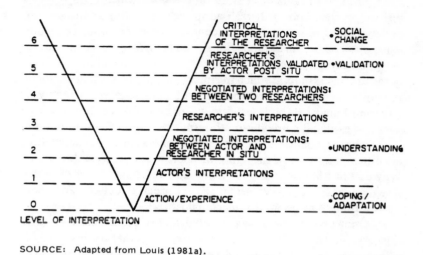

LEVEL OF INTERPRETATION

SOURCE: Adapted from Louis (1981a).

Figure 4.1 Levels of Interpretation in a Research Process

actions. For instance, in level 2 the researcher and actor in the organization would negotiate an interpretation of an event or experience. During the interview, they would discuss and decide on the meaning of the event or experience. This level of interpretation might be employed for any number of reasons. For instance, joint in situ negotiated interpretation could be used if the researcher felt that the actor's responses were implausible or if the researcher sensed that the actor did not have relevant information that the researcher did have and was able to share.

Of the six interpretive levels shown in Figure 4.1, not all are appropriate in a given study or for a given researcher. The researcher needs to be clear about which levels of interpretation are relevant in a study and why, and to specify which interpretations will be considered materials of study. Such specification affords the researcher a chance to anticipate pockets of bias and to seek out supplemental sources and perspectives. It also affords the consumer of research an additional means of judging the strength of a work and estimating the significance of its results. Issues of interpretation come into play whether one is studying culture in the field, the laboratory, or through the mail.

Specific forms of interpretation enter in through metaphors and analytic categories. Though they are prevalent across organizational studies, they are potentially more influential (and their influence may be far more subtle) in the case of cultural studies.

In terms of metaphors, it is useful to notice which metaphors the researcher finds him- or herself adopting in thinking about a setting under study. The key, then, is to identify the source of the metaphors. Have they come from organizational members, from the researcher, or from competitors or clients of the unit under study? In addition, one needs to notice points at which the metaphors break down or do not fit. If a unit is like a family, perhaps it is like a particular type of family—a fatherless family or a homeless family—or even unlike a family when it comes to explaining orientation to resources or outcomes. In terms of interpretation, it matters whether the metaphors one finds oneself using are different from those the unit's members use to describe themselves. Why and in what ways are the metaphors different? What does that reveal about the (observed versus the experienced) culture, and about the researcher's projections or personal issues?

Additionally, several aspects of analytic categories bear consideration. Again, what is the source of the categories that the researcher is using to describe and understand a particular organizational site and its culture? For instance, who decided that leadership was an issue to invoke in characterizing a setting and situation? The timing of category selection is a related issue. Did the category emerge from field observation, or was it selected a priori, before firsthand or on-site work? Finally, the status of the category bears explication. Is the category taken to be universal or particular to the site in question? Recall the contrast drawn earlier between the work of Schein (1985) and that of Kilmann and Saxton (1982). The former invokes universal categories established a priori by the researcher, while the latter researchers search out the particular categories indigenous to a setting.

A final note on interpretation concerns how those by group members may be affected by inquiries into culture—one aspect of ethics attendant to investigating workplace cultures. If culture refers to tacit and fundamental meanings shared by a group, what impact do investigators' questions, observations, and feedback have on the group and its culture, and on its store of previously tacit meanings? We know that asking a question (e.g., about job satisfaction) may alter an individual actor's attitudes and feelings. But what happens at a group level? When an investigator asks a question or makes an observation about a group's orientation (e.g., some aspect of shared meaning), it likely causes some reflection among group members. It is further likely that some of the substance or content of a given culture may not be well aligned with the ideals of all its members. As long as the substance remains tacit, inconsistencies may not be experienced as such. However, asking questions or reporting findings may precipitate an awareness of heretofore nonproblematic inconsistencies. Thus the investigator must be sensitive to the risks associated with awakening a recognition of gaps between an individual's interpretive set and the interpretations and meanings shared within the group of which the individual is a member.

Sampling: Accessing Tacit Knowledge

It is generally agreed that workplace cultures encompass tacit understandings, difficult-to-detect negotiations, and other intermittent and intersubjective processes, as well as more accessible physical and linguistic symbols. While linguistic and physical symbols may be readily observable, the more deeply shared meaning systems for which they are a shorthand may be largely inaccessible or indecipherable to nonmembers. The challenge for the investigator trying to uncover a culture, then, is to look for and/or provoke conditions under which tacit understandings and processes are accessible. Suggestions and illustrations for looking and provoking are discussed here in terms of natural occurrences (where to look) and field stimulations (how to provoke). This discussion is meant to trigger ideas of other possibilities rather than to represent a complete catalog of options.

Some natural occurrences of situations in which culture may be more accessible include disruptions or crises. For example, consider the situation in which several new members enter a stable work group in the same month, or perhaps a merger situation. Such situations are likely to be characterized by more ready access to cultural material on the part of established members. Thus observation in such situations is likely to yield more insight into "what really matters around here and why" than would observation in situations of "business as usual." The investigator might well decide, then, to purposefully sample such situations of disruption rather than to observe normal situations in which the tacit is neither threatened nor flagrantly operative (see Figure 4.2).

Another strategy for accessing tacit knowledge is to search out individuals who are experiencing high degrees of "contrast," who have a role to play two or more settings. For instance, consultants, boundary spanners, newcomers, staff members, and even field researchers covering multiple sites concurrently may have access to the tacit understandings of several groups in which they are operating. The culture in each setting is often thrown into relief by the contrast between different settings and groups.

In addition to searching for natural occurrences of largely unobservable phenomena, an investigator may want to try to provoke conditions that highlight a culture. Such efforts are termed "field stimulations." As an illustration, one could engage a group in the collective production of

	WHERE TO LOOK: NATURAL OCCURRENCES	HOW TO PROBE: FIELD STIMULATIONS
SITUATIONS TO SAMPLE	DISRUPTION OF ROUTINES -- MERGER -- NEW CEO -- WORK GROUP WITH NEWCOMERS	COLLECTIVE PRODUCTION -- COLLAGE -- CARTOON -- BIOGRAPHY
INDIVIDUALS TO SAMPLE	CONTRAST EXPERIENCES -- NEWCOMERS -- BOUNDARY SPANNERS -- CONSULTANTS -- FIELD RESEARCHERS	GUIDED REFLECTION -- GROUP INTERVIEW -- CRITICAL INCIDENT

Figure 4.2 Strategies for Accessing Tacit Knowledge

any number of items to reveal aspects of group cultures. A group could be given the task of providing a collage, a biography, or a humorous questionnaire that epitomizes the group. This approach centers on an intact group in which a situation is generated to provide insight into the group's set of shared meanings. The investigator would then record the session on videotape, debrief at length with group members individually and as a group (again videotaping the group session), and attend to the process of production as well as the product. Replication of the activity with other groups and comparisons across groups could be employed to yield a better understanding of various aspects of how group cultures work across particular settings.

Another type of field stimulation requires the sampling of individuals from different settings. This treatment may involve a critical incident interview format in which significant visual and verbal recall of a powerful experience is elicited which serves as a foundation for broad reportage. More interactive versions of "guided reflections" include group interviews in which recall of a common incident is stimulated and diverse approaches and experiences elicited, thus highlighting the differences across settings.

Thus one can select situations that have a higher potential yield in the search for cultures. Alternatively, one can set about to provoke such situations. In either case, the investigator tackles the issue of sampling in a manner that recognizes the special nature of workplace cultures as shared tacit understandings.

SUMMARY

The aim of this chapter has been to call attention to some basic, though typically overlooked, issues associated with studying workplace cultures. The discussion identified choice points, typical assumptions, and alternatives in terms of the investigator's purpose and definitions, the determination of experiential sites and boundaries of workplace cultures, the delineation of a conceptual focus of study within the topic of culture, and the role of interpretation and sampling vis-à-vis cultural investigations.

NOTE

1. Individual differences in the level of "cultural participation" (Louis, 1980b) should not be overlooked as a contributor to variances in interpretation. The extent to which variance reflects heterogeneity of the culture, rather than lower levels of cultural participation on the part of individuals, is a matter to tease out using traditional analytic procedures.

PART II

CAN ORGANIZATIONAL CULTURE BE MANAGED?

JOANNE MARTIN

"Can culture be managed?" is a question with the capacity to annoy anyone seriously interested in the topic. Cultural pragmatists and purists, however, find the question annoying for very different reasons. At the risk of overdrawing those differences, extreme versions of both points of view are described below.

Cultural pragmatists generally see culture as a key to commitment, productivity, and profitability. They argue that culture can be—indeed, should be and has been—managed, and they often offer guidance as to how to do this. Their prescriptions for this admittedly difficult task range from the active (seven steps to managing cultural change) to the relatively passive (culture as relatively unmalleable, a potential obstacle to desired strategic change that must be anticipated and "worked around"). From this perspective, it is arrogant or ignorant to question whether culture can be managed.

Cultural purists, on the other hand, find it ridiculous to talk of managing culture. Culture cannot be managed; it emerges. Leaders don't create cultures; members of the culture do. Culture is an expression of people's deepest needs, a means of endowing their experiences with meaning. Even if culture in this sense could be managed, it shouldn't be, particularly if it were being managed in the name of increased productivity or the almighty dollar. From this perspective, it is naive and perhaps unethical to speak of managing culture.

The authors of the chapters in this section lie between these two extremes. They are not as likely as the pragmatists to offer guidance to would-be culture managers, nor are they as reluctant as the purists to consider the possibility that culture could, and should, be managed. Within these common limitations, however, the authors vary widely in their answers to the question, "Can culture be managed?" This divergence in opinion becomes more understandable when the authors' interpretations of the question are contrasted.

The authors work from quite different definitions of culture itself. Some emphasize deeply rooted, even unconscious sources of culture, while others emphasize relatively superficial cultural manifestations, such as.espoused values, reward structures, and dress codes. Some of the authors discuss culture in broad terms, including cognitive, emotional, and behavioral aspects of organizational life, while others focus on a single aspect of culture, such as views of an organization's history.

The authors all, with varying degrees of explicitness, distinguish the process of cultural change from the deliberate management of that process. However, they differ in the extent of the cultural change contemplated. Some are concerned with massive cultural overhauls, while others contemplate changes of a more limited scope. All of the authors make some form of a contingency argument, refusing to answer the question in yes or no terms. Rather, they prefer to rephrase it as, "Are there conditions under which culture can be managed?"

Not surprisingly, the authors' answers depend on how they approach the question. If they choose a relatively superficial definition of culture, or if they focus on a relatively limited scope of change, then they are more likely to echo the pragmatists' conclusion that culture can indeed be managed. The authors who define culture in unusually deep or broad terms, and who contemplate massive cultural changes, are less sanguine about attempts to control the trajectory of a culture's evolution. In spite of this divergence, however, there is remarkable agreement among the authors about the kinds of conditions that facilitate and hinder the culture management process.

In the first chapter, Martin, Sitkin, and Boehm define culture as a socially constructed reality and focus on a single manifestation of it— namely, the varying perceptions and interpretations of key events in an organization's history. Based on a content analysis of historical accounts of the company's early years, Martin et al. offer a portrayal of the culture creation process that emphasizes influences beyond a founder's control. From these data, it appears very difficult for a leader to create a personal cultural legacy that reflects his or her own values and vision for the future.

Siehl also presents data from an organization undergoing cultural change. However, she comes to a somewhat different set of conclusions about the feasibility of culture management. Siehl works from a broader definition of culture, collecting data on an unusually wide range of observable cultural manifestations. Operating within a single unit of a corporation, she focuses on the unit manager's attempts to change three well-defined cultural values. The manager appears to be a relatively successful culture change agent, since he creates considerable commitment to two of the new values. This commitment is mirrored in employee behavior, ranging from changes in dress to improved sales figures. Siehl attributes the success of this effort primarily to the fit between the manager's objectives and his employees' prior value preferences.

Dandridge offers a conceptual framework that puts the results of Siehl's study in a broader context. Building on an extended metaphor of exploring the legend of King Arthur, Dandridge delineates four patterns of belief. The first is the unquestioning stance of the true believer. The second involves retaining one's own beliefs while acknowledging that other people may have other beliefs. The third substitutes rationality or "provability" for a belief system that is seen as having no basis in fact. The fourth stage is a suspension of disbelief, where a person acts as if he or she believed because of a need to feel and express a connection to a particular value. Dandridge uses this fourfold distinction to explain, in an innovative way, why some culture management efforts are more likely to succeed than others.

Like Dandridge, Krefting and Frost are open to symbolic aspects of cultural understanding. However, unlike all the other authors in this section, they focus on aspects of culture that are deeply rooted in the unconscious. From this perspective, they use metaphors as a way of expressing, and perhaps changing, cultural understandings. Because their conception of culture is grounded in the unconscious, they offer a picture of the change process that can be uncontrolled and tumultuous—more like wildcatting than contemplating the ruins of King Arthur's castle. Krefting and Frost offer a significant paradigm shift for cultural researchers used to thinking of the change process in relatively superficial and rational terms.

Eschewing metaphors, Lundberg offers an integrative framework for understanding the process of cultural change. Whereas Krefting and Frost stress the unconscious and "irrational" aspects of this process, Lundberg offers a rational reframing of cultural change as organizational learning. He then outlines the internal and external contingencies that facilitate and hinder efforts to intervene in this change cycle. Lundberg works from a broad definition of culture, including both unconscious assumptions and more superficial manifestations. The portrait that emerges is complex and dynamic, with a sensitivity to the history of institutions and the stages in their life cycles. This conceptual framework, with its historical perspective, seems to be that rare contribution: a theoretical abstraction that can add a new depth of understanding to case studies, including those presented by Siehl and by Martin et al.

In the final chapter of this section, Nord attempts the near impossible—a synthesis of the chapters described above. Without doing injustice to their differences, Nord builds a clearer picture of the often tacit agreements that link the chapters. Then, taking the argument an important step further, he uses these agreements to pinpoint that which was not (but should have been) said about the process of managing cultural change, concluding that the explanation lies in an understanding of magnetism rather than surfing, King Arthur, or wildcatting.

5

FOUNDERS AND THE ELUSIVENESS OF A CULTURAL LEGACY

Joanne Martin
Sim B. Sitkin
Michael Boehm
Stanford University

Organizational studies of the culture creation process offer a seductive promise to entrepreneurs: namely that a founder can create a culture, cast in the founder's own image and reflecting the founder's own values, priorities, and vision of the future. Thus a founder's personal perspective can be transformed into a shared legacy that will survive death or departure from the institution—a personal form of organizational immortality. Thomas Watson at IBM, Steve Jobs at Apple Computer, or William Paley at CBS: Whether seen as villians or saviors, it is the leaders who provide the center of gravity around which all else revolves.

This chapter offers a critical view of this seductive promise. We systematically analyze the culture creation process in one organization and offer a more complex and constrained portrayal of a founder's ability to impact the trajectory of a culture's evolution.

THE SEDUCTIVE PROMISE: INTEGRATION

In organizational studies of the culture creation process, summarized briefly above, whatever happens is credited in large part to the founder's

Authors' Note: Portions of an earlier version of this chapter were presented in two symposia at the annual meeting of the Academy of Management, Dallas, Texas, August 1983. The first presentation was titled "Entrepreneurial Control of the Culture Creation Process?" in Organizational Culture and the Institutionalization of Charisma (J. Martin,

unique personal attributes and actions. Consider, for example, Kimberly's (1979: 454) assessment of the impact of a founder on a new medical school: "Whether one chooses to call him an entrepreneur, a leader, or a guru, the fact is that his personality, his dreams, his flaws, and his talents were largely responsibile for the school's early structure and results." Schein (1983b) extends this point of view in an analysis of the impact of three entrepreneurs on the organizations they founded. He concludes that the founders' personal assumptions became shared by their employees and remained so, even when the firms grew dramatically, modified aspects of their businesses, and changed leaders. Other studies offer variations on these themes, descriptively portraying founders as the prime movers behind historical events or prescriptively urging leaders to articulate a vision and create a culture (see, for example, Selznick, 1957; Clark, 1972; Pettigrew, 1979; Peters and Waterman, 1982).

Although there are important differences among these studies, they share three interlocking assumptions. First, organizational culture is defined as that which is shared, and the picture of culture that emerges is monolithic. Consensus and harmony dominate, as the founder and the employees tend to share a common viewpoint. Second, these studies give founders credit for having deliberately guided, if not totally controlled, the process whereby this shared understanding emerged. Founders are portrayed as culture creators. Third, these studies argue or assume that shared understandings tend to mirror the personal value preferences of a founder. Thus organization is the founder "writ large," without mortal limitations.

These interlocking assumptions provide the conceptual backbone for organizational studies of the culture creation process. The portrayals of culture that emerge from these assumptions emphasize founder-generated harmony and integration. Research in related domains, how-

---

chair) and the second "Wild-Eyed Guys and Old Salts: The Emergence and Disappearance of Organizational Sub-Cultures" in Many in One: Organizations as Multi-Cultural Entities (S. Barley and M. Louis, chairs).

We are very grateful to the founder and the employees of the company that participated in this study. They indulged our attempts to understand the culture creation process with patience, concern, and a refreshing openness. They also gave of their time, a precious commodity in short supply in any new company. We especially appreciate the assistance provided by the director of Human Resources and his staff. Without their help the study would not have been possible. We are also grateful to Janice Beyer, Peter Frost, John Kimberly, Meryl Louis, Jeffrey Pfeffer, Louis Pondy, and Edgar Schein for their helpful comments on an earlier version of this chapter, and to Mary Jo Hatch, Tom Kosnik, and Tracy Smith, who assisted in the early observational phase of this study.

ever, suggests that each of these assumptions is misleadingly over-simplified.

A COPERNICAN REVOLUTION: DIFFERENTIATION

Such rosy portraits of organizational culture gloss over the internal conflict and differentiation that are characteristic of complex institutions. For example, a top management team may primarily focus its attention on profits, while lower status employees may be more concerned about job security and pay levels. Such divergence is often reflected in distinct subcultures. Some are countercultures that challenge core values of a dominant culture, as was seen in the DeLorean division at General Motors (Martin and Siehl, 1983). Other subcultures reflect occupational and hierarchical differences (e.g., Van Maanen and Barley, 1984). From this perspective, organizations are not accurately described as having a monolithic dominant culture. Instead, organizations are umbrellas for (or even arbitrary boundary lines around) collections of subcultures (e.g., Louis, 1983; Gregory, 1983).

Given the cultural complexity that emerges from this perspective, it is not surprising that these portrayals stress that leaders are not the only ones who generate the values, understandings, and behavioral norms that become part of organizational cultures. Other organizational members play an active role in the culture creation process. The content of a given culture or subculture can also be influenced by the task or technology used by employees, by the constraints of the organization's stage in its life cycle, or by external factors such as major changes in a firm's environment (see, for example, Kimberly, 1979; Bass, 1981; Schein, 1981; Spender, 1983; Van Maanen and Barley, 1984).

Even when researchers or employees give a leader credit for having influenced the culture creation process, that credit may be misplaced. Two social cognition biases, salience and attribution, make it particularly likely that retrospective accounts overestimate a leader's impact on events. Simply because of the role they fill, rather than their unique personal attributes or actions, leaders are salient to large numbers of people in a wide variety of circumstances. Salience causes leaders to figure prominently in people's memories of events, and that sheer availability in memory tends to cause assumptions of responsibility (see Nisbett and Ross, 1980).

In addition, attribution research suggests that people may have only minimal awareness of the situational determinants of a leader's behavior (e.g., Weiner et al., 1971). Self-enhancing biases may make leaders more likely to see themselves as responsible for successes than for failures (e.g., Miller and Ross, 1975; Bradley, 1978). Indeed, a skeptic might describe a leader's task as seeking credit for successes and avoiding attributions of responsibility for failures. For all these reasons, leaders may be given undeserved credit for having created cultures.

Taken as a whole, these points of view suggest a change in the focus of studies of organizational culture, from the search for universally shared cultural elements to a focus on differences in perspective. If one's location in an organization affects one's interpretation of events, then 100 percent agreement on any issue or value should be a relatively rare occurrence. Dissensus, conflict, and differentiation should be the norm.

If contextual factors and people other than the founder can influence the content of what is shared, then the understandings, values, and behavioral norms that constitute cultures should reflect the personal perspective of a founder only to a small extent. Rather than being the gravitational center around which all else revolves, in a Copernican revolution this second perspective on culture portrays the founder as simply one among many planets orbiting a sun. Rather than creating a culture in his or her own image, the founder is cast into a system molded by forces beyond his or her individual control. Even accounts of observers who give the founder credit for being the center of this cultural system are discounted, as cognitive biases may account for an overestimation of a leader's centrality and impact. In this second perspective on the culture creation process, the founder plays a relatively minor role.

EXPLORING THE PARADIGM CLASH: THE PRESENT STUDY

Two very different views of the culture creation process have been presented. The first, a paradigm that emphasizes integration, portrays organizations as homogeneous and consensual, having a monolithic, dominant culture. The founder is seen as the primary progenitor of that culture, the content of which reflects the founder's own personal understandings and values. The second paradigm emphasizes differentiation. Organizations are portrayed in terms of heterogeneity and dissensus, being composed of overlapping and nested subcultures, some of which may endorse conflicting viewpoints. The founder is only one of many sources for the shared understandings and values that constitute the content of these various cultures.

In the present study, we set out to observe the culture creation process under conditions that should be ideal for the emergence of data consistent with the founder-centered integration paradigm. At the same time, we focused on a manifestation of culture—versions of an organization's history—that would permit detection of the differences in perspective characteristic of the differentiation paradigm.

More specifically, we decided to study the culture creation process by focusing on how the members of a relatively new organization recounted and interpreted key events in their company's history. With this data, we addressed such questions as: What historical events, if any, were seen in the same ways by people throughout the organization? Could subcultural differences in perspective be detected? If so, what aspects of a person's position in the organization were associated with subcultural differences, and what substantive issues were affected? To what extent was the founder's perspective shared by his employees? Again, what was the content of the agreements and disagreements? Had the founder left a personal cultural legacy, at least among some subgroups of employees? The next sections of this chapter describe our reasons for focusing on organizational histories, the setting and the subjects we chose to study, and the methodology used.

AN EMPIRICAL APPROACH TO A SOCIALLY CONSTRUCTED REALITY

Events in an organization's history are raw material that members of a culture can mold into a form that both reflects and reconstitutes the culture itself. Underlying this view is the recognition that both cultures and organizational histories are socially constructed (Berger and Luckmann, 1966). Far from being objective descriptions, accounts of key events in an organization's history reflect differential attention, selective perception, and incomplete recall. As organizational members arrive at mutually acceptable interpretations of events, distortions and omissions multiply. By the time accounts have ossified in the form of organizational stories, legends, and sagas (Clark, 1972; Wilkins, 1978; Martin, 1982b; Martin, Feldman, et al., 1983), a new reality has been socially constructed.

Unfortunately, the social construction of reality is generally used as a descriptive phrase, a synonym for assumed consensus, rather than as a topic for systematic empirical investigation. We needed a way to assess the extent to which members of an organization shared the same view of their company's history. We wanted to be able to quantify the extent of agreement while retaining information about the content of that which was, or was not, agreed upon.

Our solution to this methodological dilemma was to collect versions of an institution's history from the founder and a variety of his employees, recording each person's position within the organization. These historical accounts were then systematically analyzed in a manner that permitted calculation of the degree of agreement about specific content issues between the founder and employees, and among specified employee subgroups.

The Setting

We decided to study a culture in the process of being created—that is, in a relatively new organization. We expected that a founder would have maximum ability to impact the cultural development process during the start-up stage in the organizational life cycle, when the inertia of tradition and habit had not yet been established (see Sarason, 1972). A relatively small number of employees should minimize the expanse of the realm over which the leader must exert control and, particularly if the leader had hired a relatively homogeneous group of people, should maximize the chances of creating the consensus that characterizes the integration view of the culture creation process.

The organization studied was an electronics manufacturing company located near Silicon Valley, California. When the study began, the firm had been incorporated for one and a half years. The study continued for one year. During that year, the firm grew from 200 to approximately 700 employees.

The Initial Observation Period

Approximately six months of unstructured observation preceded the design of an interview schedule and sampling procedure. During this initial observation period, pairs of researchers spent a minimum of two and a maximum of twenty hours a week engaged in such activities as observing meetings, joining informal groups during lunch and coffee breaks, and helping with menial tasks such as packing boxes. During the initial observation period, employees were told that the researchers were studying new companies in the electronics industry.

The founder requested a more detailed description of the purpose of the study and was told that we were studying "the culture creation process." In response, he observed that he was deliberately creating a culture. His view of this creation process, however, was subtle: "Creating a culture is like surfing. You cannot make a wave. All you can do is wait and watch for the right wave, then ride it for all it's worth." Although surfing is clearly an active and dynamic sport, it is passive in the sense that the surfer takes advantage of a naturally occurring change in the water, rather than creating that change. The passivity of this imagery puzzled the researchers because it contrasted starkly with the "take charge," "can do" tone of the founder's interactions with us and with his employees. The appropriateness of the founder's metaphor became evident only when the present study was completed.

A Stratified Random Sample of "Native Views"

Only one portion of the data collected during the initial observation period is relevant to the present chapter. Some researchers (e.g., Gregory, 1983: Van Maanen and Barley, 1984) have suggested that subcultures should be identified using "native view" distinctions that organizational members make among themselves. During their observations, the research team noted three recurrent subgroup distinctions in employees' conversations.

Employees distinguished "wild-eyed guys" from "old salts." "Wild-eyed guys" were members of the old guard, who had joined the company during its first nine months. These entrepreneurial types often referred to themselves as "cowboys." They thrived on pressure, coped well with crises, and preferred informality. In contrast, the newer hires were professional managers and technical experts who regarded the chaos, disorganization, and ambiguity associated with the old guard as problems they had been hired to solve. New guard members were referred to as "old salts" because of their experience in similar jobs at larger, more established companies. In addition to length of tenure with the company, employees distinguished four levels of hierarchy: the founder himself, the top management team, the other managers, and "everyone else." References to functional distinctions were also common, usually occurring in the form of divisional identification: domestic marketing, international marketing, research and development (R&D), manufacturing, or administration. Thus employees made at least three "native-view" subgroup distinctions based on length of tenure, level of hierarchy, and function.

After the initial observation period, a structured, open-ended interview questionnaire was designed and pretested and a random, stratified sample of 64 employees was selected.[1] Approximately half of the subjects were members of the old guard; the rest were new guard members. Within each of these two groups, approximately one third were members of the top management team, one third were middle managers, and one third came from the lower levels of the hierarchy. Representatives of all five divisions were included in the sample.

Collecting Histories: The Interview Procedure

The founder and this sample of employees were interviewed individually by members of the research team. In accord with Pettigrew (1979), these interviews focused on key events in the organization's history. Rather than having the researchers select those events, however, the founder and each employee selected whatever events he or she considered most important.

The founder was interviewed first. His interview began with the following request: "Please tell us about the events which were important in shaping what the company is like today or what it will be like in the future." After the founder finished listing the events he considered most important, he was asked: "Would you please rank order the events in terms of their importance?" The remaining questions were repeated for each event separately, beginning with the event the founder considered most important and continuing until the one-hour interview time had expired:

- Can you give me more details about exactly what happened, as you know it or heard about it?

- (Asked only for those events in which the interview respondent was a main character.) To the best of your ability to recall, what meaning did you intend to communicate by your actions?

- What does the event mean to you? That is, what message did you get from the event? Are there any other meanings or lessons to be drawn from this?

Employees' interview schedules contained the same structured, open-ended questions. However, in order to focus on shared elements of the company's history, rather than on personal anecdotes, the employees were told that "the event should have happened to someone other than yourself."[2]

NATIVE VIEWS OF AN ORGANIZATION'S HISTORY: RESULTS

Selecting the Key Events

The founder selected five events as particularly important: one concerned the origins of the company, two involved quality control problems, and two concerned past or anticipated departures of key employees. The employees recounted a total of 339 events, which were classified into six topic categories, presented in Table 5.1.[3] Of the 339 events, 72 percent dealt with the same three general topics as the founder's events: origins, quality problems, and turnover.[4] Only 9 percent dealt with topics not mentioned by the founder: all-out efforts to improve certain products ("upgrades"), and the company's move into more spacious quarters. The remaining 19 percent of the 339 event histories, labeled "idiosyncratic," were unique. For example, the starring character in one of these idiosyncratic events was a dog that spent time in a secretarial office.

The details of the event histories were systematically content analyzed.[5] The remainder of this chapter is a qualitative overview of a subset of these data, exploring the content and extent of agreement between the founder's event histories and those of his employees. A minimum of supplemental quantitative information is presented, as this is available elsewhere (Martin, Sitkin, et al., 1983). In the next section the perspective of the founder is contrasted with the viewpoints of the employees. Subsequently, the employee data are broken down by subgroups.

The Company's Origins

The founder's version of the origins of the company focused on the introduction of the company's first product in a "tremendous ballyhoo of publicity:"

> I threw down the challenge to the industry and said they were all full of shit; this is the way they ought to do it. [I] used enough inflammatory rhetoric, around what was basically the truth, to make everybody listen.

The founder's account described how he manipulated the media to create a barrage of free publicity. Although the purpose of that publicity

TABLE 5.1 Types of Event Histories

Types of Event	Number of Event Histories	Percentage
Shared (with founder)		
Origin	62	18
Quality control	39	12
Turnover	143	42
Subtotal	244	72
Shared (not with founder)		
Product upgrades	17	5
Moving	14	4
Subtotal	31	9
Not shared (idiosyncratic)	64	19
Total	339	100

was to draw attention to the company's product, it was ironically difficult to tell, from the founder's account of the company's origins, what that product was.

Of the employees' accounts of the company's origins, 57 percent shared the founder's emphasis on publicity. (Percentages cited are based on a total of 62 origin event histories.[6]) For example:

> [The founder] orchestrated a—and I use the word orchestrated advisedly—circus atmosphere in a way. The product itself didn't make a lot of difference. The whole thing about the introduction was an attempt to shock the industry.

A total of 36 percent of the employees' origin event histories did place strong emphasis on the company's product. For example, an engineer said:

> It was the first time anyone saw a full, complete [product with its special attributes] and at an incredible price. . . . Where others were selling the same thing for, you know, twice as much, here was somebody offering the same package at this low price, and it wasn't considered a toy. It was truly a [product] to be taken seriously. The fact that [it had these special attributes] was really a tremendous selling feature.

Every one of the employee accounts of the company's origins featured the founder as a central character, and most of these origin event histories placed primary or substantial emphasis on the unique personality and actions of the founder. For example, a supervisor in manufacturing described the origins of the company in these words:

> Part of the success of [the founder] is his own, is the fact that he's so controversial. He's just determined to show everyone else he can be a success. He just wants to show everyone else he believes in himself. He's that kind of person. I think if he hadn't been, I don't think that the product—I think that if the product had not made it, the poor man would have been crushed.

In addition to describing each event in detail, the founder and the employees were asked what lessons, meanings, or values were communicated by the event. The founder said that the company's origins illustrated the importance of being controversial in order to gain the media's attention. In addition, he interpreted the event in terms of its efficacy in problem solving and motivating others to achieve:

> The real message is that if you are right in perceiving the nature of a problem, then you can address a solution to [that] problem.

> You have a few people, maybe 15 or 20 people, reading about themselves wherever they turn. It's likely to give them a tremendous sense of achievement and spur them on to do more heroic deeds.

In all, 24 percent of the employees' origin event histories echoed the founder's stress on the importance of being controversial, but they did not allude to efficacy in solving problems or achievement. Instead, the two most popular interpretations involved the importance of meeting customer needs (34 percent) and producing an affordable product (26 percent).

Quality Control

The founder was eloquent about the extent of the company's early quality control problems:

> We were getting reports that 30% of all units were arriving at the dealers dead on arrival, that 80% of all units being shipped were requiring service work under warranty. An examination of why this happened showed that . . . the method used was to scream at an engineer until he agreed to have it fixed by the morning, whether he could or couldn't, whether he knew what was happening or not.

Two of the founder's event histories focused on efforts to resolve these quality control problems. In the first, the founder blamed the problems on the company's increasing bureaucratization:

> Problems which we encountered and addressed were known to people at the lowest levels of the company long before management realized the nature of the problem. It occurred to me that we were already beginning a bureaucracy, whereby the information I received [was] filtered through levels of management, suitably laundered at each step on the way, so that by the time it got to me, I was hearing only what they wanted me to hear.

The founder then described his solution:

> I decided to totally short circuit that by appointing five quality circles, five people in each circle, five people drawn utterly at random from the ranks of the non-supervisory personnel so that nobody, under any circumstances, could manipulate who would be on which quality circle. The moment that happened, I started to get all kinds of information. It had a tremendous effect internally, externally, and caused a number of very interesting incidents to occur.

The founder offered two interpretations of this event history:

> [Quality circles give non-supervisory personnel] a much greater sense of self-awareness and self worth . . . Because they're not giving anybody any orders, they feel they are somewhat impotent to right wrongs.

> It also makes management seem much more human; therefore [non-supervisory personnel] feel more ready to communicate problems which I may never hear about.

In the founder's second quality control event history, individuals were seen as the source of the problem, and individual action by the founder was the solution:

> It was clear that there was rank incompetence riddling the manufacturing operation, so I just had to come in and perform surgery. The first thing I did was I took quality assurance [responsibilities] away from Noah Woodstock [a pseudonym] . . . I was going to take personal responsibility for solving the problem.

The founder interpreted this event in terms of the company's rapid growth and again emphasized efficacy in solving problems:

> We were growing too quickly and had not kept pace with our growth.

> If you see a problem, solve it now, irrespective of wounded feelings. If you do approach the problem with that alacrity, it's amazing how quickly you can solve it.

The employees' versions of quality control event histories generally echoed the founder's analysis, citing the product failure rate (51 percent) and the poor procedures (26 percent). (Percentages are based on a total of 39 quality control event histories.) The antibureaucratic tone of the founder's account was not present in the employees' versions of these events. Relatively few of the employees' quality control event histories mentioned the poor flow of communication from well-informed lower level employees (8 percent) or the laundering of information that did reach management (3 percent). Instead, the employees' accounts of these events went into great detail about the design, production, and vending of the product, citing specific problems such as relations with distributors (31 percent) and suppliers (44 percent). For example:

> [The machine] was getting too hot, and . . . there were three or four issues all related to the plastics (of the machine case). So they basically went two or three months without shipping any product because we did not have the plastics. Maybe if it [the company] had done a better job and done a proper evaluation of the product from the beginning, it could have had a better start-up and continuing flow.

The disparity between the perspectives of the founder and the employees was even more evident in the descriptions of the resolutions to the quality problems. None of the employees' event histories mentioned the quality circles that were apparently so important to the founder. Instead of blaming individuals, or regretting the increasing bureaucratization of the firm, employees' quality control event histories frequently called for more bureaucratization, arguing that improvements in formal procedures (23 percent) and job definitions (15 percent) would solve the quality control problems. Rather than citing the founder's attempts to take personal responsibility for solving these problems, some of the employees' quality control event histories (15 percent) focused on something the founder never mentioned: their own willingness to work hard, beyond the call of duty. For example:

> A lot of bad [component of the product] was going out. I had to test [this component]. Everybody put [in] lots of hours, late hours, and they had shifts all night. Everybody really pulled together and made it work and fixed the whole thing.

The employees interpreted the meaning of the quality control event histories quite differently from the founder. Less than 5 percent of these employee event histories mentioned the themes of management being human, nonsupervisory people feeling powerful, the company's rapid growth, or efficacy. The employees' interpretations of these events were more likely to focus on the quality of the product itself (54 percent), the importance of admitting mistakes (36 percent), the need to maintain credibility with customers (39 percent), and the desirability of rushing less and planning more (21 percent).

In summary, the employees' quality control event histories were more product- and customer-oriented than those of the founder. The employees did not seem troubled by this difference in perspective. The founder performed myriad activities, and the employees chose to cite those aspects of his behavior that were most congruent with their own beliefs and priorities. For example, a manufacturing manager's quality control event history portrayed the founder as deeply concerned about the quality of the product:

> [The founder] was very conscientious about making sure that the product was corrected. He's always stood behind that. I think that one of the things that has made it a success was because he would take 'em back without questioning . . . again and again and again until it was corrected. Even though [the founder] was trying to be a success and get as much out in the market as he could, he was definitely concerned about the fact that he wanted his name to be on a product that worked right.

A top-ranking sales manager's quality control event history described the founder as personally concerned with customer relations:

> [The founder] sent a mailgram off to the dealers and just admitted that there was a major problem, that he was personally taking over quality assurance. [The founder] said, "If you've got any major problems, give me a personal call."

As these examples illustrate, the employees often attributed to the founder concerns about the product and customer relations that he seldom mentioned in his own accounts.

Turnover of Key Personnel

The founder told two turnover event histories. The first concerned a high-ranking old guard member:

> While he had done an excellent job while the company was small, it was now over his head and he was protecting himself by hiring only highly incompetent people and keeping out anyone who was competent for fear that they would know a lot more than he and disclose him. I therefore had to step in and move him out and start replacing him with people I'd hired. He then became extremely resentful and rationalized that he had made the company go and [now he] was going to be removed . . . He started negotiation with competitors and we had to fire him.

The founder interpreted this event in terms of trust:

> If you place that implicit trust in everyone working for you there will be occasions when that trust is betrayed. But that is overwhelmed by the number of people who will return that trust with their best efforts. And [he] was one of those few instances where the trust was betrayed.

The founder's second turnover event concerned his own plans to resign:

> I'm in the process of hiring a president at the moment to replace me as president and I'm going to become Chairman of the Board. And a great deal of the day-to-day operations, which I've been looking after, I'm going to turn over to somebody who I believe is qualified to do it because I don't think I am anymore. And by doing it with me I'm hopefully setting an example so that everybody else perceives what I'm doing and understands that it may happen to them and to take it in the spirit it is intended.

The founder summarized his accounts of these turnover events with this caveat:

> A very rapidly growing entrepreneurial company goes through many phases. And the people who did a very good job at one time tend to become incompetent very soon thereafter. You're constantly faced with the need to tell somebody, "You did a fabulous job. You're now incompetent and must be replaced by somebody else." . . . Nowhere in the company can anyone consider they have tenure. And that even a job well done in the past is no guarantee that they will keep it in the future because the company is changing so quickly.

The founder interpreted these turnover event histories as indicating the primacy of profitability over more humanitarian concerns. He justified this potentially discomforting conclusion in terms of the firm's serious concerns about its financial viability:

> The management in this company is dedicated to achieving financial success of the corporation, rather than soothing the egos of any individuals at the top of the company or anywhere else within it.

> We're not playing a game. This is a business and we intend to succeed.

The employees' turnover event histories (there were 143 of these) echoed many of the founder's concerns about the suitability of the skills of the people who left, or planned to leave, the company. The departing personnel were described as lacking "big business skills" (30 percent), having a style conflict with employees who remained at the company (22 percent, and/or being entrepreneurial "cowboys" or "wheeler-dealers"

(18 percent). For example, one employee described the founder's plans to resign in these words:

> He is in fact an entrepreneur . . . He did not feel that he was suitable from an operations standpoint to run the company as president. And I totally agree with him. I think the party is kind of over. Once you get a compnay to a certain size, and particularly when it is growing as fast as we are, you have to have significant amounts of control.

There were several differences between the founder's turnover event histories and those of the employees. Perhaps because the founder was planning to resign, his turnover event histories never described the people who were to replace those who had left or who were planning to leave. In contrast, the employees went into some detail about the new employees, most frequently describing them as having "big business skills" (27 percent). The founder hoped his own plans to resign would set an example for employees. Of all the employees' turnover event histories, 19 percent mentioned relevant implications for "other" employees, and 5 percent mentioned the personal relevance of these events.

A total of 54 percent of the employees' turnover event histories, like those of the founder, interpreted the turnover in terms of the changing needs of a growing company. Some of the employees' turnover event histories mentioned the founder's concerns about trusting employees (6 percent), the primacy of profits over humanitarian concerns (14 percent), and/or the seriousness of the company's concerns about financial viability (14 percent). However, the employees also offered interpretations not mentioned by the founder—in particular, the need for implementing more formal control systems (16 percent).

Employee-Generated Event Histories

Although the product upgrade and moving event histories represent only 9 percent of the total of 339 events, they are important because they represent shared employee priorities that were not mentioned by the founder. The product upgrade event histories described employees coping valiantly to meet management deadlines for the release of an improved product. The employees who were the stars of these event histories successfully overcame overwhelming obstacles in order to release the improved product—generally in a rush and/or late. All but one of these seventeen product upgrade event histories concluded with a recital of the positive outcomes of these struggles, such as the implementation of improved systems for organizing work (38 percent) or for distributing the product (31 percent).

The moving event histories (there were fourteen of these) focused on transfers from one office location to another, generally from a number of small, dispersed buildings to a new corporate headquarters. These moving event histories consisted primarily of details about the old and new spaces. The only surprising aspect of these event histories was the extent to which the new space was considered disappointing. This was one of the few indications, in any of the event histories, of employee discontent or low morale.

The interpretations of the product upgrade and moving event histories were quite similar to the interpretations of the other types of event histories. The product upgrade event histories were most frequently interpreted in terms of the need for rushing less and planning more (59 percent), producing a high-quality product (47 percent), meeting customer needs (47 percent), and maintaining credibility with customers (47 percent). The moving event histories were most often seen as indicating the changing needs of a rapidly growing company (57 percent) and the need to rush less and plan more (29 percent).

So far, the analysis of the event histories has treated the employees as a single, undifferentiated group. In the next section, event histories from specified subgroups are contrasted as we seek evidence of subcultural differences.

The Effects of Tenure, Hierarchical Level, and Function

In contrasting the event histories told by members of different subgroups, we relied on three "native view" distinctions encountered during the initial observation period: old guard versus new guard, hierarchical levels, and functional (i.e., divisional) membership. Previous research on subcultures has been conducted in relatively mature organizations. These studies have generally found that subcultural boundaries are likely to emerge along hierarchical and functional lines (see, for example, Dearborn and Simon, 1958; Lawrence and Lorsch, 1967a; Gregory, 1983; Louis, 1983; Martin and Siehl, 1983; Van Maanen and Barley, 1984).

Because we were not studying a mature organization, we expected to find a different pattern of subcultural evolution. Because interpersonal relations in a relatively new organization are generally characterized by close and informal contact, we thought that awareness of hierarchical differences would be minimal and that clear functional distinctions, based on formal job descriptions and clear divisions of responsibility, would be incompletely developed. In addition, we expected that the crises endemic to a start-up organization would blur hierarchical and functional boundaries as, for example, accountants, secretaries, and vice presidents join in packing boxes to meet a shipping deadline. For reasons such as these, we anticipated that subcultural differences between levels of the hierarchy and among functional specializations would not be well developed in a relatively new organization.

At the same time, we expected that other subcultural differences, such as those between old and new guard members, might be *more* important at an early stage in an organization's life cycle. In addition, we anticipated that support for the founder's perspective would be greater among members of the old guard, most of whom he had chosen himself, than among new guard members. To our surprise, none of these expectations were confirmed by the data.

The content analysis results for old guard members were contrasted to those for new guard members. Only one significant difference between the old and new guards was found: The event histories of old guard members were more likely to have central characters who were members of the old guard. Except for this tendency for the old guard to focus on themselves, no evidence of subcultural differences due to tenure were found. The old guard members were not more likely than the new guard members to tell event histories similar to those of the founder.

Hierarchical level was associated with many differences in the content of event histories. Employees' event histories tended to focus on tasks and personnel from their own, rather than other, levels of the hierarchy. In addition, the event histories of top management personnel were more likely than those from other levels of the hierarchy to focus on the founder, tell event histories similar to those of the founder, and interpret events in the same terms as the founder (e.g., citing the importance of being controversial and stressing the need to trust employees). Thus hierarchical differences in the content of the event histories reflected a tendency to self-focus and, among top managers, to share the founder's perspective.

Functional distinctions among the event histories were also well developed. Employees were more likely to tell event histories in which their division played a prominent role and to include more details relevant to their division's functions. The founder had invested considerable time in marketing; hence, event histories from the marketing division were more likely than those from other divisions to be similar to the founder's. Here again, functional differences in the content of event histories again reflected a tendency to self-focus and, among members of the marketing division, to share the perspective of the founder.

WEIGHING THE EVIDENCE

Support for the Integration Paradigm

The integration approach to the culture creation process emphasizes consensus. It is founder-centered, and it suggests that the content of a culture will reflect the founder's personal values and interpretations. Our content analysis of organizational histories produced some evidence that supports the integration view, although some caveats about the limitations of the evidence are conceptually important.

In any study of a socially constructed reality, there is a question that can only be answered arbitrarily: How much agreement must be present before "consensus" is attained? How many issues must be agreed upon? Is 50 percent agreement a cup that is half full or half empty? If we take the arbitrary position that majority agreement (over 50 percent) represents a substantial degree of consensus on any one issue, then it is clear that, in accord with the integrationist paradigm, organizationwide consensus has emerged on several issues.

First, the employees interpreted many key events in terms of the company's changing needs, due to its rapid growth. In accord with the leader-centered emphasis of the integration paradigm, the employees always mentioned the founder as a central character in their event histories and usually held him primarily or substantially responsible for event outcomes. In accord with the third aspect of the integration paradigm, for each of these issues the employees expressed a viewpoint congruent with the personal perspective of the founder.

However, it cannot be assumed that the founder caused these similarities between his perspective and the viewpoints of his employees. Rather, cognitive biases may account for some of these similarities. For example, a leader's actions and the effects of a firm's extraordinarily rapid growth should be salient to all employees, not just to certain subgroups. Thus salience (and hence, availability in memory) may explain why these particular themes were broadly shared. If this explanation is correct, even the tendency to focus on the founder can be largely attributed to the prominence of the leadership role rather than to the unique attributes or actions of a particular leader.

The founder's perspective on a number of key events was significantly more likely to be shared by members of the top management team and the marketing division, suggesting, in accord with the integration paradigm, that the founder may have created a personal cultural legacy for these subgroups of employees. However, again the source and direction of causality remains unclear. The marketing personnel and the top management team may have influenced the founder's perspective rather than the other way around. It is also possible that external factors, such as the importance of quality control in this particular industry, may have caused the founder and these groups of employees to share similar viewpoints about some issues.

In summary, the results of the historical analysis provide some support for the integrationist portrayal of the culture creation process. A few issues did engender consensus, and some overlap between the perspectives of the founder and employees was observed. However, due to availability effects and the possibility of attribution errors, it is not and cannot be clear whether the founder deserves credit for having created these shared viewpoints.

Support for the Differentiation Paradigm

Although some of the data are congruent with the integration paradigm, other findings from the analysis of the organizational histories are more easily interpreted within the constraints of the differentiation paradigm. Consensus was relatively rare, subcultural differences were frequent, and the perspective of the founder on most issues differed considerably from that of most of his employees. Factors other than the unique attributes and actions of the leader, such as salience and organizational life cycle stage, can account for most of these differences in perspective.

For example, there is a salience explanation for many of the differences between the founder and his employees. Each had different tasks and responsibilities. Not surprisingly, the founder was more concerned than many of his employees with publicity and the quality circles which enabled him to receive otherwise unobtainable information. Similarly, because the founder planned to resign, he was less concerned than his employees with the qualifications of newly hired employees. In contrast to the founder, the employees focused more on their own areas of responsibility, such as the characteristics of the product and its distribution to valued customers. Thus many of the differences in perspective between the founder and his employees appear to be task-driven dissimilarities in what was salient.

Some of the subcultural data are also congruent with a salience explanation. Each functional division and level of the hierarchy was more likely to focus on its own activities and personnel. Thus task-driven differences in what was salient may have contributed to the creation of hierarchical and functional subcultures. Salience alone, however, cannot fully explain why so few subcultural differences due to tenure were found, or why hierarchical and functional differences were so well developed. A second contextual factor, stage in the organization's life cycle, may also be relevant.

Some of the differences between the founder and subgroups of employees have an ideological flavor. For example, the founder interpreted events in terms of the classic concerns of an entrepreneur (see McClelland, 1961; Filley et al., 1976). The founder believed strongly in individualism, blaming individuals for problems and seeing individuals as solutions to problems. He emphasized efficacy—that problems could be solved "with alacrity," and that even low-level personnel had the power to "right wrongs." He was concerned with the firm's financial viability, placing profitability above more humanitarian concerns for "soothing egos." He deplored what he labeled the firm's increasing "bureaucratization." It seems unlikely that all of these values, particularly the emphasis on profitability, would be shared by employees.

In contrast to the founder, employees seemed to welcome bureaucratization. They deplored the lack of formal quality control procedures and the pressures that caused them to rush, instead of planning carefully. Rather than seeing problems and solutions in terms of individuals, the employees sought solutions in the form of bureaucratic controls, such as formal job descriptions and systems for quality control and for maintaining efficient relationships with suppliers, vendors, and customers.

Organizational life cycle research suggests a reason that this particular conflict—between the entrepreneurial concerns of the founder and the more bureaucratic preferences of the employees—surfaced at this point in the firm's development (see, for example, Greiner, 1972; Sarason, 1972; Kimberly and Miles, 1981; Perkins et al., 1983). The creation phase in the organizational life cycle is generally characterized by a founder who is technically oriented, who disdains management activities, and who focuses on marketing a new product. The transition from creation to the second phase of development is particularly problematic:

> Thus the founders find themselves burdened with the unwanted management responsibilities. So they long for the "good old days," still trying to act as they did in the past . . . At this point a crisis of leadership occurs, which is the onset of the first revolution. Who is to lead the company out of confusion and solve the managerial problems confronting it? Quite obviously, a strong manager is needed who has the necessary knowledge

and skill to introduce new business techniques. But this is easier said than done. The founders often hate to step aside even though they are probably temperamentally unsuited to be managers. So here is the first critical developmental choice—to locate and install a strong business manager who is acceptable to the founders and who can pull the organization together [Greiner, 1972: 42].

Once a new leader is found, the organization turns its attention to bureaucratization, that is, structural differentiation, implementation of systems (such as accounting), formalization of communications, and centralization of authority. This life cycle research suggests that the organization we were studying had already begun this transition to the bureaucratic phase, causing a discrepancy between the entrepreneurial values of the founder and the increasingly bureaucratic priorities of the employees.

The subcultural data support this life cycle interpretation. Hierarchical and functional subcultures were already well developed, while differences between the perspectives of the "wild-eyed guys" of the old guard and the "old salts" of the new guard were few. Support for the founder's perspective was not significantly stronger among members of the old guard, as compared with the new. Instead, the founder's view was echoed by the top management team and the personnel of the marketing division, where the founder had invested much time and effort. These subcultural data strongly suggest that this organization had begun to enter the bureaucratic stage of its life cycle.

So far, then, the disjunctions between the founder's and the employees' perspectives, like the conjunctions congruent with the integration paradigm, can be explained by contextual factors—such as salience and life cycle stage—that are not dependent on the unique attributes or actions of this particular founder. If the life cycle explanation is correct, most organizations should experience during this transition phase a conflict between the founder's entrepreneurial values and the employees' more bureaucratic ones. This particular founder, however, had a distinctive response to this particular value conflict.

The Elusiveness of Cultural Legacies:
Riding the Wave

The key to understanding the founder's response to this value conflict lies in the details of the turnover event histories. Both the founder and the employees most frequently described departing employees (including the founder himself) as lacking big business skills or as being entrepreneurs, "cowboys," or "wheeler-dealers." In contrast, the newly hired employees were most frequently described as having the skills that their old guard counterparts had lacked.

This founder was clearly aware of the clash between his own entrepreneurial values and the more bureaucratic preferences of his employees. He was also frank about his personal response to this value conflict. He candidly espoused his opinions about individualism, efficacy, and the primary importance of financial survival, expressing his distaste for bureaucracy with equal candor.

However, the founder apparently did not let his personal value preferences interfere with the company's incipient bureaucratization. He led, through his own plans to resign and through his firing of a prominent old guard member, a purge of the entrepreneurial "wild-eyed guys." Many of the old guard employees who left were high-ranking members of the top management team. Thus the purge eroded support for the founder's priorities and values where it was strongest: at the top levels of the hierarchy.

Because replacements for the "wild-eyed guys" were selected for their big business experience, it is reasonable to presume that the new hires joined the chorus calling for increasing bureaucratization. Thus the purge may have erased whatever subcultural differences existed between the old and new guards. The old guard members who did not resign may have adopted, or decided to tolerate, the more bureaucratic perspectives of the new guard. Thus, rather than creating a culture cast in his own image, this founder initiated turnover policies that decimated support for his own values and priorities.

It is impossible to determine, even from the founder's own account whether he intended his actions to have these effects. Perhaps he saw the conflict between his perspective and that of the new guard and decided that it would be impossible to change the direction of the firm's evolution toward bureaucracy. Having seen the handwriting on the wall, he may have concluded that he should resign before the conflict got worse. Or he may have accepted the direction of the firm's evolution, since it contributed to the company's financial viability, but did not want to be part of it, since his skills and values lay elsewhere. Although it is clear that the founder did not leave a cultural legacy cast in his own image, it is impossible to determine the extent to which he contributed to the organization's movement toward bureaucratization.

Although this founder will not achieve a personal form of organizational immortality, his planned resignation is consistent with his values. He gave the financial survival of the organization priority over his personal loyalties, even to himself. He saw the rise of bureaucratic concerns, and rather than try to perpetuate his own personal perspective, he announced that he would step aside in order to give precedence to the new guard members, who would strengthen the firm's bureaucratic orientation. This approach is captured well by the founder's own metaphor for the culture creation process: He didn't create the wave; he just waited for the right wave and took a ride on it.

The distinctive response of the founder of this firm allows us to distinguish between creating a wave and recognizing a wave that already exists. Had the founder responded more typically to the value clash of the transition period, our conclusions could have been quite different. For example, the founder could have tried to epitomize the values of the new guard. If the founder had successfully exercised this alternative, the employees' values would have been similar to his own. Under these circumstances, the culture would have been cast in the founder's own bureaucratic image, and it might appear as if he were responsible for the direction of the firm's evolution. However, organizational life cycle research suggests that such an evolution toward bureaucracy would probably have occurred anyway. Thus, if the founder had chosen this alternative, an observer might mistakenly give the founder credit for having created the wave that he was simply riding.

Other responses by the founder are possible. To cite one more example, the founder could have attempted to strengthen support for his entrepreneurial perspective. Had he successfully accomplished this, the organization would have avoided the transition to bureaucratization. This third alternative would have produced a culture cast in the founder's own image. However, organizational life cycle research suggests that firms rarely escape bureaucratization as they grow. Therefore, it seems reasonable to argue that the founder who succeeds in implementing this alternative has indeed exerted control over the culture creation process. Because this outcome is rare, though, the entrepreneur who chooses this alternative is likely to fail. While he may have created the wave, it is unlikely to provide an extended ride.

Balancing the Tension Rather Than Choosing a Paradigm

This evidence of the elusiveness of a cultural legacy is congruent with the differentiation paradigm. Many of the concerns and interpretations of the founder were not shared by his employees, and those that were could be explained by contextual factors, such as salience and life cycle stage, rather than the unique actions or attributes of the founder. To the extent that the founder had an opportunity to choose his actions, his range of choices was severely constrained by the momentum of the organization's evolution toward bureaucracy. These constraints and complications are serious, and a personal cultural legacy thus remains elusive. However, in accord with the leader-centered integration paradigm, the founder's choice among this limited set of options made a dramatic difference in how people interpreted the meaning of events.

This analysis contains elements that are congruent with both the differentiation and the integration paradigms. As Lawrence and Lorsch (1967a) point out, organizations need both integration and differentiation. Granted that the relative weights given these two forces can and should vary, depending, for example, on environmental pressures. Nevertheless, neither force in isolation is likely to be as effective as balancing the tension between both. This suggests that both the integration and the differentiation portrayals of the culture creation process may be simultaneously accurate.

As Greiner (1972) suggests, there may be predictable stages in an organization's life cycle when crises of leadership occur, when the unique attributes and actions of a leader can make a critical difference. If this explanation is correct, most organizations should experience some conflict between the founder's values and the employees'. To the extent that the content of this conflict is predictable by the stage in an organization's life cycle, it is congruent with the differentiation paradigm's deemphasis on leaders. However, within the constraints of this predictable value conflict, and in accord with the leadership focus of the integration paradigm, a founder has to choose among several alternative courses of action. Which alternative is chosen may have a dramatic impact on the trajectory of a culture's evolution.

NOTES

1. The original random, stratified sample was composed of 71 subjects, but for reasons unrelated to the purpose of this study (e.g., faulty recording and transcription), seven interview schedules were either not obtained or not usable.

2. If the employee's three most important events were not the same as the founder's, the employee was prompted with similar questions about three of the founder's most important events. This prompted portion of the employees' interviews was designed to tap the latent sharing of cultural knowledge not spontaneously expressed during the first half of the interview.

3. Due to a two-hour limitation on the length of an interview, there was little variance in the number of event histories told by the employees (mean = 6.36, standard deviation = 0.63). There were no significant differences, due to tenure, level of hierarchy, or division,

in the number of event histories told. Therefore, the event histories, rather than subjects, were used as the unit of analysis.

4. Some 68 percent of this overlap between the founder and the employees was latent; that is, employees shared their knowledge about the company's history after prompting from the interviewers but did not include it spontaneously in the first three event histories they recounted. Of those first three spontaneous accounts, 40 percent (192 event histories) were coded as dealing with origins, quality control, or turnover.

5. Most coding categories were abstract noun phrases which could be instantiated by a specified set of less abstract expressions. Intercoder reliability was calulated using percent perfect agreement and Winer's (1962) analysis of variance method. Both exceeded 93 percent agreement.

6. When percentages are reported, they sometimes do not sum to 100 percent because some event histories contained content relevant to more than one coding category.

6

AFTER THE FOUNDER
An Opportunity to Manage Culture

Caren Siehl

University of Southern California

The question of whether organizational culture can be managed has led to much debate among both academics and practitioners. Some researchers suggest that organizations should be conceptualized as cultures (e.g., Goodenough, 1971; Geertz, 1973; Smircich, 1983c). They favor the view that culture is part of what an organization is rather than something an organization has (Smircich, 1983c). Those researchers who argue that culture is a socially constructed system of shared beliefs and values would find it inconsistent to think of systematically managing or attempting to control the phenomenon. As Weick (1983) states in responding to a recent article on managing corporate culture: "Organizations don't have cultures, they are cultures, and this is why culture is so difficult to change."

However, other researchers, particularly those searching for predictable means of organizational control and improved methods for organization management, would seem to hold a hope, if not a rigorously tested belief, that culture can be managed, at least to some degree. Researchers who propose that organizations produce cultures usually define culture as the social or normative glue that holds an organization together (Baker, 1980; Siehl and Martin, 1983). Culture consists of values and beliefs that some groups of organization members come to share (Louis, 1983). These values can be expressed through a number of different means, including a special language or jargon (Edelman, 1977; Hirsch, 1980); organizational stories and scripts (Wilkins, 1978; Martin, 1982b); rituals and ceremonies (Gephart, 1978; Deal and Kennedy, 1982); physical arrangements such as dress and decor (Pfeffer, 1981a; Peters and Waterman, 1982); and organizational practices such as recruiting, training, and reward systems. From this perspective, culture is viewed as a powerful means of implicit control (for example, see Wilkins, 1983b). The ultimate end product of culture research would be statements of contingent relationships that have applicability for those trying to manage organizations (Smircich, 1983c). Therefore, in spite of a lack of convincing evidence, there exists an interest, and perhaps a need on the part of some researchers, to believe that culture can be managed and to understand just how this process might occur.

It would seem that rather than striving for an unequivocal yes or no in response to the question of managing culture, a more fruitful approach would be to explore the conditions under which it would be more likely that culture could be managed. In other words, the question should be changed from "Can culture be managed?" to "When and what aspects of culture can be managed?" This chapter will attempt to do the following: first, suggest a set of conditions that might be conducive to managing culture; second, propose how and what aspects of the culture might be managed under those conditions; third, describe an exploratory study that was conducted to address the propositions; and, finally, present preliminary results of the study.

TIMES OF TRANSITION AND/OR CRISIS

Organizations face times of transition and/or crisis throughout their existence. Because of the interdependency between an organization and its environment and the inherent uncertainty of parts of that environment, it is inevitable that change, in the form of a transition or crisis, will occur.

Some transitions may produce circumstances that facilitate the management of culture. Lundberg (this volume) has identified five classes of events that can function as triggering mechanisms to culture management and change. The five classes include environmental calamities and opportunities, internal and external revolutions, and managerial crises. An environmental calamity, such as all types of natural disasters or a sharp recession, is something that cannot be ignored in an organizational environment. Environmental opportunities include technological breakthroughs, the discovery of a previously unknown or untouchable market niche, and newly available venture capital. Two classes of revolution also possess the potential for culture management. One is an external revolution or something that happens external to an organization with major consequences, such as being taken over by another corporation. Internal revolutions, such as the installation of a new management team, can also act as triggers. Finally, a whole class of managerial crises, such as an inappropriate strategic decision can encourage the management of culture (Lundberg, this volume).

The research on organizational life cycles looks specifically at the predictable transitions through which organizations evolve (e.g., Cameron and Whetten, 1981; Kimberly, 1979; Miles, 1980a). As Cameron and Whetten (1981: 527) explain:

> Organizations begin in a stage, labelled "creativity and entrepreneurship," in which marshalling resources, creating an ideology, and forming an ecological niche are emphasized. The second stage, the "collectivity state," includes high commitment and cohesion among members, face-to-face communication and informal structures, long hours of dedicated service to the organization, and an emerging sense of collectivity and mission. The organizational emphasis is on internal processes and practices, rather than on external contingencies. In the third stage, "formalization and control," where procedures and policies become institutionalized, goals are formalized, conservatism predominates, and flexibility is reduced. The emphasis is on efficiency of production.

Of particular interest to the research described below is the transition from the entrepreneurial, creative stages to the formalization and growth stage. This time of transition will be used to illustrate how times of transition in general may create a condition under which culture could be managed.

There are several reasons why the potential for managing culture would exist at this particular time. Employees themselves may feel a need for change from a culture based on entrepreneurial values to one based on values of long-term growth and stability (Martin et al., this volume). Some may be looking for a new direction and may be open to attempts to move the culture accordingly. In addition, the transition from the entrepreneurial to the growth stage is often accompanied by the resignation or replacement of the founder of the company. Such a resignation sends a clear signal that a transition is occurring. This change could breed the opportunity for other changes, such as those accomplished by managing the culture.

Particularly if employees have been dissatisfied with the past, a transition creates an opportunity to manage the culture in ways that would appear to be leading to a brighter future. Finally, transitions give rise to a condition analogous to the unfreezing stage necessary for socialization. During this time, a void exists that can be filled by the management of the culture in order that refreezing can occur with the values cast in a new, predetermined image. Lest this argument seem obvious, it is worth noting that the opposite point of view is also plausible. It may be precisely during a time of transition or crisis that employees would cling to the stability of the past in order to maintain some degree of certainty in the midst of change.

HOW MIGHT CULTURE BE MANAGED?

For the reasons outlined above, the transition from the entrepreneurial stage to the formalization and growth stage may create a set of conditions under which culture could be managed. It is necessary to understand what aspects of culture might be managed under this set of conditions, what means could be used in managing these aspects, and what players might be involved in the management. Referring to the definition suggested above, culture consists of several different aspects, including shared values and the beliefs and ways of acting that reflect and express those values. It would be possible in attempting to manage culture during a time of transition (for example from an entrepreneurial founder to a new growth-oriented CEO) to change only the beliefs and behaviors expressing the shared values, with the values themselves remaining the same, or it may be possible to change both the values and their expression.

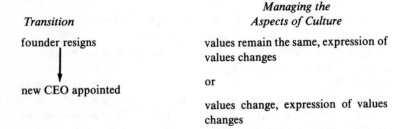

Transition	*Managing the Aspects of Culture*
founder resigns	values remain the same, expression of values changes
↓	or
new CEO appointed	values change, expression of values changes

If a company has not been successful prior to the founder resigning, and/or employees are unhappy and dissatisfied with the currently shared values, then one would expect an attempt at managing culture to involve replacing both the shared values and the beliefs and behavior expressing the values. In other words, the management of culture would involve the creation and support of a desirable new culture. If, on the other hand, the company has been generally successful, the employees have not been dissatisfied, and the founder has resigned with his respect intact, then the management task becomes more complex. For example, one may attempt to change both the values and the expression of the values in order to refocus the company toward a longer term, growth-oriented strategy, only to find that employees are loath to change their shared values because of past success. If, during the transition from the entrepreneurial to the growth stages, the values can continue to guide the company forward, it may be more appropriate to leave the values untouched and to manage the ways in which the values are expressed.

In addition to considering what aspects of culture may be managed, it is important to suggest what means could be used to manage culture. As described above, research has shown that values are expressed using a number of different forms, including special language, rituals, stories, and organizational practices. These could all potentially be used to manage culture during a time of transition. It has been proposed, however, that the most effective ways to manage culture are through one-to-one verbal communication and role modeling. Role modeling provides employees with an opportunity to observe a specific instance of behavior from which they can then begin to develop new minitheories and scripts concerning situations in which this behavior would be appropriate.

According to research carried out by social learning theorists, new behavior is acquired through the influence of stimuli that cue behavior-reinforcing responses in a particular setting. This process has been found to occur through the observation and imitation of others, known as "modeling" (Bandura, 1969). Role modeling and one-to-one communication can provide relevant, current information in a timely fashion. Because times of transition are characterized by ambiguity and uncertainty, this feature would seem to be particularly important.

Finally, the question of who might be involved in managing culture during a time of transition should be raised. The set of potential managers would include the CEO, middle managers, and members of work groups or subcultures. It would seem that if any of these players had an explicit interest in managing the culture, the time of transition would give them an opportunity to do so, and their attempts could have a significant effect. The CEO, because of his or her position and the resulting focus on that position, would be likely to have the most influence. However, if strong subcultures exist, such influence may be mitigated, if not obscured, by the values shared within the subculture. In addition, the influence of the CEO may be overshadowed by the influence of more immediate personnel who are explicitly attempting to manage the culture.

AN EXPLORATORY STUDY
OF THE MANAGEMENT OF CULTURE

The focal organization (LSI) is a microcomputer company located in "Silicon Valley" in Northern California. The company researches, designs, manufactures, and markets a microcomputer product. LSI is the worldwide leading supplier of Unix-based microcomputers. When the study began, LSI had been incorporated for six months. The study continued for two and a half years, and during that time a number of events occurred which signaled that LSI was facing the transition of moving from the entrepreneurial, creative stages to the formalization and growth stages. These events included the extremely successful initial public offering of the company's stock, which raised over $90 million, a move to a substantially larger headquarters building, and the restructuring of the corporate hierarchy. In addition, the founder of the company resigned during the course of the study. He was replaced by a CEO whose business experience was composed solely of working for large bureaucratic organizations.

The study was conducted in two major stages. The first stage consisted of sixteen months of observation and interviews. Three researchers, working alone or in tandem, spent an average of ten hours per month at LSI. This time was allocated irregularly, so that the range of hours of observation for each researcher varied from zero to ten hours per month.

During this phase, the researchers spent time observing randomly selected employees from each of five departments during the working day. In addition, the researchers attended company social events. For example, one of the researchers was a guest at the company's first Christmas party, hosted by the founder and attended by 90 percent of the employees. Interviews were also conducted with all members of the top management team, as well as a group of lower level employees. The purpose of this phase of the study was to learn as much as possible about the culture of the organization and to become familiar with the different organizational roles and the people who filled those roles.

During the sixteenth month of observation, the founder resigned and the company was reorganized. Due to the reorganization, the marketing, sales, and support functions were grouped together and divided into two regions for the entire United States. Figure 6.1 depicts the new organizational structure.

The Western regional director was explicitly interested in managing the culture of his region. He was concerned about some of the values that he felt were shared among company employees, including a focus

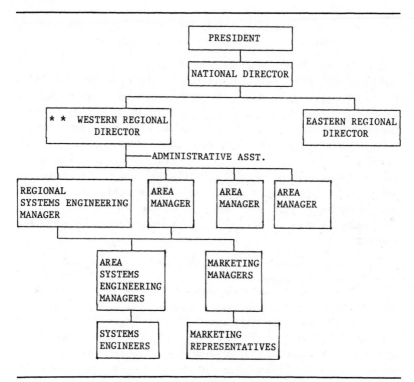

Figure 6.1 Organizational Structure After the Reorganization

on short-term results and individual superstars. He believed that several of the values had outlived their usefulness, and he wanted to introduce a new set of values. He was able to articulate three values which he embodied in the following slogans:

(1) *Feed it or shoot it.* This slogan refers to the value of focusing on the long-term, particularly on productive customers with much potential. In the past, employees had focused on short-term results, often sacrificing long-term business relationships in favor of a quick return.

(2) *Professionals think success.* This slogan refers to the value of behaving in a professional manner. By implication, if an employee acts professionally, he or she will be rewarded and thus achieve success. In addition, the slogan is a play on words, because it is also saying that in order to be professional, one needs to act with self-confidence and to define oneself as a success.

(3) *We have a responsibility to the rest of the company.* "We" is used here in reference to the employees of the Western Region. Historically, employees had felt responsible primarily to themselves. The focus had been

on individual effort rather than on the team, the region, or the company as a whole.

The regional director wished his employees to believe in these values and to behave accordingly. During the second stage of the study, each employee in his region was interviewed on two separate occasions. In-depth, structured interviews were conducted with all 45 employees of the Western Region. The first interview took place immediately following the reorganization, before the regional director had the opportunity to express and reinforce the new set of values. The second interview took place six to eight months later, after the director had attempted to manage the culture. The study will continue for another eight to twelve months, with additional interviews.

The structured interviews were composed of questions that addressed the following:

(1) Employee awareness of values being espoused by the regional director.
   Sample: What values do you think the regional director would like to have guiding your behavior and beliefs?
   Sample: Have you been told that the following values are important? To what degree? By whom?

   (a)   *"Feed it or shoot it."*
   1   3   5
   unimportant   very important

(2) Employee commitment to values being espoused by the regional director.
   Sample: To what extent are you personally committed to the following values? How have you expressed your commitment?

(3) Description of culture.
   Sample: What do you think is important to the top management of the company?
   Sample: What values do you think other employees believe to be important at the company?
   Sample: What values do you personally think are important?

(4) Means of managing culture.
   Sample: Have any of the following means been used to communicate values? Please circle any means that have been used. If possible, give an example of how values have been communicated using the following:
   (1) formal philosophy statement
   (2) recruiting
   (3) role modeling
   (4) reward system
   (5) company stories
   (6) training

Sample: What do you think are the key factors in getting a good performance evaluation?
(5) Key players in managing culture.
Sample: Which of the following have the most impact on what you believe to be important at the company? Why?

> your immediate boss
> peers
> regional director
> top management
> company material
> other _____

Sample: Have you felt any impact of the new CEO on the company?

PRELIMINARY RESULTS

After eight months, it appeared that the regional director had been somewhat successful in managing the culture in his region. At the time of the first interview, the employees were totally unfamiliar with the values being espoused by the regional director. By the time of the second interview, all of the 45 employees who were interviewed responded that they perceived the value embodied in the slogan, "Feed it or shoot it," to be very important to the regional director (see Figure 6.2). The "Professionals think success" slogan was also viewed by all employees as being very important. However, "We have a responsibility to the rest of the company" was rated by only four employees as very important, and by six employees as somewhat important. The majority of the employees said that they perceived this value to be unimportant to the regional director.

Content analysis of the open-ended questions produced similar results. At the time of the second interview, employees were able to articulate the meaning behind the first two values in a consistent fashion. For example, a manager of support personnel explained that "Feed it or shoot it" meant: "Customers are either for us or against us in the long-term. If you are for us, we'll give you all the help we can. If you are against us, let's part ways right now." A sales manager responded that this value could be translated into "weeding out the weak customers and signing up strong customers." A marketing manager, when asked about "Professionals think success," explained: "People make their own destiny. If you think successfully, you'll begin to do what it takes to make it happen. This can be a real morale builder because it affects people's attitudes."

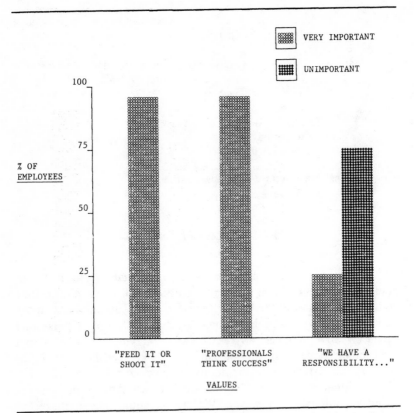

Figure 6.2 Perceived Importance of Values by Employees

At the time of the second interview, employees indicated moderate to high levels of commitment to these values. All 45 employees responded that their personal commitment to the value embodied in "Feed it or shoot it" was very high (see Figure 6.3). A similar pattern was found for "Professionals think success." However, for the value represented by "We have a responsibility to the rest of the company," employees indicated significantly lower levels of commitment.

It would seem that the regional director had met with some success in managing the culture of his region toward the attainment of a new, desirable culture. He had articulated a set of three values which he wished to become shared, and after eight months (the time of the second interview) his employees perceived that two of the three values were very important and were themselves committed to these values.

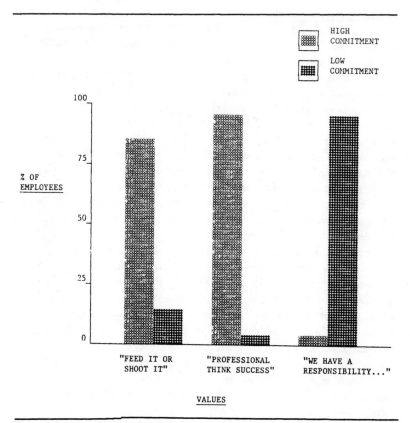

Figure 6.3 Employee Commitment to Values

In addition to the questionnaire measures of commitment, actual behavioral changes were also recorded that support this pattern of results. For example, the number of customers serviced by the Western Region dropped from 550 to 300, while the number of new orders per customer grew by 5 percent. The annual sales for the region increased from $40 million to $48 million over the eight-month period. Relating to the value of "Professionals think success," there was a noticeable change in employee dress. The regional director equated dressing professionally with the IBM stereotype of blue suits and white shirts. His employees began to emulate this style of dress and commented on the new "IBM look" in the office. Finally, there was little behavioral indication that employees viewed the third value, embodied in "We have a responsibility to the rest of the company," as being important. For example, several instances occurred where employees were offered job transfers to other parts of LSI, but such transfers met with strong resistance by regional employees. There was little interest in sharing their skills with corporate headquarters or other divisions.

This attempt by the regional manager to manage the divisional culture occurred during a time of transition following the resignation of the firm's founder. It is important to note that the employees viewed two of the three espoused values of the regional manager as being quite similar to top management values and to values held by other company employees. Only the third value, "We have a responsibility to the rest of the company," was not rated as being a good fit with either top management values or company-held values.

When questioned about the lack of similarity between this value and top management values or company-held values, employees said that the company had focused on individuals and small teams being successful without having individuals be concerned with other parts of the company. It was believed that if each individual was independently successful, then the whole organization would be successful. In other words, a major focus of the corporate culture was on doing the best you could without worrying about anyone else. This focus on individual effort is not surprising considering that the company was just beginning the process of moving from the entrepreneurial stages to the formalization stage. The regional director had difficulty in promoting a value that conflicted with shared beliefs. He was making progress, however, because at the time of the second interview, 25 percent of the employees rated this value as very important.

Employees were also asked to evaluate fifteen different means of managing culture, including company stories, jargon, rituals, formal philosophy statements, recruiting, office design, role modeling, reward systems, appraisals, management's reaction to critical incidents, training classes, dress, structure of the region, agenda items, and announcements. The regional director believed that he was using nine of the fifteen means to actually manage the culture by reinforcing his set of espoused values. He believed that he was reinforcing and expressing these three values through jargon, one-to-one communication, role modeling, a philosophy statement, the reward system, the structure of the region, dress, agenda items, and rituals. When describing the structure of the region, the regional director related the following:

> At the Los Angeles office, I reorganized and appointed a new area manager. I went with a guy who had retail experience in spite of the national director of marketing being behind another guy. I didn't think that the guy the national director wanted was professional. He would not have been a good person to demonstrate professionalism or long-term thinking.

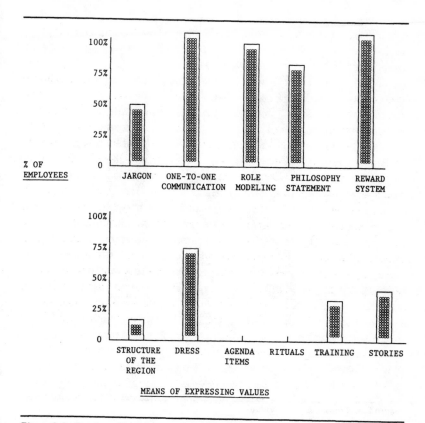

Figure 6.4 Employee Perceptions of Means Used to Express Values

The regional director used a variety of different means to consistently (and sometimes redundantly) express the same message.

Of these nine means, only seven were perceived by employees as having been used to communicate and reinforce the director's values. The employees were virtually unaware that agenda items and rituals were being used, while both the reward system and one-to-one communication were rated by 100 percent of the employees as having been used to communicate the values. These results are summarized in Figure 6.4.

Interestingly, two means that the regional director did *not* believe he was using were evaluated by the employees as having communicated his set of values. Training was rated by 33 percent of the employees as having reinforced the values of "Feed it or shoot it" and "Professionals think success," and stories were rated by 47 percent as having communicated "Feed it or shoot it."

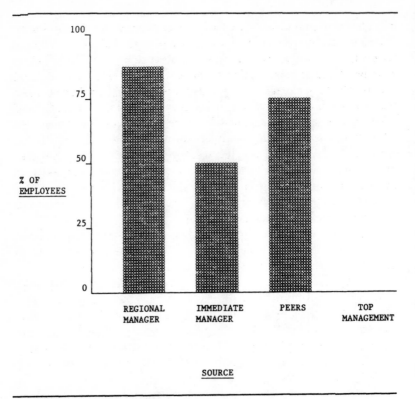

Figure 6.5 Transmission of Values

Employees were also asked from whom they had heard the director's set of values. In all, 84 percent of the employees said that they had heard the values directly from the regional director. In addition, 72 percent of the employees responded that they had heard the values from their peers, while 68 percent had heard the values from their immediate managers (see Figure 6.5).

DISCUSSION

This study has looked at the explicit attempt by a regional unit to change its culture during a time of company transition. The founder of the company had resigned, and a new CEO with vastly different skills had been appointed. The regional director felt that this would be a perfect opportunity to effect cultural change within his region. In spite of a conscious and persistent effort, in eight months his attempts were only partially successful. Two of his set of three values did become widely known and shared among his employees; however, these values were perceived as being similar to currently held values. The regional manager had not changed the shared values as much as he had changed the expression of those values. It is important to note that he himself perceived his values to be quite different from currently held values. He felt that he was promoting a dramatic cultural change. The third value espoused by the regional manager was less widely shared than the other two values. It was also viewed by all, including its originator, as being the most dissimilar to currently held values. However, the director did not consciously devote an incremental amount of time or effort toward the expression and reinforcement of this value.

Once again, we are left with an ambiguous response to the question of whether culture can be managed. It is clear that the regional director articulated a set of three values. But the other regional employees may have independently decided, or convinced each other, that these values were desirable. Thus the director may have been the "culture manager" only at the articulation stage of cultural change. Perhaps culture management is really this: articulating a possible culture, coming to agree that it is desirable, and then attaining it through the sharing of desired values. If so, all employees, not just the regional director, contributed to the management of culture.

This study suggests that during a time of transition, it is possible to manage the expression of cultural values through a number of different means. It would seem to be more difficult, even during a time of transition, to actually change the value system unless the change is desired by employees. It is important to note that in this example, only eight months elapsed since the change effort began. It was believed that this relatively short period of time would be mitigated by the fact that the company had only been in existence for three years and that the average tenure of the 45 employees was 22 months. As the study continues over the next twelve months, it should be possible to observe further changes in the culture.

Thus it would seem that times of transition are a fruitful context in which to address the question, "Assuming that culture can be managed, which periods and aspects of it are most manageable?" "Managing culture" is often synonymous with "changing culture." In addition to gaining a better understanding of the management of change, it is also important to learn more about managing nonchange. During a time of transition, it may be as important to manage stability as it is to manage change. Indeed, times of transition may offer the challenge of managing change and stability simultaneously. The research described here is a preliminary attempt to understand the management of culture from the manager's perspective and to begin to test the hope that culture can, in fact, be managed.

7

THE LIFE STAGES
OF A SYMBOL

When Symbols Work and When They Can't

Thomas C. Dandridge
SUNY at Albany

This chapter proposes the idea that there are four ways in which one can "believe" a symbol and that these ways determine one's ability to use the symbol to guide behavior. These four ways of believing can be regarded as sequential stages, as there is a logical development through the order presented. They can also be described as separate, unique ways of believing.

In order to develop a source from which examples of symbols can be drawn, I will describe a recent trip I took to southern England and Wales in search of King Arthur, Merlin, and Camelot. Near the start of the trip, in Wales, I stopped by a lake to enjoy the scene and take a break from the harrowing one-lane roads through the mountains. The lake was attractive enough for me to take a picture but was no more special than the scenery around it, as far as I could tell. Miles later, I learned that it was reputed to be the lake from which the Lady of the Lake held up King Arthur's sword, Excalibur. From then on, I reconstructed the stop as my having been drawn to the lake and, experiencing more than the serenity, having taken a picture I would not have taken under normal circumstances. I embellished and reinterpreted the facts to support a myth that I valued. In one sense, which I want to explore later, I created an illusion.

Several days later I reached Tintagel, looking for the magic of Arthur's birthplace. There I found a small tourist town, not unlike those all through the United States that depend on travelers for survival. A pilgrimage down a very dusty trail brought visitors to the sea and to a point of land on which stood the worn ruins of a "castle," since proved to be built about 800 years after the time of King Arthur, with the remains of an older monastery evident behind it. These latter ruins were little more than one- or two-room stone huts. It took all my imagination to reconstruct the castle in which King Arthur was born.

Below the castle were the famous caves of Merlin. One cave in particular attracted me, and I explored it thoroughly. It was cut clean through the cliff under the castle, as it had been formed by the tide and waves washing through it. I knew enough geology to be sure that it had changed little in 1500 years, and I was thus walking on the same stones that the magician had trod. Tourists walk straight through this cave to the sea and are satisfied. Not me. I saw a branching of the cave off to the left and knew that it was the heart of my search.

With no light, I left the bright sunlight and worked by way into the dark unknown before me—a true allegory. Walking carefully, and experiencing the power of the place, I stepped gingerly onto a flat rock between tidal pools, only to find that it was under several inches of crystal clear, icy water. Obviously a lesson from the gods of the cave, or a barrier that would have frightened other, less resolute searchers away. With one shoe full of water, I went on. My reward was eerie silence and an open space that had light such as I had never seen before. Beyond the light was the darkness of another cave. At that point, my courage failed. I was totally alone with the magic, and I couldn't make myself go further.

The town of Tintagel was full of financially healthy organizations. They apparently survived on the very desire to believe that brought so many tourists there. Parallels to modern organizations can be found in the stories of Camelot, where the knights were stimulated and guided by the symbols of the Holy Grail, the Round Table, or at a later time the Crusades to the Holy Land. Some modern organizations, like the gift shops of Tintagel, are created to take advantage of symbols. Others, like Crusading armies, are created to manage the inspiration or energy that a symbol draws forth, such as the retaking of the Holy Land.

Under certain conditions, symbols in modern organizations can be effective tools for management. This chapter will explore some ways in which symbols are believed, and how each way or stage of belief influences human actions as well as perceptions of the meanings of actions. Some readers may scoff at the tour narrative provided above as an unscientific reinterpretation of scant and unrelated data. Others may identify with such a trip and its excitement, or accept the facts as part of a legend that they never doubted. This chapter proposes that such different perspectives are actually based on different stages of belief of an underlying myth.

STAGES OF BELIEF IN A SYMBOL

In his book, *The Image* (1956), Kenneth Boulding describes the three stages in the disintegration of a social image. The same idea applies to myths or other symbols and provides the basis for the stages proposed here. In the first stage, people have a complete and unquestioning belief. This is the unself-conscious belief that Rokeach (1968) classifies as "primitive." There is only one possible conclusion. Believers "know" there is no evidence that refutes their beliefs and are not even aware of any conflicting beliefs. All data provided are "facts," and as such are unquestioned. Martin and Powers (1982: 94) describe the IBM company picnic in the company's early years in terms that fit with the stage one definition: "Until the company became too large, employees lived temporarily in tents on company grounds during the annual picnic. There they sang company songs and listened to speeches given with evangelical fervor."

In the second stage, a person acknowledges the possibility of having some other belief. He or she may see others who appear to be successful in a comparable endeavor, or happy in their lives, and who are acknowledged to hold other beliefs. Employee B tells a different story of the company origins, or laughs at those singing the company song. Employee A continues to believe the story or sing the song but recognizes that there are others who don't believe as he does.

Beliefs in stage two may depend heavily on authority. If my history book tells me that the story of King Arthur is true, and I accept this book as an authority, then I will retain my belief in the face of opposition. Similarly, my authority may be my parents, my priest, or my manager. Rokeach's (1968) authority or derived beliefs would relate to stage two. These include beliefs as to whom to believe. As our society has taught people to give ultimate authority to verifiable factual data over all else, it has also emphasized the appropriateness of questioning myths or examining the rationality of a ritual. In doing so, we are led toward the third stage.

The third stage for Boulding is the obvious result, once a person chooses to stop believing the myth or to stop perceiving any value in the ritual. Rationality or "provability" becomes the basis for accepting any belief system, and unproven myths or nonrational rituals are discarded for having no basis in fact. The disintegration of subcultural groups, religions, or class differences can be seen to follow this path from unquestioned acceptance to skepticism, and finally to rejection or disinterest.

These stages were originally described by Boulding as those involved in the disintegration of a symbol, ending in its death. However, the "spirit of Christmas," in the form of continuing tales of the founder or company president, or the survival of company emblems or rituals, provides evidence that at times there must be some stage of belief that survives despite disproof. The trek through England described above was real, and despite facts that conflict with the mythology, the motivation and the satisfaction were definite.

A fourth stage has been proposed which is a rebirth of presentational symbols (Langer, 1953) brought to life by our need for experiencing organizations as more than rational, product-oriented systems. Fox et al. (1973) propose that people need something they can project toward, an image that inspires hope. This process is facilitated by the use of symbols. The person now acts only "as if" he or she believed, because in doing so it is possible to experience closer identification with the organization. The person is more inspired or vitalized than is possible without such acceptance. Such a person might say, "I know the story isn't true, but it makes me feel good when I hear it." The person wants to feel and express connection to a particular value. Believing in the symbol as if it were fact facilitates this. In this stage, the symbol is accepted as a medium for experiencing. If the third stage is the factual, the fourth is the imaginative. Through imagination the respondent unites with the image, empowering it as a symbol. The potency of a stage four symbol thus depends on the ability of the user to imagine.

If stage three represents disillusionment, or suspension of belief in a symbol, then stage four represents the suspension of disbelief. Krefting and Frost (this volume) apply this idea to using metaphors to facilitate change. In accepting the metaphor, the user looks at the world for a moment as if that metaphor were reality, and hence takes a stage four perspective. If stages one and two represent "social blinders," as Krefting and Frost indicate, then people seeing a symbol from that perspective would have a harder time setting the symbol aside to imagine the world through a metaphor, as may be done in stage four.

Louis (1983) supports the idea of a "chosen belief." She writes: "In contrast to participation in a culture of birth, participation in an organizational culture is more temporary and more a *matter of voluntary choice*" (p. 49; emphasis added). Pfeffer (1981a: 47) adds the idea that the leader is equally subject to his or her own symbols: "Management and politicians fool themselves as well as others with their symbolic acts. If one sits in a magnificent office in a magnificent structure . . . one not only convinces others that one is in control and has power over organizations . . . one is also likely to convince oneself."

Abravanel (1983: 277) uses the idea that "membership requires that participants allow a given ideology to dominate their definition of reality," which captures the idea of stage four symbol use. The knights of King Arthur's court may have had an absolute, stage one belief in the symbol of the Holy Grail. The Crusaders may have been reinforcing their beliefs in the face of the opposing beliefs of "infidels" (stage two). The factual report of a modern historian shows that the castle at Tintagel was a crude fortress built centuries after the time of King Arthur, who probably was nothing more than an army general if he existed at all. These stage three data are disregarded by many who, while knowing these facts, look in awe into the well where the Holy Grail was supposedly thrown, just as they peer into Merlin's cave.

Pondy (1982) defines two levels of reality, one symbolic and one objective. Symbolic reality exists for those in stage four, while the objective reality of stage three can support a number of symbolic realities, depending on the perceptions and chosen involvement of participants, but it is they who permit themselves to create such a reality. (Those in stage one or two experience their data as factual, or objective.)

Piggott (1974) discusses history and our ways of treating it. He is concerned with the relations among the stages proposed here and thus distinguishes between two ways of viewing the historical past. At various times we, and historians in particular, address ourselves to the reconstruction of prior events. However, given the fact that the events of the actual past are concluded, they cannot be fully attained or actually relived. This actual past is referred to by Piggott as the "past-in-itself." What historians in particular try to construct is the "past-as-known," which is limited to the "logical handling of legitimate evidence" (Piggott, 1974: 5) and which, in our culture, leads us to stage three and no further.

Note that those in stage one or two would also profess to be handling legitimate evidence logically. By contrast, a person in stage three would recognize that data may be omitted or added in order to construct a *desired* past. Doing so creates a "past-as-wished-for" and involves the conscious or unconscious selection or elaboration of evidence to fit a pattern, of which the user may also be unconscious. While people in stage one or two of a symbol's use may be unconscious of this selection process and the underlying values desired, a person in stage four intentionally selects or creates support for the history that matches his or her values or needs. In this case, the message is more important than the symbol's verifiability, and the result is a story, treated as if it were believed.

The past-as-known uses inference based on verifiable empirical obsevation, while the past-as-wished-for uses assumption, a leap of faith chosen to achieve a desired condition. Thus we infer the technology of 1500 years ago in England based on physical evidence, but we assume the religion, laws, morals, and spiritual life of Camelot, as we lack any definitive evidence with which to do more. A stage three perspective would search for new data but would not go beyond them. The user is thus separate from the data and the event. A stage four perspective would treat ideas as data if they supported a desired pattern or belief because the user identifies with the event and feels a part of it. Martin et al. (this volume) propose that events in an organization's history provide raw material that is transformed into part of an institution's culture—surfacing, for example, in the form of shared stories about the past. This selection process supports a past-as-wished-for, a *chosen* past that represents stage two if it is unconscious or stage four if it is conscious.

Marshall McLuhan (1960) provides additional support for the existence of a fourth stage with regard to symbols. He discusses changes brought about by language and other ways of communicating. In the preliterate world, communication was through presentational symbols. As such, it took a nonlinear, unified form. By contrast, the literate world, especially since the advent of printing, is linear, patterned, and particularly rational in its description. Hence, emphasis is placed on that which can be described by talking about attributes or features.

Simultaneous communication world-wide, as well as high-fidelity audio visual communication, have led to a postliterate world that retains many of the preliterate forms. One difference is that in preliterate times, the storyteller was the carrier of the cultural thread and thus had no flexibility in the story he told. Indeed, the group members relied on the narrator *not* to innovate. This situation is consistent with the maintenance of stage one or two. However, in the post literate world, the storyteller is the creator of the cultural thread, especially in organizations with rapid changes in goals and personnel. The storyteller must now create stories or rituals and interact with the listener, who supports story or ritual changes through his or her acceptance thereof. The storyteller or ritual leader must also modify these to fit changing needs and situations.

GENERAL PROBLEMS FOR MANAGEMENT

Note that the stages described here relate directly to a person's treatment of each symbol, not to the individual's stage of development or maturation. Individuals may have some tendency either to accept everything they hear or to view everything with skepticism and look for factual proof, but they will usually treat each of a variety of potentially symbol-laden stories or occurrences in different ways. Thus managers must be sensitive not only to the symbolizing potential of a story or action, but also to the characteristics of each individual in the potential audience of the story. The member selection process for the organization alleviates this problem if the manager can select new participants with roughly similar values, orientations, or cultures. Krefting and Frost (this volume) consider the importance of selection in deliberately fostering different local cultures within an organization. Affirmative Action or Equal Employment Opportunity programs can be seen in this light as potentially eroding opportunities to use symbols to manage. These and similar programs force the mixing of cultures, symbols, and stages of belief, thus reducing the chances for a manageable local culture to develop. The use of factual data and the acceptance of cultural symbols vary among cultures and often among races or between sexes. Instead of dealing with a somewhat homogeneous group, a manager is more likely to lead a diverse group. Therefore, he or she needs to be sensitive to variation in both beliefs and stages of belief.

K. E. Vinton (1983) studied an organization that she concluded had not developed extensive symbols, appearing to operate largely at stage three. She identified three primary reasons. These were the small physical size and close proximity; the technological change in the company, which separated it from its founders; and the physical presence of the current owner. Each reason supports the concept that physical, immediate evidence is being used by participants as a basis for their operation. Details of the study also reveal that the owner/leader appeared to make no effort to nurture the use of any of the other stages. Here, the storyteller did not spin the cultural thread, and the participants used the immediate factual environment for their operation. A greater sensitivity to symbols might have added to management's control or continuity in the organization.

PATTERNS FOR MANAGEMENT

In spite of these problems, identifying these four stages and placing them in the matrix shown in Figure 7.1 permits us to consider the interaction between the person using the symbol to manage (the influencer) and the person influenced by that particular symbol (the respondent). We usually assume that the influencer is the manager;

RESPONDENT'S STAGE

Figure 7.1

however, it is equally possible that employees could use a symbol effectively to influence the behavior of their managers. This would be especially true if the manager had a stage one or two perspective of the symbol. As we consider possible interactions, we approach a more cultural view of the organization, recognizing that the meaning emerges here and is intersubjectively negotiated in the management process (Louis, 1983).

The Influencer

For any symbol, we may take the viewpoint of either the influencer or the respondent. First, consider the matrix from the perspective of the influencer. If the influencer is in stage one with regard to that symbol, he or she would completely lack comprehension of why respondents are not influenced by it—for this person, there is no alternative to believing; he or she is unaware of stages two through four.

An influencer in stage two is aware of the fact that others believe differently and may label them as ignorant (especially if they are in stage one), or perhaps as the enemy if they threaten his or her objectives or beliefs. In a company, members of a competing firm may be viewed in this way. It would be hard for a stage two influencer to differentiate between those in stages two, three, or four. A person in stage three, for example, would be seen as just another nonbeliever.

An influencer in stage three who uses symbols to manage could be described as hypocritical—not internalizing the symbol while using it to manipulate others through their beliefs. The gift shop owner in Tintagel is an example. This influencer would be likely to protect a respondent who is in stage one from conflicting ideas, and to reinforce a stage two respondent's symbols as long as these were useful to the influencer. The knights of Camelot believed in the Holy Grail, and that it could only be seen by the "pure." This would represent a respondent pattern, probably of stage one belief. A manager-king would do well to reinforce such a belief, even if he rationally rejected the myth himself. A court magician such as Merlin could provide useful tricks and rituals to reinforce the myth. This "evidence" from the magician-expert may parallel the facts provided by current stage three orientations.

The stage four influencer would use symbols imaginatively, as a creative tool, as implied by Peters and Waterman (1982) and by Deal and Kennedy (1982) in their popular books on excellence in the corporate culture. Peters and Waterman (1982: 55) point out that it is built into human nature that we "reason by stories *at least* as often as with good data. 'Does it feel right?' counts for more than 'Does it add up?' or 'Can I prove it?' " Leaders in excellent companies take advantage of this situation.

The Respondent

If we shift our focus to the perspective of the respondent, the person being managed, we can again see differences according to the person's stage in the belief cycle. We would expect people holding a stage one belief to be highly susceptible to outside influence, but only as long as the symbols used were accepted and consistent with their unquestioned beliefs. Individuals with stage two beliefs would also be susceptible, especially in situations where they had to compete with the "bad guys" holding alternative beliefs. The military organizations are examples, as are companies that have myths about how work life, ethics, objective, are to be found in competing companies. Airline pilots tell stories of other airlines, emphasizing the lower quality of service or equipment. Employees at a major hotel exchange stories that show how bad the working conditions are at other hotels and how fortunate they are to work where they do. In each case, such stories complement positive stories about the employee's own organization and reinforce the stage two belief in that company and its values.

People in the United States are most likely to take a stage three perspective toward events of their work life, a stage where the ability to influence the respondent through symbols is lost. The emphasis on rational behavior and factual information leads us to translate events, descriptions, or objects into rational messages. As a rule, Americans do not expect symbolic content and disregard or explain away whatever deeper meaning they experience. Wilkin's (1978, 1983b) studies provided descriptions of "company A," in which work participation fits this description of stage three, as does the company in Vinton (1983b).

In stage four, the individual chooses to retain, nurture, or look for symbolic content in events, descriptions, or objects. With this orientation the individual is intentionally receptive to influences by the items given symbolic importance. Wilkin's "company Z" fits this description. Respondents appear to go out of their way to find and retell stories, or to participate in ceremonies that reinforce perceptions of the organization or that have an inspirational quality for listeners.

The executive branch of the federal government provides an unusual example of behavior that may fit stage three, and that may differentiate it from stage four. Elections and political appointments routinely change the people in the top levels of a bureaucracy, and each new set of leaders bring their own symbols—heroes, pictures, rituals, and so forth. The career bureaucrats generally adopt an *appearance* on accepting these symbols immediately; they act as if the new symbols were as important as the old ones. Later, of course, they readily shift to a new set as the next change in leaders is made (Warwick, 1975). In this case the new leaders may be in stage two (ardent supporters of the winning party) or in stage four (choosing to suspend disbelief and to be inspired by the symbols). The career bureaucrats as described here may be in stage three, expressing superficial acceptance of the new symbols and using them to give the appearance of accord, much as the Tintagel shop owners used the tourists' beliefs for their own benefit.

The Interaction

Combining the influencer and respondent perspectives into one matrix, we can hypothesize the potential ability to manage a respondent, given any pair of orientations of the influencer and the respondent toward any particular symbol. The results are shown in Figure 7.2. In the cells of the upper left portion of the matrix, the potential to manage through symbols is low, although the symbols themselves may be strongly influential due to the unquestioned beliefs of

RESPONDENT'S STAGE

		1	2	3	4
INFLUENCER'S STAGE	1			0	
	2			0	
	3	H	H	0	0
	4	H	H	0	H

Figure 7.2

both the influencer and the respondent. Both parties operate without conscious selection of their symbols, and thus these are not readily the subject of conscious manipulation. Thus the belief manages, not the manager. The matrix contains a zero where the likelihood of the use of symbols in management is very low. In these cases either the respondents are not available or the influencer is not interested. An *H* indicates high potential to manage through symbols. The five cells containing an *H* are those with the highest potential for management through symbols.

Hypocritically (stage three) or by chosen belief (stage four), the influencer uses or enhances the symbols of the respondents in stages one, two, or four. Their location in the matrix indicates the ability in four of the five cases for the influencer to take advantage of the respondent—that is, to abuse the respondent's belief through representative symbols such as stories. Martin and Powers (1982: 104) confirm that stories can be "powerful and potentially dangerous tools." Respondents in stages three and four are not so enlightened as to avoid manipulation, but they are more protected by the element of awareness and choice.

The above discussion has been presented as if there were two parties, the influencer and the respondent. The issue of management through symbols is much more complicated when the multidimensional nature of the process is included. First, any individual may be influenced by a variety of symbols, each operative at any one of four stages. Second, the influencer does not often face a unidimensional audience. Among a variety of respondents, some may accept a given symbol from any of the four stages. However, neither of these concerns eliminates the potential to manage through symbols.

Having considered the interaction of stages as if they were static, we should also consider the dynamic of movement between stages. Both Siehl and Lundberg (this volume) consider the times of transition: an unfreezing stage followed by a resocialization and refreezing. It has been proposed that culture can be managed more easily during this transition. In terms of the ideas presented here, these transitions would be potential changes in one's stage of belief:

- from a stage one blind belief in the founder (hero) to acceptance in spite of conflicting evidence,
- from belief in one hero to a stage two belief in another hero,
- from acceptance to rejection of all heroes, and
- from no hero to setting aside disbelief and choosing to believe because doing so carries the desired culture and its values.

Each of these transitions can be managed. As a minimum, culture management is a matter of being sure that appropriate and consistent data or symbols, such as stories or ceremonies are available during a transition. More active transition management would create transitions by challenging or undermining existing symbols or stages of belief, thus creating desired and controllable transitions.

ORGANIZATIONAL RESEARCH

The recognition of this fourth stage is important for research that seeks to develop our understanding of organizational culture. Organizational researchers should be able to develop methods to differentiate employees or managers in stage one or two from those in stage four. With such analytic tools, new ways to track the life cycle of an organization are possible, as is diagnosis of the susceptibility to change. The potential for successful organizational change, described as unfreezing and refreezing, may be enhanced as it is related to change in one's stage of belief. On a more basic level, insight should be available from people in stage four into their conscious creation and use of symbols, and those in stage four should be capable of introspection about their use of symbols. This fourth stage is a reaffirmation of symbols and their importance to the individual, just as the study of organizational symbols is an affirmation of the potency of symbols as a source of influence in organizations.

CONCLUSION

Many miles after I left Tintagel, I came to Glastonbury and the ruins of the great cathedral. The mind's eye fills in the structure of this magnificent building. A thorn tree grows there of a type that is not found in England but is common to the eastern Mediterranean. It reportedly sprang from the staff of Joseph of Arimethea when he landed in England after bringing the Holy Grail. A sprig of the tree is sent to the Queen each Christmas. In the center of the grassy ruins of the cathedral is a grave, marked as the burial place of a king named Arthur and his queen. It shines in a light, not of the sun, but of the aura that believers create when faced with a site they want to treat as a symbol.

It wasn't until I was ready to leave Tintagel, Glastonbury, and the search for Arthur that I realized I had brought the magic with me. I didn't find it there, but I also didn't leave it there, in spite of the visual and written evidence I had accumulated that factually refuted the myths (see, for example, Alcock, 1971; Ashe, 1983; Piggott, 1974). The archaeologists still argue over sites for the ruins of Camelot and even over its existence, just as they continue to look for evidence of the Holy Grail. Meanwhile, people come by the thousands to see the existing symbols. Some look only for supporting evidence and as stage one believers never doubt the veracity of the castle, the thorn tree, or the grave. Many buy the books that disprove their existence and, as stage four believers, act as if they believed. Where symbols work, and in our modern organizations in particular, they are likely to do so on the same basis; people *choose* to believe, and as they allow themselves to be influenced by a symbol, they are not only inspired but also can be managed through it. If King Arthur encouraged his knights to "go forth," is it too much for us now to encourage managers to do the same?

8

UNTANGLING WEBS, SURFING WAVES, AND WILDCATTING

A Multiple-Metaphor Perspective on Managing Organizational Culture

Linda A. Krefting

Texas Tech University

Peter J. Frost

University of British Columbia

Organizational culture is often described in terms of shared meanings—patterns of beliefs, symbols, rituals, and myths that evolve across time and that function as social glue (Smircich, 1983a). While organizations may develop a relatively homogeneous corporate culture (Deal and Kennedy, 1982; Peters and Waterman, 1982), unique and divergent cultures may evolve for separate subgroups within the organization (Lawrence and Lorsch, 1967a; Savage, 1982; Gregory, 1983). Culture emerges at many levels to solve problems posed by life situations (Turner, 1972) and generates "learned ways of coping with experience" (Gregory, 1983). By providing frameworks for solving problems and interpreting events in everyday life, culture reduces the number of variables with which individuals must deal to levels more consistent with human information-processing capabilities.

Although culture is a social construction that both reduces ambiguity and facilitates social interaction (Luhmann, 1979), members of an established culture do not for the most part perceive their culture as a social construction; rather, they see it as an objective reality (Berger and Luckmann, 1966). Culture may thus become a set of blinders limiting

Authors' Note: The authors would like to thank Walter Nord and Joanne Martin for insightful comments on earlier drafts of this chapter.

the alternatives that individuals perceive, as well as the variables with which they must deal.

Individuals are often not consciously aware of their culture because it is familiar, taken for granted, and appears unshakably real. However, it is also possible that culture itself is rooted in the unconscious. The primary source of crucial elements of culture may be the deeply seated unconscious processes of individuals and groups. These are projected out into the external world, reflected in consciously evident frames of reference and shared meanings, and held in place by external symbols (Mitroff, 1983b; White and McSwain, 1983).

Although it is difficult to establish unequivocally that the origins of culture reside in the unconscious, we believe that exploring organizational cultures from the perspective of their unconscious antecedents and conscious manifestations raises intriguing questions and suggests implications for managing culture that ought to be of interest to both researchers and practitioners. In this chapter we examine some of the issues that emerge when this perspective is engaged, in the hope that it will stimulate debate and encourage systematic enquiry on the topic.

MANAGING ORGANIZATIONAL CULTURE

Organization is a metaphor for order and orderliness (Meadows, 1967; Smircich, 1983a). The unconscious is not necessarily orderly (Jung, 1965), and elements of culture originating in the unconscious will not always emerge or unfold in orderly ways. Thus culture interacts with organization in ways that add tension, energy, and liveliness to the orderly characteristics of organizations. If organizational culture is funneled through the unconscious and is therefore not always orderly, then it is unlikely that efforts to manage such a culture can be precisely predicted or tightly controlled. When an organization is stuck in some sense and there is a need to move it out of a rut, it may be possible to work with its culture to tap both cognitive and emotional levels of the organization to unfreeze or unblock the organization. We believe that efforts to change an organization by managing its culture will yield evolving solutions rather than those that are imposed, and that such efforts will produce outcomes that are equifinal. Because some of the consequences of managing culture are often unanticipated, the process of working with organizational culture involves risk. The challenge is magnified by the presence of multiple subcultures in a single organizational setting. Therefore, the management of culture ought to be carefully considered and cautiously undertaken.

The role of manager in this process, regardless of who adopts it, is complex, risky, and difficult. It calls for an unusual blend of skills and attitudes, as well as sensitivity, awareness, and courage. It is the manager's job to deal successfully with the implications of an unconsciously rooted, unpredictably unfolding, equifinal organizational condition. He or she needs to be able to confront or respond to organizational culture much as a therapist would, probing and unraveling the web of cultural experiences, as a wildcatter drilling the cultural terrain, to find and release hidden or blocked human resources.

Each of these approaches requires that the manager work with the capacity of an existing organizational entity to release and develop its full potential. The manager, working at levels beneath the surface of organizational culture, is likely to unleash a tide of energy and a flow of events, the content and outcomes of which he or she may not be able to predict or control. Thus the manager of an organizational culture or cultural change process is rather like a surfer who must ride a wave to its conclusion, always facing the risks of unexpected swirls from the depths beneath the wave as well as the unpredictable air movements on and above the surface. In fact, it is likely that changes of high intensity will require the manager to ride out a succession of waves, falling off some and striving to remain secure on others.

In dealing with organizational culture, a manager needs to be close enough to understand the culture and yet detached enough to see beyond the cultural blinders—that is, to see the existing culture as a social construction that can change and be changed. He or she must react, interact, and act, using symbols and imagery, to release and develop the potential of the organization, and accept the risks involved in doing so.

The difficulties and surprises encountered in attempting to manage organizational culture are likely to depend on the degree of heterogeneity in the organization with regard to the element(s) of culture being managed and their level of consciousness. The more diverse the subcultures in the organization, the wider the range of self-interests on the part of those affected by management efforts. The wider the range of self-interests, the more likely it is that the interests of one or more groups might be adversely affected, and that there might be resistance. In addition, large numbers of heterogeneous subcultures make communication difficult, because communication is based on shared meanings. If the origins of the aspects of culture being dealt with are in the unconscious rather than at or close to the surface, the web of experience will be more difficult to unravel, the wave of energy more volatile, the resources more difficult to locate, and the consequences of intervention more unpredictable.

If an organization is stuck and intervention at the level of culture is perceived as necessary, despite the risks, one approach that warrants serious examination and study is to engage organizational culture metaphorically. As relatively simple statements rich in their implications, metaphors possess great potential for capturing the complexity and occasional contradictions of organizational culture, and for doing so in its members' own terms at both cognitive and emotional levels (Mitroff, 1983b). The most vivid illustrations of strong culture presented by Peters and Waterman (1982) are metaphors used to depict managing organizations: management-by-walking-around at Hewlett-Packard, for example, or production/cast member roles for Disney theme park employees. Such metaphors are used within these organizations to convey the cultures that the organizations have developed and are working to maintain. We argue that metaphors may also serve in grasping an existing culture, framing a new culture, or generating change where current organizational culture is perceived to be less than optimal.

METAPHORS

A metaphor is usually defined as an explanation of one thing, the topic, in terms of another, the vehicle, where the topic and vehicle share some characteristics (the ground) but not others (the tension). Metaphors influence cognitive structures by succinctly "chunking" and transferring shared characteristics from vehicle to topic without enumerating them specifically, thus providing a compact *Gestalt* or coherent whole for the topic (Ortony, 1975; Lakoff and Johnson, 1980). Metaphors tend to be highly memorable because they are succinct. They can be vivid or novel, and they require the investment of thought to separate tension from ground (Ortony, 1975; Petrie, 1979; Pondy, 1984). Metaphors function to structure complex situations by naming key elements and framing relevant issues; in the process they highlight certain elements of the topic (the ground and tension) and mask others (Schon, 1979). By allowing transfer from the familiar to the less familiar, metaphors help articulate subjects for which we do not have specific language; they allow expression of what would otherwise be unexpressible (Ortony, 1975).

Since we lack a well developed language for considering organizational culture, metaphors should prove particularly useful in articulating organizational culture by providing organizational members with a vast array of possible vehicles for accessing meaning. Languages for raising culture to the level of consciousness, articulating the underlying structure, and sharing that understanding can, essentially, be borrowed. The novelty inherent in many metaphors may serve to spark playfulness in considering the aptness and implications of a particular metaphor or some alternatives, thereby facilitating the framing or reframing of an organizational culture. Playing with metaphors may also help to distinguish elements of a culture that need to be changed from those that might better be preserved (Pondy, 1984).

Metaphors have been considered somewhat controversial in the study of organizations (Pinder and Bourgeois, 1982; Morgan, 1983; Smircich, 1983a) and have not been used systematically in managing organizations or organizational culture (cf. Cafferata, 1982; Smith and Simmons, 1983; Pondy, 1984). They have, however, seen substantial use in individual therapy (Grinder and Bandler, 1976; Gordon, 1978), and many of the lessons learned and insights gained from the use of metaphors in therapy may be applicable to organizations.

Applying Metaphors to Problems of Individuals

The use of metaphos in individual therapy is most easily illustrated with an anecdote entitled "A Tale of Two Hiccups" (Gordon, 1978: 187-193):

> Willie Swenson, a therapist trainee working as a restaurant busperson, constructed metaphors to help relieve the hiccups of two of the restaurant patrons. The first instance involved a gentleman who, in a clowning fashion, asked if the restaurant bar could supply something to relieve his hiccups. Willie approached the table and asked if the individual, to rid himself of the hiccups, would listen to a story and during the story make mental images of it. When the patron agreed, Wilie told an elaborate story about a very leaky faucet and a plumber's actions to locate and replace a torn washer, timing nods of his head and drips of the leaky faucet to the man's hiccups to link the story with the problem. Willie then described testing the faucet to see if it had been repaired by turning it on, watching the water rush out, and then turning it off, finding that the leak has stopped completely: there was not a single drop of water. At that point the man's hiccups ceased as well.
>
> In the second instance, a waiter volunteered Willie's storytelling services to a woman who developed hiccups while dining. The woman was dubious and, when Willie had completed his elaborate story of the leaky

faucet, triumphantly announced that her hiccups remained. Since she seemed to need to defeat his efforts, Willie acknowledged they'd both known the story wasn't likely to work. He left the table but returned shortly to ask if her hiccups had a color; she responded that they were purple. He left again but returned shortly again to ask if she'd ever had a purple helium-filled balloon and what happens to helium-filled balloon when you let go of it. He left the table but returned quickly once more to find that her hiccups had ceased.

In telling the stories of the leaky faucet and the purple balloon, Willie Swenson helped invoke change by constructing metaphors to match the structure of the internal experience of the individual wishing to change. When the leaky faucet story failed to bring relief to the dubious woman diner, it seemed necessary for the woman to control construction of the metaphor; the choice of color for the hiccups allowed her to do so. The two metaphors provided the patrons with the opportunity to use their own internal resources, including the unconscious, to make necessary changes.

The problem in the anecdote is obvious, and the desired solution was readily apparent; metaphors that were structurally equivalent to the problem and its solution (a leaky faucet fixed or a ballon released) were relatively simple to construct. Where the problem is more ambiguous and the solution is less apparent, the construction of useful, structurally equivalent metaphors is a more complicated task (Gordon, 1978). It takes more time and skill on the part of the therapist as well as a strong desire on the part of the patient to engage actively in such problem-solving attempts.

MANAGING CULTURE WITH METAPHORS

In attempting to manage organizational culture, more than one individual is involved, problems are rarely obvious, and desired solutions are not readily apparent. Where there is relative homogeneity and the elements of culture are at a relatively conscious level, simple metaphors may be sufficient to help those involved see the existing situation, unfreeze and reframe the issue, and work toward a solution. As we argued previously, the difficulties and surprises encountered in managing culture are likely to be greater where there are heterogeneous subcultures and where the elements of culture being managed have their origins in the unconscious. These factors affect the construction of metaphors that might be useful in framing cultural issues and alternatives: The greater the heterogeneity of subcultures and the deeper the origins in the unconscious, the more complex the metaphor will need to be. For situations in which culture is more heterogeneous, simple metaphors may not adequately capture important aspects of the situation, and appropriate metaphors are likely to be extended ones.

Metaphors that tap the unconscious and illuminate the shadowy and archetypical may be necessary to deal with those aspects of culture that originate in the collective unconscious of an organization and that hold surface manifestations of the culture in place (Conrad, 1983). We now explore this homogeneity-heterogeneity/conscious-unconscious categorization (see Figure 8.1) and illustrate the function of the types of metaphors we have in mind.

To be explicit, we approach the task of managing culture in organizational settings through the therapeutic use of metaphors in terms of two constructs: the degree of heterogeneity (homogeneity) and the location of blockages (conscious-unconscious). In practices, the relative degrees of heterogeneity and the unconsciousness of crucial cultural elements may not be known at the time a blockage is identified. They may become clear only by working through alternative types of metaphors to find the most apt in activating recognition of the existing condition and in mobilizing energies to deal with it. Because the type(s) of metaphors that seem to work in analyzing a blockage may provide basic clues to the underlying dimensions of the problem, these dimensions need not be known in advance.

Conscious Aspects of Culture

We would expect that when the elements of culture affecting a blockage are at the conscious (or relatively conscious) level, the metaphor used can be relatively direct. The degree of heterogeneity of the subcultures involved will determine how extended the metaphor needs to be: The more heterogeneous the subcultures, the more complex the metaphor needs to be to structurally reflect key aspects of the problem.

Schon (1979) provides an example of a simple metaphor useful in generating new ways of coping with experience in a relatively homogeneous organizational unit. An R&D group working to perfect a paintbrush with synthetic bristles had difficulty with the rate of paint application, even after several changes in the bristles. The group's shared beliefs about how to deal with paintbrushes and innovations in brushes blinded them to many alternative formulations of the problem.

		Homogeneous	Heterogeneous
	Conscious	simple metaphors	extended or multiple metaphors
Consciousness			
	Unconscious	shadows, archetypes	shadows, archetypes

Figure 8.1 Metaphors and Situations

The problem was finally resolved when the brush was reconceived as a pump and attention became focused on the spaces between the bristles rather than on the bristles themselves. The reframed depiction of reality dissolved the creative block and mobilized the group's energies to solve the problem.

Quite a different organizational culture issue was addressed at the 1980 White House Conference on Small Business, which brought together representatives of small business and government to handle recognized problems in their relationships and to develop more fruitful ways of coping with mutual experiences. The relationship between the federal government and minority-owned businesses was addressed by a Carter Administration official in a rousing and well-received speech. He argued that the hero of the Supreme Court's landmark decision striking down separate but equal education for minorities (Brown v. Board of Education) was not Brown or her parents for filing suit, nor the courts for having the courage to overturn existing social policy, but rather the school bus, which became the instrument for implementing the changes necessitated by the decision. He went on to laud the qualities of school buses—they have room for many, provide generally safe and comfortable rides, and are efficient means of getting from here to there—and to argue that what was needed was a "school bus" for minority-owned businesses that wished to contract with the federal government. The metaphor guided the ensuing discussion of the nature of the relationship between the two sides; the alternatives considered tended to be limited to vehicles that one only needs to get on and ride (e.g., set-asides and affirmative action plans).

For situations where there is still relative consciousness but where culture is more heterogeneous, appropriate metaphors are likely to be more extended. Many situations may be too complex to be represented simply (Bohr, 1950); extended, multiple, or mixed metaphors may be necessary to capture the important aspects of such situations (Frost and Krefting, 1983). For example, the military metaphor for organization and culture can be extended to include images such as regular army versus special troops, conventional versus guerilla warfare, sabotage, passive resistance, civil defense, boot camp, and so forth. These images speak to important elements of the subcultures involved.

Metaphors may be mixed by depicting organizations as ivory towers, communities, garbage cans, and living systems. Each metaphor evokes different images and thus may access conscious cultures in important ways. Similarly, Schon (1979) contrasts health/disease metaphors for urban renewal with natural community metaphors, arguing that there is a need for a metaphor that captures elements of both to adequately frame the problem of urban renewal. Both extended and mixed metaphors allow elements of heterogeneous situations and their inter-relationships to be examined either in a holistic manner or as separate elements. They also allow consideration of elements that ought to be preserved, as well as those that might require change (Pondy, 1984).

The Game Metaphor: An Extended Metaphor

Differences between the cultures of workers and managers, and explanations of likely conflicts between them, can be examined using an extended game metaphor (Krefting et al., 1983; Krefting and Frost, 1984). Given the lack of control inherent in their positions and the limited possibilities for moving to positions with greater control, workers often develop their own control through games of "making out": They set their own levels of production, develop contests around their work, or attempt to fool management (Burawoy, 1979). Managers, on the other hand, generally have more control and greater opportunities for achieving their ends within the system. Therefore, they are more likely to play "making it" games: They determine and follow the "rules" for advancement (Maccoby, 1976; Schrank, 1978).

These differences in self-interest and local culture condition certain reactions to organizational interventions. Because interventions are at management's discretion, they are more likely to be consistent with managerial culture, more likely to have a negative impact on worker culture, and therefore more likely to meet with resistance within that culture. However, because one's own culture tends to serve as a set of blinders, negative impact and resistance are neither anticipated by management nor well understood when they occur.

Cognizance of cultural differences within an organization through the use of game metaphors can increase the ability to anticipate reactions to interventions and, where necessary, to redirect them. In this context, successful managers of culture are those who can recognize and harness the extended game metaphor. They are aware of and able to articulate the images inherent in the game metaphor that are important in each culture, and they can move between and among these images and bring them to bear, as therapists, on organizational change problems. Although worker and manager games are common, they may not be universal; the nature of the games can vary substantially from one organization to the next. Therefore, the exact cultural implications of the game metaphor will depend on the situation.

Unconscious Aspects of Culture

If culture is in fact projected from the unconscious to the external world, dealing with conscious structures may not unfreeze or unblock the organization sufficiently to generate change when it is perceived to be necessary; thus, the unconscious origins of culture may need to be explored. The two metaphorical vehicles that tap the unconscious most explicitly are shadows (nondominant aspects of personality) and archetypes (universal psychological images of idealized character types). These two types of metaphors were originally used by Jung (1959) to explain individual growth and change but have since been extended to organizations (Denhardt, 1981; Mitroff, 1983a, 1983b, 1984; Obert, 1984). According to Jung, individuals in early stages of development must work to become balanced by incorporating shadows or unconscious aspects into the overall personality. While shadows are often described in dark terms, these aspects of personality are not necessarily negative; they are simply hidden "in the shadows."

To continue to grow, the individual must in later life come to grips with archetypes in a process Jung (1959) calls "individuation." Archetypes are universal, idealized, larger-than-life symbols that contain the essence of human experience and that help individuals develop an emotionally satisfying picture of the world. Fairy tales often involve representations of archetypes; for example, the wicked witch as the "bad mother" archetype and the fairy godmother as the "good mother" archetype. In the process of individuation, individuals learn to act and deal with the world realistically, in terms of composites, rather than in idealized, archetypal terms (good guys versus bad guys).

Shadows and archetypes, we believe, can be generalized to organizations and organizational cultures. Effective cultures need a balance, which requires the incorporation of shadows or other less dominant elements. Such cultures must also deal with "problems posed by life-situations" (Turner, 1972) in complex and realistic terms rather than at the idealized, archetypal level. When organizational culture goes awry, blockage may well result from unincorporated shadows or unresolved archetypal conflicts; hence, exploring the problem in terms of shadows or archetypes may well be the way to approach it.

We expect shadows and archetypes to be useful in both homogeneous and heterogeneous cultures because they tap the unconscious origins of culture, which may be at the root of the problem, and because they provide a level of abstraction at which commonalities can be found. The greater the heterogeneity of the culture, the more extended or mixed the metaphorical exploration of the unconscious needs to be in order to fully examine the issue.

Incorporating Shadows: An Illustration

A recent organizational culture issue of *Administrative Science Quarterly* contains a description of a naturally occurring fairy tale metaphor in a reasonably homogeneous work group. Smith and Simmons (1983) relate the difficulties encountered in opening a new psychoeducational facility for emotionally disturbed children. The director of the facility had a specific dream for the high quality of care the facility should provide and the cooperative relationships that should exist among the staff, but he was unable to develop a plan to realize his dream or to accept plans proposed by others. As the opening date for the facility neared, the lack of a plan for operations, combined with pressure from conflicting constituencies, created a great deal of tension within the facility, and the ineffectual director was removed.

At one point prior to the director's removal, a staff member had a dream about the fairy tale "Rumpelstiltskin," which the staff decided captured metaphorically much of what was going on (and going wrong) in the process of opening the new facility. The director had the charisma to "turn straw into gold," but his efforts were solely individual. He was unable to delegate work, incorporate others, or develop the cooperation that the facility needed. The director's unincorporated shadow (cooperative team effort) was reflected in his organizational functioning and the developing culture. Like Rumpelstiltskin, once he was found out, the director vanished (was removed).

The conflict in the psychoeducational facility, as described by Smith and Simmons (1983), was intense and unruly. The authors write of staff members deciding to revolt, and of "council-of-war" meetings. The Rumpelstiltskin dream seemed to provide a vehicle through which the shadow side of the organization could be accessed. The actual dynamics of the conflict then moved turbulently toward resolution. As Smith and Simmons (1983: 391) observed:

> Much of the power of the Rumpelstiltskin tale . . . was that it provided sign posts to the relationship between the manifest and the unconscious. As observers, we could sense that the clinical group was dealing with primitive levels of fear and fantasy. But what were these fears? What were these fantasies?

The dream provided "a way to interpret the manifest . . . a totally different logic" within which to think about a situation that was stuck (Smith and Simmons, 1983: 391). Similarly, the metaphorical fairy tale was a naturally occurring event that appeared to serve an important therapeutic purpose.

As wildcatters, managers of organizational culture may hit upon evidence of images that allows them to confront the unconscious aspects of the culture to or for which they are responsible. Attention to such evidence of "underground activity" is very important for successful managerial action. Nevertheless, as stated earlier, we do not think that awareness of, sensitivity to, or working through such images provides control over the culture or the situation. These elements may, however, allow managers to traverse more intelligently and successfully the waves set in motion by the fear, fantasy, energy, and emotion that emerge as members of a culture struggle to incorporate its shadow elements.

As a therapist, a manager attempts to mobilize an organizational culture through the incorporation of shadow elements. This entails searching for images within the culture that will allow the process of incorporation to take place; organizational stories (e.g., Martin, Feldman, et al., 1983) and rituals and myths (e.g., Conrad, 1983; Dandridge et al., 1980) may serve as the base from which such therapeutic actions may begin. We do not underestimate the difficulty of this task, but we note the current absence of research work to guide these actions.

Confronting Archetypes

While we do not have available examples of managing organizational cultures through the confrontation of archetypes, it is our belief that profound changes in organizational culture can be accomplished only if those who wish to manage or facilitate the change process are able to tap a culture's unconscious origins. This is done by confronting, understanding, and mobilizing the archetypes that activate the minds, emotions, and energies of the members of the culture.

Some of the archetypes that may have relevance to organizations, and hence that bear investigation, are described by Mitroff (1983b). For example archetypes for homogeneous cultures may come from the Oedipus complex, since they involve images of the organizational unit as a nuclear family or maternal entity. By contrast, the archetypes that often emerge across heterogeneous cultures are suggested in the imagery of mergers and takeovers described by Hirsch and Andrews (1984). Takeovers and mergers, which pose important issues in managing heterogeneous cultures, are frequently described in language resplendent with images that hint of possible organizational archetypes. These images include the following:

> [S]uch well known popular genres as the western (ambush and shootout replace offer and actions taken), the love affair and/or marriage, warfare (replete with sieges, barricades, flak, and soldierly honor), mystery, and piracy on the high seas (with raiders and safe harbors), . . . merceneries or hired guns, . . . black and white knights. . . . In virtually all formulations the acquiring executive is macho and the target company is accorded the female gender ("sleeping beauty" or a bride brought to the altar; reference to rape is also not uncommon) [Hirsch and Andrews, 1984: 148].

Mitroff (1983b) adapts a typology of difficult people put forward by Bramson (cited in Mitroff, 1983b) as the basis for individual archetypes. Such archetypes include Sherman tanks, snipers, "clams," and the "compleat complainer." Mitroff (1983b: 132) also interprets Chrysler's financial crisis as "a modern example dressed up in the metal of the archetypal American story, Moby Dick," with Lee Iacocca playing the central role as Captain Ahab.

To dismiss these images of mergers, difficult people, and companies in distress as journalistic concoctions to catch the attention of readers or add spice to descriptions of events that in fact deserve more "serious and sober language," as some have done, is to miss the point. The evocative imagery and rich metaphors are only surface manifestations of the unconscious—keys to unlocking the deep structure of the cultures they describe. Thus it is no accident that they tend to emerge most vigorously when organizations are facing significant crises.

The astute manager, in our view, is one who pays attention to metaphors as devices for understanding and dealing with the management of unconscious elements in diverse organizational cultures, although the task is arduous and the course uncharted. The level of expertise demanded of a manager as therapist, wildcatter, or surfer is indeed high. There are, no doubt, practitioners who can fulfill these roles, who are able to recognize and confront organizational archetypes in order to cope effectively with organizational cultures. We doubt they would use the terminology we have, but they might recognize the process we've described. Certainly they operate from intuition and experience, for there is nothing definite that students of organizational culture can tell them.

CONCLUDING COMMENTS

The complexity of organizational culture, including its origins in the unconscious and the existence of multiple subcultures within organizations, makes the outcome of efforts to manage culture difficult to predict or control. Attention to metaphorical language and images may provide a way of understanding and managing organizational culture that recognizes this complexity and addresses it at the level of equivocality necessary for coming to grips with it. Metaphors may serve as models or paradigms that can help focus attention on what currently exists, frame other possibilities where change is perceived as desirable, and initiate action toward such change. They can also help distinguish aspects of culture that might be changed from those that might better be preserved, as well as pinpointing likely conflicts and communications problems in heterogeneous situations.

While the skillful use of metaphors can assist in analyzing, reframing and unfreezing, metaphors are unlikely to be sufficient to allow complete control of the change process. Metaphors help in efficiently "chunking" key aspects of organizational cultures so they can be dealt with as coherent wholes, but it is quite impossible that any metaphor or set of metaphors could capture all aspects of a given culture; the unexpected is thus always likely. Using metaphors to explore and release the potential of an organization is to use them to explore the unknown.

We think the study of organization culture from the perspective we have taken in this chapter is challenging, perhaps even daunting, given the ground that must be covered. Nevertheless, there is rich promise for developing new knowledge that will be of great benefit in theoretical and practical terms. It is our hope that this subject will become a topic of intense interest and attention in the years ahead.

9

ON THE FEASIBILITY
OF CULTURAL INTERVENTION
IN ORGANIZATIONS

Craig C. Lundberg

University of Southern California

In recent years, managers and scholars alike have given increasing attention to organizational culture. The popularity of organizational culture reflects several quite different concerns or purposes, three of which are relevant to this essay. First, it introduces a major new metaphor for thinking about organizations (Jelinek et al., 1983), adding to the prior ones of an organization as a machine or an organism. The cultural metaphor promotes attention to the generation, function, and consequences of meaning. A second use of the idea is to provide an umbrella term, some would even say a paradigm (Smircich, this volume; Brown, 1973), under which many other ideas for organizational understanding can be gathered and related. Third, organizational culture is seen by some as either the means or the target for changes that have major commitment, control, productivity, or even bottom-line consequences (Wilkins, 1983b; Sproull, 1979; Peters and Waterman, 1982; Martin, 1982b).[1]

The question of whether organizational culture can be managed has been both debated (Martin, 1982a) as well as assumed. Managers and consultants have tended to assume that it can be managed and changed. Many definitions of organization development, for example, speak of it as "a planned, managed, systematic process to change the culture, systems, and behavior of an organization" (Conference Board, 1978: 2), or as "a planned process of change in an organization's culture through the utilization of behavioral science technology, research and theory" (Burke, 1982; 10). Today, many managers blithely assume the "use of corporate culture to increase productivity and cultivate excellence" (Salmans, 1983). For all of its contemporary popularity, however, organizational culture remains a phenomenon that is as yet neither fully understood nor agreed upon. In addition, relatively little thought has been given to the feasibility of intentionally intervening to alter organizational culture.

This chapter focuses explicitly on the processes of cultural intervention and their feasibility. In the pages that follow, a framework is sketched which may enable us to consider more systematically the accumulating experience of organizational culture change. The chapter also offers some preliminary speculation on the feasibility of intervening so as to manage such change.[2]

The careful and systematic examination of conscious intervention for the purpose of changing organizational culture appears to be an important task for several reasons. In part, it is important because the popular business literature has simply assumed that feasibility is ensured; however, before costly errors and investments are made further, we ought to be better informed. In part, our focus is important because the acacemic literature has mostly ignored or only tangentially considered the change of organizational culture. By bringing attention to the systematic study of the feasibility and probable dynamics of organizational culture change, perhaps organizational scientists can enhance their work, which may in turn improve both managerial practice and consultancy. Our focus is also important because inquiry into the dynamics of organizational culture change may have a fruitful impact on the way static and cross-sectional organizational culture is investigated.

The remainder of this chapter is organized in four parts: Initially, we clarify the terms of the title and briefly note what others have stated about the feasibility of cultural intervention. Next, organizational culture change is reframed as organizational learning. A framework is then offered which outlines the conditional contingencies and cyclic change processes for cultural intervention—showing when, where, and how intervention strategy and tactics are possible. Finally, we revisit feasibility and indicate both its likelihood and its practicality.

COMING TO TERMS

General semanticists remind us that the symbol is not the thing and further caution that the same symbol is sometimes used to refer to quite different things. Such appears to be the case with the term "organizational culture." Any sampling of the literature produces a wide variety of definitions, varying in specificity and scope. Corporate culture popularizers Deal and Kennedy (1982) define organizational culture as "the way we do things around here." Turnstall (1983: 1), a practicing manager with AT&T, states that organizational culture is "a general constellation of beliefs, mores, value systems, behavioral norms and ways of doing business that are unique to each corporation." Louis (1980b: 227), a scholar of organizational culture, defines it as "a set of common understandings for organizing actions and language and other symbolic vehicles for expressing common understandings." Beres and Porterwood (1979: 141) take a somewhat different tack, defining organizational culture as "a cognitive frame of reference and a pattern of behavior transmitted to members of a group from the previous generations of the group."

Many of these definitions reflect earlier, more general anthropological ones.[3] Herskovitz (1948: 625), for example, defines culture as "essentially a construct that describes the total body of belief, behavior, knowledge, sanctions, values and goals that make the way of life of a people." Kroeber and Parsons's (1958: 86-87) definition seems to be a major progenitor of many pertaining to organizational culture: "the transmitted and created content and patterns of values, ideas, and other symbolic-meaningful systems as factors in shaping human behavior."

Obviously there are many meanings of organizational culture to draw from. In this essay, we shall follow the definitional theme indicated in the array presented above, specifying, after Schein (1981) and especially Dyer (1982), four levels of organizational culture which together form a beginning toward operationalizing the idea.[4] The four levels are:

- *Artifacts:* The tangible aspects of culture shared by members of an organization. These verbal, behavioral, and physical artifacts are the surface manifestations of organizational culture. Language, stories, and myths are examples of verbal artifacts, while behavioral artifacts are represented in rituals and ceremonies. The technology and art exhibited by members are where physical artifacts are found.
- *Perspectives:* The socially shared rules and norms applicable to a given context. Perspectives may be viewed as the solutions to common problems encountered by organizational members; they involve how members define and interpret situations of organizational life and prescribe the bounds of acceptable behavior. Perspectives are relatively concrete, and members are usually aware of them.
- *Values:* The evaluational basis that organizational members utilize for judging situations, acts, objects, and people. Values reflect the real goals, ideals, standards, as well as the sins of an organization and represent members' preferred means of resolving life's problems. Values are more abstract than perspectives, although experienced members sometimes articulate them more or less in statements of organizational "philosophy" and "mission."

- *Assumptions*: The tacit beliefs that members hold about themselves and others, their relationships to other persons, and the nature of the organization in which they live. Assumptions are the nonconscious underpinnings of the first three levels—that is, the implicit, abstract axioms that determine the more explicit system of meanings.

Turning to a second key term of this chapter's title, we choose to understand intervention, following Argyris (1970), as intentionally doing something for a particular effect. To intervene is to enter into an ongoing system of relationships, to come between or among persons, groups, or objects for the purpose of altering prior or present patterns of behavior.

Feasibility, another key term, is defined here as the ability to be accomplished. It has two meanings: Something is either *probable* or *possible*. Thus the feasibility of intervention in organizational culture change refers to the likelihood of intervention, on the one hand, and its practicality on the other.

Organizational culture change should also be explicated. Essentially, it is a form of transitional change (Lundberg, 1984b). When an organization moves from one quasi-stable equilibrium to another, such as between major stages in the organization's life cycle, a transitional change occurs since it involves a noticeably different organization character or culture. Interventions designed to alter organizational culture are therefore devices for aiding major transitions.

What guidance may we glean from the literature? The available opinions about the feasibility of intervening to change organizational culture vary considerably, whether offered by practitioners or academics. "The fashionable view holds that the biggest stumbling block on the path to adaptation is often an inappropriate corporate culture" (Fortune, 1983: 66). "Corporate culture is the magic phrase that management consultants are breathing into the ears of American executives" (Salmans, 1983). Here the clear implication is that culture is changeable by managers.

Some academics would agree that it is feasible to interfere. For example, Kilmann (1982: 12) advises that "culture is touchable and changeable through the assessment of norms." Tichy (1982a: 3) goes even further, arguing that corporate culture is a strategic variable and that managers can use "role modeling, jargon, myths, rituals as well as the use of the human resource systems of selection, development, assessment, and rewards to shape and mold corporate culture." Turnstall (1983), writing about cultural transitions at AT&T, straightforwardly lists six necessary actions.

Others take a more moderate position. While organizational culture change does occur, they say, it is usually or often the result of non-managerial forces—managers, however, can and often do guide the changes. Turnstall (1983: 2) notes that "divestiture is one of the causal factors underlying change in culture." Louis (1983) adds that changes in settings and new technologies can also lead to cultural changes. Siehl (this volume) reports on the cultural changes unleashed when a firm's CEO steps aside, while Dyer (1984: 12) states that "culture change is precipitated by unanticipated crises that stimulate leadership transitions and major shifts within firms." He goes on to state that "many of the factors involved in culture change appear to be largely beyond managements' control, thus culture change appears to be not as 'programmable' as some writers have recently suggested."

Finally, we should note that changing corporate and organizational culture is viewed by some as both feasible in general, as well as easily under management's influence, and we already know how to do it.

So what is the guidance in the literature? That culture change in organizations does happen is agreed. That it can be stimulated by exogenous factors is also strongly suggested. However, whether or not managers can initiate and fully control such change is disputed. Of interest is what the literature does not as yet provide commentary on—a systematic discussion of the external and internal conditions under which organizational culture change does occur and the probable dynamics of how such change unfolds. Intervention feasibility will no doubt be a function of these situational factors, as well as the precipitating events and the roles, influence, and practices of managerial change agents.

ORGANIZATIONAL LEARNING

Organizations change all of the time, continuously; sometimes planned, sometimes not. As Bateson (1979) observes, the constancy of any living system depends on continual change—on the continuous detection and correction of errors in the mutual adjustment of an individual's task performance. Achieving a better fit among organization parts and between the organization and its domains and environment is in fact what managers and change agents mostly try to do (Lundberg, 1980). This ongoing, negative-feedback-dominated change is familiar, expected, and common. Schon (1983) characterizes this as "zero order" organizational learning, meaning that there is not significant change in the underlying values and knowledge structure of the organization. To be sure, this order of changes is seldom perfect, and organizations do "drift" (Lodahl and Mitchell, 1980) and evolve (Weick, 1979), as evidenced by their artifacts being altered over time.

Organizational culture change is clearly more than the accumulation of imperfect homeostatic processes, more than "zero order" organizational learning. Rather, the transition involved in a managed change of culture requires real organizational learning buttressed by some degree of positive feedback so that the requisite variety appears. Most organizational members are relatively immune to attending to their present perspectives, values, and assumptions because their cognitive structures, norms, and games expressly prohibit it (Nystrom and Starbuck, 1984). Organizational learning, however, appears necessary for culture change (Argyris and Schon, 1978).

How does organizational learning occur? Given that an organization's culture provides its members with a way of viewing and understanding their experience but prohibits attention to the basis on which such meaning is generated, a predicament must be faced in order to launch real organizational learning that results in culture change. In other words, the organization experiences a surprise, "an error or phenomenon, pleasing or unpleasing, which escapes the organizational model of the world" (Schon, 1983: 11). It is this perception of surprise— an unexpected outcome of an action or a major shift in circumstances— that allows some members to discover that their unquestioned values and assumptions have been violated. The members just referred to may then function as intelligence agents for the organization, bringing attention to the fact that the existent basis of understanding is being exceeded by current circumstances. If they are influential enough and concerned enough, then organizational learning becomes possible.

Organizational learning underlies the transitional changes that are captured in the phrase, "organizational culture change." Learning, of course, is the product of inquiry. To recapitulate, organizational learning is a cycle that begins with a set of existing cultural values and assumptions which channel the attention of members to some things and not to others. Attended to phenomena (e.g., predicaments) are experienced, and the experience prompts surprise, which, if coupled with sufficient concern, prompts inquiry. Inquiry involves the discovery of previously unattended to phenomena at all levels (i.e., artifacts to assumptions) and, under the right circumstances, results in the reformulation of the cultural values and assumptions with which the cycle began. Figure 9.1 diagrammatically presents this cyclical process.

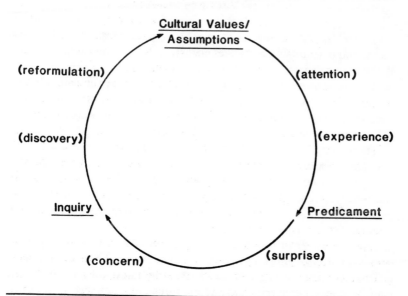

Figure 9.1 Organizational Learning Cycle

Understanding culture change as organizational learning provides guides for developing a more elaborate framework for comprehending the feasibility of organizational culture change. One, it will be cyclical. Two, it will indicate conditions at points of the cycle that enable, permit, trigger, and guide culture change. We now turn to the elaboration of such a framework.

A FRAMEWORK FOR COMPREHENDING ORGANIZATIONAL CULTURE CHANGE

Once in existence, organizations are posited as embracing a culture. Large, complex, or differentiated organizations often contain multiple cultures (Louis, 1983). Our framework begins, therefore, with the culture of an organization or subunit. For cultural change to be possible, an organization or subunit must exist under propitious external and internal circumstances.

External Enabling Conditions

External enabling conditions, of which two are posited, increase the likelihood of transitional changes occurring. Such conditions are external in that they are in the environmental domain of the organization or subunit. They are enabling in that if they exist, they indicate that the environment will be supportive of culture change. Essentially, these conditions speak to the degree of difficulty an organization or subunit will experience if it attempts a transitional change.

The first external enabling condition is *domain forgiveness*. In the relevant immediate environment there are conditions of scarcity or abundance, stability or instability, and resource concentration or dispersion, which in combination determine the degree of threat to an organization posed by its competition, input sources, and the economic cycling of its industry.

The second external enabling condition is termed the *degree of organization-domain congruence*. Too great or too little cultural congruence between an organization and its domains will make cultural transitioning seem overly risky, overly threatening, or totally unnecessary. When the congruence is viewed as modest, the challenge of the difference is more likely to be perceived as advantageous.

Internal Permitting Conditions

Other propitious circumstances must exist within the organization or subunit. Four such internal conditions that permit transitioning are hypothesized.

The first internal permitting condition is the existence of a surplus of change resources. These are managerial time and energy, financial resources, and the like which are available to the system beyond those needed for normal operating. This internal condition merely acknowledges that cultural change will require resouces, or "slack," above and beyond those necessary for accomplishing the everyday tasks of the organization.

A second permitting condition is system readiness. This ill-defined construct refers to a collective sense on the part of the organizations' members that they or some influential coalitions can (and perhaps will) endure change of the magnitude that transitioning requires. In a sense, system readiness is willingness of most members to live with the anxiety that comes with anticipated uncertainty.

Culture change requires the existence of some minimal informational linkages, of a minimal level of intraorganizational dependency. Minimal coupling is therefore the third internal permitting condition. Without such coupling of system components, transitional change would be exceedingly difficult because of the additional coordinative and integrative work necessary.

The fourth internal permitting condition has to do with agent power and leadership. Culture change puts heavy demands on the management, formal and informal, of an organization. Some reasonable stability in managerial membership is therefore needed. Likewise, some unspecified level of strategic awareness is also needed within the dominant power condition. To be sure, while the agents of cultural transitioning may include consultants and/or staff personnel, many are eventually and inevitably managers. They must hold sufficient power and possess the ability to envision alternative organization futures. Perhaps, too, some considerable skill in communicating experienced predicaments and possible futures is a part of this permitting condition.

Precipitating Pressures

As described earlier, internal and external conditions, if they exist in some as yet unspecifiable configuration, increase the likelihood of transitional change. From time to time, organizations also face factors that precipitate major change—that is, that bring pressure to bear on an organization for change. It is these precipitating pressures that set the stage for organizational members to be attentive to predicaments and to be surprised by them.

Four types of pressures seems to occur. One is "atypical performance demands" on the organization. Any unexpected greater or lesser level of organizational performance tends to be pressureful. These demands from the marketplace and the public, interpreted by the organization's intelligence systems, are perceived as pressure if the organization is unprepared for them. Stakeholder pressures are a second precipitating circumstance. Stakeholders, those claimants inside and outside the system with a vested interest in it (Mason and Mitroff, 1981), provide the main sources of organization purpose and stragegy. One or more stakeholders can exert pressure on an organization to be different in character from what it presently is.

Another kind of pressure has to do with organizational growth or decrement. An organization can be either downsizing or growing in size, membership heterogeneity, or structural complexity. Each process creates pressures in that dysfunctions and dissatisfactions build up. A fourth precipating source of pressure is in the real or perceived crises associated with environmental uncertainty, such as the unpredicability of competitor or consumer options, as well as resource deprivations or excesses (e.g., skills, materials, ideas, and so forth). Pressure is felt by key members when they notice the accretion of preferred indicators of these real or perceived crises.

In our framework thus far, we have outlined external and internal conditions, enabling and permitting respectively, and certain precipitating pressures. While such contingencies prepare the way for the initiation of transitional culture change, it should be stressed that they only describe the circumstances under which organizational learning is possible.

Triggering Events

The transition that may produce cultural change usually begins in response to one or more triggering events. The image promoted here is of tensions built up from pressures that can no longer be easily ignored. These tensions are released through the stimulus of one or more particular events. Essentially, a trigger event contains a predicament predicated by the organization learning cycle. When experienced, the predicament leads to surprise. Five classes of trigger events can be distinguished: environmental calamities and opportunities, internal and external revolutions, and managerial crises.

An environmental calamity is something severe that occurs in the organizational environment and that cannot be ignored. Examples include all types of natural disasters, a sharp recession, or an innovation that jeopardizes the organization's products or services. Environmental opportunities are like calamities in that they appear suddenly and possess much potential. Technological breakthroughs, the discovery of a previously unknown or untouchable market niche, and newly available venture capital are all examples of environmental opportunities. A third class of trigger events comprises managerial crises. Here we have in mind a major shakeup of top management, the occurrence of a substantial blunder, an inappropriate strategic decision, a foolish expenditure that loses reserve funds, and so on.

Two classes of revolution possess the potential to become triggering events. One is an external revolution. In the first case, something happens external to the organization that has major consequences, such as being taken over by another corporation or being subjected to political interference (e.g., nationalization of a foreign subsidiary, or perhaps legislation of new and more stringent governmental regulations). Internal revolutions can also be triggers. The installation of a new management team and a coup by the "young turks" are examples.

Cultural Visioning

If trigger events are perceived as surprises (i.e., hold a quality of being a predicament), the leadership of an organization or subunit will often respond by engaging in an inquiry process of visioning.[5] Leaders survey the perspectives, values, and, if possible, the assumptions of the organization's culture. In addition, they seek to anticipate future conditions and create an image of the organization within that future. This new image is in essence a more appropriate, socially constructed system of shared meanings. Leaders descriptively shape an image of a new organization culture (Pettigrew, 1979) or paradigm (Pfeffer, 1981b; Mohrman and Lawler, 1983). In still other words, key organizational members with a raised consciousness of the need to redesign their culture enter into the non-ordinary task of making their present organizational culture explicit and sketching out a more preferred one.[6] It should be emphasized that a new conception that does not reach the value and assumption levels of cultural meaning is really not true culture change.[7]

Culture Change Strategy

Creating a vision of a new, more preferred organizational culture is a necessary but not sufficient step toward that culture's establishment. The vision serves as a guide for development,[8] but once a new cultural vision exists, a strategy is still needed for its achievement; that is, a plan for transitioning. Such a strategy outlines the general, intentional process of transforming the present culture into the new one. Cultural change strategies require the agents of change to define their plans in response to three questions:[9] Will the change be swift or slow? (This concerns the *pace of change*.) How much of the organization will be affected? (This concerns the *scope of change*.) Will the change take a short time or a longer time? (Here the *time span of change* is at issue.) These questions define a more and less explicit "process plan" (Beckhard and Harris, 1977); that is, a sequencing of intentional activities. Most typically, a change strategy is made known through a series of explicit action plans.

Cultural Change Action Plans

As previously noted, cultural change results from interventions organized into a sequence of action plans for the inducement, management, and stabilization of change.[10] *Inducement action planning* involves the stimulation of organizational members and the countering or weakening of natural resistance forces. The purpose of planning inducement is to heighten system readiness for change and to prepare the organization for withdrawal from its former equilibrium conditions. *Management action planning* outlines interventions in which, for example, meaning-laden information is manipulated and additional powerful agents mobilized.

The purpose of planning managing is to intervene so that the situation of organizational members is redefined by them. *Stabilization action planning* focuses on the institutionalization of culture change. Here the interventions are designed to obtain persistence of performance to establish existence of the new culture as an accepted social fact (Goodman et al., 1980; Meyer and Rowan, 1977).

The three phases of action planning can be mapped against the four levels of cultural meaning to provide a matrix of culture change interventions as shown in Figure 9.2. While no exhaustive listing of interventions is possible, in part because the study of the cultural change of organizations is still in its infancy, we can provide examples of many of the cells of our matrix.

Assumption inducement is exemplified by the assumption-surfacing technique of Mason and Mitroff (1981). Value-level inducement can occur negatively, by discrediting existing myths and stories, as well as positively through the reconstruction of history and the creation of desirable metaphors for the organization (Lundberg, 1981), and through stakeholder analysis (Mason and Mitroff, 1981). Inducement at the perspective level often seems to happen as a result of management consulting, of long-range planning and the reformulation of an organization's strategic mission. A more pointed device is the Kilmann-Saxton culture-gap survey, which identifies both current and desired operating norms (Kilmann and Saxton, 1982). At the artifact level, inducement takes many forms, from top management exhortations to scare stories. It should be noted that when inducement artifacts are not simultaneously paired with or soon followed by inducement interventions at all degree levels of meaning, they seldom have any effect—an experience all too common in organizations. Hence, cosmetic and surface efforts remain just that.

No assumption-level interventions for managing culture change are known at this time. The value level, however, is represented by symbols of all kinds—slogans and logos, new leaders, and statements of corporate philosophy—and by the establishment of new short-term objectives. Role modeling, signs of all kinds, agendas, training program content, changes in work design, and specific criteria for personnel recruitment

LEVELS OF ORGANIZATIONAL CULTURE

ACTION PLANS	ARTIFACTS	PERSPECTIVES	VALUES	ASSUMPTIONS
INDUCEMENT				
MANAGEMENT				
STABILIZATION				

Figure 9.2   A Matrix of Interventions for Organizational Culture Change

and selection are all examples of management intervention at the perspective level. Finally, new goals and altered settings, decor changes, and the use of new jargon are typical artifact-level interventions for managing change.

Artifact interventions that persist or get reified can aid in culture change stabilization. Reward systems, policies and regulations, and other managerially designed control systems are actually interventions that stabilize at the level of perspectives. Similarly, rituals and ceremonies, as well as leader exemplification, stabilize at the values level. (Examples of assumption-level stabilization intervention are not known to exist.)

While the selection of culture change interventions will reflect the ecology and agent competencies of a particular organization for each action plan phase, two caveats should be followed. One is to intervene across all of the levels of cultural meaning, especially for the induction and management of the change effort. Intervening across these levels will most probably achieve maximum impact. The second caveat is that interventions should be both consistent and redundant (Siehl and Martin, 1982). Continuous, repeated, multiple activities are purported to be critical in the successful change of organizational cultures as well as in everyday management.

Let us recapitulate the framework presented here. It begins with the culture of an organization or subunit and requires a configuration of external enabling and internal permitting conditions. Then, if at least one precipitating pressure exists, triggering events may lead to agents engaging in cultural revisioning. A vision or image of a new, preferred culture guides the development of a culture change strategy, which in turn is translated into sequences of inducement, managing, and stabili-

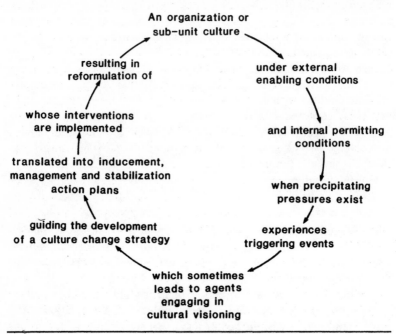

Figure 9.3 The Organizational Learning Cycle of Culture Change

zation action plans. These plans are combinations of interventions across the four levels of cultural meaning. When implemented, they result in the reformulation of the culture. Figure 9.3 summarizes this cyclic, organizational learning process.

ON FEASIBILITY

Can organizational culture change be accomplished? Clearly, this is not a simple question. While the possibility of culture change certainly exists, the probability of it happening is now seen to depend on several factors, not all of which are fully under the control of an organization's leadership. The framework presented in the last part of this essay provides a way of commenting more fully.

The feasibility of organizational culture change depends in part on three sets of contextual conditions. Unless the environmental circumstances of a forgiving domain and a modest organization-environment congruence exist, we predict that change efforts enabling transitions may flounder. Similarly, without one or more precipitating pressures in an organization's context, little energy or concern will exist. The third sort of contextual conditions are internal to the organization—the so-called permitting conditions that we posited as necessary for cultural change to be initiated. Even at the outset, feasibility is therefore a function of a benign general environment and "experienced" unfocused pressure coupled with particular internal circumstances. We conclude that these contextual factors substantially reduce the probability of culture change for many organizations. Further, if organizational culture change is initiated without them, the possibility of transitional change is severely diminished.

Given favorable contextual circumstances, our framework then specifies that culture change requires a trigger event that creates surprise because it is experienced as a predicament. The perceptual threshold of influential leaders, which acknowledges the need for revision, is likely the product of some experience factor, such as succeeding with an earlier major change or assessing the severity and timing of needed change. Feasibility turns on the impetus for and the actuality of revisioning—and what predicts the levels of concern that prompt it?

With a new cultural vision, the feasibility of culture change will depend on both an appropriate strategy and action plans; or in other words, on the selection and implementation of a sequence of sets of interventions that induce, manage, and then stabilize the new vision. Interventions that have an impact on all levels of cultural meaning will embrace feasibility as well if they are consistently and redundantly applied.

The complexity of the phenomena of organizational culture, the inherent difficulty of impacting deep levels of cultural meaning, the vision required for designing a new, more relevant culture, and the complexity of designing and sequencing the multiple interventions needed suggests that managing culture change is not often likely, even if it is possible. So much seems to be requisite, even to begin. There are so many places where the process can go awry. The demands on managers, both conceptually and experientially, are great. Yet organizational culture change does happen.

CONCLUDING COMMENT

This chapter has examined the feasibility of intervening in organizations to effect culture change. We have argued for understanding organizational culture at several levels. Culture change was conceived of not only as change across all levels of meaning but also as transitional change—real organizational learning. Given certain hypothesized contextual preconditions, a complex, cyclic process of change was presented that is initiated by a predicament, fostered by a new vision, guided by a strategy, and implemented through interventions organized in a sequence of action plans. This framework was sketched not only to aid the study and practice of changing organizational cultures, but also so that some insight into the feasibility of such change might be addressed.[11]

As noted earlier, the framework presented in this way, while informed at many points, is essentially speculative. With the popularity of organizational culture and the increasing turbulence of contemporary society, efforts at conceptualizing the contingencies and dynamics of culture change are sorely needed. Managers and scholars alike need to understand such major transitions and their feasibility as never before. No doubt the framework presented here will soon give way to more refined and validated ones as holistic and emic inquiry proceeds.

NOTES

1. There appear to be three broad models of managerial control. The earliest was the bureaucratic, wherein reward manipulation works to increase subordinate loyalty, which in turn leads to increased productivity (this model assumes that people are largely rational, economically motivated, and competitive). The second model was the human relations one. Here a satisfying work life ostensibly leads to loyalty and then to increased productivity (people are thus assumed to be primarily sociable and cooperative in nature). The third model is the corporate culture one. A "strong" culture supposedly leads to a love of the firm and its goals by members, which in turn provides increased productivity (members are assumed to be emotional, responsive to symbols, and desirous of belonging to a superior entity).

2. Let me emphasize my focus in this chapter. While organization culture change which is the outcome of exogenous factors is acknowledged as possible, and organizational members can and do intervene in ways that present or impede culture change, in these limited pages I have elected to focus on the human interventions that may proactively guide such changes.

3. Kroeber and Kluckhohn (1963) devote a rather large book to a review of the concepts and definitions of culture.

4. Martin and Siehl (1983) also specify four levels that are close, but not identical, to those presented here. Instead of what are here termed perspectives, they use management practices, which "may or may not include artifacts" (p. 2).

5. The term "visioning" is borrowed from Ackoff (1979) but here includes elements of what Watzlawick et al. (1974) call "reframing." For a further explication, see Lundberg and Finney (1984).

6. No particularistic classification of organizational cultures presently exists. However, we can map out the variety of alternatives by indicating some general choices among the epistemological structures in which culture is anchored. Two dimensions of our constructs of reality seem useful. One dimension concerns the way in which reality is conceived—as either fragmented or whole. Organizations are either conceived of as single entities (i.e., homogenetic), in which case any fragmentation is understood as arbitrary, or else as having a multiplicity of components that are in reality independent of observations (i.e., heterogenetic). The second dimension of reality classifies underlying beliefs of organizations as either essentially stability-oriented (i.e., homeostatic), or change-oriented (i.e., morphogenetic). The alternative combinations of these two dimensions are unquestionably accepted as natural, right, basic, and desirable.

7. As Elden (1983) reminds us, if values and assumptions are involved, politics are involved.

8. Let me emphasize that visioning occurs prior to action. Of course, organizational leaders and other members are subject to post hoc rationalization. When (for whatever reasons) behavioral patterns are altered, people often adjust their values and cognitions to fit. Reports of organizational culture change that are based on data gathered "after the fact" may thus be viewed skeptically.

9. Cammann et al. (1984) report four strategic choices in their study of QWL projects. Beyond scope, time frame, and pace, they add choices between top-down and bottom-up intervening and the type of consulting assistance used, if any.

10. These analytically separate but actually overlapping phases are better known as unfreezing, change or movement, and refreezing after the usage of their first exponent, Lewin (1951), and other early advocates (e.g., Lippit et al., 1958).

11. The next steps in a research agenda might take several noncompeting directions. One is to empirically ground the framework offered through multiple case comparisons. A second would be to acknowledge the relative importance of the many factors suggested. A third might be to use the framework prescriptively, thereby gaining a better understanding of the factors that seem to impede its utilization. Fourth, attention needs to be paid to inventing/elucidating interventions in all the cells of our matrix of cultural interventions (Figure 9.4), thereby enhancing the "tool kit" of practitioners. Fifth, thought should be given to the ethics of culture change, especially the manipulations of the value and assumption levels of meaning. No doubt this list could be expanded even before nonclinical methods are considered, as eventually they must be.

10

CAN ORGANIZATIONAL CULTURE BE MANAGED?

A Synthesis

Walter R. Nord

Washington University

Appointing a synthesizer was itself a conscious effort by the conference planners to manage culture. The verb "synthesize" means to make a whole out of the parts. In contrast to the discussant or respondent, a synthesizer considers the chapters collectively and interactively rather than individually and sequentially. I have taken this direction seriously; my central focus is on building a whole that is rich enough to encompass the parts that the individual chapters represent. Just as Dandridge's search for King Arthur was a product of his choice to believe, I chose to believe in a whole that would encompass the chapters in this section of the book, and I was controlled by this belief. Although I was not successful in creating one entity, the search for a larger whole proved useful in examining the chapters.

There are important risks inherent in taking the creation of a whole as an objective. First, each part may get less attention than it deserves. Second, the uniqueness of each part is understated. In fact, because the meaning of components is affected by the whole that they form, the individual parts may be changed in the process. Third, it is possible that the components might be more meaningful if assembled into several entities rather than one. However, because synthesis was my primary goal, I gave little attention to these possible risks.

The results of my efforts to synthesize are summarized in two parts. In the first, I attempt to synthesize by accepting the authors' frame of reference. I look at common themes that the chapters address and examine the various stances on these themes. In essence, this approach first lists the dimensions that would exist if these chapters were added together and then specifies the range that is represented on each dimension. Also in the first section, I suggest several implications that particular chapters have for conceptualizing and studying organizational cultures. In the second section, I step outside the frame of reference of this set of authors. I consider how certain omissions and assumptions of the current set of chapters reveal flaws in current applications of the concept of culture. This approach suggests the need for an expanded framework.

A SYNTHESIS FROM COMMON THEMES

Two concepts, although not formally addressed in any of the chapters, underlie my synthesis. These ideas—deviation-amplifying and deviation-counteracting processes in mutually causal relationships—will be explored before addressing the more explicit common themes.

Maruyama (1963) describes what he calls "mutual causal systems." The fundamental property of these systems is that the elements within them influence each other either simultaneously or alternatingly. Some mutually causal relationships are deviation-counteracting in that changes in some elements of the system produce changes in other elements that tend to return the system to its original state. By contrast, deviation amplication is a positive feedback process through which an initial change produces a new, and often more structured, system. For example, the development of a city can begin with an arbitrary choice by a single farmer to locate a farm on a previously homogeneous plain. This choice influences where other farmers locate and where shops, streets, and other facilities are built. Ultimately, it shapes the dynamics of a complex social system.

A number of deviation-amplifying or deviation-counteracting feedback loops may be built into complex systems. Depending on the nature of these loops, an initial change (i.e., a deviation) may produce systems that either differ greatly from the original system or hardly differ at all. While the prediction of specific outcomes requires a detailed knowledge of these components and their interactions, these concepts summarize the dynamics of both change and stability in mutually causal systems, including organizations.

Viewed in Maruyama's terms, we realize that the management of culture requires the ability both to introduce change and to maintain the status quo. In other words, managing organizational culture involves understanding both the conditions where a small change (e.g., a deliberate intervention) in a complex system can produce a self-sustaining (i.e., deviation-amplifying) change in the complex system and the conditions where the change will be overwhelmed by the system (i.e., deviation-counteracted).

The core question that these chapters address is, "Can culture be managed?" Because deviation amplification and counteraction are central to such management, it will be useful to keep these systems concepts in mind as we examine several specific themes that these chapters share.

Five themes or issues are addressed more or less directly by almost all of the authors: (1) their conceptualizations of what organizational culture is, (2) their relative emphasis on changing cultures, (3) the time period their analysis addresses (that is, the formative period versus a time after initial formation), (4) the degree to which culture is manageable or subject to planned change, and (5) what constrains the management of cultures.

Conceptualizations of Culture

Smircich (1983a) observes that theorists have tended to link culture to organizations in two ways. Some argue that organizations can be understood *as* cultures. In contrast, others treat culture as something that organizations *have*. Smircich suggests that whereas the former view tends to focus attention on how organization is accomplished and what it means to be organized, the latter tends to focus attention on what organizations accomplish and how they accomplish it more efficiently. Although in practice most writers deal with both aspects, it is useful to employ Smircich's distinction to reveal the primary focus of a culture. This distinction often boils down to which set of dependent variables a writer is most concerned with—results or the elements of process. Because the authors in this section are all concerned with managing cultures in order to improve organizational performance and health, it is to be expected that their dependent variables would consist primarily of results. I believe this to be the case for every chapter—culture is of interest as a tool to achieve some desired outcomes through an organization.

Emphasis on Changing Cultures

While change is a common issue, the authors differ substantially in the degree to which they are concerned with creating change or preventing it.

For the most part, Lundberg and Siehl, and Krefting and Frost focus exclusively on changing cultures. Dandridge, as well as Martin et al., focus on change but also on nonchange. For example, Dandridge notes how people can choose not to change while Martin et al. postulate an overdetermined pattern by describing how life-cycle forces might make it impossible to maintain an entrepreneurial shop even if one wanted to. In this sense, although change occurs, the new state is not subject to deliberate change. To some degree, Lundberg, whose primary concern is with change, is also concerned with the stabilization of change (that is, nonchange after change). Still, all of the chapters in the section are primarily concerned with changing organizations by changing culture.

In contrast, Peters and Waterman, authors of *In Search of Excellence* (1982), suggest that what "excellent" organizations have done can be instructive for deliberate changes in other organizations. Thus they provide more insight into how organizations with successful cultures sustain those cultures rather than how new cultures can be created. Because this book seems to be viewed by so many managers as a guide for change, I think this distinction should be highlighted.

Although some of Peters and Waterman's concepts, particularly that of transforming leadership, focus on creating new patterns, many of them illustrate processes that may be more useful in dampening change than in amplifying it. For example, socialization, values, philosophy, common language, stories, and so on are apt to function to maintain a system the way it is, although the content of these items could support change. For example, it is possible to envision socialization processes that promote deviation, but it would seem that much of the socialization provided in the "excellently managed" firms makes for flexibility by ensuring homogeneity on central dimensions. In fact, many of the mechanisms that Peters and Waterman reveal may be effective because they reduce the chances for deviation (should it occur) to be amplified. For example, openness, tolerating failure, and concern for individuals all seem to remove the probability of rallying points for resistance to and/or dampening of specific changes. Moving quickly and emphasizing homegeneity in hiring and socialization also reduce the chances of there being enough people to rally against something even if an opportunity occurred. I believe that interpreted in this way, Peters and Waterman's contribution to our thinking about change has not been emphasized enough. Successful management/change is often a function of what does *not* happen; typically, however, we focus on what *does* happen. Peters and Waterman show us that culture can be useful in accomplishing management's objectives by reducing the opportunities for undesired deviation amplification. In some ways, Martin et al.'s notion of waves may be pointing to a similar matter—what makes it so difficult to reverse a wave is the absence of support that allows "counter ripples" to develop and be amplified into waves.

In short, the chapters seem to focus on changing organizational cultures. However, when examined more closely, in the light of the dynamics of mutually causal systems, they seem to be concerned with both deliberate change and the deliberate avoidance of change.

Time Period Addressed

A related theme involves the time or point in an organization's history. The chapters range widely along this dimension. Martin et al. and Siehl examine early stages in the life of organizations, when we would normally expect maximum change to be possible. The others, for the most part, focus on older systems, with Dandridge covering both by suggesting that the past can be recreated. In any case, their concern with culture directed all of the authors to be much more involved with history than is customary in much work on organizational behavior.

One of the most useful contributions that the concept of culture can make to our field may be that it induces a historical perspective. Organizational behaviorists are notoriously ahistorical in their analysis of particular organizations and of the evolution of organizations in a social system. Such a state is very difficult to maintain if one takes culture seriously, because the desire to understand a system's culture drives one to a concern with the process by which the past has been mapped into or stored in the present. Following scholars such as Gutman (1977) and Green (1980), I expect that such historically informed understanding will produce a very different perspective on organization than now dominates our field. This change will include a greater awareness of both the tensions and struggles that took place prior to the emergence of present organizational forms, and of the role of organizations as forces for social control in society. The emphasis on culture will move organizational behavior to be relatively less reliant on the empirical analytical sciences and more dependent on the historical-hermeneutic sciences (Habermas, 1973).

Although these particular chapters deal primarily with individual organizations, rather than social trends, all of them emphasize how the events of the past are embodied in the structures, beliefs, and practices of the present. This emphasis has important methodological implications for students or organizations; to understand such developments, the researcher must be close to the organization and recognize the dangers of reification. In other words, borrowing from Geertz's (1973) description of the work of anthroplogists, we do not study organizations; rather, we study *in* organizations. We must understand how the particular processes within organizations have shaped systems of meaning and structural forms at the level of the individual system. However, because these micro level events within individual organizations are expressions of and contributors to the evolution of larger entities, the historical study of individual organizations can provide data useful for understanding human development more generally. Returning to Geertz (1973: 23): "Social actions are comments on more than themselves. . . . [S]mall facts speak to large issues." In short, these chapters (and most of the others in this collection) point unequivocally to the importance of history in the study of organizations and, I suggest, of the role of organizations in the study of history. This emphasis could have farreaching consequences for the methods, the substance, and the importance of organizational study. Our subject matter may be far more important than our current ahistorical microlevel focus allows us to comprehend.

Action Issues

What would you do to manage and change culture? This issue is addressed by all authors in this volume. Moreover, what specifically does a focus on culture lead you to do differently compared with other perspectives? In short, does culture add anything new to the analysis of change?

Except for Dandridge and Lundberg, these chapters focus almost exclusively on what leaders or managers could or could not do, and what they did or did not do. While there is great variation in the degree of success anticipated, there is also considerable agreement on what to do. Almost all advice can be summarized as efforts to aid organizational learning: chunking, using symbols, raising consciousness, using rolemodeling rewards and repetition, action planning, one-on-one communicating, and matching perspectives. Perhaps the most novel idea is Krefting and Frost's appeal to archetypes (another example of the relationship of small events to larger processes stimulated by the cultural metaphor).

Are these significant additions to conventional approaches to management? In many ways, the answer is no. For most part, there is not much that is new here. However, there is a difference in emphasis; symbols, metaphors, and history become more central. Is this a major difference? I'm not sure, but maybe the size of the difference is less important than its existence. To illustrate this point, consider the clever radio advertisement for Chapman's ice cream. In the ad, someone attempts to pass off an ordinary brand of ice cream as Chapman's to a rough, tough cowboy named Black Bart. Bart immediately detects the difference and becomes enraged. Fearing for his life, the seller tries to calm Bart down by saying that there is only a little difference between this ice cream and Chapman's. Black Bart retorts, "It is the subtle little difference that is *all* the difference."

The use of culture as a mangement tool may represent such a "subtle little difference." Indeed, systematic, continuing attention to the components suggested in these chapters may one day have a major impact on the knowledge and management of organizations. Attention to culture may, via deviation amplification, produce major changes—not immediately, but over an extended time period. In a sense, if we view culture as a tool, it may inform theory in important ways. For example, it could become a sixth and overarching coordinating mechanism in Mintzberg's (1979) framework.

Constraints on Managing Culture

All of the chapters indicate a number of limitations on the degree to which culture can be managed. A partial list of these constraints includes: life cycles, conflicting interests, a lack of willingness on the part of some actors, different saliences attached to issues, different meanings, poor communication, lack of subordinate development, bad timing, a leader getting trapped by his or her own rhetoric, and complexity. As would be expected in a series of chapters that center on culture as a managerial tool, most of the attention here seems to be on how these constraints counteract change—that is, how they keep an initial deviation from amplifying.

Summary

Overall, a rich entity can be developed by searching for commonalities and synthesizing these chapters under five headings, informed by the concepts of deviation amplification and counteraction. Such a synthesis reveals that the authors adopted a tool view of culture, were concerned with both change and nonchange, were deeply conscious of organizational history, relied primarily on an organizational learning framework to understand and manage cultural change, and implicitly viewed the failure of deviation amplification to occur as the prime explanation for the inability to change in an intended direction.

TOWARD A RICHER SYNTHESIS

In developing the synthesis in the first section of this chapter, I accepted the mainstream conceptualization of culture that others assume uncritically. I focused primarily on what the chapters addressed rather than what they omitted. In this section, I change my perspective—I attempt to step outside the frame of reference of the authors and explore the implications of this analysis for the use of culture as a concept in the analysis of organizations. Two themes emerge—current views of organizational culture underemphasize the tensions and dynamism of organizations; they also underestimate potential problems in understanding culture through normal science.

The Static View in Current Perspectives

As I suggested earlier, these authors approach organizational culture as a managerial tool. Although they explicitly acknowledge the influence of competing values and interests within an organization, they tend to regard these factors as problems to be overcome by management rather than as items to be viewed as interesting in themselves. This approach seems to result from the rather explicit focus on leadership and from the less explicit belief in the existence of a pervasive organizational culture. The view is consistent with the metaphor of culture acting as a glue that binds the parts of an organization together.

Unfortunately, these assumptions are conducive to a rather static view of culture. Moreover, they fail to dignify the importance of countercultures within complex systems. Complex organizations contain conflicting values, perceptions, and interests (Burawoy, 1979; Edwards, 1979). Just as the value of an overarching culture is more informative about a society on a small, remote Pacific island than about a society such as the United States, so it may be more useful for understanding smaller, more homogeneous organizations such as those described by Martin et al. and Siehl than for the analysis of large, complex organizations where the resolution of conflict is a more pragmatic course than the elimination of its roots.

When we consider these more complex organizations, the deficiencies in the conceptualization of culture as a glue become clear. The many parts of these systems are constantly changing, both themselves and their relationships to each other. The existence of the larger entity depends as much on a dynamic tension among the parts as it does on their similarity. Certain units can be expected to exert considerable force against the values of others, and components are differentially bonded to each other—for example, there are a number of coalitions. Moreover, alignment may vary across different issues. The bonding does not come about purely from something between the parts, but rather as a function of the dynamic relationships of changing components. These considerations led me to be uncomfortable with the popular glue metaphor, and thus to consider some alternatives. I concluded that magnetism is a more informative metaphor.[1]

Adequate conceptualization of the bonding process that holds complex organizations together must be able to encompass repulsion as well as attraction; it must allow for changes in the parts; and it must treat the patterning among the parts (e.g., coalitions). If there is such a force, magnetism seems to a better analogy than glue. The magnetic metaphor encourages examination of the dynamics through which the various parts arrange themselves in the field, of how various parts attract some parts and repel others, of how the magnetic field itself (via induction) may change the structure of the individual components, of the operation of some elements that are nonmagnetic, and of others that are antimagnetic and that may lead to the destruction of the field. Undoubtedly other metaphors could serve equally well or perhaps better in this regard. The point is to recognize the limitations of the glue metaphor. If culture is seen as a powerful integrating force in complex organizations, viewing it as glue is apt to lead to understatement of the autonomy of the parts and thus to understatement of the causal roles they play. It also encourages overstatement of the integrating and understatement of the disintegrating forces, and it may produce less dynamic models than may be warranted.

Culture, Normal Science, and Expanded Synthesis

One major contrast among the chapters suggests a significant epistemological issue in the study of culture. All of the chapters except parts of Krefting and Frost's seem to assume that culture can be understood using conventional research methods—in all probability relatively clinical and qualitative approaches, as opposed to routine and quantitative.

Krefting and Frost introduce the Jungian notion of archetypes. Following Jung, archetypes refer to elements that are, in principle, unknowable to the human mind. These unknowable forces structure the phenomena that we as social scientists study.

At this point, we are driven beyond normal science. Thus we are in the same position of the astronomers in Jastrow's *God and the Astronomers* (1980). Jastrow argues that the "big bang" theory has achieved widespread acceptance in accounting for the formation of the universe. According to this theory, the universe was produced by an enormous explosion of a very dense body that contained all matter. In principle, from a time after the big bang it is impossible to understand the origins of that body. Scientific methods can never lead to an understanding of the origins of the universe; hence, the scientist can never discover history prior to the big bang. If Jung was right, the introduction of his work by Krefting and Frost and other recent authors into our analysis of organization culture forces us to a very different level of knowing. Normal science will not be a helpful approach here. Rather, a synthesis that includes this view would imply that treatments of culture need to consider the existence of some cosmic spirit that is mapped into the human components of an organization. It is tempting to draw an analogy between such pervasive, pattern-inducing force and a magnetic field. Although such a step might be the ultimate in synthesis, I cannot bring myself to take it.

NOTE

1. There are serious issues involved when the administrative sciences draw on the physical sciences for metaphors (Pinder and Bourgeois, 1982). Because glue is also such a metaphor, magnetism is no more or less prone to these problems. My suggestion that we consider magnetism as a metaphor to describe bonding is based on my judgment that it corresponds better to the dynamic processes we observe in organizations than does glue. Of course, a variety of bonding processes could coexist, and it may be reasonable to see culture as analogous to a gluing process and magnetism as analogous to something else. At the very least, the proposal of an alternative metaphor may help to uncover some of the previously unrecognized limitations of current conceptualizations of culture.

PART III

HOW SHOULD ORGANIZATIONAL CULTURE BE STUDIED?

CRAIG C. LUNDBERG

There is a story about a "wonder scholar" of organizations, who on his deathbed whispers to one of his disciples, "Organizations are like bagels." The disciple mentions these words to his colleagues and they spread quickly throughout the community of organizational scholars. Finally, they reach the ears of the newest and most naive student, who asks, "What does it mean, organizations are like bagels?" This question spreads back through the community of scholars until it reaches the bedside of the wonder scholar. "Scholar," his disciple asks, "What does it mean, organizations are like bagels?" "Oh," the scholar says, weakly shrugging his shoulders, "so organizations are not like bagels."

Thus, by the timely intervention of a naive mind, we are saved from a metaphor. We do not have to work at our scholarly careers as if the phenomena of interest were seamless circles without beginning or end, seemingly substantial but actually empty at the center. Not every discipline or field is fortunate enough to have divinely appointed irreverence that keeps nature from mimicking its pseudoscience. On the contrary, our views of the world are so dominated by powerful metaphors that we often turn similes into identities. Organizations cease to be *like* bagels and *become* them. Organization studies have long been captive of two major metaphoric "bagels": organizations are like machines, and organizations are like organisms. With the advent of the study of organizational cultures, we seemed to be released, at last, from the confines of seeing organizations as either machines or organisms. The first organizational culture studies sidestepped paradigmatic metaphors by bringing us face to face with meanings.

The study of organizational cultures, with its emphasis on meanings and its relative newness, holds the potential for becoming the most self-reflective branch of organizational studies. Quite naturally, we are led to examine the culture and meanings of studying organizational culture. The chapters in this section have this as their common concern. To be sure, all of the authors agree on the significance of cultural phenomena and the utility of understanding the meaning of life in the workplace. All are willing to be unfettered by conventional research strategies and methods as they tackle the conventional myths of managerial behavior and organizational research. In one sense, then, the authors in this section have adopted a stance of caring and informed irreverence that allows each of them to follow a unique thought path as they explore several significant considerations for studying organizations.

In the first chapter, Mirvis relates a case study of changes in a corporate culture following a firm's acquisition. He focuses his attention on the many conflicting personal and professional roles he experienced in this action research project. As he points out, managing research while researching managers raises many practical and moral issues as well as questions of partisanship, the efficacy of interventions, and the potential loss of integrity. This richly descriptive account not only sensitizes us to the complexities of the culture researcher's role and relationships but leads us to consider the risks, benefits, and harms of culture research for researchers, organizations, and their members.

The second chapter, by Adams and Ingersoll, also focuses on the human side of culture research, and especially on the aesthetic choices of personal involvement. The authors relate their struggle to discover a way of relating to cultural phenomena that are antianalytical and phenomenological. Woven into their tale of discovering a personally appropriate path for how to research cultural phenomena is the equally gripping tale of the discovery of their phenomena of interest—managerial metamyths. Adams and Ingersoll find that they cannot separate the study of organizational culture from its host culture—a point echoed at several other places in this book. They would go further than the self-reflectiveness of Mirvis, arguing for an aesthetic self-reflexiveness by culture researchers. It is important to note that both Mirvis and these authors consciously underscore that their experiences as cultural researchers are still unfolding before them; thus they are open to the nuances of such work, as well as to the wonder of their findings.

Jones, writing as a folklorist concerned with applications of his craft, argues for a sensitive action research. He eloquently reminds us that older culture researchers have often been hamstrung by taking a stance of ethical neutrality. Jones argues that ethics are not the issue.

If we are to go beyond technical, structural, quasi-rational perspectives on organizations and truly embrace a symbolic, meaning-laden one, then passive inquiry alone is insufficient. Active involvement in the preservation and change of cultures is not only nice, but necessary.

When Jones states that ethics are not the issue in cultural research, he clearly does not exclude ethical considerations in organizational culture research. Deetz's chapter agrees with this point and elaborates the research agenda of cultural researchers by urging us to understand the dynamics and features of organizational culture not only theoretically and epistemologically but also ethically. Deetz argues for a reversal in conventional thinking. Whereas many of us assume that organizational culture and ethics reflect the wider culture, Deetz shows how societal ethics are the result of organizational behavior and decisions. Deetz, like Mirvis, Adams and Ingersoll, and Jones before him, is persuasive in arguing that organizational culture research has to be more than hermeneutical. In fact, it cannot help being so, because it opens up choice through exposure. If this type of research begins, then ethical considerations are not only of interest but vital.

The final chapter in this section, by Butcher, is a passionate plea for organizational culture to become more than the subject or means of inquiry; it should be a training ground, too. Butcher, an executive himself, is impatient with what he perceives to be the high frequency of antisocial and unethical business practices. He recognizes the real power of business leaders and advocates that managers examine more carefully the consequences of their behavior as partial causes of cultural norms—believing that most unethical business practices will be eliminated in this way. Needed are not only more and better studies of organizational culture but also the active collaboration of managers. Butcher, in his direct fashion, adds to the considerations for cultural research his clear concern for its import regarding managerial education.

The chapters that follow all upend conventional expectations for treatises about studying organizations. They neither reflect nor mention the dominant unidirectional causal paradigm that is still rampant in the organizational sciences, the popular research strategies fawning toward classical experimental designs, the "tried and true" tool kit of research methods, or the ubiquitous concerns for measurement, validity, and sampling. The considerations written about here are interestingly congruent with the study of organizational culture itself. Each essay seeks a fresh meaning of the roles, relationships, and processes of inquiry into meaning and consensual realities. It is tempting to liken this set of essays to an exotic smorgasbord—depending on your appetite, nutritional needs, and taste preferences, you can fill your plate in many ways and even come back for extra helpings. Having been cautioned in the story that began these introductory remarks to be careful with metaphors, however, let us conclude with the observation that these chapters are more than bagel fare.

11

MANAGING RESEARCH WHILE RESEARCHING MANAGERS

Philip H. Mirvis

Boston University

I began to study the DC organization, a 1000-person U.S. manu-facturing firm, some eight years ago. First experiences taught me that, with some diligence and care, research relationships could be openly and productively managed and my research done ethically and well. The study involved the preparation of an audit of quality of work life (QWL) based on personnel records and findings from a companywide ques-tionnaire survey (Mirvis and Lawler, 1984). Initial research agreements established the rights of DC people in the study and protected their welfare as research participants (American Psychological Association, 1973). Completion of the survey was voluntary; all participants were ensured of the confidentiality of their surveys and records, and each was given a written and oral summary of the QWL findings. Agreements also gave me the right to "sign off" that the audit procedures and summary were fair and to publish professional papers on QWL measurement at DC.

I filled a dual role in the research: as an impartial auditor of QWL in the company, and as a consultant contributing to action strategies and plans developed from the survey feedback effort. As a researcher, I worked with DC people to ensure that the survey design included questions of interest to personnel at all levels and functions, and that the feedback addressed their various concerns. As a change agent, I actively participated in planning sessions and debriefings throughout the organization.

These actions were consistent with the accepted standards of professional practice and of morality in organizational research. Stanley Seashore and I have described these standards and have based them in an analysis of research roles and relationships (Mirvis and

Seashore, 1979). Figure 11.1 illustrates (from our approach) the role system developed in organizational research. It shows researchers linked with many interests in a client organization, including research participants and various stakeholders both within and external to the firm. We charged researchers to work jointly with these interests to clarify research roles and to address role conflicts in an open and mutual fashion. We also proposed that certain ethical norms—regarding freedom, self-determination, due process, equity, and the like—need to be addressed in research agreements and advanced in research relationships. This makes the development of a research contract and the resolution of practical and moral quandries in research a matter of concern to all parties.

This conception also links researchers to their professional role system, with obligations to represent their profession, their discipline, and potential users of their research findings. In this study, "DCers" took an active hand in developing the research contract and readily agreed to provisions of both confidentiality in data gathering and a full disclosure of results within the firm. They were interested in contributing to management knowledge about QWL measurement and were pleased to have the study methodology and findings published. This made it easy for me to represent my professional interests and to uphold standards of professional practice in organizational research.

Another obligation of researchers in action studies is to examine the values advanced in a change effort (Mirvis, 1982). I was very candid with DCers that the survey feedback method would "open up" the organization and "empower" people by giving them voice in strategy and action planning. This approach was welcomed, for DC's culture is based on the "authority of knowledge" in problem solving and consensus decision making when it comes to implementing solutions. There were some fears that the survey would heighten expectations and that the feedback might provoke unworkable levels of conflict. We talked over these concerns and agreed to manage them mutually as the study progressed. There was a shared commitment to collect valid data on QWL in DC, to involve all DCers in its interpretation and problem solving, and to make QWL audits both a scientifically and organizationally valued activity. The first audit went very well, and it was agreed to continue them every two years.

Two years later, however, circumstances had changed. DC had been acquired in a "white knight" acquisition by a conglomerate we shall call GrandCo. DCers told me that the acquisition had created problems in their firm. GrandCo was much more financially driven than DC and

© Philip H. Mirvis. Drawn by Laura Santi.

Figure 11.1   Research Role Systems

exercised authority from the top down. Several DC policies and systems, integral to its people-oriented philosophy, had been changed at GrandCo's insistence. There was bad blood between the two company's leaders. Top managers in DC also noted that they were more "uptight" and less communicative with DC work force.

At the meeting to negotiate the upcoming QWL survey, I proposed to expand its scope and focus in-depth on the impact of the acquisition. The subject would be changes in top management's behavior and in the culture of the firm. This would require in-depth interviews and analyses of pertinent documents and memoranda. I would then prepare a history of the acquisition that could be used alongside the QWL data in action planning.

"Damn near suicidal" was the DC reaction. Major concerns regarding privacy; the amount of employee participation in such a study; control over the release and publication of data; and the potential risks, benefits, and harm, as well as the overall value of the study came to the fore. Plainly, old research guidelines were not applicable to this new situation. This conclusion applies, in my view, to most studies of corporate culture. This chapter details the formulation of research guidelines and the management of research relations in our study of DC. Its lessons apply to the study of any organizational culture.

OLD RESEARCH GUIDELINES,
NEW RESEARCH PROBLEMS

Research Relations in Studies of Corporate Culture

The model of research relations presented in Figure 11.1 can be applied to show how any effort to clarify roles and values in a study of corporate culture is fraught with vagary. Part of the problem can be traced to the research role. Culture researchers are a diverse group; some work in academia, others in consulting, and many are employed in both. They come from different intellectual heritages and have had varying degrees of exposure to and socialization in the ethics of research traditions. In practice, they may be called upon to be anthropologists, sociologists, psychologists, political scientists, and erstwhile management practitioners. They may assume both action and research roles. This combination of professional identities is a prime source of ambiguity for researchers as they manage client relations and fill multiple roles (Seashore, 1976).

Furthermore, cultural researchers are, to this point, marginal to the research "establishment." They lack common methods for studying culture and a common paradigm for interpreting their findings. Many, by temperament, are also marginal in values from the profession. They see themselves as research entrepreneurs, breaking new ground in methods and content and in how they approach their work. This makes messages from the profession as to appropriate role conduct seem distant and hazy. Many culture researchers prefer to choose their own ways and make their own peace with chosen ethical standards.

All of this leaves such researchers free to shape their own roles in a study of corporate culture. They may self-style themselves as detectives, prophets, storytellers, even searchers of the deep. Such self-styled roles are based in societal models imbued with distinct investigative traditions and ethical guidelines. However, when scientists become detectives, consultants become prophets, researchers become journalists, and landlubbers find themselves in the deep, they discover that the traditions and standards of these personal identities clash. Researchers encounter role conflicts and find themselves unprepared to contend with the practical and ethical demands of so many conflicting roles.

This situation sends mixed messages to organizations as to what culture researchers define as standards of practice and what the investigation is really all about. A second source of problems in culture research, then, can be found in the organization. Clients bring experienced-based expectations to organizational studies. Many know what to expect from researchers and have (admittedly stereotypic) views of what researchers study, how they study it, and for whose interests they work. Thus they become skilled in working with and around researchers that fit their molds. Clients have a harder time working with unsocialized research mavericks. They get nervous and do not know how to behave.

Researchers whose roles, methods, and purposes seem uncertain or foreign can be threatening to clients. Such researchers can become magnets for organizational "craziness." The result is a cycle of defensiveness and counterdefense—in clinical terms, transference and countertransference. Threatened clients may erect psychological, strategic, and political barriers to protect themselves (Argyris, 1952; Guskin and Chesler, 1973). When researchers strive to break through such defenses, or to bring them to light in search of ever-more relevant data, they introduce their own personalities into the study and engender even more anxiety. Managing research becomes an exercise in managing mutual craziness. Researchers may be called upon to become therapists—another role they are not trained for—or else find themselves in need of therapy!

All of this manuevering is complicated by the high stakes implied in studies of corporate culture. Several features of culture studies raise the stakes for both researchers and clients when compared with more commonplace organizational investigations. First, the studies focus on corporate leaders and their behaviors rather than managers, supervisors, hourly personnel, or MBAs. Many researchers itch to study the "big shots" in corporations but are nervous lest they appear unworldly or, worse, academic. In the same way, many corporate leaders are eager to contribute to management knowledge, yet they are guarded as to what they say and attentive as to how they will be portrayed. Second, culture research is "hot" today. Researchers are beginning to compete for leadership in this intellectual area, and companies are concerned that they appear to be searching for excellence (Fortune, 1983). Third, culture research touches on the roots of power in organizations. Researchers with a bent toward action know that promoting changes in culture is fundamental to enduring changes in corporate behavior (Beckhard, 1969). In the same way, corporate powers and power seekers know that myths, symbols, and beliefs are key to their control of an organization (Peters, 1978).

Most of all, the very subject of organizational culture raises the stakes in such a research effort. Values are the foundation of corporate culture, and the learning of those values is central to cultural identity (Schein, 1983a). Values are also central to researcher's identities (Berg, 1980). As culture studies force researchers and clients to clarify their roles and expectations, they also force them to surface and confront their own identities. As such studies provoke conflicts over the roles and purposes of the parties involved, they also create conflicts over individual and collective identities. To reach inside a culture requires researchers and clients to reach inside themselves. Researchers may be tempted to retreat to more traditional methods, molds, and research morays (Devereux, 1967), and clients may be tempted to retreat from the study altogether. Such temptations run deep when, as in the present study, the organization seeks to keep its culture sacred and the researcher wants to make it profane.

Research Relations in the Acquisition Study

Figure 11.2 depicts research relationships in this acquisition study. It shows the researcher's role to be ambiguous and potentially disruptive

© Philip H. Mirvis. Drawn by Laura Santi.

Figure 11.2   Research Role Systems in the Case of a Corporate Acquisition

to the client organization. I brought multiple professional identities to that research role. For one, I was to continue as a researcher, but now studying both quality of work life and the impact of the acquisition on DC employees. I had never studied an acquisition before and, though vague notions of organizational crises and cross-cultural relations came to mind, I truly had no definitive research agenda, nor was I certain what research methods would be most appropriate to the investigation. In addition, I would continue serving a consultative role at DC. This change agent role had been clearly delineated in my work as a survey researcher, but it was more difficult to specify in my function as a historian.

Furthermore, I brought multiple personal identities to the research. I would be a detective, storyteller, prophet, and searcher of the deep. I was not prepared, however, to have my detective work circumscribed at the outset, nor later to have my searchings invade privacies, my prophesies read as fantasy, and my storytelling cast into the deep. Messages from colleagues and guidelines from the profession would prove hazy as to whether my research choices were defensible and how to handle the conflicts they evoked.

My clients at DC were just as uncertain about their own roles in the study and faced their own roster of conflicts and concerns. From the start, Bruce Bates, head of Human Resources, and Lester Richardson, president and CEO, supported the need for an in-depth study of the impact of the acquisition on their organization. Yet both had concerns over its breadth and how the data would be used. One major concern centered on GrandCo. The acquirer was portrayed as a bureaucratic "octopus" that wanted to engulf DC. Another concern was that DC's managers, supervisors, and the bulk of the work force might be further upset with GrandCo as a result of the research. One "tiger" we had to address was whom to involve in the study. Another was whether and how to make public the results.

Bates and Richardson could not initially define an action role for me in the study. That would have to await my findings. As it happened, they and some of their peers invited me to review my historical report with them and participate in their action planning. Later, however, others would find that my history lacked action implications and my consultative would be seen as unessential. DCers would become confused about my role and their own roles in the study. They too would lack models for participating in a study of their culture that would prove to be upsetting and threatening.

A sampling of the kinds of ethical and practical conflicts that arose in this study will anchor them in the mainstream of most cultural research:

Rights to privacy. Those who study corporate culture favor an in-depth probe of the organizational psyche and seek to turn the tacit into the explicit, the hidden into the conscious world of the known (Louis, 1981b). Accounts of cultures depend on thick descriptions that lay bare a social structure's bones (Geertz, 1983). When does an organization have a right to keep its secrets private? How can this right be weighed against a researcher's right to know and tell the truth?

Free and informed consent. Culture researchers know that information, freedom, and even choice is mystified in organizations (Meyer and Rowan, 1977) and becomes part and parcel of political processes (Pfeffer, 1981b). Procedures to ensure voluntary and informed involvement by the parties at interest in a research study assume that all can make voluntary, informed, and rational decisions. When politics and mystery intervene, what standards of free and informed consent should be upheld?

Freedom from harm. Those who intervene in organizational cultures know that the consequences of their actions are unpredictable and never fully under their control (Michael and Mirvis, 1977). Cultural studies can evoke anxiety, fear, and even danger along with hopes, fervor, and dreams within a firm. There is a potential for some to benefit from actions developed from studies of corporate culture; there is also risk that some could be harmed. What should be done to ensure that the benefits outweigh the risks? What can be done to manage and minimize the harms?

These and many other issues concerning partisanship, the efficacy of interventions, and the potential loss of integrity for the researcher, the research participants, and even the client organization all came to the fore in this research. But such issues are endemic to cultural investigations. To see them arise in this study, to examine their resolution, and to evaluate the moral and pragmatic justifications of the parties involved requires a review of my efforts at managing research while researching managers.

COMING INTO A CULTURE: THE RESEARCH CONTRACT

I was the one who proposed doing a study of the impact of DC's acquisition to Bates and Richardson; they had come to the "contracting" meeting only to make plans for the upcoming QWL study. I offered three purposes to such a study: (1) to contribute to our understanding of corporate acquisitions; (2) to help DCers learn from their own experiences in an acquisition; and (3) to educate other managers and scholars about the phenomenon. Such purposes were also advanced for the QWL study, but in this context they raised the stakes of the research.

We all talked about the "mania" over acquisitions in the country and the many problems that managers encountered in coping with them. Bates and Richardson warmed to the idea of studying the impact of the acquisition at DC.

Next I noted that a more in-depth study would be required. I proposed interviewing the people most involved in the acquisition and a sample of others at DC. I also said that a review of pertinent memos, meeting agenda and notes, as well as other relevant documents could all contribute to the preparation of a history of the acquisition. Bates and Richardson saw value in this methodology and added that tape recordings of some key meetings were available that would add richness to my investigation.

To this point, the meeting was animated and all of us were in agreement. Then it turned serious. Bates said that we had to make a distinction between the QWL study and the study of the acquisition. The former could continue as usual, under the old ground rules, with full DC participation and debriefings. The acquisition study, however, would have to be limited to a few key informants, and the reporting of results would have to be limited to top management. His rationale was that many at DC saw top management as "obsessed" by the acquisition and "copping out" to GrandCo when it came to adopting their policies and business systems. He described months of fighting with GrandCo during which DC sought to keep its own policies and systems but had been forced to make many changes. Supervisors and the rest of the DC work force had not been told that such changes were mandated for fear of souring relations with GrandCo. An open and visible study of the acquisition might reveal that fact and show the basis for top management's obsession. That had to be avoided, according to Bates.

Richardson then cited two "tigers" that we had to address. One was GrandCo's involvement in the study (I had proposed that GrandCo be involved). Richardson saw this proposal as "damn near suicidal." The "cover your ass" orientation at GrandCo, he said, would put a stop to the study. I challenged this position and said that DC and GrandCo might come to work together more effectively through participation in the study. Richardson said that the norms of our research, with the emphasis on openness and problem solving, were contrary to GrandCo's ways. Their style was to be "nice and genteel" and to sweep problems under the rug. I pressed further and stated that perhaps GrandCo could learn something from the study. Richardson said that GrandCo was a bureaucratic "octopus" that would use such knowledge to exert even more control over DC. Bates remarked that he had seen no evidence that GrandCo was interested in learning anything from DC.

He added that, as things stood, he could not maintain his integrity and involve GrandCo in our work. Richardson then summed up his views:

> I am reluctant to come to this conclusion because I really place a value on informed choice. . . . In effect I'm saying that I'm going to deprive GrandCo of a choice. In my judgement, its a choice I don't want to bother them with. . . . We are so deviant already . . . We have to use our shots carefully.

The second "tiger" was over my rights to publish the findings. I had promised to protect the anonymity of DC and of individual participants in the study. "Is that possible?" queried Bates. We discussed ways to disguise the identities of the companies from public recognition. Still, DCers would recognize their firm, and GrandCo executives might discover themselves and the acquisition story in publications. "The sands of time would cover up this archaeological dig," noted Bates, unless that data gathering started right away. Thus I proposed:

> There might be a way out of this box. There could be a moratorium on publishing the results a number of years. I take to heart, as we all do, the notion of academic freedom, but I also have an equal respect for the rights of parties I study. Its one of those dilemmas. I'm willing to make this kind of commitment.

It was agreed that the study of the impact of the acquisition could commence. Publication of the results would come later—when relations between DC and GrandCo had settled down, when careers were certain, and when the passage of time had healed raw feelings.

Comments on Entry

This short description shows how researchers and clients negotiate a culture study. In terms of role theory, it is an exercise in role making wherein distinct roles are created for several sets of interests. The DC work force would continue to register their views on quality of work life through the survey. They would also be given a briefing on the results. In addition, top managers would be involved in a study of the acquisition's impact. They would be asked to reveal more of their lives and, in return, be given a "for their eyes only" history of the acquisition. Another interest, GrandCo, was not given any research role.

I was to assume distinct roles in relation to each of these interests. For the work force, I was to continue as a survey researcher and consultant. For top managers, I would function as a historian and in an as-yet-to-be-defined change agent role. Formally, I was a nonperson in relation to GrandCo.

It was recognized that my role in the acquisition study would limit the validity of conclusions. I would gain a one-sided, certainly distorted, and possibly self-serving picture of the acquisition. There were moral hazards as well. I was ripe for cooptation by top management at DC while denying information to the rest of the DC work force. I was also colluding in the disenfranchisement of GrandCo. Finally, I was agreeing to participate in a study under ground rules I did not favor.

Culture research often poses such conditions. In some research disciplines, workers are encouraged to "go underground," and deception is accepted as simply one of the rules of the game. Detectives operate in much the same way. The high stakes of the studies seem to necessitate accommodations. My colleague, Stanley Davis (1984), has found his access to divergent interests in organizations to be limited and has had his rights to publication restricted. Peters and Waterman (1982) make no mention of their contacts with union officials at Dana Corporation, and countless other researchers leave out key interests and viewpoints in their reports. Many consultants intentionally limit their debriefings to top management, and some researchers conduct no debriefings at all. There is no single research role model for culture researchers. Here I was an entrepreneur, and to get started I had to develop a situation-specific role.

The craziness at DC also shaped research roles. Bates and Richardson acknowledged that they were obsessed with the acquisition, paranoid over GrandCo, and worried as to how this would "play" in their own firm. We were all anxious over the new ground rules. Bates compared our negotiation process to that between DC and GrandCo. Strategy and defensiveness overwhelmed our efforts at openness and problem solving. This was out of character with our past research relationship, but it was too risky to proceed in any other way.

Can this research contract be defended? It represents an uneasy accommodation to competing values. Values regarding privacy—an organization's right to protect its interests and its members' right to control their self-presentation—were weighed against values favoring openness in research relations, the search for truth, and the timely publication of data. Values protecting participants' rights to be free from risk and possible harm were cast against values allowing other claimants to make an informed choice before being excluded from a study. The top managers at DC agreed to pursue the study under the negotiated ground rules. Top managers generally favor secrecy and control when the stakes are high. Was I justified in agreeing to do the study?

My choices had some basis in moral guidelines for researchers regarding respect for privacy, control over self-presentation, ownership of data, and the weighting of risks and benefits (Kelman, 1979; Pinkard, 1979). I also empathized with DC's top managers and saw that my own interests could be served under the study's ground rules. My choices may look pragmatic, like a cop-out, or like a conflicted effort to address competing value claims in the design of cultural research. They were made at the expense of learning the whole truth, a high research principle, and of incorporating all relevant interests into the research study, a particular principle of my own. I trusted Bates and Richardson and the rest of top management to make good use of the history; I also reasoned that the QWL audit would make them accountable to the work force for how they used its results. I did not know what to expect from the data gathering and feedback itself.

DOING A CULTURE STUDY: DATA GATHERING AND FEEDBACK

The data gathering proceeded slowly and cautiously. I read through key memoranda, listened to tapes of meetings, and did background interviews. Then began my acquisition interviews. I adopted two broad guidelines in the interviews to respect the privacy of interviewees. One applied to the tape recording of interviews. It was agreed that all conversations on tape could be quoted with attribution to the speaker. Interviewees could, however, turn off the tape and provide background information without attribution. Finally, they had the right to give me information completely "off the record." This was to be for my own understanding and to be held in strictest confidence. No one used this final option in the first year of data gathering; they would two years later.

The second ground rule allowed for "time outs" during the interviews. Here, either party could stop the conversation and address immediate "process" concerns. Several interviewees called time outs when questions turned to their career concerns and plans. They felt the questions were "off base." I used this as diagnostic data about the level of anxiety and uncertainty engendered by the acquisition. Sensitivity to such interviewing cues is integral to diagnosis and, later, intervention (Alderfer, 1968). Other time outs were used for clarifications and easing of discomfort—both the interviewees and my own.

These two guidelines may have cost me some data. They also prevented me from catching interviewees off guard, a favorite technique in diagnostic efforts. Still they did lessen anxiety, make the revelation of privacy a personal matter, and let people know that I valued what they chose or chose not to say. All told, more than twenty people participated in interviews over a few months, and nine hundred completed QWL surveys.

Round One Findings and Feedback

The QWL data were returned to DCers some months after survey administration. The ratings showed a sharp decline. Some attributed the declines in communication to management's closed-mouth handling of the postacquisition changes. Managers were quick to point out that declines in participation in decisions began at the top, where GrandCo operated from "command power." The increasing sense of pressure found in the survey was traced to GrandCo's "meatgrinder" attitude and DC's strategy to keep the numbers looking good lest GrandCo intrude further on the organization.

The history of the acquisition was prepared and sent to Bates and Richardson following the survey feedback effort. It covered the stage of crisis management at DC after an initial takeover attempt and the sale to a "white knight" GrandCo. It delved into negotiations between the two companies concerning reporting relationships, the integration of financial control systems, and the resolution of policy differences. Two factors, the pervasive sense of loss at DC and management's reactivity to control by GrandCo, were seen as contributors to DC's strategy of resistance and noncompliance. That strategy had set the stage for win-lose conflicts between the firms that DC lost (Mirvis, 1984c). Finally, the report focused on differences between the DC and GrandCo cultures. Interviewees had made sharp distinctions between the values, philosophies, norms, and business operations in the two firms. DCers' views of GrandCo, the report concluded, were ethnocentric and polarizing. These slanted views, DC's crisis management, and its militant strategy were contributing to continuing problems between the companies and were ripe for reconsideration.

The history was read with interest by Bates, Richardson, and other top DC managers. They asked that I join them in reviewing the history, reconsidering their actions, and developing a new strategy for relating to GrandCo. The meeting went well, and DCers left with a mind to work more openly with GrandCo, ready to accept their status as a subsidiary, willing to "reality-test" their perceptions of differences in the two firms, and eager to avoid fights for fighting's sake. The history was praised by the top managers and my contributions at the meeting were credited as helpful. In a letter to the work force, DC's top managers discussed their plans for becoming more active in dealing with GrandCo and moving the business ahead. Two years later, another QWL survey, another round of interviews, and another chapter in the history of the acquisition would be undertaken.

Round Two Findings and Feedback

The next QWL ratings were higher—not to the level they had once been, but moving in a positive direction. Interviewees reported greater flexibility in their dealings with GrandCo and had found areas of compromise. Conflicts were not as sharp, the new strategy had been successfully implemented, and the sense of crisis and loss had given way.

The acquisition history for this round focused on DC's integration with GrandCo. It concluded that in many key areas, DC had attained its goal of maintaining its culture and gaining acceptance of that culture by GrandCo. In other areas, mostly having to do with financial policies and systems, DC had been assimilated into GrandCo. The question that the history raised was whether DC could maintain this balance of integration and assimilation and still preserve its cultural integrity. There were conflicts between DCers' espoused values and those embedded in its new business systems. There was also the matter of how to "read" the two major changes in the DC organization.

One of the changes involved the selection of a new executive vice-president. DC traditionally made such selections through an open and participative process. For this one, GrandCo had joined in. The two leading candidates were Bates and the head of a key operating division. Bates was identified with DC's participative management philosophy and people orientation. The other candidate was linked to its operational strengths and was seen as less supportive of "too much" participation. After some months of deliberation, the operating manager was named to the post. Some interviewees saw this as a straightforward business decision. They were pleased that the traditional selection mechanism had been supported by GrandCo. Others, however, said that GrandCo had "stacked the deck" and used its power to sway the decision. One interviewee told me, off the record, how the decision had been made.

The second change had DC forming a "super" division that combined several smaller ones. Richardson was against the move, as it meant a loss of "smallness" in divisions and less chance for participation in decisions.

Other top managers saw the combination as a profitable business move. I cited this and the vice-presidential decision as examples of DC putting finance ahead of its philosophy—adopting GrandCo's values at the expense of their traditional ones. That people had so many different interpretations of these changes suggested that DC had lost a common myth and belief system; the firm was at risk of "deculturation" (Sales and Mirvis, 1984).

The second round of the history was again read with interest. Bates and Richardson favored a meeting to reconsider DC's values and strive to incorporate these organizational changes into a new value system. However, the new vice-president and a new accounting official in top management were against such a meeting. For them, the report seemed vague and without action implications. The QWL scores looked good, they reasoned, and there was no need to dwell on the acquisition any further. Top management was split in its opinion over the value of a meeting, so none was held.

Comments on Data Gathering and Feedback

Carrying out this study of the acquisition moved me and DC's top managers into the action realm. Action researchers have been charged to work openly with clients in order to clarify the purpose of action studies and to consider the link between means and ends (Kelman and Warwick, 1978; Walton and Warwick, 1973). DC's top managers and I agreed that the collection of data from those who managed the acquisition could be a useful guide to action. They wanted to maintain their culture and hoped to use the data to learn how they were managing the transition—what aspects of their culture had been lost and what had been retained. My purpose was to study the impact of the acquisition on them and the DC culture and to contribute to their learning and actions. At the outset, I felt no conflict between my research and action roles. We defined compatible roles and values for the first round of investigation.

Argyris (1970) contends that the collection of valid data, free choice in the review of data and the implementation of action plans, and conditions that promote psychological commitment to chosen directions are the key ingredients of effective intervention. The two ground rules for the collection of data from interviews were devised to increase the validity of gathered data. The collection of data on organizational culture helps people to learn about their cultures and their own identities. It makes their tacit understandings explicit (Louis, 1983) and can "unfreeze" them from their past beliefs about their companies and themselves. As such, it can also arouse anxiety. The interview methodology allowed people to protect their privacy and control their disclosures to others. Indeed, in "time outs" interviewees asked how the data would be presented to their fellow managers. These procedures sought to convey my acceptance of the participants' rights in the study. This same conveyance is essential to the gathering of valid information and the maintenance of a helping relationship (Rogers, 1961).

DC's top management found my report to be informative and chose freely to review its findings and include me in developing action implications. They left the meeting committed to the implementation of a new strategy for working with GrandCo. This was a sign to me of the integrity of DC's commitment to openly examine information, to manage on the basis of the "authority of knowledge," and to operate on the basis of members' consensus.

What happened in the second round? More DCers spoke off the record during interviews and refused to make known to others their private information and views. I had no say in the decision to abandon the planned debriefing meeting. DC exercised its freedom of choice to not hold the meeting when top managers failed to come to a consensus on its relevance. It was as though the "authority of power" had prevailed, but no specific power had cancelled the meeting. Instead, top management simply made no decision and the meeting was never held. Self-study was no longer on top management's agenda. My study had lost its value for them and my action role in this work was countermanded.

Mirvis and Berg (1977) urge change agents to reflect on their failures and strive to learn from them. I believe the second round report provided valid information to DC. It emphasized the company's success in implementing its new strategy but also acknowledged GrandCo's power over DC (see Pfeffer, 1981b). It raised the question of the misalignment of DC's values with its new business systems and challenged DCers to examine the mystery in the vice-presidential and division-combination decisions. The inference was that DC was losing its culture and at risk of ethnocide.

One possibility is that this conclusion was simply too much for DCers to cope with. My conclusion implied that GrandCo had unimagined powers and that DCers might be fooling themselves by thinking that their culture could be retained. By extension, I was challenging their capacities to preserve their own identities. Change agents know that they must consider the readiness of clients to handle threatening data. My work smacked of "reality therapy," and my methods lacked empathy (and, ultimately, effectiveness).

A second possibility is that my conclusions were mistaken. I was closely identified with Richardson and Bates and the "old" DC culture. Thus my views may have represented only my "reality" or the slice experienced only by the two of them. Change agents must also respect divergent views and interests and incorporate them effectively in developing action steps. My work may have been overly introspective and not geared to the action orientation of the vice-president and his supporters in top management. As such, it truly would have lacked action implications for them.

A third possibility, of course, is that I was caught in a power play. My work may have been a threat to the new vice-president and his power bloc. Their resistance to a meeting to review the round two history would keep the mysteries secret and put a stop to further discussion of the implications of organizational changes. Change agents have a responsibility to "mirror" conflicts in a social system and must avoid taking sides to be effective (Argyris, 1961). I challenged DCers to look at the split in top management, but I had clearly taken sides in the eyes of one camp. There is moral justification in partisanship (Laue and Cormick, 1979; Alinsky, 1971), but I had not intended to fill such a role within DC, nor was it consistent with the agreed-to purposes and means and ends of my action research work. I was unable to fill that role when the meeting was cancelled, anyway.

Researchers have an obligation to know their values and to use good sense when working with client organizations (Mirvis, 1982). The nondecision regarding the meeting broke the ground rules. It made me angry at first. Then it helped me to examine my own values and my own integrity as an action researcher in this case. Bates could not keep his integrity and involve GrandCo in this study. Could I keep my integrity and continue this research?

THE DECISION TO STAY OR TO GO

Richardson left DC between the second and third rounds of the acquisition study. Upon his departure, the vice-president became DC's new CEO. Richardson was of two minds about the future of DC. Part of him is a strong believer that the culture of a company reflects the values of its chief executive. He found the new CEO's values more in line with those of GrandCo and felt that the GrandCo value system would work its way into DC under his leadership. Yet another part of him believes that culture is ingrained in people, ideas, and traditions. He felt that

DCers would hold on to their beliefs and traditions; they would resist becoming more like GrandCo.

The QWL results, some five years after the acquisition, continued to improve. Ratings of communication and participation were nearly back to preacquisition levels. Morale, in general, was high. Still, there were reported pressures to improve productivity, and DC veterans—those who had lived through the development of the old culture—were less satisfied than newcomers with the DC organizaiton. The QWL survey included questions relating to the new CEO. Some people reported that he would make the company more profitable and future-oriented. The majority, however, felt that the company would become less participative and people-oriented.

My interviews about the acquisition continued. This time they were introduced simply as part of the ongoing research. There were no provisions for any report or meeting on the results. In that sense, the study was going "underground," though without duplicity and with top management's assent. It was referred to as *my* research. Interviewees made no comments on the reasons behind Richardson's departure. My opinion was that this area was best left unaddressed. Richardson had explained the circumstances to me. Interviewees expressed a sense of loss and wished him the best.

Top managers also commented on the changing norms in their group. More and more of their deliberations were taking place prior to meetings and in private offices; as a group, they were not as involved in decisions. There was also less discussion of their management process and relationships. Several commented further that GrandCo seemed to have greater influence with the new CEO.

Nonetheless, there was also excitement among interviewees and a sense that DC was "moving again." New products were being introduced and profitability was on the rise. Bates was named head of the super division and was doing a great job. The mood was very upbeat, and the acquisition seemed like old history to many of them.

Nevertheless, I sensed division in the group and less commitment to DC's traditional values. What is more, I found that no clear set of values had supplanted them. I arrayed survey evidence to suggest that DCers lacked clear principles and a vision for the future. This summed up the QWL briefing, and a manager said that we were now "feeling an elephant." I then drew an elephant to illustrate my views. The elephant could sit on people or it could use its trunk to vitalize them; it could stand on its hind legs and lead or it could use its head, listen to people, and lead in that way; the elephant had to walk through tall grass to be profitable, but it also had to carry DCers on its back if the company was to be successful. Top managers liked the elephant symbol. They concluded the QWL briefing with a plan to hold an off-site meeting and articulate DC's values as they understood them.

Two months later the top managers sent to all DCers a copy of the new corporate vision. Participation, people orientation, and the like make up the first point. The rest cover customers, productivity, innovation, and other values that companies follow when searching for excellence.

Comments on the Decision to Stay

I am now back in my initial role at DC as an auditor of QWL and a consultant as to how to improve it. There is no longer a sharp distinction between that study and interviews about the acquisition and state of the DC culture. My action role, however, is limited to the QWL work. The acquisition study is now seen as my work and regarded as simply for scientific purposes. I no longer have any contract to prepare a history of the acquisition for DCers nor to meet with top managers on its implications. And they have no obligation to meet with me.

I am not fully satisfied with this role definition. Maybe I miss working with the "big shots" on important matters and contributing directly to their planning efforts in relating to GrandCo. Maybe I just miss having this part of my work, once our research and now my research, no longer so highly valued. I do feel strong ties to the DC work force and believe that the QWL work holds top managers accountable to them to manage the DC culture well. Therefore, I accept and live with my new role definition and contribute to maintaining the old DC values through my work on QWL.

I have gone underground in my study of the acquisition. It may also be that I have gone native and lost my personal integrity in continuing this research. I do find my values incongruent with the new CEO and resent that my findings on the continuing impact of the acquisition are no longer relevant to top management's learning. Clearly, I try to work them into my QWL briefings. The irony of this is that I am becoming more influential as an action researcher in DC. Every DCer got to see the picture of the elephant, and top management finally began to articulate their values as a step toward reculturation at DC.

I am now trying to learn from my experiences in this research. Other studies of acquisitions show that companies are often split following a sale and divide into camps more and less favorable to the acquirer (Nord, 1968). That helps me to understand what has happened at DC. I am also exploring the roots of my own identification with Richardson and Bates, my problems relating to the new CEO and his camp, and my strong connection to the values and myths in the old DC culture (Mirvis and Louis, 1985). This process helps me to understand what is happening to me. Finally, I am trying to come to peace with DC's efforts at reculturation. One collegue says that my action orientation is geared to the participative/interpersonal competence emphasis of the 1960s, while change in the 1980s is geared toward symbolic management and philosophies that espouse the search for excellence.

I retain power at DC and remain accountable to all of its members in my QWL work. I am a symbol of commitment to people through that work and have the power to tell my story of how the company is changing in "elephant" ways. I have less influence among top managers, but I still have a role to play in the organization. This means that I am less privy to some of the secrets at DC, but it also lets me continue to contribute to the QWL work and to continue my study of the acquisition and its impact on the organizational culture of DC.

The study of the acquisition is not over. My colleagues and I have begun to prepare papers on the research, and these are being reviewed by top management to ensure factuality and to protect the anonymity of the firm. Significantly, the new CEO sent these papers to his boss at GrandCo. How the boss will react to the data remains to be seen. Richardson has warned me that this could create problems. He also projects that my study may never end. Still, I plan to continue this research. I am trying to be less judgmental about and more open to changes in the DC culture, and I am trying to improve my action work. I am also trying to keep my own integrity while doing culture research. My judgment is that more good than harm will come from continuing. Of course, that judgment may be "damn near suicidal" as well.

12

THE DIFFICULTY OF FRAMING A PERSPECTIVE ON ORGANIZATIONAL CULTURE

Guy B. Adams
Virginia Hill Ingersoll
Evergreen State College

A man cannot really be grasped except on the basis of the gift of the spirit . . . which determines the person.

(Martin Buber)

The Sacred is surely related to the beautiful.

(Gregory Bateson)

Why not "aesthetics in science"? Whence comes the implication that to find aesthetics in science is like finding poetry in a timetable? The answer lies in the sad history of Western culture which, over the last two centuries, has so narrowed the concepts of both Science and Art as to leave them diminished and incommensurable rivals—the one an island in the sea of knowledge not certified as science; the other an island in the sea of skill not certified as art.

(Geoffrey Vickers)

The study of human activity in organizations carries with it a fascinating, if frustrating, difficulty. On one hand, studies of organizational symbolism and culture can reveal the richly textured fabric of meaning and attachment that persons associate with their work life. For the participants, the story of organizational life is one that arises from closely felt personal cares and concerns. On the other hand, students of organizational life often feel constrained to maintain a posture of distance and detachment from the object of their inquiry. The story of organizational research is a cool and dissociated account. The field of organizational studies is moving toward offering more true-to-life versions of organizational culture. As it does, we cannot help but take notice of the seeker who works to interpret those cultures, for the seeker's approaches to understanding and interpretation are inseparable from the picture he or she paints. Who are we and what do we do when we look at organizations? This chapter is an exploratory visit into this problematic territory.

What vision of a present or future world do we attempt to realize in organizational research? Our values, backgrounds, styles, and assumptions, whether explicitly stated or implicitly held, have a powerful impact on that vision and thereby on all that we do. Though this seems a truism, the changing nature of organizational research requires that we give it a closer look. This is what we aim to do in this chapter. Part of the chapter describes our own experiences with organizational research, the greater part of which was the product of an implicitly held vision. We also attempt to state explicitly what we have come to believe is valuable about the study of organizations. At the same time, the chapter is another piece of research representing a moment in a research dialectic—a dialectic that embodies the tension between ideals of organizational research and successive attempts to realize them.

IMPORTANT PREDISPOSITIONS

Sometime during the early seventies, *Psychology Today* published an interview with the accomplished ethologist, Nikko Tinbergen. The interview recounted some of Tinbergen's triumphs in discovering the secrets of the herring gull, as well as his own philosophy of research. In the interview he said something that one rarely hears from a researcher: that the way he first began to learn about herring gulls was to love them. Until he loved them, Tinbergen said, it wasn't possible for him to understand them.

Sentiment, attachment, and affection are words one rarely hears in the context of conducting social science research. Likewise, one seldom reads reports of hatred, passion, or anger in the work of those who study organizations. One does hear, occasionally, of the emotional highs and lows associated with the conduct of research—with research as a life's occupation—and one hears of the sometimes bitter competition among rivals in the research arena. But it is unusual to read about intense attachment to or care for the subjects of research. Indeed, one of the chief caveats for the social scientist has been to establish objectivity, to refrain from becoming involved, to maintain some sort of scientific distance from what one studies.

And yet, as anyone who has belonged to a work organization can attest, such organizations are full of meaning for those who participate in them. Organizations are center stage for the action in a drama that includes and evokes a wide range of emotions, dreams, and dark desires. The workplace isn't incidental to anyone who spends a third of his or her life there; it matters very much. It influences physical and mental health, it affects families, it determines where people live, and it provides key sources of a person's identity, sense of self-worth, and social need satisfaction.

To penetrate a situation in which people are so deeply engaged demands personal involvement. It is not possible to understand something of this importance by simply standing outside and looking in. This means, of course, that one will be subject to influence and bias, but that is a natural consequence of examining a human phenomenon. The social world is, after all, much like a storm of competing explanations, each awaiting acceptance by those who would act on it.

It is also true that research, like any human act, is projective. That is, every act is a projection of the person who originated it and in some measure constitutes the world for that person. Therefore, all of our actions reveal us and in so doing determine our future, for who we are depends on who we have been and what we have done. Moreover, any act we engage in projects a vision of the world in which we think we live, would like to live, or fear to live. Research, of course, is no more immune to this than any other human activity. Whether signing one's name, walking across the street, or ending an argument, we all do it in a unique way. Likewise, when we do organizational research, we can't avoid telling the world something about who we are and the kind of organizational life we would choose for ourselves.

Yet in a fundamental sense, our unique actions are shared with and mean something to those around us. Meaning—whether it be the meaning of life in the workplace or the meaning of our own research—is a social as well as an individual phenomenon.

Thus both the people in organizations and those who study them share a predisposition to care about their attachments and identifications, and to project these out into the world. These key predispositions, caring and projection, are social as well as individual phenomena.

AN OLD PROBLEM: A STARTING POINT

From the time of Heraclitus and Democritus, philosophers have puzzled over the problem of the "one and the many." Is "being" (i.e., all that exists) a single stream, a flowing, changing river, or is it many beings, many atomized entities? The metaphors evoked by this problem have infused not only philosophy but political theory, physical science, religion, and social science. Is society, for instance, a collection of individuals—much like marbles in a bag—who need to be protected from one another, or is the notion that there are individuals an illusion? Are what we call "individuals" simply manifestations of the real being—society? And, more specific to this book, are organizations aggregations of members' actions, or do members' actions transcend individual control and express the organization of which they are a part.

Though this is a very old problem, it represents an important metaphor for the study of meaning in work organizations. The very definition of "work organization" demands that one take a position on this problem. For instance, a researcher who implicitly believes that "being is one" will also believe that work organizations—one dimension of being—are more than simply collections of individuals. Likewise, a person with this belief will hold that meaning is not an idiosyncratic phenomenon (that is, something unique to each person who lives in an organization) but that it is somehow shared, perhaps even transcending individuals altogether. This in turn raises important questions: If it is shared, how broadly is it shared? Within a single work unit? Across organizational boundaries? Nationwide? Worldwide? On the other hand, if one believes that "being is many," then meaning, including meaning in the workplace, is idiosyncratic. If it is idiosyncratic, what can a social scientist—or anyone else, for that matter—say about it?

If we carry the metaphoric polarity of the one and the many further and look at the question of meaning in the workplace, it appears that the organizational researcher who exemplifies being-as-many would function as a reporter, making known the subjective experiences of individual people who work in organizations. In this case, the outcome of research would be reports of organizational incidents as seen and felt by particular individuals. Social phenomenologists and ethnomethodologists in particular, do this sort of work. In the strictest sense, they take the position that whether being is one or many is ultimately unknowable, that only particular incidents or occurrences are really knowable, and then only by those who experience them.

Conversely, researchers who manifest the being-as-one approach begin with the assumption that there are some universal laws, patterns, or commonalities that cut across all organizations, and that if a researcher samples organizations appropriately, seeks out the right variables, and collects observations carefully, he or she will ultimately uncover the generalities that make all organizations manifestations of some underlying, singular reality.

An interesting contradiction emerges when one stands back from either of these poles and examines the stance that they represent for research. One discovers that the phenomenologist's form of observation is to see the subject of interest—the research being—as one. The phenomenologist tries to keep intact the fabric of the experiencing subject in a situ and yet to describe it in detail. In so doing, the phenomenologist yields research that depicts a piecemeal, largely unknowable universe, in the sense that one can only know that with which one had had immediate experience, something which the human condition sorely limits. On the other hand, the inductive researcher, in seeking meaningful generalizations about the organization as a whole, breaks down the phenomenon in the process of gathering observations, thus construing the organizational being as many. This approach is meant to yield generalizations about the underlying, shared reality of all organizations.

Our own research is predisposed toward the being-as-one pole. While our focus is on the organization, we see the individual, the organization, and other phenomenon in the world as reflective of the essential unity of life. This unity manifests itself—albeit imperfectly—in a variety of ways and settings. But the meaning of this unity, inchoate as it may be, is the centerpiece of our concern.

ADDITIONAL COMPLICATIONS: THE NATURE OF MEANING

The study of meaning is a figurative slough of despond into which many scholars have journeyed, never to be heard from again. To uncover the meaning of "meaning" is a task that has stymied philosophers, linguists, psychologists, and critics alike. To some, meaning is a purely subjective phenomenon; to others, such as Osgood et al. (1957), it is a function of some concept's location in an n-dimensional semantic space. Some people equate meaning with relative importance or significance, while for others it is a transcendent quality that imbues certain particular entities with a reality that they cannot possess on their own.

What, then, might an organizational researcher study in approaching the phenomenon called the "meaning of worklife" (Smircich, 1983a)? There are several possibilities, each offering opportunities and drawbacks. First, one might adopt a phenomenological approach and describe one's own work life experience or help others in the workplace to describe their personal experiences. Such popular works as Studs

Terkel's *Working* (1974) and Robert Schrank's *Ten Thousand Working Days* (1978) attest to the interesting and useful outcomes of this approach. However, this approach possesses an important drawback: As our discussion above indicates, this work is by its very nature a treatment of the idiosyncratic. Whatever generalizations it yields appear only as the kind of loose, "me too" remarks evoked when one recognizes some of one's own experiences in such accounts.

While it is important to recognize the convergence of one's experiences with those of others, the meaning of work life is more than this. Such an approach enables the researcher to say a lot about individual experiences but not much about organizations, for the latter are not simple aggregations of experience but rather devices that structure experience. On the face of it, many organizations have elements in common, suggesting that there is some systematic ordering of experience that issues from membership in a work organization. Wholehearted focus on the individual and the idiosyncratic cannot uncover this; thus the problem becomes one of addressing the appropriate unit of analysis.

As a second approach, one might study those elements that are held in common—the shared anchors for meaning that are the focus of much research in organizational culture: language, stories, myths, visual and other symbols, and images. To study these is to study a system's map for meaning, the internal raw materials that serve as reference points for any person's interpretation of organizational life. These are valuable in that they are characterizations of organizations; thus they augment any study of personal experience in an important way. However, unless one posits some kind of organizational archetype system (e.g., Mitroff, 1983a), there is no reason to believe that there is any relationship between the symbol systems of one organization and those of another. To learn about one system, or even several such systems sequentially, does not necessarily provide knowledge about organizations in general.

Third, researchers might examine the foundations and sources of meaning in the workplace. To do so means to look outside of individual organizations and into the larger system in which they are embedded— into the encompassing culture and subcultures that give rise to organizations and their members. The advantage of this approach is that it can yield the raw material of organizational symbolizing across a large portion of a national culture; therefore, its outcomes should provide insight into any work organization within that culture. A disadvantage is that it addresses the question of meaning for an individual person in only an oblique way. Hence it must be seen as an adjunct to the other two approaches. This is the route that we have chosen. How we came to make that choice is our next topic.

A PHENOMENOLOGY OF
STALKING THE MANAGERIAL METAMYTH

One belief that many researchers use as an implicit criterion in assessing their colleagues' work is this: Researchers choose a method on purely rational grounds based on its suitability for the research subject. In fact, we all develop rationales, almost always reconstructive, for the methods we use, and chapters such as these constitute such rationalizing. But researchers' choices of methods are more complicated than this. Their choices are conditioned by factors such as their habits of mind, their facility with certain methods, the acceptance of those methods by the scholarly community, and the ease with which their use can be explained, to say nothing about present resources and researchers' own courage. Sometimes the methods used yield useful, interesting insight and understanding; sometimes they yield tedious exercises in ersatz researching. But as Kuhn (1970) and many others have made clear, the paths to knowledge are by no means equivalent to pristine searches for truth, wherever that may lead, and often peculiarities of circumstance are as responsible for the form that research takes as any reconstructive rationale provided by the researcher.

Peculiarities of Circumstance

A discussion of our research should include a description of how we came to use the approach that we did. We came to our work from quite different backgrounds. One of us was trained in public administration, with emphasis on a phenomenological perspective; the other was trained in communications and organizational psychology, with a strong orientation toward empirical methodologies. Still, we are more alike than different. Early on in our careers, both of us chose to put teaching before research. Because we were both attracted to a situation that would enable educational experimentation, we joined a four-year college deeply committed to interdisciplinary, nontraditional teaching but only modestly supportive of faculty research. Both of us have long been fascinated with work organizations. Though we have not spent the bulk of our time researching them, we have each experienced several organizations and have worked as academic administrators. In addition, we both spend a substantial amount of our energies thinking and teaching about work life. Both of us have questioned the extent to which most organizational research says much of value to us or to our students, who work in both public and private organizations. Thus we have had to improvise using unconventional sources and resources to provide useful classroom material for our students.

Our teaching has served as the gestation for our research. We needed to find some form of organizational research that could be done on a very small budget, without research assistants and in the few hours per week that we had available. We knew that without special support, firsthand research in an organization outside the one in which we worked would be difficult. However, our teaching experience provided us with one vehicle, because we both emphasize the social and cultural context of management as a part of our regular curriculum. We noticed in our recollection of the material we had read with our students that there were some fairly consistent ideological trends in modern management literature. Looking further, we became aware that these trends extended beyond the academic literature into publications intended for working managers, and into the literature and mass media offerings used by the public at large.

The Managerial Metamyth

What we saw and later documented (Adams and Ingersoll, 1983) was an extraorganizational manifestation of what other scholars have observed in modern work organizations (for example, see Weber, 1968; Mouzelis, 1967; Weick, 1983)—namely, a repeated bias toward rational-technical values. We labeled the configuration of beliefs informed by these values the "managerial metamyth" (the prefix *meta* in this case meaning "to stand behind"). The metamyth is characterized by three tenets: (1) Eventually, all work processes can and should be rationalized—that is, broken into their constituent parts—and so thoroughly understood that they can be completely controlled. (2) The means for attaining organizational objectives or ends deserve maximum attention, with the result that the ends quickly become subordinated to those means even to the extent that the ends become lost or forgotten. (3) Efficiency and predictability are more important than any other considerations in the conduct of worklife.

We proposed further that the metamyth was a kind of deep structure to the managerial belief system, and that the surface beliefs or myths that managers and others in the workplace held would largely map onto this metamyth. That is, the metamyth underlies many of the official, espoused beliefs that people have about work and work organizations. We gave examples of the metamyth's presence in the literature generated by three levels of culture: the academic subculture, comprising those who teach, study, and consult from an academic vantage point; the managerial subculture, constituted by those who actually manage work organizations; and the macroculture, embracing our national culture. We also noted that the metamyth was antithetical to such qualities as spirituality, mystery, and the numinous—qualities one finds in the myth systems of earlier cultures.

Later we explored in more detail the presence of the metamyth in the larger culture (Ingersoll and Adams, 1983). Specifically, we examined American mass market children's literature, aimed at children under the age of six, that had been published before 1965 (so it would be part of the heritage of today's managers and work force) and was still in print (indicating in a rough way that it had sold well and, therefore, had reached a large audience). A thematic analysis of thirty stories that met these selection criteria revealed an orientation toward work life that could have been dictated by many management textbooks and that was fully consistent with the metamyth. Briefly, the stories emphasized the importance of their characters' fitting into the social system, the importance of submerging the unpredictable dimensions of one's personality, and an orientation to problem solving that portrayed problems not as complex and messy but as easily solved by strong individual effort or by some authority figure. Work life was depicted as a series of invariant routines performed on rationalized tasks.

The experience of preparing these two papers did much to clarify our assumptions and values about organizational research. Organizations seem an imperfect manifestation of the essential unity of being-as-one. Indeed, our own research seems an imperfect manifestation of this essential unity, but the experience better enables us to characterize our underlying ideal.

The aim of our research is to bring into the open some aspect of organizational life that presently lies concealed. In one sense, this is the underlying aim of all research—to bring some concealed or unnoticed aspect of being into appearance. Social science and management research have had their own particular way of bringing forth concealed phenomena—a way informed by the same rational-technical value system that informs the managerial metamyth. This way usually involves a challenging posture toward such phenomena:

> When man, investigating, observing, pursues nature as an area of his own conceiving, he has already been claimed by a way of revealing that challenges him to approach nature as an object of research [Heidegger, 1977: 300].

The danger lies in construing this particular way of opening hidden aspects of phenomena as the sole or best way to do so.

The rational-technical approach tends to bring forth hidden aspects of phenomena in order to predict and control various other processes and phenomena in nature. We would like to see research pursue another way of revealing concealed aspects of phenomena, that is, bringing forth the essential unity of life. This approach has both a critical and a constructive aspect. Our caring and concern for ourselves and for the organizations we live in and study leads us to be critical of part of what we see, but we are also to look for the aesthetic, ever-more positive manifestations of the essential unity of life. It is a life's work; indeed, it is perhaps the fundamental work of our species.

SEEKING AS AESTHETIC

We like to think of what we do as something aesthetic, as an art form. Research as art is an informative metaphor for several reasons. First, both are acts of self-expression. Art, of course, is created not to perform some task but to reveal the artist and, in so doing, to reveal a unique perspective on the world. As indicated earlier, organizational research cannot avoid being an expression and projection of researchers—of their experience and their unique identities. Second, the stance that an artist takes toward his or her subject is one of intense involvement—in some cases of communion, a level of care that we advocated earlier for researchers. The artist does not stand back from a subject, objectifying it. Rather, he or she tries to penetrate it and so transform it in the process of expressing it, even if the subject is something quite abstract. Third, the artist's intense relationship to a subject often yields a series of creations provoked by that relationship. It is not unusual to see a visual artist do a series of paintings or sculptures on a particular subject. We know a painter, for instance, who made a dozen or so paintings of the sky to capture the unique qualities of light near Puget Sound. We also know a sculptor who made a series of perhaps twenty magic wands, depicting in a fascinating way the everyday objects that people use to transform their actions into something other than what they appear. Likewise, we see many researchers who look at some phenomenon from many points of view, exhaust it for themselves, and move on to something else. Once they have exhausted themselves with one aspect of being, they move on—not to the next scientific task, but to the next aspect that they find interesting.

Apropos to this last point, Bateson, in *Mind and Nature* (1979), develops a thesis that ties the researcher to the artist even more closely. Bateson proposes that nature itself in its evolutionary process is a form of mentation and that the human mind, as part of the natural world, acts very much like evolution. That is, both rely on the presence of random or unpredictable events that make certain actions more beneficial to a system than others and that therefore result in those actions being taken. These courses of action represent natural selection and favor the development of new species in nature and/or new directions in human thought. This new milestone, be it in the course of biological evolution or in the evolution of thought, is then "unpacked" or elaborated until it can no longer account for a new set of random events, such as an ice age for certain living organisms or an anomalous "fact" in the world of knowing. Once again, a new species or a new paradigm standing in the wings is pressed into action, which in turn runs its course.

What is especially interesting in Bateson's work is that he does not simply make an analogy between knowing and the workings of nature. Instead, he asserts the necessity of an underlying pattern that is common to the process of each. Whether the pattern he proposes is the best depiction of what actually occurs is a matter to be judged against the evidence he offers—and he offers quite a lot of it. That formal similarities exist is a fundamental assumption on his part—something very difficult to disprove and not unique to Bateson (see Jung, 1958; Mitroff, 1983a; Levi-Strauss, 1964) but very tantalizing to anyone who holds that being is one rather than many.

If Bateson's "pattern of patterns" is a close depiction of the processes of both mind and nature, one would expect both the work of an artist and of science to follow it. Kuhn (1970) suggests that science does proceed according to this pattern (indeed, Bateson uses Kuhn as a wellspring for part of his argument). It also appears that the work of artists might follow the pattern of "new concept-unfolding-new concept." Our conversations with several artists suggest that some unpredictable (random) event often leads an artist's attention from one preoccupying image or idea to another.

An aesthetic posture on the part of the seeker offers an appealing consistency with Bateson's notion of a pattern of patterns. Moreover, an aesthetic approach embodies the predispositions of care and projection as it seeks to express the meaning of a subject. Assumptions concerning the one and the many are made in the aesthetic dimension as well. The essential unity of life is an elusive ideal but one that finds meaningful expression aesthetically.

CONCLUSION

In this chapter we have characterized how we work. We discussed the predisposition of care or communion with a subject; the process of projection, of the philosophical question of one and many; and the metaphor of the artist. We believe that this approach is fully appropriate for work in a field that is trying to find a way of expressing hidden aspects of meaning and organization. The chief thrust of our work is twofold: First, it embraces the idea that culture is one and that work organizations as symbolic entities reflect that culture in a thoroughgoing way. Second, it affirms what many others are saying as they try to interpret, rather than objectify, the meaning of life in work organizations—namely, that work organizations are dynamic artifacts of human activity and interaction. As artifacts, they are best known through acts of respectful appreciation.

This chapter has been crafted with care and offered as a gift to strangers. In it, we have explored the difficulty of seeking—seeking to represent organizational culture and the meaning of life in the workplace. The problem of accounting for the seeker with the same richness and importance with which we characterize the meaning of work life is largely unexplored territory. Our experiences and suggestions are not a map, but they may help other seekers through this territory. We join Vickers (1978) in asking: Why not aesthetics in science?

13

IS ETHICS THE ISSUE?

Michael Owen Jones

University of California, Los Angeles

"I contend that it is no business of the folklorist to engage in social reform," insists Richard M. Dorson, "that he is unequipped to reshape institutions, and that he will become the poorer scholar and folklorist if he turns activist." Dorson published his remarks twelve years ago at the end of a special issue of the *Folklore Forum* journal entitled *Papers on Applied Folklore* (1971). Among the several articles about improving educational systems, health care, housing, and urban planning through a study of tradition, only Dorson's essay challenged action research. "We cannot afford much diversion from our primary responsibilities as scholars to seek and record the truth about man and his ways," he continues. Beyond being an educator, he concludes, "I hesitate to give advice on how to make the world better, or happier, or freer, through folklore" (Dorson, 1971: 40-42).

Many folklorists today agree with Dorson. We should confine ourselves to pure research, they insist, because we lack the skills to apply inferences and hypotheses to solving practical problems. Scholarship will suffer neglect if we divert our energies to mounting interventionist programs, and the true mission of folkloristics is not that of changing conditions but of understanding behavior. Others contend that action research raises the specter of manipulation and exploitation, and for this reason they either challenge the concept of applied folkloristics generally or denounce specific programs of application, such as consulting with management to bring about changes in an organization. Some even question the techniques and procedures entailed in field studies, whether the research is pure or applied, insisting that the use of interviewing, tape-recording, participation observation, and so on is fraught with ethical problems of such magnitude as to cast doubt on the desirability of conducting fieldwork at all.

I disagree with Dorson and others about our mission and how to carry it out. It is my contention that through their studies of organizational symbolism and corporate culture, folklorists and others can enhance our understanding of human behavior. By recommending or implementing a plan of social management, they can also enrich organizational life. I believe that action research is not inimical to pure research, as Dorson suggests, nor is interventionism inherently unethical, as others insist. Rather it seems to me that many of the "ethical" problems arising in field studies are less a matter of ethics than they are a function of the human element in fieldwork. Their solution requires realizing that the word "results" embraces not only tangible effects and impersonal products but also outcomes that are intangible or intensely personal.

If there is a threat to human dignity and the general welfare, it is not in undertaking action research, consulting with organizations, or observing people's behavior firsthand; rather, it is the tyranny of methods. Too many researchers, managers, and administrators depend on a priori models and assumptions, thus failing to engage in genuine inquiry or to seek simplistic solutions to complex problems. The moral imperative, therefore, is not to challenge applied folkloristics or to ferret out examples of questionable conduct in fieldwork, but rather to assess and reevaluate the methods and assumptions on which both research and interventionist strategies are based.

Why object to action research? Should we intervene in organizational life? What can applied folkloristics accomplish? Why has field research sometimes raised questions about ethics? How can we avoid the tyranny of methods? Is ethics really the issue? These concerns are discussed below.

APPLIED FOLKLORISTICS: CONCEPTS AND CHALLENGES

Folklore and Action Research

Interventionism is not a new topic in folklore studies. In 1899, the English folklorist Edwin Sidney Hartland published an article entitled "Folklore: What Is It and What Is the Good of It?" Like others of the period, and in contrast to most modern folklorists, he viewed folklore as a survival of culture found among peasants and savages whom he called "the folk." He insisted that a study of folklore, therefore, could help in reconstructing the past, serving as a key to understanding the mental growth of mankind and revolutionizing conceptions of human history. For folklore is, he wrote, "the science of Tradition" which is concerned with "the mental and spiritual side of humanity."

The traditions of savages and peasants were ways of thinking and behaving out of which the upper classes of his day had slowly evolved. Hartland urged civil and military officials, as well as missionaries, to document the folklore of those dwelling in colonial possessions. He quotes a former governor of British Guinea: "It has been felt that no man, or body of men, can rule justly and wisely a people with whose customs, usages, and inner life they are unacquainted." Anticipating readers' objections that they are not colonial administrators, he asks what other practical value the study of folklore has: "Well, what I have been saying about Government officials and missionaries applies . . . to everybody who has to do . . . with the peasantry and the uneducated classes of our own countrymen. The more perfect your interest in and your sympathy with them," contends Hartland, "the more completely you can identify yourselves with their modes of thought, the greater your influence for good upon them" (Hartland, 1899/1981: 231, 247).

Some date the beginning of folklore studies to at least a century before Hartland published his notions of folklore and a justification of its study. One William Thoms coined the Anglo-Saxon compound "folk-lore" half a century before, in 1846; he intended it to replace "popular antiquities," which had been in vogue for the preceding fifty years. Other designations include "oral traditions" (used as early as 1777), the French *traditions populaires,* and the German *Volkskunde* (literally the "goods of the folk," coined in 1803). In 1909, a decade after Hartland considered what folklore is and why it should be documented, Sven Lampa at the University of Lund lectured on *folkliv,* the Swedish equivalent of the German *Volksleben* and the forerunner of "folklife," which was championed in the United States by Yoder, among others (Yoder, 1963, 1976; Dorson, 1972).

To distinguish the subject matter of folklore from its documentation and analysis, "folkloristics" began to be used in the mid 1960s (Dundes, 1965, 1966). By the early 1970s, "applied folklore" had found currency; however, the term "applied folkloristics" seems more appropriate, suggesting the application of general scientific principles to the solving of particular practical problems (Jones, 1981). In some instances, of course, applications of inferences and hypotheses might also entail precipitating or perpetuating certain kinds of expressive behavior and thus truly be "applied folklore."

Whether they refer to their field as folklore and mythology studies, folklife research, or folkloristics, most folklorists today would probably accept the definition of folklore given by Georges (1983). According to him, folklore consists of those communicative processes (e.g., narrating, singing, playing, dancing, and music making) and expressive forms (proverbs, rituals, customs, argot, games, objects, festive events, and so on) "which seem, because of the similarities they exhibit, to be frequently imitated or emulated, repeated or reproduced, modified or transformed" (1983: 134). Thus they can "be viewed as traditional phenomena or simply as traditions; and they are worthy of documentation and study because they constitute evidence of continuities or consistencies in human thought or behavior through time or space respectively." Moreover, folklorists today are likely to agree with Georges that "the traditional communicative processes and forms which folklorists focus upon" are not survivals from the past or found among culturally or geographically isolated populations, but rather are "an integral part of human social existence," playing fundamental roles in the lives of all human beings.

Regardless of how they refer to or define their field of study, many folklorists bristle at the mention of applied folkloristics and interventionism. Their reasons for objecting to the notion of social engineering are not difficult to discern. Five come to mind immediately.

Limited Resources

One reason for Dorson's insistence on pure research and teaching, and for his contention that applied research will detract from scholarly objectives, is probably the fact that even today folklorists is not well established in academia. The University of California at Los Angeles, the University of Pennsylvania, the University of Texas, and Indiana University alone offer a Ph.D. as well as an M.A. degree in the field, while the University of California at Berkeley, the University of North Carolina at Chapel Hill, and Western Kentucky University all have M.A. programs. A few other institutions permit concentrations in folklore within various departments on both the undergraduate and graduate levels (Baker, 1978).

Dorson, who headed the program at Indiana University from 1957 until his death in 1981, championed folkloristics in academia (Dorson, 1950b) and even defended it to Congress (Dorson, 1962). In chronicling and praising the work of the nineteenth-century British folklorists, of whom Hartland was one, Dorson lamented that the "great team" lacked academic connections, for this fact impeded the development of folklore studies as a scientific field until the midtwentieth century (Dorson,

1968). To be preoccupied with applied folkloristics, then, would have meant to Dorson that the teaching of folklore studies would suffer. Also, for him and others the study of traditions needs no justification; it can be defended, however, because of the understanding of human behavior that ensues rather than because the field is or must be "practical."

Nationalism

A second reason for Dorson's loyalty to research concerns politics. For all the importance given to the pure research of folklore in understanding history, culture, or the psyche, the fact remains that in the past much of the documentation of traditions was inspired by nationalism and/or put to the use of colonialism and political control—the other side of the coin shown us by Hartland 85 years ago. The 1960s and 1970s witnessed the publication of a spate of books and articles warning against the use and abuse of folklore, holding up as examples Nazi Germany's exploitation of the Aryan myth, Soviet Russia's glorification of its power elite as heroes, and Red China's indoctrination of children in its government's philosophy through folk songs, dance, and puppetry (see Bazgöz, 1972; Eminov, 1975; Haque, 1975; Klymasz, 1975; Mieder, 1982; Oinas, 1975; Ortutay, 1955; Snyder, 1951; Wang, 1935; Wilson, 1976; Yen, 1964; Zemljanova, 1964). Conscious of the political abuse of folklore and the perversion of the study, several generations of folklorists can perhaps be forgiven for questioning the propriety of using folklore or applying inferences from the study of traditions.

Commercialism

A third reason for challenging folkloristic endeavors outside of academia is that folklore has been exploited for commercial as well as political purposes. In condemning this practice, Dorson (1950a) coined the term "fakelore" to designate the fabrication of stories, songs, and other "traditions" for financial gain, whether in the form of advertising, popular "treasuries" of folklore, television hootenannies, or community boosterism (Dorson, 1956, 1978; Greenway, 1968; Stekert, 1966; Bausinger, 1969). In 1971, Denby came up with "folklure" to refer to the appeal of folklore in the mass media, especially advertising. Others, too, have written about the use (or abuse) of folklore in advertising (e.g., Falassi and Kligman, 1976; Sullenberger, 1974; Mieder and Mieder,

1977); the creation of "protofestivals" or "ethnic display events" (e.g., Gutowski, 1978; Ivey, 1977; Moe, 1977; Danielson, 1972); mail order magic (Snow, 1979); and commercialism in folk religion (Teske, 1977).

Populist Sentiments

A fourth reason for objecting to some forms of interventionism, especially those involving organizational development, grows out of an implicit mandate in such fields of study as folkloristics and anthropology for researchers to be champions of the common man (Freilich, 1970). Folklorists spend much time interacting with people while doing fieldwork that requires qualitative methods. They get to know individuals, often sharing in community and family activities, and sometimes identifying with the subjects of study (Georges and Jones, 1980). In addition, folklorists document and analyze behavior in everyday life rather than the great monuments created by a few geniuses. They are justly proud of their role in bringing accolades to unheralded bards (Georges and Jones, 1980: 151-152), of challenging the elitism that once pervaded the arts and distorted the study of history (Jones, 1975; Bronner, 1982), and of finding in the daily activities of every person the key to humanity that unlocks our understanding of the species (Georges, 1983; Jones, 1980a, 1982b). Combined with a heightened awareness of the potential for manipulation and exploitation of symbolic behavior for political and commercial ends, this appreciation of human achievement has made many wary of programs intended to alter the way people interact, communicate, think, and do things.

The Power of Symbols and Expressive Behavior

The fifth reason for questioning folklore's use and challenging action research and interventionism is the fact that it can dramatically affect beliefs and behavior in organizational life and at work. "Employees need to be wary of the potentially powerful impact that a seemingly innocuous story can have," write Martin and Powers (1982: 103-104): "Management, indeed anyone, could use the power of a story to manipulate beliefs about a policy and generate commitment to an organization when the information is, in fact, corporate propaganda. As this caveat indicates, symbolic forms of management, such as the telling of organization stories, are powerful and potentially dangerous tools."

As far as the manipulation of attitudes and values in an organization is concerned, it must be realized that there is never an isolated story, metaphor, or ritual; rather, the bulk of our behavior is expressive and symbolic. Many stories are told about people and events, the interpretation of which depends on the specific situation. A variety of traditional speech forms are used to characterize feelings and conceptions of oneself and others, and most activities are customary and ritualistic. The creation and dissemination of a heroic narrative, or the staging of a banquet honoring achievement, is not going to convince organizational participants (although a visitor might be impressed) that a company has their best interests in mind if other events and activities in the organization contradict this message.

To summarize, objections to applied folkloristics grow out of several concerns: that action research efforts will detract from pure research and the teaching of folklore studies in a field that is still not well established in academia (despite having existed for two centuries and made important discoveries about history, culture, and behavior); an acknowledgment of the political abuses of folklore, whether for nationalistic ends or by totalitarian regimes; an awareness of the exploitation of folklore for commercial gain; populist sentiments arising from field studies of the common man rather than a concern for great literature and the fine arts; and the realization that expressive, symbolic behavior is powerful, serving as a form of communication and affecting attitudes in a way that other sources of information do not.

Detractors of applied folkloristics should be reminded, however, that the situation is complex and not at all one-sided. Without the many reports of traditional behavior in the nineteenth century prepared by missionaries, colonial administrators, and civil servants, the armchair scholars would have had little about which to theorize. A number of leading folklorists in the United States and abroad have been performers or writers who documented traditions initially in order to add material to their repertoires. Some of the most respected scholars in the country today were inspired by and participated in the folksong revival of the 1960s (Reuss and Lund, 1975). They made records incorporating traditional materials from informants into their performances, formed companies to produce records of singers and storytellers, and became promoters of folk festivals or purveyors of folksong collections (Legman, 1962; Seeger, 1962). In addition, for the past fifteen years, scores of folklorists in the United States and Canada have been employed by government to promote local and ethnic festivals, celebrations, and exhibits (Carpenter, 1975; Carey, 1976; Camp, 1977). Their jobs have entailed applied folklore in the true sense of the word, but not without controversy (Carpenter, 1975, 1978; Henderson, 1973; Degh, 1977-1978; Chinn, 1983). When conducting field studies to document and analyze traditions, many researchers are motivated by a desire to satisfy requirements of their jobs or aspirations of advancement rather than by scientific inquiry (Georges and Jones, 1980: 1, 3, 23, 41-42, 135). In this regard, or when they publish textbooks appealing to a large market or articles in popular magazines, they can be considered to be using folklore for personal gain.

IS ETHICS THE ISSUE?

Given the five objections to action research discussed above, is ethics the issue? Ethics has nothing to do with a preference for pure research, nor is it inherent in populist sentiments. Commercializing folklore, whether by publishing popular articles or by incorporating traditional materials into one's own performance is no more unethical than encouraging ethnic pride in traditions, a phenomenon common to many nationalistic movements. Introducing rites of passage marking accomplishments and changes of staus in an organization, or telling stories at orientations to communicate the organization's philosophy and objectives, is not inherently unethical, either. What, then, is behind the concern about ethics? For that matter, what is ethics? Further, what constitutes unethical behavior, and why?

Several threads run through the objections to applied folkloristics—manipulation of behavior, utilization, and alteration. Manipulation is not necessarily reprehensible. Experimentation in science sometimes requires orchestrating events, setting up situations, and in other ways getting people to do something they might not otherwise do. The same might be said of childrearing practices. "Exploitation" is defensibly charged, not when something is used, but when the utilization is unfair. Alteration is amoral; it is immoral only when something cherished is lost.

What emerges, then, is a possible definition of "unethical conduct." It is not manipulation, utilization, or alteration. Rather, it is an act that results in someone else being embarrassed, harmed, or deprived. Manipulation is unethical when an individual is not informed immediately afterward of the nature and rationale of an experiment and therefore suffers embarrassment later. It is also unethical when an experiment harms a person participating in it, or when participation is forced. Change is reprehensible when it disregards the value of what preceded and when it becomes a value—an alleged good—for its own sake, without consideration of the consequences. Dictionary definitions of ethics refer to moral principles, precepts, or rules of conduct which in turn are defined in part by reference to "right conduct," the rightness or wrongness of actions, and the goodness or badness of motives and the ends of actions. What makes conduct "wrong," and therefore unethical, is that someone suffers embarrassment, harm, or deprivation because of another's actions. Similarly, what makes motives "bad" is the presence of an intent to cause embarrassment, harm, or deprivation.

USING SYMBOLIC BEHAVIOR

These points notwithstanding, the mere mention of studying organizational folklore for the purpose of improving work life, management, and corporate leadership is enough to raise the eyebrows of many folklorists and to invoke the ire of some. In 1981, for example, I chaired and gave a paper in a session of the California Folklore Society meeting devoted to "Folkloristics & Business/Industry/Government: Confronting the 80s Together?" Most of the discussion time was given over to defending the notion of applied folkloristics (which was under vociferous attack by several people) rather than defining areas of mutual concern.

In 1983 I was principal director of the conference, "Myth, Symbols and Folklore: Expanding the Analysis of Folklore," which brought together for the first time folklorists, organization behavioralists in schools of management, and representatives of corporations. Among some of the individuals invited to participate were leading specialists in occupational folklife, one of whom flatly refused. "I find it incredible and somewhat cynical that you were not sensitive to this aspect of the situation," he wrote, referring to our emphasis on improving managerial effectiveness. Because unions were not involved, and because of a focus on white-collar rather than blue-collar traditions, he had inferred that the intent of the conference was to suggest how management could increase productivity. As the program developed, however, none of the 23 presentations and half a dozen workshops had the exploitation of labor as its goal.

Initially, some of the individuals in attendance assumed that an interventionist perspective was part of the normative culture of management and were critical of this appeal. Sensing these feelings, Barbara Kirshenblatt-Gimblett remarked at the final session of the three-day conference that she too had "wondered about the possibility of co-opting or appropriating and then controlling the expressive life of workers. I worried about issues of ethics and issues of responsibilities." She also observed, however, that a lot of folklorists, when they intervene at all, do so not to foster change but preservation. . . . Folklorists are more likely to be preservationists, attempting to stabilize an endangered species, than they are to be fostering change to make things work better." She continued: "As a folklorist, as someone who studies expressive behavior, I'm really very noninterventionist in my behavior." But she has also served nonprofit organizations, she said, and puzzled about how to remedy the mismanagement rife in some of them. And she admitted that as an administrator—the head of performance studies at New York University—she has created folklore to improve the organization. "When I began to chair the department, I instituted the "Seventh Annual" Winter Solstice Party. That was the first time it had been held," she joked. Nevertheless, "it has now become the tradition that it is every year the *Seventh* Annual Winter Solstice Party."

I too have used traditions both at home and in the workplace to intervene in situations that I felt needed changing. We all do. Being reflective and introspective, we realize through our native intelligence that storytelling involves listener and teller alike and therefore has the potential to illustrate principles and persuade others of a point of view that print alone or simple discourse lacks. Likewise, proverbs encapsulate the wisdom of many, ritualistic activities hold great symbolic meaning and significance, and festive events are joyful occasions with the power of generating a sense of community.

Without turning this article into an exercise in confessional journalism, I would note that as vice-chairman of the Folklore and Mythology Program at UCLA, and as acting chairman recently, I was aware that the ambience of our organization was not what many desired, for a multiplicity of reasons. The situation was not unusual or extreme; any organization's performance, like that of any of the individuals within it, sometimes may be lackluster. People can become inured to conditions, their sense jaded and sensitivity diminished. As specialists in the study of traditions, we are aware that the species can be called not only *homo sapiens* (man, the wise) but also *homo narrans* (man, the storyteller), *homo festivus* (man, the celebrator), *homo faber* (man, the creator), and *homo ludens* (man, the player) (Jones et al., 1983). However, in pursuing our professional goals, we often seem unable to do anything about the fact that we are denying some of our humanity in our everyday lives.

Among other things, some of the faculty and students were taking for granted the development of skills and the successful completion of degree requirements, so that passing foreign language exams, the M.A. comprehensive, or the Ph.D. qualifying exam was not celebrated by the organization as a whole. Analyzing the situation, it seems that public approbation and rites of passage were needed to provide closure to events in the continuum of human existence and to acknowledge accomplishments. For a while we did not have organizationwide celebrations; indeed, we had no parties. Our fall orientation for entering and continuing students was devoted to brief introductions and a review of facilities and policy. We interacted as the occasion dictated, offering little more of ourselves. Over time, our ritualistic behavior had become increasingly negative, as had the themes in our narratives and the metaphors we used to characterize ourselves and our relationships with others. Now, however, the ambience was different—not because of some large-scale social system change, but because several organizational participants made a concerted effort to institute appropriate celebrations, rites of passage, and rituals honoring achievement among other forms of traditional behavior. The *feeling* of the workplace had changed. More doors were left open, welcoming others inside the offices, and Pride in the appearance of the suite had become more important; even the seminar room was freshly painted and the walls adorned with portraits of some of the major figures in the history of folklore and mythology studies.

These changes were brought about by several of us acting in concert and in response to a felt need; we analyzed expressive behavior (both positive and negative, noting both what was present and what was absent) and consciously implemented a program of social engineering based on our folkloristic research, thus initiating or perpetuating certain forms of expressive behavior. Coincidentally, but perhaps meaningfully, the changes were wrought by some of us who later participated in the conference on organizational folklore. This conference was intended to sensitize both scholars and managers to fundamental human needs and ways of fulfilling them.

APPLIED FOLKLORISTICS AT WORK

"I'm just really excited about the conference," said Dan L. Smith, manager of Human Resources Development at Southern California Edison. "From my perspective as part academician, part consultant, and mostly corporate manager, this is the weirdest conference that I've ever been at," he joked. "But also one of the ones that left me more enthusiastic and excited about possibilities than before." Smith was speaking at the same panel as Barbara Kirshenblatt-Gimblett, that of "Expanding the Analysis of Organizations, with Applications for Corporate Leadership." He summed up the event by telling about events at Southern California Edison that, as a result of his having attended the conference, he had come to understand and appreciate in a different light.

Most of these narratives addressed motivation to excel, commitment to quality, and concern about safety. Some were humorous, others frightening, and some inspirational. Concluding one story, Smith asked, "Do you feel this in me? That pride. And you might have the same feeling." In regard to this account, Smith added, "What strikes me is the deeper appreciation of what that kind of story means in the larger perspective of things." Later he said, "I'm sharing with you a rich lore of stories that I'm coming to appreciate as stories that tell us about our company. . . . I'm very, very excited about the possibilities of the whole thing"—that is, studying organizational folklore. He then mentioned several applications. Among them were new employee orientation, management development (leadership and decision making), and executive assessment. "Now we have a way," said Smith, "to get at the kinds of cultures that have been created and that can be created—a powerful application."

Diagnostic

Smith's questions about what has been and can be created lead us to the more general concern of what applied folkloristics can accomplish in organizational settings. Why study organizational folklore, what programs should be implemented, and how? Some of the answers to these questions have been implied in our discussion of ambience. Obviously, folklore as one output of people's interactions can serve as a measure or index of attitudes, values, and feelings. In this way it can be of enormous value when other records are lacking or inadequate, as is typical of the "informal culture" of an organization. Not only is expressive behavior the principal source of information about these matters in everyday life, it is also compelling and thus tends to strengthen or reinforce the feelings and attitudes that are expressed. In this sense, folklore is both social and dramatic. Narrating, for example, is a social activity and communicative act (Georges, 1969) as well as a cognitive process and physiological experience (M. O. Jones, 1983). It commands attention, absorbing auditors, precipitates interchanges among all participants in the event, and conveys ideas as well as sentiments and feelings through a multiplicity of channels.

As a rule, ritualistic acts transcend mere repeated motions or even habit and custom, conveying meaning that far exceeds the rationale usually given for engaging in such activity. Celebrations typically include many forms of expressive behavior (Humphrey, 1979; Moore, 1983; Trice and Beyer, 1983). Those involved must ignore their differences and accept their fundamental similarities in order to establish a common basis for interaction, identification, and sharing (Jones et al., 1983). Traditional beliefs and practices gain potency from the recognition of their venerable history. The manufacture of objects, even those principally utilitarian in nature, often requires considerable investment of self; the objects themselves are an expression of identity, capability, and personal philosophy and aspirations (Lockwood, 1981). This is why close scrutiny of the ways in which individuals decorate space at work and at home can lead to inferences about self-conceptions, hopes, and accomplishments (Faulds, 1981; Jones, 1980b). In sum, various forms of expressive behavior can serve as sources of information not otherwise obtainable through the use of quantitative methods.

A New Perspective

More broadly, the study of folklore and folk art relates to organizational development in the orientation it embodies and in what it uncovers about human nature. It is recognized in folklorists, for example, that the subjects of research are experts and "star performers" in their own right. Put in terms of organizational behavior research, this observation yields the perspective that even those individuals carrying out the most limited and specialized assignments are quite capable of solving technical problems; developing suitable tools, procedures, and spatial arrangements for undertaking their duties; and in general imagining how to proceed in efficient and effective ways (Bell, 1976, 1981; Jones, 1980a). A machinist in a large manufacturing plant in Los Angeles, for example, proposed in one year's time more than 100 different improvements in fabrication techniques and dozens of ways of reducing costs.

One of the many results of folkloristic research is the realization that fundamental to being human is the capacity to master technique, the desire to perfect form, and the impulse to have satisfying social and sensory experiences. This suggests that in an organizational setting it should be presumed that most participants are self-motivated and self-controlled, capable of cooperating with others, able to judge the skills and performance of others, and qualified to select their own "leaders" if such are required; hence, quality circles and participatory management techniques have much to recommend them.

Areas of application, then, are numerous. One is based on ascertaining day-to-day relationships among people as expressed through narrating and narratives, ritualistic interaction, the personalization of space, and so forth—paying attention to both what is present and absent in regard to the form and content of expressive behavior. Are interactional rituals those of avoidance? Are there really any joking relationships (Swanson, 1978; K. L. Vinton, 1983)? Do people celebrate minor holidays, birthdays, and small successes in their everyday work (Collins, 1978)? In the course of describing events and telling stories about their experiences in an organization, people often suggest or imply changes that they feel are needed. They will also reveal their conceptions and perceptions of the objectives, philosophy, and identity of the organization. This information can be used as the basis for clarifying and communicating organizational goals, whether during a time of rapid expansion—with its consequent loss of a sense of common identity—or in times of acquisition and merger.

Once organizational objectives have been discerned, and after stories and descriptions of activities consistent with this view of the organization have been documented, orientation programs can be assessed and enhanced (Siehl and Martin, 1982) and management training shaped to include attention to expressive behavior (Jones et al., 1983). By sensitizing managers to the range of folklore in organizational settings, and to different ways of interpreting symbolic interaction, leadership can be enhanced. Even decision making and problem solving can be enriched (Frost and Krefting, 1983) through a study of the metaphors that individuals commonly employ to affect attitudes and behavior.

Qualitative Methods

The specific nature of an application depends on the circumstances, of course. Whatever the problem to be solved, the research will likely entail the use of qualitative methods and techniques or a combination of survey instruments, on one hand, and participant observation and in-depth interviewing on the other (Siehl and Martin, 1982). Fieldwork is essential to applied folkloristics, for expressive behavior is best studied at firsthand in the environments in which it naturally occurs. This approach helps us to understand how such behavior is generated, why it is perpetuated, and what it means.

Because of the mandate implicit in field studies—to get the information—many assume that there must be a "best" or "right" way to proceed, and that there is a logical method that should be followed to achieve their goal (Georges and Jones, 1980: 2). Thus some fieldworkers might deliberately employ strategies to accomplish preplanned objectives. In the process, however, they may alienate those who are the objects of such "manipulation." Other researchers feel that the quantity or quality of their records will suffer should their attempts to use film or magnetic tape be rebuffed. Thus they may fail to disclose that an interview is being taped. Still others require a written report in which they review the alleged causes of problems as well as their solution, overlooking the possibility that such a document might embarrass organizational participants or lead to their censure or reprimand. Promising everyone anonymity may seem to be a standard procedure, but some employees might be denied the respect and accolades they deserve if they are not identified by name. As Georges and I indicate in our book, *People Studying People* (1980), there are no simple answers to many questions that arise in fieldwork.

As noted earlier, getting information is the primary reason for carrying out field studies. One seeks to learn, and then to report observations and analyses to others. But observing and interviewing require more than knowing what information to elicit and how to record, process, and present it. Fieldworkers have to explain their purposes to others, gain cooperation, and maintain mutually acceptable relationships. These requirements creat dilemmas, produce confrontations, demand clarification and compromise, and evoke reflection and introspection that cannot be fully anticipated or prepared for in advance. Because even in pure research there are always personal motives for doing fieldwork (despite claims to the contrary of dedication or commitment to inquiry), there is always a concern with results. Usually results are conceived of as a final product such as a report or a film or, as in the case of organizational development, some tangible evidence of change. There is justification, however, for defining "results" more broadly to include the intangible and human as well as the tangible and impersonal (Georges and Jones, 1980: 135-136).

Because some fieldworkers feel compelled to get information in order to produce results in tangible form, they commit themselves to procedures that they later regret or that others may criticize. This inflexibility, along with a conception of results as a product rather than as something intangible and personal, has resulted in many fieldworkers being castigated for their use of various techniques to elicit or record information. At the same time, insisting that the fundamental issue is one of ethics implies that a standard of conduct can be devised and legislated, when in fact the circumstances of fieldwork differ so greatly, and the specifics are so varied, as to suggest that promulgating standards is virtually impossible. The basic issue thus appears to be a matter of rights and responsibilities, not absolutes in behavior. Given the necessarily pragmatic nature of fieldwork, the notions of broadening our conception of results to include the human and the intangible, and of challenging the implicit mandate to get information (seemingly at all costs), appear to be highly defensible.

Reassessment of Concepts and Assumptions

The subject of fieldwork techniques leads to a consideration of methods in general. As noted earlier, many suppose that there is one "best" way to observe and record behavior at first hand. Some may also believe that certain assumptions, concepts, and perspectives should prevail in analysis. All of us are biased, of course, but this is not usually cause for alarm. At worst it makes our reports interesting, while at best it precipitates discussion over apparent disagreements in interpretation. There is danger, however, of falling victim to the "tyranny of methods" as long as we (a) entertain assumptions about and conceptions of phenomena that restrict rather than enlarge research perspectives and our understanding of human behavior, (b) subscribe to a point of view in the face of disconfirming evidence, or (c) rigidly follow an approach simply because others have employed it in the past.

Some researchers insist on distinguishing workers from managers and labor from management. The conceptual implications are that managers and executives do not work, and workers do not manage or execute. While such a conclusion is absurd when stated this way, the propensity to follow a "natural language" usage of terms does result in our viewing these two groups as having different needs and different ways of attending to them (Dewhurst, 1983). Combined with a commitment to the notion of a hierarchy of needs, this orientation in research leads to a focus on achievement rewards for white collar workers. It also fosters the assumption that blue collar workers are motivated only by money and that they seek pleasure at work in such "trivial" activities as ritual interaction, joking, and so on. Indeed, "play" and "work" have long been dichotomized. Some researchers, as well as managers and administrators, have assumed that only serious endeavors constitute work, while play is the reward received after hours or on weekends for complete dedication to an enterprise eight hours a day, five days a week; suspicions are aroused if employees appear to be enjoying themselves on the job. Research has demonstrated, however, that the arbitrary dichotomy between work and play is neither behaviorally based nor defensible (Jones, 1980a; Dandridge, 1983; Runcie, 1983; Fine, 1983). Rather, playing is a natural and vital part of working.

It is often supposed that an existing system or culture in an organization is dysfunctional; hence, organizational development should require intervention with large-scale social system changes. However, what may be needed is the preservation or conservation of values and the perpetuation of certain kinds of expressive behavior. The task, therefore, is to enhance and communicate the features that have long distinguished the organization. In addition, research might be undertaken to highlight work and social routines already in place, and to elicit recommendations for small changes that take advantage of the dynamics of these situations, thus improving the ambience of the organization (Jones et al., 1983). Many assume that programs must be conceived at the top, and that "grass-roots" participation merely entails lower-level employees implementing what has already been mandated. However, a growing number of both consultants and clients have come to realize that recommendations must involve *all* levels of organizational participants, and that even those with the most circumscribed tasks are quite capable of designing better ways to carry them out.

CONCLUSION

I could continue to list assumptions that impede rather than facilitate research and the improvement of conditions in the workplace. I might raise questions as well about some of the cherished concepts we hold, such as "folk" and "culture" and "organization." All I want to suggest at the moment, though, is that of all the issues examined in research of organizational culture and life in the workplace, perhaps the most compelling ones are conceptual and human. Of course, ethics is not the only issue; there are other concerns. Ethics might not even be an issue at all in some instances. Objections to action research often arise from an admixture of motives and concerns in which the question of ethics either is absent or subordinated to other matters. Fieldworkers, some of whose techniques for eliciting or recording information have been challenged, are not necessarily unethical individuals; in a few cases they have simply been overly zealous in their desire to get information and have failed to consider the intangible, human results of their actions. In conclusion, it seems to me that the moral imperative in regard to the study of organizational folklore is twofold: One goal is to inquire, with all the implications and ramifications that this word entails. The second is to participate in efforts to improve life in the workplace whenever one's assistance can contribute to designing environments that provide pleasant social and sensory experiences, purvey good will, and promote a sense of well-being.

14

ETHICAL CONSIDERATIONS IN CULTURAL RESEARCH IN ORGANIZATIONS

Stanley Deetz
Rutgers University

In discussing ethics, cultural researchers must feel something akin to what 5-year-olds do when discussing Santa Claus with their peers. No one wants to appear naive; to be a grown-up in the real world is to be cynical, or at least objective. The real issue is the goods. Secret hopes and beliefs are best worked out in one's own conscience. For all practical purposes, conventional agreement on practices will do. Of course, even at 5, everyone is entitled to his or her own beliefs as long as those beliefs aren't forced on others.

I happen to believe in Santa Claus. I believe there are human constructions that are very real and that help to make us what we are as human beings. The fact that they are really fictions is a problem of ontology, not human conduct. After all, what more is an organization than a construction (a coordinated fiction) that members uphold and maintain in some way? My metaphorical Santa Claus concerns ethics. I have what Rorty (1982) would call an "unjustifiable hope in the possibility of human solidarity"—a belief that agreement can be reached on fundamental ethical principles and a conviction that such a belief makes a difference.

We have all had our dose of relativism with the accompanying resolution that the notion of ethics resides in the individual conscience while the external world works on principles of economics and power. If you feel pretty good about what you do (i.e., if you can sleep at night), there's not issue. There have always been ethics committees and text-book chapters to help people feel bad about the right things. (Similarly, if you make it too clear that you don't believe in Santa Claus, parents will withhold presents just to keep you humble. Flaunting is always bad.) The weakness of these premises is evidenced in the frequent placement of these chapters at the end of the books (possibly to have more heady discussion at the end) or, even more vividly, in statements like I heard the other day as I walked by a colleague's classroom: "This isn't just a matter of ethics; it's the law."

I don't believe we have to bring back the "white bearded man" to recognize that ethics is not just a matter of opinion, even collective opinion. *Ethics is really a form of socially produced practical knowledge, and discussion of ethics is as necessary and potentially as productive as discussion of any other knowledge claim.* This doesn't mean that discussions of ethics or ethical decision making can be made easy, but rather that they are little different from discussions of other forms of knowledge and decision making. Just as concepts of social good are ascertainable, if changeable, so differences in ethical positions should signal the beginning of productive discussion rather than a frustrating end.

This chapter is not intended to discuss the many philosophical debates and positions regarding ethics. Several such reviews exist, and I have responded to several of these issues elsewhere (Deetz, 1983a). Here I wish to show that ethical issues can and should be discussed in relation to organizational theory and practice. Ethical considerations are as much an intrinsic part of organizational study as theory. Consequently, the treatment of ethical positions as merely an external constraint on research has always been in error and degrading to the role of ethical concern. Ethics is not just a nice thing to have; indeed, research is fundamentally weak without it. If explicit ethical discussion were central to research, perhaps we would begin to break the paradoxical anxiety of applied social science research—namely, the simultaneous fear that such research is having no influence on organizational decision making, and then again that it might.

The theme developed here is a remarkably simple one. Organizational practices have major effects on human development. Anything that influences the continued formation or deformation of the human character has ethical implications. While no one is in a position to suggest what the human character ultimately should be like, we can suggest that the full representation of differing people and their interests is the central characteristic of holistic development. Social and organizational practices frequently limit such representation and distort human development. The ethical responsibility of cultural research is to isolate limitations on representation, to facilitate greater interest representation through understanding and critiquing organizational practices, and to contribute to continued cultural formation. We first examine a conception of cultural research in organizations and then develop the issue of ethics around it.

CULTURAL STUDIES IN SOCIAL CONTEXTS

My conception of and concern with cultural studies in organizations is somewhat different from that presented in many other papers. My concern is not principally with how organizational cultures work within organizations, but rather with the impact that organizational cultures have on the wider society. Work is an important aspect of what we are as human beings. Much of our time and energy is spent either within or thinking about our workplace. For many, no aspect of life occupies as much time and energy. Clearly, our work is an important part of what we are as people. The workplace culture has important, if not easily specifiable, effects on the human character and the wider culture.

Cultural studies tend to be descriptive of social beliefs and activities as they occur in the workplace. An important motive for this has been to help managers cope with this elusive thing called culture. The primary criteria for justifying these studies over the more restricted quantitative studies they replaced remain increased productivity, lower turnover and absenteeism, and increased commitment and morale (Deal and Kennedy, 1982; Peters, 1978). This should come as no surprise, since effectiveness criteria derived from managerial goals have long dominated organizational theory (Hall, 1980).

Studies of the impact of organizational practices on the social environment have been even longer in coming than those of the impact on the physical environment, and for many of the same reasons. Organizations are primarily committed to their own interests, and the short-term perspective of managerial decision making underestimates the reciprocal impact of environmental change on the long-term health of an organization.

Changes in society frequently have more impact on productivity, motivation, and morale than any managerial decision (Deetz, 1979; Nord, 1978; Goldman and van Houten, 1977). Major cultural changes strongly influence the kind of person who comes to work for an organization. *Rolling Stone* magazine (O'Rourke, 1982: 58) offered a pithy account of the changing perception of work:

> In a Sixties good job, you changed the system while realizing your own potential as a person. In a Seventies good job, you discovered the best way to change the system was by becoming successful within it while realizing your own potential in a leisure context. This led to the Eighties good job, where you make lots of money and get to screw off.

I hear some of the same analysis in my colleagues' jokes about our "prewealth majors." The climate of work in general creeps into every organization, but little has been done to investigate such changes or the contributions made by organizational structure and job design. Quality of life and "meaning" studies linked to limited organizational objectives underestimate both directions of this two-way process. Organizations help us to define what it is to be a human being, and human beings come to organizations to work. Organizational study that omits the impact of organizations on society is responsible neither to organizations nor society.

Ethics in the Social Context

What has all this to do with ethics? Let me begin by making a distinction between two kinds of ethical concerns. The first type are those most often treated in management texts and that are central to both Jones (1984) and Mirvis (1984b). These concerns involve professional ethics and personal integrity; they include a number of the critical existential concerns facing any decision maker in an organization. For example: "Am I being fair to the people here?" "Did I violate their confidence?" "Is my work being coopted?" "Do I have enough information to make this decision?" "Is this practice hurting people?" "Should I report the deception?" "They'll fire Joe if I make a full report. Should I?"

These are, without a doubt, serious personal questions. I do not want to diminish their importance, but neither do I wish to treat them here. My fear is that focus on these concerns could lead us to overlook more central ethical issues in favor of discovering an equation of ethics for "being a good person." Ethics in this sense gets confused with a kind of private morality, since the focus is on the individual decision maker and his or her sense of goodwill.

The second set of ethical concerns has little to do with private morality but a lot to do with social good. While private morality is primarily based on personal (if socially shared) beliefs, I wish to consider the concept of "social good" with regard to the discursively produced principles that guide social praxis. Such principles differ from the first type of ethics in that they are rationally reconstructed from actual human behavior rather than being assumed, and they are directed toward action choices and the structures that enable them rather than toward evaluations of personal intentions.

An example of the intuitive separability of these two types of ethical concerns may help to clarify this point. Some time ago, an alumnus of an institution for which I worked wrote a stinging letter to the editor of the student paper. The letter forcefully posed the following question to the students: "How can you criticize normal business practices and environmental choices which are necessary to keep America competitive while you live in co-ed dorms and engage in permissive sexuality?" The reader can guess the student replies. The debate over whether private or public ethics is more important, independent of the criteria for judgment in either, is familiar.

Ethics and Human Development

The concern about a public ethic is not with what is good or right but with the preferences we share, or can come to share, regarding human development. One of the most stark realizations of modern times is that human beings lack a fixed nature, and that if we are not responsible for our own "becoming," there is certainly no "motor" of history (no matter how personified) that will be. With no nature or motor to appeal to or to limit our own productive and destructive choices, we are collectively responsible for our own fate. Choices that affect our collective historical development pose ethical concerns in this second sense. Organizations thus have a place in total social development and must be critically examined in that role (Deetz and Kersten, 1983).

The guiding ethical questions might be stated as follows: *If we innovate in this way, if we manage in this way, if we create this kind of product, what kind of people will we become?* This issue is, or should be, at the heart of any public, social ethic. Given people's current belief structures, the existence of a strong private morality in no way assures or contributes to the conditions for positive social development. Indeed, the focus on private ethics frequently diverts attention away from the discussion and actions necessary for the formation of these conditions.

Developing an Ethical Sense

The privatization of ethical principles leads to great difficulties in productive discussions of this second type of ethical concern, and even greater difficulties (and ethical concerns) in teaching them. There are reasons why the ethics chapter appears last in most management, public relations, and advertising texts. Ethics has not been treated as a subject amenable to rational discussion or as a form of knowledge. When it is treated like the modern version of other nonrational (subjective) bases for decisions such as "tact" and "taste," discussion has nowhere to go.

Recent philosophical discussions of tact and taste (e.g., Gadamer, 1975; Apel, 1980) show how poorly these concepts, like ethics, have been treated in postenlightenment philosophies and in the public mind. Ethics is like "taste" properly understood. Perhaps an image of wine tasting is more appropriate than one of mere "taste." There are two kinds of knowledge about taste in wine—data about purchasing patterns, and reports of wine tasters. We use this second kind of knowledge to make determinations about the quality of a wine, which is not determined by sales but by its appeal to the eye, nose, and palate.

It would be in error to consider this appeal as merely "subjective." A public vote on wine preference would not replace a judgment of quality by an "informed" judge. In these matters we clearly recognize the nature of acquired tastes and acculturation. Most people only gradually learn to like beer or acquire a palate for quality wines. Wine tasters are not a simple elite with power; they are accepted as representing the potential for taste in each one of us, what our palate *could* become. For all their limitations, disputes, and changes, they have a handle on one small aspect of the continued development of human sensitivities and sensibilities.

Ethics is like this, too. It is a form of knowledge that is acquired in ways more similar to acquiring taste or even wisdom than to learning rules, tables, and theories. Experience and apprenticeship are certainly critical to this kind of learning. Unfortunately, rather than working to build this kind of knowledge, teaching tends to focus on that which can be reduced to a formula. Further, the inability to reduce ethics to anything other than trivial formulae leads to its not being taught at all.

The teaching of ethics is frequently reduced to value clarification exercises or moral dilemmas. While these methods may spark discussion, they are often designed to prohibit reasoned consensus. Perhaps they teach tolerance, but they also teach value neutrality and the false sense that ethical discussions cannot be resolved.

Such discussion and education is not easy (even wine tasters disagree). But ethics, like wine tasting, is gutted of meaning if it is treated as subjective and reduced to opinion polls or matters of power. The faith that an agreement can be hammered out in discussion, and that such a reasoned discussion can be improved, need not be elitist in the least. Instead, it is a critical, if perhaps unjustifiable, act of social hope. At the very least, it is a place to start, and we are certainly better off for doing so.

The question is how to sensitize our ethical "feelers," our metaphorical ethical palate. How are people to be cultured in such a way as to improve their ethical sense—that is, how are they to become more caring of human development and more aware of how decisions influence human development? Cultural studies in organizations need to be guided by such sensibilities if they are to be ethical in this public sense just as they need to contribute to sensual development by focusing on the influence of organizations on the holistic human actor. Cultural studies sensitize our understanding of human experiences in some of the same ways wine tasters guide and educate the human palate.

But enough metaphors. How are we going to study organizations in terms of this ethical concern with organizational influences on the kind of people we become?

ASPECTS OF A PUBLIC ETHIC FOR ORGANIZATIONAL STUDIES

I doubt that I need to forewarn anyone that working out such ethical concerns is filled with dangers—much like plowing a fertile field filled with mines. The dangers of rushing to a conclusion or being too tentative seem equally grave. Everyone has a vested interest, and the political implications are, at times, all too clear. To be too shallow or to sidestep too much hardly makes the enterprise worthwhile. The subject of public ethics is inherently and deeply political. While private ethics issues such as the impossibility of legislating morality, or the need to separate church and state, can be put aside, questions of human development are issues of public as well as private policy. While a public ethic must consider power and politics, it cannot be reduced to that.

One of the most difficult distinctions in modern social philosophy is the difference between ideologically and nonideologically based cultural development. Such a distinction was easier to draw when people shared a relatively fixed notion of the nature of man and the proper direction of history. Criteria could be drawn for "true" and "false" development. However, as such criteria were shown more and more to be merely the reflection of powerful sectional interests rather than universal conditions, the line blurred. Every culture could be seen as having an ideology.

All disputes over the direction of development can only be settled by power, since no basis for "right" can be maintained. This is a preferred resolution for the politically powerful, and in organizational studies it neatly supports managerial interests. A culture is good because of who it serves rather than its support of human development, because who it serves *defines* good development. The privatization and fragmentation of ethical principles in the name of tolerance and openness make such domination complete and diffuse dissent. Perspectives like that advanced by Connolly et al. (1980) help to open organizational analysis to the view of different "constituencies" but fail in the end to provide any criteria at all.

I wish to hold on to a distinction between natural, nonideological development and distorted ideological development. Unlike earlier positions, this does not rest on criteria from either a definition of human nature or insight into the end of history. Rather, the focus is on a process of open expression of interests and of representation in decision making—the public's self-formation. Ideologically based development rests on sectional interests being universalized as "the way things are" (see Giddens, 1979: 188ff; Deetz and Mumby, 1984). Under such conditions, experience is predetermined and partial, beliefs and values that are unwittingly opposed to personal interests are uncritically accepted and expressed; and the expression of interests is arbitrarily (because of power relations) limited by structures and opposing power interests. Development is by necessity skewed and partial. The point is not that human development should follow this path or that one, but that no single set of interests should have an arbitrary advantage over others in the "human dialogue."

Neither liberal democracy nor a new elite, whether of intellectual or economic origins, can assure this participation and nonideological development. Liberal democracy, like many organizational participation plans, fails owing to the ideological formation of public opinion, structural constraints on the distribution of critical information, and skill differences among participants (see Mason, 1982). The cultural researcher is not posed as a new elite to make ethical judgments but, as I will develop later, can isolate instances of arbitrary oppression, aid the fuller representation of interests, and expose restrictive cultural practices.

Representation of Interests

The goal of nonideological self-determination is based on the representation of interests rather than simply people or groups. Human interests reside in people, but they cannot be limited to that which anyone can possess or know. Rather, they are defined more by the orientations and actions that one takes (people positions) than by what people think they want. Here I wish to isolate two conceptions of human interests that need to be explored.

Different literatures have meaningfully discussed issues related to representing "sectional" and "cognitive" interests. Sectional interests refer to the differences among social groups and the available means for expressing and acting on them. Works by Dahrendorf (1959) and Abrahamsson (1977) are good examples of such studies. Most "participant-interest" theories of organizational effectiveness also present a clear conception of sectional interests (see Keeley, 1984). Cognitive interests refer to the complementary and at times competing interests that are part of all human conduct, such as the logics of play and work. Critical theorists of the Frankfurt School, particularly Habermas (1972), have worked extensively with this latter conception. I can only develop each briefly here. I will begin with the representation of cognitive interests.

Representing cognitive interests. Habermas (1972) distinguishes three basic cognitive interests: technical, practical, and emancipatory. Each of these can be seen in the workplace as well as in the larger society. The technical interest is seen primarily as a drive for control, instrumental gain, and material or economic growth. While its origin rests in biological survival, the move toward control can exceed that necessary for survival. The practical interest is a natural complement to the technical interest. It focuses on the meaning of existence and the satisfaction of social and symbolic needs. Finally, emancipatory interests arise from the interplay between the first two types.

Both technical and practical interests generate a particular type of reasoning and decision making. Technical reasoning is instrumental; it tends to be governed by the theoretical and hypothetical, and focuses on the future and "means-ends" chains. By contrast, practical reasoning is consummatory, governed by the practical and immediate, and focuses on the goodness of the means as ends in themselves. Each evokes a particular morality and concept of moral development. Gilligan (1982) examines the difference between male and female moral development in the United States. His study could easily be applied to these two interests by a focusing on rules rather than caring.

While no universal preference can be given to either of these interests during particular historical periods, a society may be dominated by one or the other. In so-called primitive societies, for example, the technical interest is subordinate to the practical one. The fulfillment of economic development is less essential and therefore subservient to the fulfillment of symbolic necessities. In modern society, the opposite is true. The pursuit of economic goals has become the end to which other goals are subservient, with the control and domination of people and nature being the principal end of science and organizations (Adorno and Horkheimer, 1972). Technical reasoning is regarded as primary, although technical domination—the overrepresentation of the technical interest—can lead to one form of what was earlier called ideologically distorted development. Still, the expression and action preferences are given to technical thought.

Many organizations today reproduce (and produce?) these same interest preferences. The long-term conflict between various versions of the scientific management and human relations approaches to management are in part the legitimate offspring of this interest struggle. However, it has never been a genuine choice, because technical reasoning has always prevailed. Thus concerns with economic growth, organizational survival, profit, and productivity have always been the ultimate criteria.

Meaningful work, participation in decision making, and the growth and development of personnel have rarely been treated as goods in themselves. Rather, these notions answer to the same criteria. Work is pushed to be labor, and effort that might be exerted in the pursuit of self-actualization is channeled into accomplishing production objectives in exchange for economic gain (Guerreiro-Ramos, 1980: 152). Braverman's (1974) demonstration of "de-skilling" has touched all levels of work organizations and the professions (see Heydebrand, 1977). If continued technological innovations are introduced following this singular logic, the process will surely continue. *Rolling Stone* once described changing views of work as natural, if potentially negative, consequences.

The moral implications of this narrowing and hardening of the human character through the distorted representation of interests are significant. The ethical demands placed on cultural studies are clarified here, though they have yet to be developed. The investigation of "practical interests" and how they can be better realized in organizations is critical to human development. At the same time, however, cultural studies can be coopted in the same way as other bodies of knowledge and technology, only more covertly. The apparent concern with meaning of life issues in the workplace could thus become merely a new means of tapping into a reservoir of unutilized human talents and energies without considering human beings and human development as ends in themselves.

Let me pause lest I seem unduly critical of material growth and the essential elements of organizational survival. Am I not advocating the addition of extrarational value criteria that are beyond any organization's mission and potentially detrimental to its survival? At this point, I want to make three supplementary points: (1) The problem is not the tendency to value economic growth and productivity, but rather the current dominating and exclusionary character of this tendency. (2) While each organization pursues increased productivity, the means of doing so ultimately results in all organizations collectively creating social conditions that decrease productivity and limit human development. (3) Organizations already act on numerous extrarational values, but few that are supportive of holistic human growth and development.

Economic growth and productivity can and do coexist with the development of the total personality. While human relation factors rarely have a simple positive correlation to productivity, they even more rarely have a negative one. Any supposed threat to productivity from positive work climates, job enrichment, and employee involvement thus seems ill founded. Resistance to such changes appears to be motivated more by private and unexamined values of managers and workers than by production costs. From an ethical standpoint, the changes should be seen as goods in themselves, and their attainment should be as essential as that of profits, environmental protection, and economic growth.

Quite apart from the ethical issue, many of the current organizational practices that developed from a technical rationality may pay off in the short term but eventually decrease the quality of the work force. Job designs enabling the easy and quick replacement of lost workers create jobs that stimulate personnel development only minimally. Specialization in a changing environment reduces adaptability, while centralization and bureaucratization reduce commitment and foster fragmentation and alienation. Current conditions of work have created a social condition that Habermas (1975; see also Deetz, 1979) characterizes as a legitimation crisis on the social level and a motivation crisis on the individual level. Alcohol and drug abuse, absenteeism, high rates of turnover, low quality control, and reduced productivity are merely surface expressions of a general disenchantment with work, or of work motivated only by economic payoff. Negative cycles of individual organization solutions creating social problems which lead to more such solutions seems to be the rule of the day.

Ethical concerns with human development may appear to some to be extrarational values imposed on a necessarily rational production process—an intrusion of noneconomic concerns into economic spheres of social life. To some extent this is true, if rationality is conceptualized only as technical rationality. But let's put this notion in context. Organizational decision making is always accomplished within areas of considerable uncertainty. Under these circumstances, beliefs and values have nearly always tipped the balance. More importantly, however, extrarational values have enjoyed considerable influence on all organizational decisions.

Many of these extrarational values are technical interests that have gone astray. Organizational decisions are frequently influenced as much or more by perceived effects on managerial careers than by any determinable relation to profit or productivity. Managers continue to increase their power, incomes, and work loads as their health and general life satisfaction decreases. Technological innovation and increased size are often values for themselves or to maintain a posture. If state-of-the-art equipment purchases and takeovers were as much in need of justification as job enrichment and personnel development programs, such decisions would be much more infrequent. For example, how many hospitals looked closely at their balance sheet when CT scanners became available? The point is that extrarational value systems are already at work in organizations and are protected from careful examination. Facts are always produced within a context of values. The question is not whether noneconomic values have a place in organizations, but rather which ones will occupy that place.

The emancipatory interest mentioned earlier becomes critical in periods of either technical or practical interest domination. This interest promotes the conditions necessary for human reflexivity and autonomy. Its logic involves critical examination of an organization's warrants for decision making. Concern here is with analyzing the "blockage on productive activities and the distortion of communicative praxis" (Schroyer, 1973). Blockages and distortions arise when beliefs and values are acted upon that have been accepted without assessment. Through emancipatory reflection, implicit decision making is opened to explicit consideration. The emancipatory interest fosters a reconstructive approach which allows "discursive penetration" (Giddens, 1979: 5ff) into the structural workings of organizations and society. A decisive "moral-ethical imperative" serves as the *telos* of such reconstructive study (Bernstein, 1983). In the face of technical interest domination, this task falls to cultural studies in organizations.

Representing sectional interests. Since various conceptions of sectional interests have received considerable attention in the literature about organizations, I will be brief here. March and Simon (1958), following earlier work by Barnard (1938), carefully develop the concept of "participants"—members of various groups that hold an interest in an organization. These include employees, investors, suppliers, distributers, and consumers, as well as the wider society.

Dahrendorf (1957) notes that participants' roles generate natural vested interests and intergroup conflict. The full variety of these interests, however is rarely represented in organizational decision making. As Abrahamsson (1977), among others, has demonstrated, managerial interests dominate organizations by dominating not only the decision process but also the criteria for determining the quality of decisions. Other individuals are marginally represented, if at all, through the translation of their interests into purely economic terms (e.g., the price of labor or capital funds, sales, or resource costs) or through largely advisory groups such as unions, consumer groups, or professional associations. The influence of such groups, as of stockholders, is at best occasional and usually negative (stopping rather than initiating action).

The reason for this distorted representation of interests has little to do with the available power or intelligence. The structural features of modern organizations continue to reproduce such domination against attempts for representation by any other group, no matter how powerful. Clegg (1979; Clegg and Dunkerley, 1980) identifies and analyzes some of these structural determinants, but most cultural studies sidestep the issue completely by looking only at surface power features (Astley and Sachdeva, 1984; Riley, 1983; Conrad, 1983; Deetz and Mumby, 1984).

One unexamined reason for the current valuing of managerial domination probably rests in the organic relationship that once existed among capital/invention, ownership, and management. But why should managerial interests dominate decision making in the large public organizations of today? Few ask whether managers are prepared to make the best decisions even on economic questions, let alone in regard to the full variety of human interests; nor, whether in economic or broader terms, whose interests are advanced by managerial decision making. Organizational goals are always advanced by some; however, questions like "Whose goals count for how much?" are now being taken seriously in determining definitions of effectiveness (see Cameron and Whetten, 1983).

The ethical concern advanced here is not that managers as a group make decisions that are intentionally or carelessly detrimental to the development of the human community. The singular representation of any sectional interest cuts off many voices that are essential for the human dialogue, whether the interests expressed be those of union members, stockholders, or consumers. Under current conditions, however, managerial logic has been internalized by other potential participants; contrary conceptions are rarely thought and less often spoken. Further, this ideological domination is largely built into the structure of organizations and protected from rational assessment. Hence we have ideologically based organizational decision making and one-sided effects on the development of the human community.

The most neglected sectional interest in organizational decision making is the wider social community. The community's interests are in the utilization of resources, the type of goods and services produced, the environment, and the development of its citizenry. These social interests are insufficiently represented by commercial and governmental regulations owing to organizational (managerial) control, crude negative constraints, time lags, limited information, and governmental bureaucracy.

The problem of partial representation of interests extends beyond the problem of managerial interests. The presentation of and response to the interests of minority groups and women are frequently limited by employment practices, a disregard of legitimate counterinterests, and a preference for modes of expression that makes certain aspects of human experience difficult to express.

Research in the Service of
Representation of Interests

The task for cultural research in light of interest domination and the subsequent distortion of human development is both important and difficult. The ethical imperative is for theory and methods to be based on a normative foundation, such as the open formation of the human character. While the actual conditions of social existence are always at some distance from this ideal, such a principle serves as a touchstone for critically examining the practices of organizations and organizational research.

Technical and managerial interests dominate workplace decision making. This situation contributes to certain legitimation and motivation problems at the social level (Habermas, 1975) and creates systematic distortions in human development. Do we as a society like or want to be what current organizational practices recommend for us? Is there any way we or anyone else can have a say in the matter? In what ways is wider representation possible? To me, these are the critical ethical questions.

Unfortunately, as a citizen I have little influence on organizations. In fact, if we look at the partial representation of different sectional interests, it is the general social good that is most neglected. In many respects, novelists, singers, and poets have done more than anyone to describe the changing human character and the role of organizations in that process of change. Academic researchers have largely accepted a managerial perspective and thus aid and support the representational domination. The research questions asked and the type of studies conducted make sense only with prior acceptance of a technical, managerial interest. There are, of course, exceptions (e.g., Keeley, 1984).

There are many good reasons why academic researchers, and particularly those in organizational culture studies, have special responsibilities and opportunities. Most (though clearly not all) are paid to represent the wider culture through their employment in public institutions of higher education. Further, their disposition, training, and work activities support and allow cultural reflection and consideration of long-term effects. Perhaps the image of "cultural wine tasters" is too grand, but it is more appropriate than one of "support personnel" for organizational managers.

An Agenda for the Study of Organizational Culture

How, then, should we conceptualize the task of organizational culture researchers? Their principal ethical task is much like that of the anthropologists they so often wish to imitate but it is also more. It is like that of the anthropologist who, having become disenchanted with missionaries and empires, primarily works to record and preserve a human possibility, a human voice, so that we may interrogate it and it us. Preservation serves to enable dialogue with a way of being human, to expand human self-understanding before it is silenced by change, domination, or fatigue. Giving representation to that which cannot represent itself owing to current conditions constantly undermines the arrogance and one-sidedness that ultimately reduces adaptability and skews all development.

The modern cultural researcher participates, albeit unwittingly, in the practice of giving voice to the silenced aspects of human dialogue. He or she brings to expression and consideration that which may have been overlooked or lost from a discussion. But preservation is not passive; there are always forces that work for discursive closure. Action research (Susman and Evered, 1978) or, even better, what has been called participatory research (Brown and Kaplan, 1981; Brown and Tandon, 1983), is necessary to find the "lost voice" and a means for its suitable expression. Such research may at times be in the service of one interest or another, but the guiding principle is not a political vision. The removal of domination and the presence of open participation is central to the formation of any vision.

Elsewhere, I have discussed in depth the basic goals of such research (Deetz, 1982; Deetz and Kersten, 1983) and the essential communication conditions for open participation (Deetz, 1983). These goals involve understanding, criticism, and education. I will merely highlight how each serves the ethical task.

Understanding. Nearly all cultural studies purport to have a hermeneutic goal of a richer understanding of naturally occurring events.

Understanding is perhaps the purest form of preservation. It involves (1) recording stories, metaphors, symbols, statements of beliefs, and behavioral practices; (2) synthesizing from them a logic or social reality that makes sense of them and displays their functions; and (3) playing them back to organization members for consideration and reflection.

Of course, this process in itself has little ethical import. Such knowledge may be used to produce coherence in the face of contradiction and to reinforce existing relations of domination. Merely understanding the means by which consensual realities are formed and perpetuated says little about whether such a consensus adequately represents different competing interests. Nevertheless, understanding often provides insightful discursive penetration, which in turn allows organizational members to reframe knowledge and develop choices that were previously hidden by accepted knowledge standard practices, and existing conceptions. Without such reflected knowledge, members continue to respond out of meaning structures that were developed in response to past situations and historical power arrangements and that have been unknowingly perpetuated in members' talk and actions.

Critique. This goal involves examining the conditions of consensus. It means, as Frost (1980: 503) suggests "to bring individuals to full awareness of the repressions associated with power distributions." An organization's language and accepted means of expression usually enable easy, rapid expression of some things and yet block alternative expressions. Power politics is packed into every expression (Deetz and Mumby, 1984). Whom do such preferences serve, and what is lost by them? Every organizational story produces an account and fixes responsibility, thus closing off alternative narrative accounts. Critique involves looking for the story that did not get expressed, both to explain its absence and to consider how interests are lost to expression. Technical innovations such as microcomputers may aid efficiency in some fashion, but who gets left out and what is no longer or less adequately expressed? What is the impact of such innovations on the human character? Why are those impacts not considered? To whose advantage is the trade-off?

If understanding is in the service of preservation, then critique is in the service of demythification. That which has been glorified and held above scrutiny is brought under examination. The fictions are not thrown out, but they are shown to be fictions. Their evaluation is done for the purpose of separating arbitrary advantages from discursive contributions. All organizational structures are fictions. The question is, which ones enable representation and which ones essentially block it?

Education. Irrational belief structures often arise in areas of inability and ignorance. The formation of conceptual systems that enable greater representation is itself a liberating activity. New structural arrangements and forms of decision making are essential if issues of meaning and economics are to coexist. Continued cultural formation, which enables fuller interest expression and overcomes the development of new discursive blocks, is an ongoing project. Skills in expression and decision making are important if new decisional models are to meet the demands of either productivity or human development. Cultural researchers can help provide skills in developing less restrictive environments. Verbal and symbolic enrichment is useful in many cases where the natural language of an organization must be made capable of expressing a wide variety of interest.

CONCLUSION

I began this chapter by suggesting that commitment to discussing and actualizing ethical principles is often based on unjustifiable hope for human solidarity. This hope is rekindled in every act of cooperation, every instance of love and friendship, and every resolved argument. My concern is not about a lack of assurance, but that people will have no say in what they become or, worse, that they will not care. Cultural research can signal not only a theoretical and epistemological break, but an ethical one as well. Opening up human choices strikes me as more important than constricting them. Someday, perhaps, we will hear: "It's not just a matter of law, it is a matter of ethics."

15

UNETHICAL BUSINESS BEHAVIOR MUST BE UNDERSTOOD

Charles Butcher

Butcher Polish Company

I have advocated for some time that schools of business administration should engage in a scholarly examination of the causes of ethical business behavior on the one hand and of antisocial business behavior on the other. I am struck by the potential for achievement in this area which is inherent in the study of business culture. I urge you to examine why otherwise ethical human beings sometimes conduct their businesses in ways that hurt both the people they work with and those they seek to serve. A short story from my own experience will help to define the kind of behavior that I have in mind.

A disease that can be fatal to humans, known as aplastic anemia, can be caused by the ingestion or inhalation of a chemical substance that contains a benzene ring in its structure. Not everyone is susceptible, but approximately one-quarter of the populaton can contract the disease by ingesting or inhaling chemicals containing the benzene ring.

When my first child became ill at 2½ years of age, his symptoms appeared to his doctors to be those of a child suffering from aplastic anemia. In an effort to confirm the diagnosis, his doctors asked if he had

Editors' Note: We asked Charles Butcher, Chairman of the Board and owner of the Butcher Polish Company, Marlborough, Massachusetts, to translate the notes from his address to academics at the Conference on Organizational Culture and the Meaning of Life at Work (University of British Columbia, April 1984) into a statement for this book. Mr. Butcher has retained in this piece the strong personal tone of his earlier address. His thoughts and ideas are a passionate and direct plea from a concerned businessman to scholars to make the relationship between culture and ethical behavior in organizations an important item on their research and education agendas. The format of the chapter is different from others in the book. Nevertheless, we believe that the message and the style of communication are important contributions for the reader to encounter.

been eating crayons. They explained that some childrens' crayons were manufactured with dyes that contained the benzene ring. "Did the manufacturers of the crayons know of this problem?" I asked. "Oh, yes," they replied. "We have told them all. Now some are using safe dyes and others are not."

I was shocked. How could anyone knowingly do this?

I learned that a very large, nationally prominent dye manufacturer, from whom I bought dyes used in a floor wax that I manufactured, sold dyes containing the benzene ring. I questioned these people about the dye I was using and found that it contained the benzene ring. Naturally, I had my employees tested for possible contamination and began thinking about what else I should do. I wrote an irate letter to the president of the dye company asking why my company was not warned of the danger.

The good news was that my child did not have aplastic anemia, my employees were okay, and I adopted procedures to keep both my employees and my customers out of danger. The bad news was that the president of the dye company sent a benign letter saying that I must be mistaken, they had no problem with the benzene ring, and no employees of his had ever died of aplastic anemia. After further investigation, I found that his company had avoided the problem simply by firing employees who got sick with symptoms that suggested they might have the disease.

This is the kind of unethical behavior on the part of management which must be understood and eliminated. There is simply no logical reason for tolerating it. The dye could be safely used in most instances (our use of it being one of them), but not unless the user knew of the problem.

All societies breed a few law breakers whose behavior is openly and blatantly against the social norms. A few of these people become business leaders. They know they are cheating their employees and the public, but they don't care. Fortunately, they are a small group in any society, and most systems of criminal justice are designed to deal with them. These individuals are not responsible for the unethical behavior I am talking about.

Business leaders who act immorally and who affect a large portion of the dollar volume of national and international business are a major problem to society. They think of themselves as social and political leaders, and yet they run their businesses unethically. They are responsible for a large amount of suffering in the world for which they are rarely held accountable.

Studies of organizational culture in business indicate that ethical considerations provide the underpinning and driving force of most of the attributes of successful companies. *The Art of Japanese Management* (Pascale and Athos, 1982) places shared values at the center of the seven most important keys to success. *In Search of Excellence* (Peters and Waterman, 1982) emphasizes the basic philosophy and central beliefs of good companies as the force underlying eight characteristics of success. Companies that have these attributes and that are driven by shared ethical values will find it difficult to behave in an unethical manner.

There is a lot of evidence that the strength of an organizational culture can be traced to the character of the founder. A strong ethical leader will not succumb easily to temptations that could lead to unethical behavior and corruption. In fact, such a leader would probably tend to see corruption as a sign of failure and thus strive even harder to work within the system to achieve his or her goals. Therefore, the nurture and training of ethical behavior should be a priority of those who teach organizational culture in schools of business administration.

Work on the myths and symbols of organizational culture suggests that they can be very strong motivating forces. Properly emphasized, they can drive the behavior and determine the goals of a business. The right symbols can dominate a business culture so thoroughly that unethical behavior would be unthinkable.

Let us consider some ways in which unethical behavior gets into business and then examine how organizational culture affects the outcome. Frequently, the leader of a successful business is confronted with a new discovery which makes the promotion and sale of one or more products unethical. Cigarettes, asbestos, and crayons manufactured with dangerous dyes are examples. If the leader had built a strong ethical cultural climate, it would be impossible to ignore the problem; he or she would be forced to find an ethical way to transform the business.

The power to place substantial orders is often vested in someone who is not the recipient of the goods or services being purchased. Sellers can get orders by offering benefits to the purchaser instead of to the recipient or real buyer. The temptation to corrupt those who individually or jointly wield this power for companies, institutions, and other organizations is well known. The wonder is that there are not more corrupt deals made. The reason must lie in the strength of the organizational cultures involved.

The classic form of corruption by restraint of competition between sellers, for which the "robber barons" became famous, is a temptation to most manufacturers. The comforting fact is that it is often less rewarding to conspire in the restraint of trade than it is to do a good, honest job of filling a niche. Again, however, strong organizational cultures will not succumb to this form of corruption.

When governments are the buyers and citizens/taxpayers are the ultimate recipients of goods or services, opportunities abound for both personal gain and the misuse of power. Buyers and sellers can share in these rewards, which are tremendous. Admiral Carroll of the Office of Defense Information has estimated that most of the major weapon systems purchased by the U.S. Department of Defense are acquired under contracts planned by industry and Defense Department personnel working together to mislead or deceive both Congress and the public. Billions of dollars are spent by towns, cities, counties, states, and nations under a similar cloud of corruption. There seems to be a presumption that business and government leaders know what is best for the public. Unfortunately, the cultural constraints on their actions seem to break down under these conditions.

Large business organizations sometimes see themselves as invulnerable fortresses of power. They can use their almost limitless earnings, equity, and borrowing power to do whatever they please. They can enter a business arena, hire the best managers and operators, use any means fair or foul to get the equipment and know-how they need, disrupt the lives of thousands of employees by pirating them away from their present employers, and, in the end, abandon the whole project without a trace of concern for what they have done. The cultural climate in a business that behaves this way must be substantially weaker in an ethical sense than that of one that "plays by the rules." A study illuminating these differences might do much to eliminate unethical behavior.

It may be possible to ascribe unethical behavior to the profit motive if it were not for the fact that making money without hurting others is relatively easy in our culture. The rules for success are well codified, and any person of moderate intelligence and energy can follow them. Members of social minorities often find it more difficult to become successful businessmen, but even their chances have improved over time. Furthermore, it is usually harder to make money when you decide to violate the cultural norms. Ordinary crooks work harder to accumulate and keep what they get than do most honest people.

Similarly, it is doubtful that a desire to break or circumvent the law is at the heart of the matter. Most businesspeople dislike some laws and regulations, and all have an aversion to taxes, but they find that obeying regulations and paying taxes is the best way to minimize these annoyances. In fact, a smart businessperson will usually find a way to make regulations and taxes work in his or her favor.

Is it possible that we have come to accept antisocial behavior in business as the norm? Do we ignore it because we take it for granted? Perhaps. I know people who say that it is part of human nature and that there is nothing we can do about it. I disagree.

Not all people in business behave this way. They sometimes have mixed motives, but they behave in business the way they behave in other areas of their lives. Their behavior can usually be rationalized as enlightened self-interest. They put real value in what they sell, because that is the way to get referrals and reorders. They don't cover up hidden dangers, because it doesn't pay in the long run. Rather, they find myriad ways to make socially acceptable behavior profitable to them.

If antisocial business behavior is not necessary to make a profit, and if it is not a necessary part of human nature, why does it keep occurring? Is it a function of the size of an organization? Or is it related to the power that the organization grants to its leader?

The work that is being done on organizational culture can supply answers to some of these questions. Perhaps it will show that size and power are not always causes of unethical behavior. This can be done by identifying companies that are both honest and successful and whose characteristics of success are tied to their ethical standards. Maybe the source of these standards can be traced to the character of the founder or present leader, whose beliefs are propagated by the myths and symbols that ethical companies often make a dominant part of their working environment. Thus it can be shown that ethical behavior in business is not only possible but may be a strong component of success.

PART IV

HOW ARE ORGANIZATIONAL CULTURES AND THE WIDER CULTURAL CONTEXT LINKED?

LARRY F. MOORE

Previous sections of this book have been primarily concerned with developing a cultural perspective at the organization level. In this section the focus of attention is enlarged to consider the broader cultural context in which organizations are embedded and from which organizational cultures are at least partially derived.

Culture (as shared meaning) is not genetically inherited; it is learned. Individuals learn cultural values and beliefs from parents, peers, and other significant individuals. Group culture develops as a social learning process, and organizations generate their collections of meaning by drawing on and adopting (learning) the mores, archetypes, metamyths, and values which form the fabric of the host society. Thus, organizational culture cannot be understood without reference to aspects of the wider culture. As noted recently by Sir Adrian Cadbury, chairman of Cadbury-Schweppes:

> One thing I'm totally clear about, whether we're talking about structure of organization or whether we're talking about methods of involving people in the business, is that the way it's done must be related to the culture; the way people manage and expect to be managed in those countries.

The six chapters contained in Part IV, although very different in many respects, have in common a concern with the need to include in the analysis of organizational culture a careful consideration of the wider cultural influence system. In exploring the linkage between organizational culture and the manifestations of culture at the broader societal level, we have grouped the chapters according to three perspectives.

The first perspective is from inside organizations looking out. The focal point in this perspective is the question of fit between the cultural variables in the organization and the variables constituting the cultural context outside the organization. In Chapter 16 ("Organization Change as a Symbolic Transformation Process"), Berg notes that a traditional approach that organizations have taken to incorporating cultural considerations into formulating strategy has been to attempt to develop and manipulate various symbols such as slogans, language, and colors in order to promote corporate identity and legitimate change. Berg believes that this approach is quite limited and proposes an alternative perspective in which organizational culture is seen as a symbolic field made up of objects, properties, images, languages, and sagas that constitute the collective representation of an organization's reality. Organizational change, then, would be accomplished through a transformation of the underlying symbolic field. Berg discusses how strategic planning can be enhanced by making use of the symbolic field paradigm.

Chapter 17 ("Culture Collisions in Mergers and Acquisitions"), by Walter, is concerned with what happens to an organization and its culture when another organization's culture is superimposed as a result of a merger or acquisition. Walter points out that an organization's culture is really a balance of six competing values, and that a merger or acquisition upsets this balance, generally in favor of those values concerning the enhancement of capitalistic rather than human dimensions of organization.

The entire culture of the acquiring firm is sometimes forced upon the firm being acquired. The degree to which assimilation of new cultural folkways is accomplished is dependent on several things including task similarities, type of merger (whether horizontal, vertical, concentric, or conglomerate), prior events, and so on. Usually, much time and pain is involved before a new synthesis is achieved in this dialectical process. Walter argues that paying attention to the overall cultural effects when two organizations are melded together can contribute much to cost effectiveness on both financial and human levels.

The next two chapters in Part IV address the nature of the linkage between organizations and the wider culture from the perspective of outside organizations looking in. What can we learn about organizational culture by attempting to use analytical frameworks that may be appropriate for understanding culture at a broader level? In Chapter 18 ("The Transformation of Organizational Cultures: A Competing Values Perspective"), Quinn and McGrath present a conceptual framework designed to provide consistency and structure to the environment of human perceptual values while at the same time illuminating the fundamental tensions and paradoxes that often exist among values. The authors illustrate the models' analytical power by using it to map a major facet of organizational behavior-leadership—as a framework of competing values—and by showing how different types of organizational forms must be congruent with their cultural surroundings if organizations are to be effective. The model provides a capacity to explore cultural relationships consistently at different levels of analysis such as society, organization, or management. It can also be used to investigate parallel facets of analysis such as information processing, leadership style, and motivation. The approach advocates using multiple perspectives and developing counterintuitive insights when exploring cultural linkages.

In Chapter 19 ("Linking the Host Culture to Organizational Variables"), Beck and Moore employ a modified version of Quinn's and McGrath's competing values framework in exploring the linkage between some important dimensions of a national culture (Canadian) and one of that culture's major commercial institutions, the major chartered banks. Available materials from several domains such as art, literature, and folklore were drawn on in identifying cultural components that are potentially important to understanding organizations. The competing values model provides a frame for displaying such cultural features as either complementary or competing concepts.

To furnish data about the organizational and managerial cultural levels with the banking system, Beck and Moore conducted in-depth interviews with branch bank managers based on critical incidents and metaphors. The underlying assumptions, attitudes, and values held by these managers were located within the competing values framework previously constructed for the broader Canadian culture. This made it possible to explore for consistencies, inconsistencies, or absences at the various cultural levels, as briefly illustrated in the chapter. The authors regard the identification of linkages between the host culture and organizational cultures as a first step in understanding the deep significance of business behavior in a given country or region and why that behavior may differ from behavior in another cultural milieu.

The final two chapters in the section are written from a perspective of being outside organizations. That is, neither chapter centers its attention on organizational cultures per se. In Chapter 20 ("A Cultural Perspective on the Study of Industrial Relations"), Davies and Weiner explore the relationship between the external culture and some major cultural dimensions of trade unions. For them, examining the culture of trade unions is particularly important because unions historically have demonstrated a strong capability to exercise social and political force as well as economic force. Furthermore, unions often act as major agents through which external influences are brought to bear on an organization. The authors highlight the need for congruence between cultural values and the technological and economic aspects of the work setting if industrial relations are to be stable.

Chapter 21 ("Culture as Culture") concludes Part IV with a reminder that the most widely held notion of culture is that associated with the arts, letters and communications, theoretical science, recreation, religion, and education. The author, Mavor Moore, is a leading Canadian playwright, actor, producer, and critic who believes strongly that attempts by governments or business organizations to deliberately channel or constrain the free development of culture may in fact be anticultural and antisocial because of the danger of stifling human creativity. Moore wonders if social scientists are becoming too concerned with the use of culture as an instrument of business rather than treating it as the essence of individuality. According to Moore, organizations that stimulate the impulse to create will achieve more than those which try to find and impose a formula.

Some themes seem to run through all of the chapters in this section. First, there is a consensus that culture is a multidimensional concept. As such, it can be explored using the notion of levels, processes, or domains. The linkages between dimensions are made up of complex interaction and influence patterns. Although consistencies often appear, paradoxes and tensions are also likely. Second, all the essays, in one way or another, focus on context and characterize a need to develop ways of framing the broader culture so that linkages may be observed and studied. Finally, all of the authors in Part IV would probably agree that it is desirable for the culture of an organization to be in congruence or harmony with at least some dimensions of the broader culture in which it is embedded.

16

ORGANIZATION CHANGE AS A SYMBOLIC TRANSFORMATION PROCESS

Per-Olof Berg

University of Lund

STRATEGY, STRUCTURE, AND CULTURE

Corporate Culture and Strategy

While there are a number of studies on corporate culture and organizational symbolism, few studies have explicitly dealt with the issue of cultural change and development. This is surprising, as many consulting organizations claim that they are involved in corporate culture change activities, and there is much evidence of organizations that have carried out "culture revolutions," with SAS, the Scandinavian airline, being one of the best known examples in Sweden.

One of the main characteristics of the studies that exist is that they stress the "fit" between strategy and culture (e.g., Burgeois and Jemison, 1982; Kilmann, 1982). According to this view, a strategic deviance from a culture can be seen as a "cultural risk" (Schwartz and Davies, 1981) that should be minimized or avoided, possibly through an elaborate corporate culture diagnosis (Kilmann, 1982, talks for example about the Kilmann-Saxton culture gap survey). In the literature, this fit refers to intraorganizational issues (the fit between strategy and corporate culture), as well as to the fit between a strategy and the symbolic context in which an organization exists (Scholz, 1984).

One problem with this approach is that it presupposes a split between strategy and culture, thus focusing attention on the implementation of change, with little reference to the way in which change emerges as a result of the character of culture. According to other experiences (e.g., Berg, 1983a), strategy should be treated as a more or less synthesized abstraction of the aspects of corporate identity that a company wants to promote.

Another characteristic feature of the fit perspective is its focus on the way in which management uses symbols to legitimize change; that is, the use of symbols as "political tools" (Karlsson, 1984). The assumption here is that dominant groups within the organization develop powerful symbols, with the help of which they can control or manipulate the organization or the context in which it exists (for example, through language, categorizations, or "sacred" objects).

Many authors in the "cultural engineering" tradition tend to reduce culture to concepts that are easier to handle; for example, basic values (Peters and Waterman, 1982), shared understandings (Sathe, 1982), normative systems (Silverzweig and Allen, 1976), and norms (Kilmann, 1982). However, these authors give little guidance as to how to change culture as a whole. As the holistic perspective of organizations is one of the major advantages of the cultural approach, such a "reduction"of the whole drastically diminishes the value of this approach as such. Thus there seems to be a need for exploring cultural change in organizations (or rather organizational change when seen from a cultural perspective) as an issue of strategic fit. This can be done using an approach that takes corporate culture concepts seriously rather than reducing them to the scope of traditional organizational development (OD) variables.

Corporate Culture and Organizational Change

It has been argued that theories of organizational change are essentially "different ways of describing theories of action in organizations, not different theories" (March, 1981: 563). Thus, whether we look at theories of "natural" organizational change processes or of planned change, they all have at their core a particular conception of organizations and the ways in which they act.

In this chapter, the issue of organizational change will be addressed from the perspective of viewing each organization as a culture. However, as Smircich (1983) has shown, the culture concept entails a number of approaches, each with a particular perspective on organizations (spanning from classical, "functional" management theory to the understanding of organizations based on their "unconscious" processes). Thus I have an uncomfortable feeling that the concept of culture can be somewhat misleading, as it evokes images of cultural manifestations (norms, values, attitudes, habits, and the like) rather than of deeper, underlying, symbolic patterns.

Another problem is that when talking about cultural change, one assumes that it is actually possible to change (or develop) a culture in a planned way. This might well be the case, but as of today we are not yet certain, as we lack a clear theoretical conception of what a culture is, as well as empirical evidence of successful change efforts. Thus the aim of this chapter is to carry out a discourse on the concept of organization change from a symbolic perspective, rather than to discuss the more or less visible manifestations of cultural change processes. It is clear, then, that our conception of organizational culture comes close to what Smircich (1983a) calls the "organizational symbolism" approach to the study of corporate cultures.

This chapter proposes an alternative perspective of organizational change, starting from a view of organizations as "symbolic fields." The main argument here is that organizational change can be seen as a symbolic transformation process whereby the form and/or content of a symbolic field is altered. The transformation takes place in two dimensions: the diachronic-syntagmatic dimension of symbols and sagas, and the synchronic-paradigmatic dimension of metaphors and myths.

This perspective leads to a redefinition of certain strategic concepts—for example, from environments to contexts; from strategies and structures to identities, profiles, and images; from products and markets to business "concepts"; and from strategic planning to rites of renewal. Finally, a number of salient features of a culturally based paradigm for organizational strategy development may be defined. The discussion so far can be summarized with the help of Figure 16.1.

If organizational change is studied out of a traditional strategic management perspective, the major issue in the strategy-structure-culture relationship will be that of the fit between these variables, and the culture will be reduced to basic values, norms, assumptions, and the like. If, on the other hand, one starts from what will later be referred to as a symbolic perspective on organizations, the focal issue will be that of "transformation"—that is, the way in which the instrumental aspects of a culture, such as the structure and strategy, are changed in form and/or content. According to this perspective, the strategy and structure of the organization are seen as more or less conscious means of stressing certain aspects of corporate culture in a given business context, and not as ends in themselves.

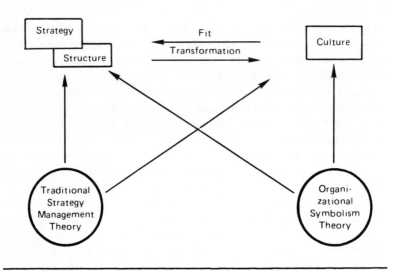

Figure 16.1

ORGANIZATIONS AS SYMBOLIC REALITIES

The Symbolic Field

According to Cassirer (1944), a person is an "animalum symbolicum" rather than an "animalum rationale." His basic argument seems to be that it is the capability for intellectual manipulations (e.g., abstract thinking, theory building, and image creation) which separates humans from animals. This ability to discriminate between an object as a physical phenomenon and the meaning assigned to that object (the creation of a symbol) makes it possible for people to deal with the world on a different level of consciousness. Following the same line of thought, Steiner (1975) and Asplund (1970) examine the creative potential in seeing the world other than it is and the need to "make alien" (that is, question) something familiar. After all, the reality in an organization as it appears to its members is essentially a symbolic construction in which the physical world is transformed into a "symbolic universe" (Cassirer, 1944: 25).

One consequence of this perspective is recognition of the wide spectrum of dimensions (cognitive, aesthetic, ethical, emotional, and so on) in which people experience or "live" the world. Another consequence is that the collective reality in which man exists is a living, symbolic universe that exists only as long as it is enacted by members of the collective (Witkin and Berg, 1984).

This last point—that humans are symbolic animals who live a symbolic reality—puts us in a difficult spot when it comes to defining the structural properties of the symbolic universe. A structure is essentially a way of ordering the world, and what most characterizes symbolic animals is their attempts to order experiences in a more or less consistent framework. This ordering process is crucial when it comes to understanding how their world is constructed.

It has been argued (e.g., Berg and Faucheux, 1982) that the structural dimension of a corporate culture can be seen as a symbolic field. This field is essentially a "holographic pattern of clustered symbolic representations" which constitute reality in the organization. It is this pattern that gives various organizational phenomena their meaning.

The symbolic field has three important characteristics. First, it consists of coded and stored collective experiences, ordered according to a certain logic. The fact that the field is a collective phenomenon is important, as it emphasizes that collective processes are involved in its creation and maintenance (i.e., through rites, rituals, and ceremonies; see Berg, 1983b).

Second, the symbolic field is the result of symbolizing and "symboling" processes by which experienced reality is transformed into symbolic reality (Witkin and Berg, 1984). By "symbolizing" we mean the conscious, purposeful, and rational creation of symbols, rituals, and the like to accomplish a certain task or achieve a certain effect. The result of the symbolizing process is essentially a set of abstract concepts, models, theories, and routines linked together with a rational logic (i.e., concepts categorizations, and languages). "Symboling" refers to the fixation of predominantly affective experiences (symbols, settings, images, and so on) in the symbolic universe. This process is manifested in the corporate myths, heroes, and fantasies that make up the most potent points of reference in the symbolic universe of the organization.

The third point is that the symbolic field is not "reality" as it once appeared but the collective symbolization of that reality. The symbolic field is essentially the result of an attempt to interpret experiences in one reality using objects, properties, and symbols from another reality. This is an important point, as it argues that organizations must be seen as similar to (but not the same as) something else. In this sense, when we talk about the organization, we refer to a metaphor of human experience, an image, a complex symbolic construction with links to the physical or objective reality.

Before discussing the dynamics (change processes) of the symbolic field, it is important to take a closer look at the two dimensions along which the field is shaped. Evidently, every organization has a history which gives meaning to its operations in the present. The way the company was created, the personality of the founder, and legends about "big battles" or other crisis situations in the corporate history are all examples of collectively stored historical experiences. In the terminology used here (partly borrowed from the linguists), these elements will be referred to as the "diachronic (through time)-syntagmatic (systematic arrangement)" dimension.

The second dimension, called the "synchronic (together in time)-paradigmatic (patterned example)," basically refers to the underlying pattern given by the war stories, horror stories, and so on that exist at any given point in time within a company. The idea is that these stories convey the basic values, beliefs, and norms upon which the organization rests in its daily operations.

The Diachronic-Syntagmatic
Dimension of Reality

Every organization has its own history and traditions which give it a sense of development and evolution; thus the organization "learns." This is what is referred to as the "diachronic" aspect of corporate life. What in fact seems to characterize organizations that successfully adapt to changing environments is their ability to share, evaluate, and store collective experiences, while rigid organizations tend to lack this ability. Like human languages, the symbolic field also has a syntagmatic logic for building up pieces (whether of history or a text) into a meaningful whole.

The saga of an organization, with its heroes and scapegoats, battles and victories, and the like gives members symbolically loaded points of reference, organized in time. This symbolic reorganization of the company history thus functions as one dimension in a complex coordination system. The diachronic-syntagmatic dimension essentially explains how organizations attempt to fixate their experiences by creating points of reference in the symbolic universe.

Quoting Plato, Ricoeur (1971: 532) argues that this activity in the social system fulfills the same function that writing does in the context of language: "to come to the rescue of the weakness of discourse." It is in fact through such fixation or "situating" that the meaning of an action is detached from the actual event. Of course, some actions make stronger imprints over time than others and eventually become points of reference in the organization's document of its history. Another way to express this notion is to say that in the life process of the organization, actions that form the essence of human experience are fixated to attributes from other realities, thus creating a fabric of meanings held together in a complicated pattern. This important aspect of culture is widely recognized in the literature and referred to as an organizational saga (Clark, 1972), an organizational story (Wilkins, 1983b) or a corporate legend (Levy, 1980).

It is important to note once again that sagas are not the same as the objective history of an organization; rather, they constitute the interpreted and reinterpreted meaning of historical events. As such, they often have some factual data in common with the historical event, but the meaning assigned to these points of reference might be quite different. Expressed another way, one can say that powerful actions create imprints that can be used to activate or mobilize a culture long after the event takes place. Thus fixated events become reference points in the symbolic universe within the organization—reference points used to guide the interpretation of present time and thus to monitor actions.

The earlier experiences stored in symbolic form also represent learning by an organization. Every organization has more or less elaborate systems for interpreting, categorizing, and storing collective experiences which are later used to guide actions. In every day language, clusters of these representations are often referred to as habits, traditions, or customs, indicating their strong influence on general and organizational behavior.

Symbolic reference points may consist of any number of objects, concepts, images, gestures, or persons that have appeared in the life of an organization. A piece of craft may come to stand for the way in which technology is viewed; an image (e.g., the corporate logo) may represent the very essence of the corporate identity; or a key person may represent an epoch in the evolution of the company.

The Synchronic-Paradigmatic
Dimension of Reality

The reality of an organization is very much influenced by values, norms, and assumptions that cannot easily be traced to its history. Seen together, all of these basic assumptions about the company and its environment form a paradigm out of which the organization operates. This paradigm, or pattern of underlying assumptions, governs the organization, both its structure and operations, at any given point in time. If the diachronic dimensions provide the symbolic field with its content, in terms of reference objects, then the synchronic-paradigmatic dimension provides the organization with the code for interpreting those points of reference.

There have been a number of attempts to approach this paradigmatic dimension from a symbolic perspective. One uses the argument that organizations are dominated by "myths" (Jonsson and Lundin, 1977). Another proposes that organizations are ruled by "root" metaphors which provide members with a reference system for interpreting reality. The major argument in both cases is that there exists a commonly shared, underlying perspective or frame of reference, a particular way of viewing the world. Like linguistic codes, this system exists out of time and space, providing the logic behind the corporate reality. It is a system, or a structure, used to interpret the actions that will later be fixated in the symbolic universe. Thus it is only a condition for communicating meanings, containing no meanings in itself.

What characterizes this synchronic dimension when viewed as a metaphor is that a meaning (meta) is carried (pherein) from one reality to another. The metaphor basically operates in the cognitive-aesthetic dimension of experience, while, as we show later, the dominant myth operates in the ethical-emotional dimension. What gives a metaphor its power is not the fact that two things are the same, but that they are similar. Morgan (1980) discusses this aspect of the metaphor, arguing that a powerful metaphor has a certain distance which is necessary to create tension—and thus understanding. If the metaphor is the same as what it is set out to capture, it is dead (Charlton, 1975) and fails to serve as a generator of meanings.

What characterizes the synchronic-paradigmatic dimension when seen as a dominant myth is that it links the organization to a larger context, an ethical universe, thus giving believers a sense of direction and purpose. This teleological aspect of the myth has been underlined by many authors (e.g., Cassirer, 1944), often combined with the notion of the extreme stability of the myth over time. Another property of the myth is its emotional load and its close connection to the value system of the organization. As the saga is the source for many of the historical reference points, so the myth is the most fundamental generator of values, and thus of policies and plans.

ORGANIZATION CHANGE AS SYMBOLIC TRANSFORMATION

Using the terminology developed above, organizational change can be seen as a transformation of the underlying symbolic field; that is, a change in the points of reference for human action. When seen from a symbolic perspective, organizational change has more to do with the transformation of mental-symbolic patterns than with their structural or strategic manifestations. Changes in the symbolic field means changes in the two dimensions of experience. In the diachronic-syntagmatic dimension, this essentially means changes in symbolic representations (the sagas, legends, and so on). In the synchronic-paradigmatic dimension, it means changes in the root-metaphor or the dominant myth of the company.

Changing Sagas

Essentially, the diachronic-syntagmatic dimension of an organization stands for the codified, accumulated, and stored experience upon which the organization relies for interpreting the present. Thus, redefining the roots of the organization essentially means to question earlier corporate experiences and the way they have been processed and stored. Making the company more aware of its roots clarifies its identity and gives a better perspective for the future.

Changing symbolic representations of experience can either be done through a redefinition of old points of reference (rewriting or reinterpreting the corporate saga; DeMarco, 1984) or through the collective creation and processing of new experiences (renewal or purification).

Below are some examples of how this might take place:

- the mere review of the corporate saga, as it may appear in anniversary speeches, in jubilees, as parts of an organizational analysis (DeMarco, 1984), and so on;

- the marking out of a new era in the life of the company through celebrations (e.g., opening up a new plant, rebuilding the office, changing name and logo, or changing top management);
- the redefinition of the corporate history by publishing "old time stories" in corporate papers, by "deifying" the retired president (or making him into a scapegoat), or reviving historical heroes (technological or managerial); and
- the marking out of a particular activity or event, such as launching a project or rewarding a particular deed.

All of these examples show how an organization more or less consciously attempts to change its own identity by manipulating the roots on which it feeds, either through an active questioning or emphasizing of the old symbols or through the creation of new ones. The basic assumption, in fact, seems to be that by doing so, or even by making certain features in the saga more visible, one creates new coordination points to guide present and future actions.

Changing the Root Metaphor

As mentioned earlier, the synchronic-paradigmatic dimension can either be seen as a root metaphor or as a dominant myth. Metaphor is basically a linguistic concept, meaning the property of expanding reality by likening one thing to another. Compared with metonymy, the metaphor opens up a phenomenon to a number of connotations on various levels. This makes it easier for interpreters to attach their particular connotations to a certain metaphor and thus to find images or associations that convey the essence of the culture. Thus metaphorical thinking (as compared to traditional linear/logical thinking) produces a holistic image in the mind of the interpreter.

What characterizes a metaphor even more is that it contains a paradoxical element. By likening a thing, a phenomenon, or a state to something familiar (but different) in another context, certain properties in the primary phenomenon will be highlighted. Rather than changing the object or phenomenon studied, one changes the context in which it is studied. Thus one of the most active elements in metaphorical operations is this contextual replacement.

The metaphor concept has been used in at least two ways to convey the basic characteristics of the synchronic-paradigmatic dimension. The first is to view it as a key to model building; that is, a more or less conscious attempt to get a condensed image of the essence of the organization (or various organizational or environmental phenomena).

Stevrin (1983) talks, for example, about "generative metaphors," those with the ability to generate meanings to human actions and that can therefore be used as control devices. What characterizes a living metaphor is that it constantly generates meanings. In the organizational change context, we may talk about business ideas or business concepts as more or less powerful metaphors to generate meaning in complex and ambiguous situations. A dead metaphor, on the other hand, has lost its capability to generate meanings. It is no longer seen as alien to the context but is taken for granted—its meaning is commonly shared and understood, with no degrees of freedom for interpretation.

The second way in which the metaphor concept is used is as a root metaphor—"a fundamental image of the world from which models and illustrative metaphors may be derived" (Brown, 1976: 170). According to this perspective, the metaphor is essentially a synchronic ordering device according to which organizational experiences are coded and sorted. Changing the root metaphor makes a profound difference in the symbolic field, which will effect not only the overall frame of reference of the members, but also the content and form of the organizational saga. A change in the root metaphor may be manifested in many ways, including:

- a change in the overall business policy of the organization, as expressed directly in policy statements or indirectly through the norms and values connected to "doing business," such as business ideas, business concepts, or service style;
- new "guiding images" in the form of corporate logos, slogans, or espoused basic values; and
- a complete redefinition of the corporate mission and vision through a redefinition of the context in which the organization exists.

All of these examples indicate that the company has changed the structure or form of the symbolic field so that it interprets reality differently than previously.

Changing the Dominant Myth

One of the basic thoughts in organizational theory has been that people come together in organized forms to do something together. Thus they are forced to develop a common understanding of what to do and how to do it. However, what has not been discussed so much is that in coming together, people also form assumptions about the very character of their organization and what it represents in a larger context (e.g., in society). In the previous section, one aspect of these assumptions was discussed—the root metaphor—but there is also another way of conceptualizing the synchronic-paradigmatic dimensions of reality: the myth.

One assumption often connected to the myth concept is that myth is a manifestation of deeper archaic-symbolic patterns. These patterns have a "grammar" of their own according to which the message in the myth can be coded and interpreted (see Broms and Gahmberg, 1979). In the same way, the symbolic field can be said to have structural properties of a "mythological" character, containing symbolic actors (heroes, villains), events (battles, encounters), and activities (rescue missions, flights) ordered in a particular way.

Even though there seems to be relatively little agreement as how to view myths in organizations, a general assumption is that myths express values. Viewed in this way, they have a certain teleological dimension (as opposed to the archaeological function of the saga), thus giving the organization a sense of direction into the future.

Myths are not easy to change. They are emotionally and ethically loaded, expressing codes of conduct in strongly value-loaded terms; that is, they express the value-logic of the organization. The value system is also connected to the teleological dimension; that is, the way in which it expresses an underlying, unconscious, deeper purpose of the organization and its members.

There have evidently been many attempts to manipulate corporate myths, and "mythmaking" is even considered to be an active instrument in organizational change (Boje et al., 1982). Others, however, argue that "to control the corporate culture by changing the stories [or] myths . . . is undoubtedly a very difficult, if not impossible, task" (Kilmann, 1982: 13). The latter viewpoint seems more likely, mainly because a myth is not only at the very core of the emotional and ethical systems of an organization, but also because a true myth follows patterns of reality beyond the scope of the organization and its immediate context. As myths have their roots deep in the archaic symbolic patterns of the world, they are not easily accessible.

IMPLICATIONS FOR PLANNED CHANGE

Redefining Strategic Concepts

As mentioned earlier, few studies have explicitly addressed the issue of cultural change in organizations relative to the large number of studies on corporate culture in general. There are even fewer examples or studies of organizational change seen from the perspective of organizations as symbolic realities (with the possible exception of Broms and Gahmberg, 1979, who study the relation between strategic changes and the underlying symbolic-mythological structure). Thus organizational change becomes an issue of redefinition (if it concerns the content of the symbolic field) or reframing (if it concerns the form of the field). By redefinition is meant a change in the meaning assigned to concepts, objects, categories, and historical persons, as well as the introduction of new symbols, without changing the form of the overall symbolic field. By reframing is meant "a change in the conceptual and/or emotional setting or viewpoint in relation to which a situation is experienced, and the placing of it in another frame that fits the facts of the same concrete situation equally well or even better and thereby changes its entire meaning" (Watzlawick et al., 1974). Expressed in the terminology of this chapter, reframing is essentially a change in the overall structure of the symbolic field, either through a replacement of the context or through changes in the root metaphor or dominant myth according to which the organization operates.

A first step in applying the theoretical framework outlined in the preceding pages is to develop strategic concepts that are consistent with this symbolic perspective. It is, for example, evident that the concepts of structure and strategy no longer sufficiently capture the symbolic character of the strategic change process. Neither is it adequate to add culture as a third element to the structure-strategy formula. Rather, we need to seriously question the character of the strategic concepts that are to be used in monitoring strategic organization change processes.

From Environments to Contexts

Bearing in mind the view of organizations as living metaphors, the relation to the environment becomes somewhat problematic. It is evident that the traditional market, domain, and niche concepts will no longer adequately cover the character of the organization-environment interface. Thus, rather than talking of environments, one can talk about contexts; that is, the definition of the background (or frame) that gives the organization its meaning.

The corporate context stands for the symbolic reality in which an organization chooses to exist. Thus the context is a matter of definition rather than of a factual environment. The environment in our terms is more a sense of definition and choice than something given beforehand or predetermined. Thus the context is the "framing" of the company, and the problem of strategic change becomes mainly an issue of reframing, of creating a different context. "Contextual dependency" essentially means that the view of the organization and what it stands for (its mission and vision), its identity (its character and properties), is dependent on the context in which it is seen. If a company, for example, moves from a national to an international context, the national-cultural character of the company (which previously was completely neglected) will be of the utmost importance. Thus a focal issue is that of contextual choice, the conscious construction and/or selection of the background in which the company forms the figure.

For a long time we have been aware that organizations create their own environments (Starbuck, 1976), but we have not been very successful in showing how. What is suggested is that this takes place through "contextual redefinitions"; that is, that the organization redefines the domain or niche in which it exists. This could explain why some organizations experience changes in the environment as a serious threat whereas others (in the same industry) might perceive them as golden opportunities.

What is argued here is that by treating the environment as a context, it becomes a matter of definition—a symbolic reality—rather than being something unambiguously given beforehand. This does not mean that environmental restrictions can be defined away, but rather that the mission and vision of the company may be seen in another light when changing the context. Consider the traditional example of the company that changed its purpose from making watches (a product) to measuring time (function). Such a redefinition of the context in which one exists, from the watch-producing to the time-measuring business, will have a profound impact not only in the way the company structures or segments the market (moving into all types of time-measuring businesses like the space industry, laboratory equipment, and so on), but also in terms of the products that are created.

From Products and Markets
to Business Concepts

Given the view of organizations as symbolic realities and environments as contexts, the question is immediately raised of how to treat traditional strategic concepts such as products (product groups), markets (market segments), service styles, and business logics, as well as how to relate to the large number of more or less advanced strategic tools based on these variables (product-market matrices, life cycle curves, and the like).

I have chosen to introduce the idea of the business concept as one way of dealing with this issue. A concept is essentially a way of gathering a thought or an idea through a general notion; that is, an inclusive way of communicating the essential idea behind what a company is attempting to do in a particular context. A business concept basically stands for an integrated whole consisting of markets, products, delivery systems, business logics, service characteristics, and the overall lifestyle of the company. The basic assumption is that finding, or defining, a business concept helps the organization to integrate all of these strategic considerations into a whole, which in turn helps it to interpret reality and focus strategic action.

One example of a business concept is the SAS business class (or Euroclass) concept, which not only stands for a certain market segment—the business traveler—but also for a completely new set of products (e.g., special check-in counters, special lounges, and limousine service) and a special service (business) philosophy, including a number of catchy phrases and particular ways of treating the customers. Another example would be IKEA, the Swedish (now international) furniture store chain, which relies on what they call the "IKEA concept," standing for a "Scandinavian" lifestyle characterized by thriftiness, unconventionality, and smart (in terms of design) solutions.

From Strategies and Structures to Identities, Profiles, and Images

Traditionally, strategy and structure have been key concepts in theories of organizational change. When applying the symbolic approach outlined in this chapter, the application of the strategy and structure concepts becomes problematic. The structure that is important in the above framework is, for example, not the physical, logistic, or authority structure outlined in a chart of plant outlines but the collective meanings or mental structures existing in the mind of the organization's members. In the same way, the strategy in a symbolic perspective becomes nothing but a conscious formulation of (a part of) the underlying corporate myth. A strategy is not seen as a plan but as a collective image that can be acted upon.

Thus, rather than talking about structures as static manifestations of present and future states, I will introduce the concept of identity, and rather than talk about strategies as directions for action, I will talk about profiles as consciously developed mental guidelines. Finally, the contextual dependency of the corporate culture has led to the introduction of the "image" notion to conceptualize the way the company is perceived by the public.

The corporate identity essentially means the significant properties of a corporate culture in relation to a given context. What characterizes the identity of an organization is that it contains not only the character of the symbolic field (its saga, root metaphor, myths, and so on), but also the mechanisms developed to maintain and change that field (rites, rituals, and celebrations). The corporate identity is essentially a collective identity, a commonly shared understanding of what the organization is all about and how it should operate.

The strongest strategic advantage of introducing the identity concept is that it immediately links into the historical (diachronic-syntagmatic) dimension of the organization. This dimension is often neglected in the synchronically oriented strategy-structure discussions that seem to characterize traditional strategic thinking. Another important advantage is that the identity concept leads to "individuation," the process through which a social system develops its potential and reaches qualitatively higher levels of functioning. This is particularly important in that one well-recognized disadvantage of the present strategic paradigm is its lack of qualitative appreciation for corporate functioning (most strategic models focus on strength and growth rather than on excellence).

The profile of the company incorporates the conscious attempts of management to support certain aspects of identity. In developing the profile, the company draws attention to particular aspects of its identity that are considered to be important for its existence and legitimization in the wider society. Compared with the traditional strategy concept, the profile includes not only the business philosophy (and business logics) but also the management philosophy of the company. Thus the concepts broaden our understanding of strategic actions and point at the importance of a consistency between what a company should do (the business philosophy) and how it should do it (the management philosophy).

The corporate image is the way in which a company is seen by the public. The image is often different from the profile that the company tries to project on the outside world. However, it is not only a distorted projection but also a contextually loaded image, a metaphor, which has borrowed properties from other companies in the same industry or from unintended public exposures, scandals, hero- or success stories, and so on. There are some things that seem to be more powerful in forming a sense of corporate image than others, such as the corporate logo, symbolic characters in the organization, its saga and creation, present public persons and their appearance, and successes or losses. Again, when we talk about the corporate image, we refer to a symbolic construction rather than a fact. It is the meaning of the company and its actions when seen from the perspective of the outside world.

From Strategic Planning to Rites of Renewal

According to our theoretical framework, a strategic change program is a symbolic operation of a highly ritualistic character. More precisely, if correctly performed it is a "rite of renewal" by which the organization attempts to gain insight into the very reasons for its existence and to collectively reaffirm or renew itself (Berg, 1983a).

By introducing the concept of rites of renewal rather than strategic planning, three factors in the strategic process are emphasized. The first is the collective character of the activity. A rite is always a collective process, an activity in which a number of people participate simultaneously. If strategic change, when seen from a symbolic perspective, essentially calls for a change in shared images (or symbols), then involving collective processes is a necessary step for such change. Thus it is a collectively performed undertaking in which members from different parts of an organization can participate.

The second factor is the emphasis on the link between what emerges and the identity of the organization. A rite of renewal is thus founded at the very core of the company, and the strategy that results is expressed as root values or basic beliefs rather than as operationalized plans for actions.

The third point is that the rite is not a simple forecasting process but an undertaking that questions the corporate mission and vision. Thus the rite also challenges the social and political system in a company. The outcome of a rite cannot be entirely predicted, and a serious strategic change program is therefore an exploration of the unknown, where traditional frameworks and maps do not suffice.

TOWARD A NEW STRATEGIC PARADIGM

In this chapter I have argued that taking the corporate culture concept seriously means a requestioning of many of the major strategic concepts, and not adding the culture concept as just another variable in the organization equation. Using a theoretical framework built on the assumption that organizations can be seen as symbolic fields, the analysis has proposed four important changes in strategic thinking.

The first is the enlargement of the environment concept, from domains and niches to contexts, thereby indicating the symbolic and relativistic character of the reality in which the organization chooses to exist. The second is the introduction of business concepts to emphasize the need for consistency between not only markets and products but also service styles and business logics. The third proposal is that of introducing identity, profile, and image as supplements to strategy and structure in the change process. Finally, I have argued that a true strategic change process should be a rite of renewal wherein the organization questions the basis for its own existence.

What has been said above can have a strong impact on management thinking and managerial actions. I now summarize three of the more important consequences in the form of slogans:

You can't change a culture! (but you can facilitate a development of its identity). By definition, a corporate culture cannot be pressed down upon a collective, nor can it be controlled or manipulated at will. A true strategic change program does not impose anything but makes people aware of and illuminates certain aspects of the culture in which they exist. In this sense it is also a creative process; by bringing values, principles, and behaviors to the surface, and by providing people with a framework with which they can interpret what they see, a creative and emancipatory process is started. The step between emancipation and manipulation is, however, not a very long one. The basic difference is the quality of the dialogue that is created rather than in the content of the outcome. To interpret a culture requires a dialogue between different levels of an organization. A true dialogue, one where the parties are really open do not know what will come out of it, requires risktaking and courage. It also requires an "opening" (as opposed to open) attitude, a will to go deep into a joint exploration of the company and what it stands for.

Issues are smarter than people. This phrase captures the dilemma of strategic corporate culture development in a nutshell. It essentially says that the corporate symbolic universe follows a logic of itself, more powerful than the intentions of individual members or groups. By framing an issue in a particular way—for example, by linking it to powerful symbols in the history of the organization—the collective logics get activated and the development will follow its course.

Thus the obvious consequences for management will be to focus a lot of attention on formulating and framing strategic issues (rather than developing strategic plans), and to trust that the syntactic logics of these issues will be interpreted and acted upon in a way that is consistent with the corporate culture. Another way of saying this is that the strategic managerial emphasis will be changed from managing people or money to the management of meaning (see Bednar and Hineline, 1982).

Images are more potent than plans. Beck and Moore (1984) report how companies and managers use images to convey meanings to their employees and to the public. They have even shown that there is a direct relationship between the quality of the imagery and managerial performance. This suggests that the manager who has the ability to think symbolically and to develop and use images to convey his or her thoughts will be more efficient than another who lacks this ability. Strategic images are "broadband" conceptualizations of the future, whereas plans are narrower descriptions of how to get there. By leaving the way open, but by creating a powerful and corporately "grounded" image of a desired state, there are more opportunities for the creative search process to succeed. The image-creating ability is particularly important during periods of organizational change, when the members of a company need a concise sense of the direction in which they are moving.

Manage your symbolic resources. I stated earlier that the change that is really important is that in the collective mental imagery rather than in political, economic, or social structures. Thus one consequence for strategic change is that the target of change is this mental imagery and the context in which it exists. According to this view, strategic plans and new organizational structures are means through which this symbolic collective reframing takes place, and not ends in themselves.

At the base of any strategic change process there must be a clear conception of what the organization is in relation to its wider context (its mission) and what it is aiming at (its vision). Thus the emphasis in strategic management is likely to change from managing people or money to managing "symbolic resources."

17

CULTURE COLLISIONS IN MERGERS AND ACQUISITIONS

Gordon A. Walter

University of British Columbia

Mergers and acquisitions are important and powerful means by which corporate leaders create and implement strategy. The popularity of mergers and acquisitions is at least partially the result of their usefulness in bringing dramatic corporate changes. Unfortunately, few organizational issues related to mergers and acquisitions have received scholarly scrutiny, and organizational culture will probably be one of the last aspects to be closely and systematically studied.

Organizational research is problematic because the power dynamics of mergers and acquisitions often require secrecy and celerity, thus making longitudinal comparisons difficult. Information, which exists in abundance, is generally in the form of post hoc, retrospective sense making. A second source of information is public manifestations of conflict and dissatisfaction, the true meaning of which must remain in doubt. This chapter explores cultural conflict in the aftermath of mergers and acquisitions. It is believed that information does exist that is useful to academic analysis, and one feels the need to make a stab at some salient cultural dynamics associated with mergers and acquisitions. Two general categories are used to explore this topic: types of mergers and acquisitions, and major values and cultural themes. The second issue is further subdivided into six pairs of concepts to allow discussion of some relevant organizational dynamics.

CULTURE AND MERGERS

Culture is taken to be the shared attitudes, values, beliefs, and customs of members of a social unit or organization. For focus and economy, it is held that values are to the individual what culture is to the organization. As Bougon et al. (1977) point out, values are the basis of action but are not tightly coupled to action the way goals are. The challenge for individuals is to find goals that are meaningfully linked to values. That is, while goals can be pursued, their value is determined by the individual. Goals determine the "what" of organizational activity and are tightly linked to the "how"; values pertain to the "why" of activity for an individual. The perspective taken on culture in this chapter involves something beyond sense making (of a merely cognitive interpretive variety) and extends to the creation of meaning as well. Still, our definition of culture as shared attitudes, values, beliefs, and customs by members of a social unit is a rather standard view of culture (G. R. Jones, 1983).

This chapter accepts the finance field's current notion that mergers and acquisitions are best understood as a manifestation of the struggle for corporate control rather than merely the search for immediate profits (Jensen and Ruback, 1983). The significance of such an explanation is potentially enormous, and this chapter pursues one of several possible avenues of inquiry.

THE CENTRAL CONFLICT

In the spirit of Hegelian dialectic inquiry, let us consider two fundamental and antithetical value systems. The first centers on individuals (humans) and the second on capital (property).[1] Other value bases such as "preservation of nature" might also be relevant to mergers and acquisitions but will not be explored here. Radical humanists would argue that human rights are primary and the only legitimate rights and that property rights are derivative (Burrell and Morgan, 1979; Walter, 1984). By contrast, economists assume that property rights are central. It is by mobilizing, preserving, and managing property that other utilities (especially leisure) are realized and enjoyed (G. R. Jones, 1983). The reality of organizational culture is that some concept of a balance between these competing value bases tends to exist in stable systems. Thus this chapter assumes that, prior to a merger, there is a distinctive cultural reality in a given organization. This cultural status quo is broadly acknowledged, if not enjoyed or fully embraced.

A synthesis or coexistence of the two polarities described above is assumed to exist in the culture of any organization prior to a merger/acquisition event. Since mergers and acquisitions represent the assertion of power in the service of property rights, it is inevitable that this status quo be disturbed. A new thesis is asserted which in turn invites and perhaps even generates a new antithesis position on behalf of human rights. Ultimately, a new synthesis is formed. This process appears to take five years or longer. The way in which the actual synthesis might be effected is beyond the scope of this chapter.

Our present goal is to elaborate some of the major issues in the conflict between human rights versus property rights. The pivotal human rights elements of concern here are freedom, self-esteem, and equality (Walter, 1984); the corresponding property rights elements are control, performance, and primacy. Figure 17.1 summarizes these points and shows six values for the "human" position: security, privacy, identity, inclusion, comparable competence, and self-determination. Property rights are reflected in the notions of flexibility (in the use of capital and labor), scrutiny, substitutability, segregation, superior competence, and organizational direction. The figure provides a paired comparison of these antithetical value expressions (see Martin, Feldman, et al., 1983, for a different sense of such polarities). The discussion that follows treats the specific themes and issues arising from mergers and acquisitions as they pertain to these fundamental value expressions.

Security Versus Flexibility

The importance of security for freedom and self-esteem is quite obvious. Freedom from pain, anxiety, and deprivation is desirable and contributes to self-esteem. In this sense, security is survival. The property value expression that stands as the antithesis to security is flexibility. Efficient use of capital requires making staffing adjustments, altering investment priorities, and so forth. These acts require a degree of flexibility that often runs counter to the security of the individuals affected (see Figure 17.1).

Of fundamental importance is the fact that an acquisition is, in essence, a capital reallocation. A significant cultural issue then arises: How cruel or kind will one's employer be (Martin, Feldman, et al., 1983)? Following an acquisition, this question blazes in target company employees' minds. A takeover is generally based on the acquiring management's belief that they can utilize capital in the target more efficiently than is currently the case. This is the economic justification for premium payments in a takeover, which average about 18 percent (Jensen and Ruback, 1983). Such efficiency must come from doing the same task at less cost or from doing it better at the same cost. Either way, target company managers are right in expecting increased performance pres-

Value Basis	Human			Property		
Pivotal Elements	Freedom	Esteem	Equality	Control	Performance	Primacy
Value Expressions	Security			Flexibility		
	Privacy			Scrutiny		
	Identity			Substitutability		
	Inclusion			Segregation		
	Comparable competence			Superior competence		
	Self determination			Organizational direction		

Figure 17.1 Value Contrasts

sure and reduced autonomy. They are also right in expecting increased coercion from above (Martin, Feldman, et al., 1983; Walter, 1982). In fact, this may be the best set of circumstances that they can hope for, since wholesale elimination of target company management is often the practice of acquirers (especially in horizontal takeovers). By contrast conglomerates often impose financial performance standards but otherwise keep their hands off for six months or a year. By this point any required levels of coercion are internally justified by unacceptable financial performance ("We gave them a chance to pull up their socks"). Under such pressures, target management often "draw the circle tighter," but there is little evidence that anything more than an illusion of security is created by such practices (Janis, 1972).

Finally, many acquired companies experience the new owner's control as occurring between an entire replacement of top management and hands-off financial policies. Visitations of varying frequency by acquiring company executives and technical experts can shorten time frames for adjustment by the head office and at the same time intimidate the acquired company's managers (O'Day, 1974). It is also not unusual for managers to be "parachuted" in to the acquired company from the head office. This action precipitates real anxiety and a paranoiagenic climate (DeBoard, 1978; Kets de Vries, 1984). The paranoia is constantly stimulated and exacerbated by the in-group/out-group dynamics between the old guard and the occupational troops. Thus these management moves serve the needs of capital for a timely response to required shifts in capital utilization following a takeover, but they simultaneously undermine the security of managers at the acquired company. It is not surprising that, following a takeover, often the one or two target company managers whom the acquirer would like to have retained (who are also the most mobile) leave and take their chances with a new employer rather than get trapped in such takeover dynamics.

Privacy Versus Scrutiny

The significance of privacy for freedom in an environment of power imbalances has been well argued in law and the behavioral sciences (Breckenridge, 1970; Walter, 1984). Freedom means pursuing one's own goals, but power imbalances give others the ability to thwart those goals (sometimes for irrelevant reasons). Thus an executive with an alcoholic spouse might keep that information private lest negative attributions about the cause of the spouse's problems or possible complicity with those problems be made. There is little appeal in industry for permitting such factors to affect the judgment of superiors. Rather, it is in the interest of capital to scrutinize anything and everything that pertains to the dispensation and utilization of capital. Does the manager's spouse need expensive care or time- and energy-consuming attention from the manager? Will this result in an increased probability of theft or a reduced capacity to perform?

Following a takeover, increased reporting is virtually always expected and demanded. This reporting initially may involve accounting, financial planning, capital decision making, and basic performance statistics, especially for holding company acquirers. However, the trend toward group management structures (even within conglomerates) indicates that far more scrutiny is desired by representatives of property. Strategic plans, explicit manpower succession charting, electronic data processing and other technical interchange, multiple reporting relations between subsidiary and parent companies, as well as top management contact and involvement via visitations between acquirer and acquired companies are all ways by which more scrutiny can be exacted. It is also not unusual for acquiring companies to require managers in targets to undergo rigorous psychological testing (two days), with follow-ups (two hours) at regular intervals (quarterly). Since acquirers often suffer from limited expertise and insufficient operations knowledge as to the business of acquired companies, there is a tendency to desire any and all fragments of information that may prevent these shortcomings from being exploited by the acquired company's management.

Identity Versus Substitution

Man's search for meaning in life and at work can be conceptualized in many ways. The notion of identity seems appropriate to this level of discussion, since identity includes the values inherent in one's "being and action" (Frankl, 1966), as well as the explicit qualities attributed to oneself. Further, to identify with one's work, community, and employer implies that in these domains a congruence exists between self and context. Martin, Feldman, et al. (1983) discuss reactions to fit and lack of fit around such core values as "identification" and "distancing," for which sociologists typically substitute the term "alienation" (Geyer and Schweifzer, 1981). Identification means caring, and organization members inevitably pose the question, "I care—do they?" (Martin, Feldman, et al., 1983). That such caring is often directed at an organization's official, or even unofficial, mission rather than at profit per se is obvious

By contrast, capital primarily values the substitutability of elements, since it is through substitutions that the flexibility is achieved which allows maximum capital utilization. Here, the bureaucratic principle of division of labor may come to mind as an outgrowth of property values and a hunger for substitutability. However, another bureaucratic notion is even more relevant: the notion of impersonality in dealing with employees, since it is impersonality, more than the division of labor, which facilitates personnel substitutions. The division of labor makes substitutions practical (the "can" component), but impersonality makes them emotionally tolerable (the "may" component). It also serves the need to think of people as expressions of capital (manpower, human capital, "bodies"). Thus it is congruent with a need to legitimize adjustments that are eminently practical in terms of nonhuman objects.

Returning to Martin, Feldman, et al.'s (1983) notion of identification/distancing and the question about caring, one sees substitutability as antithetical to personal identification. Imagine a $50 million per year company that has been bought and sold three times in two years. Imagine a meeting between the managers of the acquired company and the chairman of the new owning company. When told by the chairman that "he cares," management incredulity is boundless. Reciprocity is central to normal power relations in commercial intercourse (Blau, 1967), but this requirement is simply swamped by the acquiring company/target company power asymmetry. The injection of massive reporting requirements that adhere to standardized reporting conventions (none of which are tailored to the realities of the "business" of the target company) further underlines the substitutability/impersonality of the new relationship. No illusions as to what or who is important remain for target management. It is not one's unique contribution to the target's mission that matters but a more abstract, impersonal, and ultimately substitutable emphasis on overall capital efficiency. And this emphasis has been escalated.

Horizontal mergers such as that of Northeastern and Pan Am Airlines emphasize the substitutability issue, for in this case the integration of operations to improve economies of scale and route synergies required transcending the corporate identifications of thousands of employees. Pan Am employees felt more elite, Northeastern employees were more down to earth, and so forth. Two years after the merger, questions of seniority rights, bargaining unit representation, and a host of other "local" issues were still frightfully tangled. That many workers felt "distanced" from the new merged entity is an understatement.

Other factors also reduce identification with organizations and jobs. When a target company accounts for less than 3 percent of sales of the total enterprise, it tends to be ignored by top management (Kitching, 1967). In capital terms, this may make a great deal of sense, but when top management ceases to report to a board and becomes trivial in the eyes of the new parent company's top management, the alienation can be profound (Mirvis, 1984a). Requirements of standardized and formalized reporting and explicit succession plans further deemphasize the uniqueness of management in the subsidiary while signaling top management's desire to make such a unit and its elements highly substitutable. Thus, "I care—do they?" has an obvious answer in the aftermath of a takeover.

Inclusion Versus Segregation

The fourth major expression of pivotal values in terms of social units is the desire for a sense of belonging or inclusion. This feeling serves primitive psychological needs and relates to one's identity, security, and self-determination. Much management is conducted within mutual loyalty patterns, the establishment of which involves inclusion within one or more coalitions (groups with values, norms, and vested interests). At one level, this can be thought of in terms of the affiliation component of an organization climate or culture (Litwin and Stringer, 1964), but it also speaks to the stabilization of power relations and thus has power implications (Pfeffer, 1981b).

In most cases, takeovers assault "cozy" relations. Multiple reporting channels (accounting, human resources, and so forth), plus revised procedures, fractionate the old ruling coalition of the target firm. Thus, while previously the coalition attempted to "manage the board," this becomes less and less feasible. Intensified performance pressure, heightened scrutiny, and visitations from headquarters emphasize coercive power and thus further destabilize the coalitions. Holding company "hands-off" niceties can have the paradoxical effect of intensifying bonding among members of the ruling coalition, but this can have the undesirable effect of excluding others (subordinates) from management's increasingly insular machinations (bunker mentality; Mirvis, 1984a).

If a holding company's segregation of each subsidiary and its function is effective, the coalition will be fragmented and cease to yield a united front. The power dynamic guarantees a climate shift away from affiliation and toward power and achievement. Most probably, efficient utilization of capital is served by such a shift, but inclusion and related identity needs tend to take a beating. In horizontal mergers, such as the airlines noted above, inclusion can and must be managed to create both viable power groupings and to meet social needs of employees. Corporate name changes and other symbolic acts can help here, but mostly it takes time.

Comparable Competence Versus Superior Performance

According to economic theory, individuals sell their leisure time to employers. This model captures the idea that individuals often consider their job rights and compensation as pertaining to their trade-offs and effort (inputs) rather than to exactly what they accomplish (outputs). Such is the logic of labor's position in collective bargaining (G. R. Jones, 1983). For many it is hard to imagine maintaining self-esteem without some faith that "good enough" *is* good enough. That is, one does not have to be superior in order to be adequate. Thus college graduates (and not just honors graduates) are "highly educated" people, and an average doctor is trusted by most. Unions further enshrine this notion by pursuing seniority rights in jobs rather than in performance evaluations so that they can insulate members from competitive pressures that could undermine esteem and security.

By contrast, corporations in a competitive economy find that no insulation from competition exists. Average performance is often *not* good enough, since better performing firms eventually tend to overwhelm average competitors. Superior performance becomes required, as the Japanese car invasion of North America attests. If the takeover firm is a holding company, the expression of pressure to improve performance is experienced as the efficient use of capital. That is, holding companies can "win" because greater subsidiary scrutiny allows better capital allocation decisions than would occur in other circumstances. This means that employees and managers of subsidiaries face superior performance expectations and related pressures after a takeover. Moreover, since selling a subsidiary is the ultimate coercive act, holding companies are able to make performance demands credible. Unfortunately, abundant evidence exists that such corporations are rarely able to help subsidiaries perform better because of a lack of relevant expertise, but one might argue that substitutability often makes up for scrutiny.

By contrast, concentric acquisitions (where companies have similar technologies, as will be elaborated later) and horizontal acquisitions often yield situations where such expertise and the related ability to scrutinize do exist. Here too, however, superiority also can become the drive, since the acquirer is often "bigger league" than the target. More importantly, there is a presumption of superiority by the acquirer's staff, so that any "occupational troops" sent in to help the target may find themselves in an ingroup-outgroup competition. Often, acquirer personnel deal with this competition by denegrating people and procedures in the target company. For such dynamics, a little goes a long way, and the esteem of the "inferior" subsidiary staff generally suffers. Some outputs can always be criticized and generally are, but in takeovers superiority assertions create unusually intense criticism.

Self-Determination Versus Organizational Direction

The final way in which fundamental value positions find expression involves control (Martin, Feldman, et al., 1983). Behavioral science widely documents autonomy and actualization needs. Further, the freedom ethic in Western nations is central to such needs for human well-being. By contrast, the management of capital is avowedly focused on control and direction. The management of people requires a balance. Since acquisitions represent an assertion of capital, it is reasonable to expect greater direction and control to be central to the designs of takeover corporations. In concentric and horizontal mergers, adequate expertise exists to direct and control the most minute aspects of subsidiary operations, which leaves the power of subsidiary management and staff seriously undercut. They may perceive themselves as technocratic pawns rather than as leaders or originators of their enterprise's evolution (Nord, 1984). The pressure for increased control in such situations, especially during the first year after a takeover, is so common that this is probably why, almost immediately after a takeover announcement, the most talented and self-directing often leave a target organization. Such desertions, plus the breakdown of social networks, further undermine a sense of self-determination in target company management. Thus it is not surprising that target management describe takeovers as "Saturday night massacres" or "rape" and worry about the acquirer "milking" (that is, misusing) subsidiary profits.

Holding companies tend to impose less direct and more long-term external direction. They often have a "wait and see" approach. This, however, can produce immobilizing levels of fear and uncertainty. For example, since ultimate standards are determined far away from operational reality of the subsidiary, little sense of a linkage with relevant response alternatives can be hoped for. When the parent is affected by factors beyond the scope of the target, the feeling of unimportance is accentuated. That a sense of insignificance and powerlessness can go together is obvious. Performance in the firm can thus decline and the control sought by all concerned can, paradoxically, be lost.

MERGER AND ACQUISITION DYNAMICS

The manner in which the central conflict is expressed can now be explored a level further. Using four merger and acquisition types, this section will scrutinize specific values or cultural elements in target organizations that are assaulted via merger and acquisition implementation dynamics. Cultural elements imposed on new "partners" or subsidiaries will be simultaneously highlighted and related to Figure 17.1. Further, the mechanisms for inducing change following the merger or acquisition will be discussed as they pertain to the central value items treated.

Merger and Acquisition Types

Two areas where there has been some clarification of thought involve types of mergers and acquisitions and strategic goals. These are important focal points for the discussion that follows on possible organizational research issues, and as a starting point for serious scholarly study of the phenomenon. Four merger types are useful when organizational issues are of paramount interest: vertical, horizontal, concentric, and conglomerate (see Kitching, 1967). They are defined as follows:

- *Vertical:* mergers in which a buyer-seller relationship exists or could exist between two firms (Federal Trade Commission's [FTC] vertical merger)
- *Horizontal:* mergers between firms with identical products operating in the same or different markets (FTC's horizontal mergers plus FTC's market extension-conglomerate mergers)
- *Concentric:* mergers between firms with highly similar production or distributional technologies (FTC's product extension-conglomerate mergers; Thompson, 1967; Perrow, 1970)
- *Conglomerate:* mergers between two firms with *no* buyer-seller relationship, technical and distributional relationship, or identical products (FTC's pure conglomerate mergers)

Vertical Mergers and Acquisitions

Vertical mergers generally serve the purpose of reducing dependencies (Pfeffer and Salancik, 1978), vulnerabilities (Klein et al., 1978), and/or costs (Williamson, 1975). In terms of the value contrasts of Figure 17.1, perhaps the most striking change for the target company is the shift in control. Target management must shift from serving the market to linking with the acquiring or parent firm. Self-determination is reduced and replaced by parent organizational direction. Subsidiary executives are essentially demoted to middle management roles. Entrepreneurship must make way for responsiveness to bureaucratic control mechanisms such as rules, hierarchy, goals, and plans. Cultural elements that replace those valued when self-determination was higher include those related to bureaucratic systems—alignment skills, politics, reward seeking, and rule sensing. There is often an increased emphasis on cost control and a reduced ability to invest in market adaptation sensing and opportunity seeking. Thus a general trend appears toward conservatism or, in Miles and Snow's (1978) terms, a shift away from prospecting and toward defending.

Horizontal Mergers and Acquisitions

Horizontal mergers are not as easy to approach as vertical mergers because they involve many complex and varied issues and strategies. Some of these points were touched upon earlier in this chapter. These mergers can seek to consolidate operations and thus serve two firm's clients with little more than one firm's resources. At the opposite extreme, when two similar firms from different geographic locations combine forces, quite different dynamics are involved. Most horizontal mergers involve elements of both examples, with redundancy of facilities and personnel and integration at linkage points being major organizing issues. Personnel redundancy at high levels is often a major factor in these mergers. Thus the compatibility of styles and values between management and staff becomes central in personnel decisions. Since most mergers involve one party being more than equal, it is reasonable to speak of the acquiring organization as having the majority of control over these matters.

Often the entire culture of the acquiring firm is forced upon the target. All of the standard bureaucratic control mechanisms discussed for vertical acquisitions are relevant here, but there is also the likelihood that the acquiring firm will send in "occupational" management who understand the business and can rapidly impose personnel adjustments to ensure that the "right" approach is followed. Simultaneously, physical settings and all associated symbols of the target organization are stripped away and replaced by those of the acquirer. Survivors in the new endeavor rapidly learn the ways of their new corporation and assimilate its culture. In terms of Figure 17.1, the substitutability of staff and facilities in horizontal mergers diminishes the ability of members of the target firm to maintain group solidarity and thus meet either inclusion or social identity needs. The task similarities also increase the ability of acquirer managers to scrutinize target organization personnel, and thus the self-determination of target personnel is further reduced.

Concentric Mergers and Acquisitions

Concentric mergers are highly similar to horizontal mergers in that the similarity of task expertise makes the imposition of occupational managers practical. Unlike horizontal mergers, physical facilities are seldom consolidated, although other corporate symbols may be comprehensively changed. The most important change factor, which is unique to concentric mergers and acquisitions, is for a few highly skilled representatives of the acquiring firm to analyze the new subsidiary. Such analyses tend to yield serious and highly public criticism and often involve charges of incompetence. The important issue here is that such scrutiny is used to emphasize particularly valued skills from the acquiring company culture. If target personnel were to argue that they had skills that the acquirer lacked or that their skills in the areas emphasized by the analysis team had always been adequate, they would be missing the point, since the critique serves primarily as an intimidation ritual (O'Day, 1974).

The criticism of areas presumed to be adequate and the discounting of skills which are special sources of pride combine to diminish the self-esteem of target personnel. This process seems to reduce the capacity of target company personnel to resist the cultural change demands of the acquiring firm. Clearly, self-determination and identity are reduced. One particularly relevant source of change in concentric mergers is the way in which the acquiring company's reward system comes into play. Following the initial destabilization period, the reward system serves to legitimize the central skills valued by the acquirer. That earlier events also served to legitimize a change in the dispensation of rewards also deserves emphasis here.

Conglomerate Mergers and Acquisitions

Conglomerate takeovers tend to be the most benign of all the sources of cultural change discussed in this chapter. Few outward changes are forthcoming, and control tends to center on financial reporting. The latter generally requires significant upgrading of the financial reporting capacities of subsidiaries and often a shift in the internal power structure toward the financial accounting function at the expense of marketing and human resources. The small cadre of executives at the top of subsidiaries thus experience the greatest dislocation following a merger. In a sense, one can think of conglomerates as a special case of concentric mergers in which the central shared technology and related skills are financial manipulation and reporting. On a long-term basis, of course, the fundamental shift in top management priorities tends to be translated throughout the subsidiary.

The uniqueness of conglomerates probably lies in the heightened pressure to perform and the reduced security of members in the new subsidiary. It is the flexibility of the conglomerate form which allows "do or die" demands to be made of subsidiaries. The lack of scrutiny on dimensions other than financial can be a problem, but conglomerates tend to be organized in group management structures that compensate enormously. Further, consulting psychologists are more than willing to sell their services for incredibly close scrutiny of many of the most important determinants of managerial functioning. In the final analysis, these approaches to scrutiny are consistent with the impersonal, competitive, rational culture sought by many conglomerates and thus undermine attempts of subsidiary personnel to insulate themselves from the dominant cultural shift.

CONCLUSION

Mergers and acquisitions are profound disturbers of organizational cultures. By and large they represent an assertion of property rights relative to human rights. Postmerger cultural dynamics pivot on target company management and staff reactions to the control, performance, and privacy or superiority assertions of the acquiring company. Once a new synthesis has been reached, these dynamics cease to be a problem. However, much time and pain and many personnel changes are involved for most acquisitions before a new synthesis is struck. Three to five years is not an unusual transition time, and it can be much longer. To date there has apparently been no analysis of the costs in either human or efficiency terms, so central is the fundamental assertion of property rights. Justification of the legitimacy of takeovers in terms of market efficiency or the efficient use of capital seems to have the focus of property rights advocates, but these efforts are insufficient. It is easy to believe that costs are as high as 25 to 30 percent of the acquired firm performance in most cases. If so, this cost factor swamps market efficiency factors in the short run and forces serious consideration of whether one primarily values humans rather than capital, or perhaps both rather than either one.

NOTE

1. Argyris (1957) uses this type of dialectic in his seminal *Personality and Organization*, although here the focus is quite different.

18

THE TRANSFORMATION OF ORGANIZATIONAL CULTURES
A Competing Values Perspective

Robert E. Quinn
SUNY at Albany

Michael R. McGrath
University of Southern California

Thinking about the dynamics between organizational culture and societal culture is like considering the interface between the sand and the sea. Usually, one of two perspectives undergrids our analysis. Sometimes in examining the interface we note the dominance of the tide (external culture) and recognize that the fine patterns on the beach (organization) are never the same at any two points in time. At other times we note the dominance of the beach, relatively constant in place, shape, and size and a powerful determinant of how the sea behaves. Occasionally, however, a third, transformational perspective emerges. Here we observe a unique storm. We see a relationship in dynamic tension, characterized by a pattern of furious opposition that leads to a transformation of the elements and of the interface itself.

TRANSFORMATION: THE NEED FOR NEW WAYS OF THINKING

In considering the construct of culture, we are interested in the phenomena of transformation. More particularly, we are interested in the contradiction, tension, and paradox that leads to transformation. Unfortunately, our present theories are not very helpful in this area. Van de Ven (1983), for example, reviews the popular book, *In Search of*

Excellence (Peters and Waterman, 1982), and focuses on the importance of paradox. He argues that while the managers of excellent companies seem to have a capacity for managing paradox, administrative theories are not designed to consider the phenomenon. In order to be internally consistent, theorists tend to eliminate contradiction. Hence there is a need for a dynamic theory that can handle both stability and change, that can consider the tensions and conflicts inherent in human systems. Among other things, the theory would see people as complex actors in tightly strung social systems, constantly interacting with a "fast-paced, ever-changing array of forces." The theory would center on transforming leadership, which in turn focuses on "the ethics and value judgments that are implied when leaders and followers raise one another to higher levels of motivation and morality" (Van de Ven, 1983).

We both agree and disagree with Van de Ven. There is a need for a theory that can explain both stability and change, that can handle contradiction, that include complex people, tightly strung systems, and transforming leadership. The problem in the above statement is that as soon as we follow the advice to consider contradiction, complexity, tension, and transformation, we tend to stop considering consistency, rational people, tensionless systems, and instrumental leadership. We fall into a trap born of our need for internal consistency and shearing away that part of reality that contradicts the things that we seek to explain.

Thinking about contradiction is not a natural inclination; it requires counterintuitive processes. The natural tendency for humans, including managers and theorists, is to be schismogenic (Bateson, 1979). For Bateson, this refers to a growing split in the nature of ideas and relationships that emerges whenever we act with conscious purpose. When a person, whether layperson, manager, or theorist, seeks to explain or make sense of a phenomenon (a conscious purpose), a logical (internally consistent) set of abstractions is constructed. This kind of thinking defines away contradiction.

The work of Rothenberg (1979) suggests that Janusian thinking, the opposite of schismogenic thinking, is what leads to great work in art and science. In a study of creativity, he found a Janusian insight at the heart of every significant leap forward in art, literature, music, and science. Named for the Roman god who looked in opposite directions at the same time, Janusian thinking is a complex process in which two apparently contradictory ideas or concepts are conceived to be equally operative. It involves the generation of a simultaneous antithesis, the integration of opposites. Einstein's observation that a falling object could be simultaneously moving and at rest is a Janusian idea. In sum,

Janusian thinking offers the resolution of psychological contradiction in such a way that the resolution generates great productive energy. There is a new whole that is greater than the sum of its parts. In the mind, new theories and insights emerge. In organizations, a new culture evolves in which "leaders and followers raise one another to higher levels of motivation and morality" (Van de Ven, 1983).

What is needed in our field is a Janusian tool, a conceptual framework that will encourage us to see paradoxical as well as linear phenomena, transformation as well as equilibrium. We need a scheme that will help us to be counterintuitive as well as intuitive in our analsysis. We need to move beyond linear analysis while simultaneously maintaining and valuing such thinking. The purpose of this chapter is to review an approach that may be of some help.

THE COMPETING VALUES APPROACH AS A JANUSIAN SCHEME

The competing values approach is a meta theory that emerged from a series of empirical studies and conceptual papers done at the Rockfeller College's Institute for Government and Policy Studies at the State University of New York at Albany. As a theory of human information processing, the CVA assumes that all abstract knowledge is organized around a consistent framework of perceptual values and that the articulation of these values can do much to further human understanding. In this section we review the basic assumptions and concepts associated with the CVA.

The Structure of Information Processing

In scanning the environment, the human perceptual system is structured to make at least two primary differentiations about the cues, data, or information patterns received. These are represented along two axes in Figure 18.1. The differentiation along the vertical axis has to do with recognition, predictability, and understanding. When we scan our environment, we ask if anything is changing; are the patterns familiar, or are they unique and uncertain? The differentiation along the horizontal axis has to do with the necessity for action. Does the perceived pattern suggest a short time line requiring immediate response?

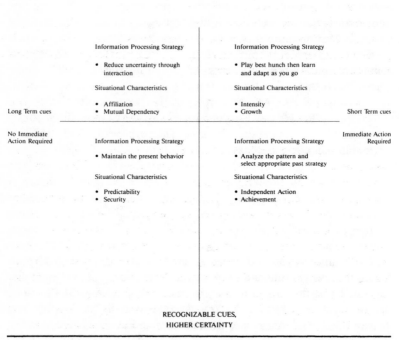

Figure 18.1 Primary Perceptual Differentiations with Related Strategies and Situational Characteristics

Once these two differentiations are made, an appropriate strategy can be employed. When the cues suggest immediate action and certainty is high, one tends to rely on previous learning, engaging a past strategy or means-ends pattern that has already proven successful. These kinds of situations lend themselves to feelings of independence (the right solution exists in one's own mind) and achievement (task closure through the utilization of a clear means-ends strategy). When the cues suggest immediate action and certainty is low, one relies on intuition, choosing a behavior that one assumes to be appropriate. One also recognizes the necessity for change, remaining open to further learning and adaptation as more information becomes available. These kinds of situations lend themselves to learning and growth. When the cues suggest no immediate action but certainty is low, one tends to reduce the uncertainty by seeking the opinion of others. This may be as simple as an infant searching a mother's expression for an interpretation of a unique event, or as complex as a team of interdisciplinary professionals bringing a new product into being. These kinds of situations lend themselves to learning and mutual dependency. When the cues suggest no necessity for immediate action and certainty is high, the more appropriate strategy is to simply continue monitoring the environment while maintaining one's present behavioral pattern. These kinds of situations lend themselves to feelings of continuity and security.

People and Information Processing Styles

People are not equally comfortable in all four of the situations identified in Figure 18.1. A person with a great need for achievement, for example, will most likely prefer situations where the need for action is immediate and cues are recognizable. A person with a great need for affiliation, on the other hand, most likely prefers situations where there are long time lines and more novel cues. Why people develop such needs or become predisposed toward a given orientation is unclear, but there are both physiological (Hampden-Turner, 1981) and social psychological theories (Forgus and Shulman, 1979) that attempt to explain this process. Using the concepts in Figure 18.1 and employing the work of people such as Jung (1971), Driver and Rowe (1979), Mitroff and Mason (1982), and others, it is possible to name and elaborate upon four styles of information processing.

The rational information processing style. Here is the preference for short time lines and high certainty, the need for independence and achievement. People in this mode tend to have a purposive orientation. They rely on a priori logic (known means-ends chains) and focus on the clarification of goals and structures. This is a very functional or instrumental outlook that tends toward the use of general principles, rules, or laws. In making decisions, people with this outlook tend to have a single purpose or focus. They make rapid decisions and once a decision is made, it is final. This perspective is achievement-oriented and tends to emphasize logical direction and the initiation of action.

The development or adaptive information processing style. Here is the preference for short time lines and low certainty, the need for variation, risk, excitement, and growth. People in this model tend to have an idealistic orientation. They rely on internally generated ideas, intuitions, and hunches. It tends to be a future-oriented approach that considers what might be. In processing information, problem cues and messages tend to be analyzed from a dynamic, longitudinal view and the subject is seen as if it were in a moving picture. In making decisions, people with this orientation tend to have a multiple focus. They make decisions very quickly but continue to gather information and adjust the decision as they go along. This subjective perspective is oriented toward creativity, risk, and growth and tends to emphasize adaptability and external legitimacy.

The consensual or group information processing style. Here is the preference for long time lines and low certainty, the need for affiliation and mutual dependence. This mode is oriented toward feelings. This is a more existential view that suggests that the world can only be known through human interaction. Meaning is discovered through process. The individual case is more important than the general rule; hence there is a much greater tolerance for individual exceptions and spontaneous events and behaviors. In making decisions, people with this outlook tend to have a multiple focus. They take the time to seek out diverse opinions and search for solutions that integrate the various positions. This perspective is oriented toward affiliation and tends to emphasize harmony and consideration of the individual.

The hierarchical information processing style. Here is the preference for long time lines and high certainty, the need for predictability and security. This objective perspective is oriented toward empiricism or the systematic examination of externally generated facts. It tends to be a present-oriented approach that describes what *is*. In processing information, problem cues or messages tend to be analyzed from a static, cross-sectional view and the subject is seen as if it were in a photograph, frozen in time. In making decisions, people with this orientation tend to have a single focus. They take a long time to gather and systematically or scientifically analyze the facts. The objective is to obtain the single best answer or optimal solution. This hierarchical perspective is oriented toward security, order, and routinization and tends to emphasize standardization and perpetuation of the status quo.

The Understructure to Human Knowledge

Because people espouse certain of the above modes of information processing, they organize their perceptions around various "axes of bias" (Jones, 1961). Eight of these are shown in Figure 18.2. Each bias is presented in juxtaposition to a very different bias. For example, idiographic contrasts to nomothetic, longitudinal to cross-sectional,

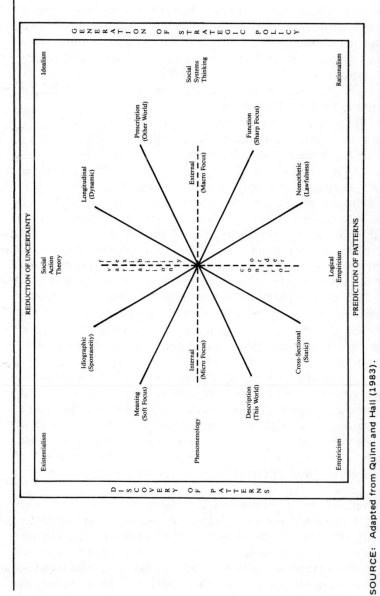

SOURCE: Adapted from Quinn and Hall (1983).

Figure 18.2 Biases, Metaphysical Orientations, and the Uses of Information

prescriptive to descriptive, and function to meaning. These biases not only have opposites, but they have neighbors or biases that are close to one another. This property makes possible the overall pattern in Figure 18.1 and constitutes the basis of what we call the "competing values framework." Notice that, as indicated along the horizontal and vertical axes, the biases to the right are more likely to be associated with the observation of external, macro phenomena, and the ones to the left are more likely to be associated with internal, micro phenomena. The biases at the top are more likely to be associated with phenomena that vary greatly, while the ones at the bottom are more likely to be associated with phenomena that are orderly.

In Figure 18.2 we also show the relationship of these biases to the framework of metaphysical or philosophical orientations offered by Mitroff and Mason (1982). In the margins of the figure we have indicated four general uses of information and how they parallel the various metaphysical orientations and biases. Those biases and orientations along the top tend to be useful in reducing uncertainty, while those at the bottom are useful for predicting patterns. Those to the left are useful for discovering patterns in phenomena, while those to the right are useful in generating strategic policy or prescribing directions.

The CVA assumes that various axes in Figure 18.2 are commonly used when people interpret social action. Jones (1961), for example, argues that the individual axes of bias (he does not conceive of them as an integrated framework) permeate the entire aesthetic production of a high culture, including painting, poetry, metaphysics, and scientific theory, and shows their presence and operations in numerous well-known works.

When people make sense of reality, whether laypersons, managers, or theorists, they abstract out those elements or facts that best fit their a priori notions. Normally, in terms of Figures 18.1 and 18.2, they have a strong quadrant, a couple of complementary quadrants, and a weak or negatively valued quadrant. This often leads a person to pursue a course of action or to build a theory of reality that is both logical and schismogenic. Those bits of reality that reflect the weak quadrant are defined away.

To researchers, the presence of these biases can be an asset. Over time, if enough people study a subject, we can expect to find all the biases represented in a field, and with the CV framework we can begin to untangle and make sense of them. This in turn allows us to identify structural similarities across levels of analysis and areas of study (Rinn, 1965; Kilmann, 1983). We can then build multilevel theories of congruence (Quinn and Hall, 1983) that help us to see the schismogenic assumptions in our fields.

A MULTILEVEL THEORY OF CONGRUENCE

The CV framework has been used to organize the literature on organizational effectiveness (Quinn and Rohrbaugh, 1983), leadership (Quinn, 1984), information processing (Quinn and Hall, 1983), organizational change (Quinn and Cameron, 1983), organizational culture (Quinn and Kimberly, 1984), and organizational decision making (Quinn and Anderson, 1984). Here we will integrate and extend the ideas from these papers. We will begin with a focus on leadership, then consider culture, and finally integrate the two.

Leadership

Quinn (1984) employs the CV framework to integrate three literatures on managerial leadership (behaviors, traits, and influence patterns). In a subsequent study, four ideal types of leaders were identified (Quinn and Hall, 1983). Here we will elaborate and integrate the two schemes.

Figure 18.3 is organized around the same horizontal and vertical axes as Figures 18.1 and 18.2. On the eight spokes we show a set of eight leadership roles. By roles we mean general clusters of traits and behaviors expected of managerial leaders. Along the outer fringe of the figure we show eight styles of leadership, and in the four corners we indicate four types of leaders. Any particular role, style, or leader type is complementary to its neighbors and is in high contrast to those with which it is juxtaposed (for an elaboration, see Quinn, 1984).

With the articulation of these roles we can consider each of the four ideal types. The rational achiever, preferring short time lines and high certainty (Figure 18.1), employs the rational information processing style, has the biases embedded in rationalism (Figure 18.2), and is very comfortable in the director and producer roles. In contrast, the existential team builder, preferring long time lines and low certainty (Figure 18.1), employs the consensual information processing style, has the biases embedded in existentialism (Figure 18.2), and is very comfortable in the mentor and group facilitator roles. The empirical expert, preferring long time lines and high certainty (Figure 18.1), employs the hierarchical information processing style, has the biases embedded in empiricism (Figure 18.2), and is very comfortable in the internal monitor and coordinator roles. In contrast, the idealistic prime mover, preferring short time lines and low certainty (Figure 18.1), employs the developmental or adaptive information processing style,

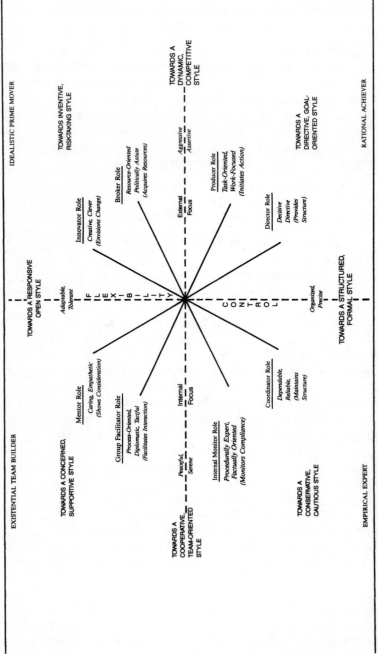

EXISTENTIAL TEAM BUILDER

IDEALISTIC PRIME MOVER

TOWARDS A CONCERNED,
SUPPORTIVE STYLE

TOWARDS INVENTIVE,
RISKTAKING STYLE

TOWARDS A RESPONSIVE
OPEN STYLE

Adaptable,
Tolerant

TOWARDS A
DYNAMIC,
COMPETITIVE
STYLE

Innovator Role
Creative, Clever
(Envisions Change)

Broker Role
Resource-Oriented
Politically Astute
(Acquires Resources)

Aggressive
Assertive

External
Focus

Producer Role
Task-Oriented,
Work-Focused
(Initiates Action)

TOWARDS A
DIRECTIVE, GOAL-
ORIENTED STYLE

Mentor Role
Caring, Empathetic
(Shows Consideration)

Director Role
Decisive
Directive
(Provides
Structure)

Group Facilitator Role
Process-Oriented,
Diplomatic, Tactful
(Facilitates Interaction)

FLEXIBILITY

CONTROL

Internal
Focus

Peaceful,
Serene

Organized,
Precise

Internal Monitor Role
Procedurally Expert,
Factually Oriented
(Monitors Compliance)

TOWARDS A STRUCTURED,
FORMAL STYLE

Coordinator Role
Dependable,
Reliable,
(Maintains
Structure)

TOWARDS A
COOPERATIVE,
TEAM-ORIENTED
STYLE

TOWARDS A
CONSERVATIVE,
CAUTIOUS STYLE

EMPIRICAL EXPERT

RATIONAL ACHIEVER

Figure 18.3   A Competing Values Framework of Leadership Behavior

has the biases embedded in idealism (Figure 18.2), and is very comfortable in innovator and broker roles.

Culture

Just as individuals process information, so also do groups and units of people. In doing so they develop collective belief systems about social arrangements. While philosophers tend to call these belief systems shared paradigms, sociologists speak of them as social reality, and anthropologists talk of cultures. The most central aspect of these cultures involves beliefs about the "appropriate" nature of transactions. Whenever an interaction takes place, valued things (facts, ideas, affection, permission, and so on) are exchanged. These transactions or exchanges determine identity, power, and satisfaction. These governing rules about the nature of transactions tend to be deeply embedded values that are usually dormant but that contain explosive potential. They include beliefs about, among other things, organizational purpose, criteria of performance, the location of authority, legitimate bases of power, decision-making orientations, style of leadership, compliance, evaluation, and motivation. In the upper portion of Table 18.1 we present the profiles of four transactional systems. In the lower portion are the characteristics of four organizational forms.

Reflected in the four cultures, as well as the four styles of personal information processing, are some implicit beliefs about desirable end states. These are embedded theories of effectiveness that not only offer different definitions of effectiveness but also specify the mode of information processing that will result in the desired outcomes. When made explicit, all four reflect easily recognized schools of organizational thought. These are presented in Figure 18.4. In rational cultures, individual information processing (goal clarification, logical judgment, and direction setting) is assumed to be a means to the end of improved performance (efficiency, productivity, and profit or impact). In a developmental culture, intuitive information processing (insight, invention, and innovation) is assumed to be a means to the end of revitalization (external support, resource acquisition, and growth). In the consensual culture, collective information processing (discussion, participation, and consensus) are assumed to be means to the end of cohesion (climate, morale, and teamwork). In the hierarchical culture, formal information processing (documentation, computation, and evaluation) is assumed to be a means to the end of continuity (stability, control, and coordination). Around the outer periphery of Figure 18.4

TABLE 18.1 Four Transactional Systems and Organizational Forms

		Transactional Expectations or Governing Rules		
	Rational Culture	*Ideological Culture*	*Consensual Culture*	*Hierarchical Culture*
Organizational purpose	pursuit of objectives	broad purposes	group maintenance	execution of regulations
Criteria of performance	productivity, efficiency	external support, growth, resource acquisition	cohesion morale	stability control
Location of authority	the boss	charisma	membership	rules
Base of power	competence	values	informal status	technical knowledge
Decision making	decisive pronouncements	intuitive insights	participation	factual analysis
Leadership style	directive, goal oriented	inventive, risk oriented	concerned, supportive	conservative, cautious
Compliance	contractual agreement	commitment to values	commitment from process	surveillance and control

Four Types of Organizational Forms

	Market	Adhocracy	Clan	Hierarchy
Evaluation of members	tangible output	intensity of effort	quality of relationship	formal criteria
Appropriate motives	achievement	growth	affiliation	security
Technology (Perrow, 1967)	engineering	nonroutine	craft	routine
Effectiveness model (Quinn and Rohrbaugh, 1983)	rational goal	open systems	human relations	internal process
Strategic orientation (Miles and Snow, 1978)	analyzer	prospector	implementor[a]	defender
Type (Oliver, 1982)	task	professional	group	hierarchic
Illustration	Theory A	Stage II	Theory Z	bureaucracy

a. See Quinn and Hall (1983).

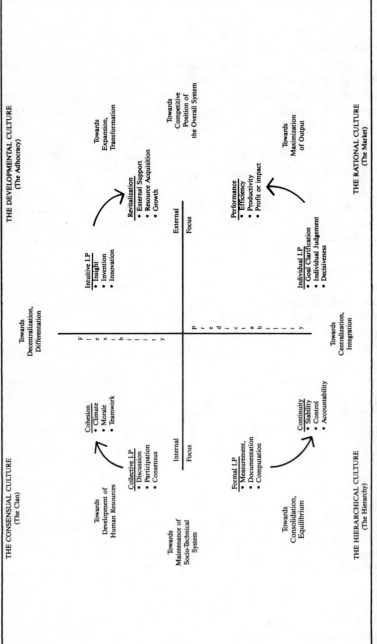

Figure 18.4 Four Cultures and Their Embedded Theories of Effectiveness

are eight more general values which help to define the values in each theory.

Notice the parallel between the four personal information processing styles discussed earlier and the four cultures described here. We have, at two different levels of analysis, models that are analogues of one another. At each level we are looking at the same values. This affords a number of analytic efficiencies (see Rinn, 1965), one of which is the capacity to consistently explore relationships at different levels of analysis.

From Fit to Congruence

In discussing the requirements for a theory that will handle contradiction, Van de Ven (1983) alludes to contingency theory but expresses doubt that it will be helpful. In its present state, we agree, there are some problems that limit its utility.

Contingency theory can be expressed as both a macro and micro statement. In the macro, socioeconomic perspective, performance improvement flows from improved decision making, which in turn flows from having the kind of differentiation and integration (form or culture) required to obtain and use appropriate data from the environment (Lawrence, 1981). A micro, psychological version argues that individuals experience an inner feeling of competence when there is a three-way fit between uncertainty (the environment), organizational arrangements, and individual predispositions (Lawrence, 1981).

While the definition of fit is very unclear (Hrebiniak, 1981), it does tend to suggest a state of equilibrium, order, and minimum contradiction. It also tends to be equated with improvement and effectiveness. This is a problem because it encourages us to value order over disorder (Lawrence, 1981: 319).

In the CVA we shift from the concept of fit to the concepts of congruence and incongruence. Because we have differentiated four types of environmental or information-processing demands, four types of leaders, and four types of cultures or forms, we can posit four diffeent types or states of congruence. The first line in Table 18.2, for example, suggests that when uncertainty and intensity are high, the most congruent form is the "adhocracy" (developmental culture) and the most congruent leader or decision maker is the "idealistic prime mover." The remaining three lines can be read in a similar fashion.

In considering the four states of congruence, notice the variation in terms of a static-dynamic continuum. In the third line, with low

TABLE 18.2   Four Types of Fit or Congruence

Environmental Condition	Organizational Culture and Form	Leadership Style
High uncertainty-high intensity	developmental culture (adhocracy)	idealistic prime mover
High intensity-low uncertainty	rational culture (market)	rational achiever
Low uncertainty-low intensity	hierarchical culture (hierarchy)	empirical expert
Low intensity-high uncertainty	consensual culture (clan)	existential team builder

uncertainty and low intensity, the hierarchical form (or culture), and the empirical expert, we have a state of congruence that suggests a very static system. In the first line, with high uncertainty and intensity, the adhocracy (or developmental culture), and the idealistic prime mover, we have a state of congruence that suggests a very dynamic, rapidly changing system. While in the former case we have a highly ordered, reasonably static system, in the latter we have a changing, dynamic system.

Table 18.2 also allows us to ilustrate extreme states of incongruence. Incongruence occurs, for example, when the empirical expert manages the adhocracy, the idealistic prime mover manages the hierarchy, the existential team builder manages the market, or the rational achiever manages the clan. Similar statements can be made about relationships between the forms or cultures and the external demands by rotating them in a similar fashion.

Congruence, then, is a theoretical state where personal information-processing styles, leadership orientations, organizational forms or cultures, and external demands are matched in such a way that contradiction and paradox are less prevalent than they are in states of incongruence. While there is a natural tendency to value congruent states, from the view of the CV framework there is nothing inherently good about congruence or incongruence. They are simply theoretical points along which we can locate the system under examination.

The CV framework is an analytic tool that maps social action and helps us to understand, as a system moves from one point to another, why tension, contradiction, and paradox are increasing or decreasing.

The logically trained Western mind, however, with its apparent need for order and internal consistency, will almost always put a higher value on congruence than incongruence; hence there is a tendency to equate fit and effectiveness. The CVA, however, provides a theoretical scheme that allows us to temper the problem.

From Incongruence to Transcendence

Real organizations probably never reach a state of perfect congruence. Because, as Van de Ven (1983) notes, they "interact with a fast-paced and ever-changing array of forces," they are always characterized by description's from all four quandrants. The most buffered hierarchy has some aspects of the adhocracy, and the most existential clan has within it some aspects of the instrumental market. In reality, the four value systems seep into one another at all levels of analysis. Hence organizations are characterized by complexity, contradiction, and paradox. If a theory defines away contradiction and paradox, it has no utility in helping us to see the transformations that can come from transcending a paradox.

Transcendence is one of four conditions that can come from the confrontation of contradiction. This is depicted as one of the four states in Figure 18.5. Isolation is a passive reaction to contradiction that seeks to maintain one of the competing positions by closing off other aspects of the dynamic, tension-causing relationship. Closure may come through denial, formalization, buffering, or some other mechanism but tends to result in separation. Accommodation is a passive approach to contradiction that suggests a problem-solving strategy resulting in compromise and perhaps the subordination of one or more of the competing positions. Dominance is a dynamic strategy for maintaining continuity and suggests confrontation and conquest of the opposing positions. The final strategy is transcendence.

Transcendence parallels such concepts as interpenetration (Munch, 1982), autopoiesis (Smith, 1984), and double loop learning (Argyris and Schon, 1978). At the psychological level, it is the capacity to engage paradox in a Janusian fashion, to transcend one's own schismogenic tendencies, to see the unities in oppositions, and to move above and reframe the contradictions. At the physical level, it is that point at which two or more elements perform at their maximum individual capacities while also reaching maximum interpretation. Here they exhibit synergy or performance beyond their natural capacities.

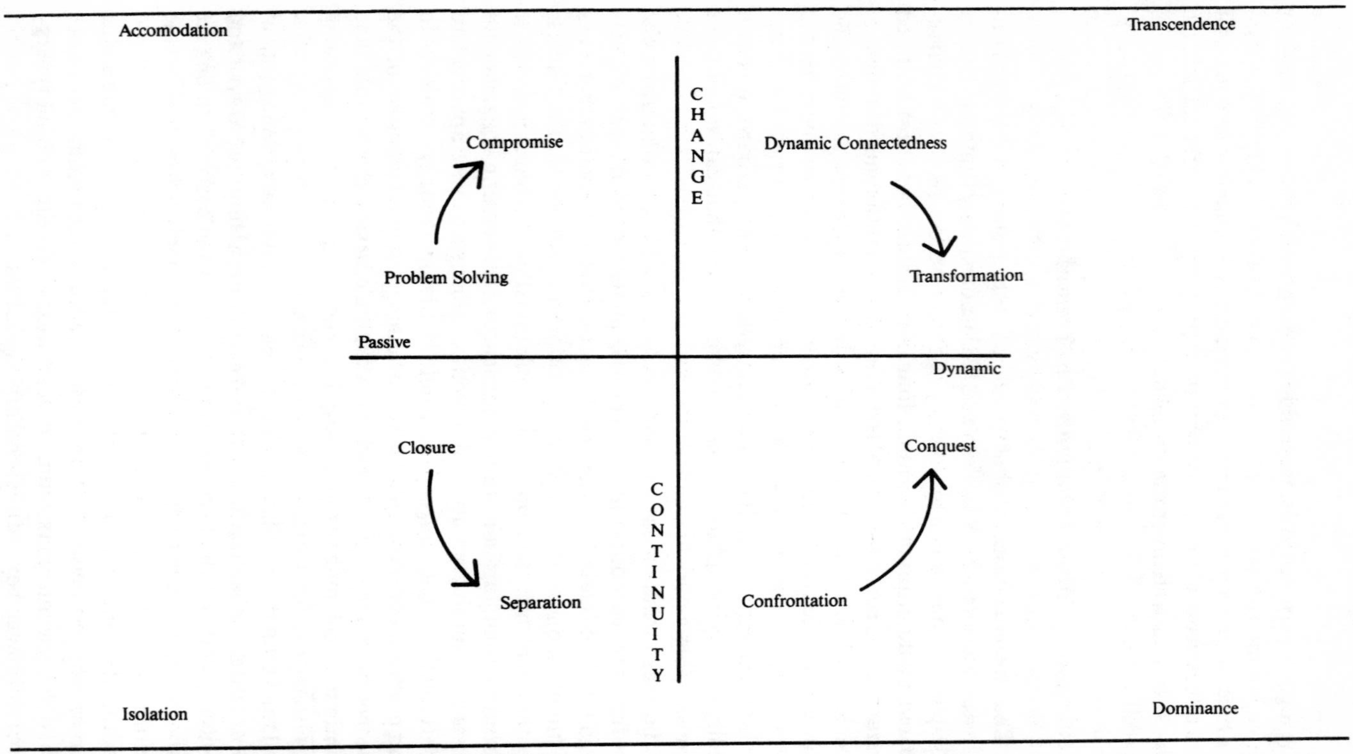

Figure 18.5 Four Reactions to Contradiction and Paradox

Schismogenic Transcendence

Once we conceptualize transcendence, there is an enormous temptation to equate it with effectiveness or excellence. This is the pitfall into which Peters and Waterman (1982) lead us. They notice that in "excellent" companies, managers have the capacity to resolve paradox. Basically they are observing transcendence and all of its exciting ramifications. Linear thinking leads us to take this exciting observation and define transcendence as the hallmark of excellence.

This focus is understandable. When one observes or engages in transcendence, there is an absolute fascination that follows. Unfortunately, people tend to put an inherent value on their insight. Transcendent thinking becomes effective thinking and transcendent performance becomes the hallmark of excellence. Linear thinking is rejected, and hierarchical systems become bad systems. Interestingly, *this rejection is an example of the very thing that is being rejected. It is a schismogenic approach to transcendence.*

Transcendence is a point in an evolutionary cycle. It is a point at which peak performance occurs, when people "raise one another to higher levels of motivation and morality" (Van de Ven, 1983). Transcendence in the organization is the solution to a paradox of some sort, and much energy is released. This can be seen in the early stages of new organizational efforts (Quinn and Cameron, 1983). Here there is a sense of innovation, mission, and collectivity. Hence people may show intense commitment, spending long hours at their work. Interestingly, this state does not last indefinitely. In case after case, these exciting organizations become increasingly formalized. Miles (1980a) provides three reasons: pressures from external constituencies to perform in more predictable and controllable ways, maturation or burnout among employees, and the psychological and social distance that comes with growth and then works to undermine the original values.

The last reason is particularly interesting. Transcendence results in dynamic growth. However, within the expansion itself are the seeds of contraction, formalization, and routinization (Quinn and Anderson, (1984). *In other words, as the values of the developmental culture or adhocracy are increasingly maximized, the values of the hierarchical culture spontaneously emerge.* This brings increasing contradiction and tension until a major shift occurs. The organization goes through the process of formalization, and the adhocracy becomes a hierarchy.

To the person who values transcendence, this process is seen as inherently negative; formalization is something to be resisted (Lodahl and Mitchell, 1980). But to someone who sees it as the unfolding of a natural process, formalization is simply a different point in the evolutionary process. Someone with this view, who also values congruence, would argue that the effective or "excellent" manager is not an idealistic prime mover who resolves paradox but an "empirical expert" who engages in a hierarchical thought process. Actually, in the cycles of organizational life the thought processes of all four types are congruent with situational demands (Quinn and Kimberly, 1984).

The point of all this is that while transcendence is a period of peak performance, we might be advised not to become schismogenic by advocating it over other states. If we are to retain our capacity to see all of reality, we cannot reject any of the quandrants at any level of analysis. Whether the focal system, like the sand and the sea, is in quiet equilibrium or furious transformation, we would benefit from tracking the competing values in any social system.

19

LINKING THE HOST CULTURE TO ORGANIZATIONAL VARIABLES

Brenda E.F. Beck
Larry F. Moore
University of British Columbia

A recent critique of research on organizational culture suggests that more attention be given to the "external societal, cultural context within which organizations are embedded" (Jelinek et al., 1983: 338). The implication is that organizational products and processes are linked in some way (not necessarily in a simple causal relationship) to a broader milieu. Popular culture represents shared substrata and understandings, sometimes highlighted by leaders or by artists and musicians but very often left to slip below the level of constant consciousness in the hustle and bustle of daily life. Cultural attitudes and assumptions provide a latent background to human action; they are like the frame on a picture, providing a reference point or a sense of clear boundaries.

All people carry with them a cultural heritage of some kind. Culture consists of a set of patterns and assumptions learned in early childhood that get gradually modified, expanded, and refined with later life experience. Furthermore, human culture never provides a completely consistent set of ranked values or action guideposts. There are always ambiguities, even contradictions, inherent in the set of traditions a society generates. Martin, Feldman, et al. (1983) point to paradoxes and contradictions existing in cultures internal to organizations. These ambiguities may become more complex in places where immigrants from foreign settings have settled and become rerooted. Even the most "traditional" culture complexes contain counterbalanced or competing viewpoints and symbols.

Cultures are also "layered." They permeate many levels of social life simultaneously. Some aspects of culture are nearly universal, like the high value placed on family bonds and good child care. Other cultural themes are characteristic of whole regions of the world. A culture becomes characteristic of a specific nation, or even of a particular social group, largely because of its linkage to specific locales and experiences. Both Canada and the United States, for example, place a very high value on law and order. The traditional symbol for this in Canada is the uniformed RCMP officer. In the United States, however, law and order are more closely linked to the Old West theme of self-defense, with direct action to be judged later in court. Sometimes latent stereotypes and the historical events that fostered them help to distinguish the cultural traditions of different locales and groups.

Once inside a nation, one quickly becomes encompassed by repetitive layers of a specific popular culture (Riley, 1983). The way members of a corporation behave in the company board room may be modeled after their image of behavior in the national parliament. A school principal disciplining a child may be compared with an RCMP officer dealing with a motorist on the open highway. But these cultural layers also work the other way around. Sometimes we use smaller units of social life as models or metaphors for bigger ones. For example, the feel of individual Canadian homes, warmly heated against the cold winter winds, can become a popular metaphor for a good business, one that is run so as to keep its earnings snugly protected from the avaricious greed of creditors. A manager beset with labor troubles in his plant might similarly think of himself as a lone voyager paddling his canoe through an icy lake during the spring thaw.

In this chapter we explore how the broader cultural characteristics and the images that managers carry with them into their work lives may be linked. We will draw, for our examples, on materials from several major domains of Canadian culture such as folklore, art, and literature, and from our research on the management style of branch bank managers. Our aim is to provide evidence that management imagery and style are closely related to the culture of a nation at large.

We begin by briefly describing a framework that we find useful fo analyzing cultural imagery. Next, we identify several features of Canadian culture that are particularly relevant to organizations in that country. Then, based on our studies of the Canadian banking industry, we provide examples of role-related imagery held by a representative regional sample of branch managers. Finally, building on this initial analytic framework, we summarize a set of tentative linkages between Canadian cultural themes at the national, organizational, and individual levels within one portion of the analytical framework.

A FRAMEWORK FOR MAPPING CANADIAN CULTURAL IMAGERY

Quinn (1984) points out the structural similarity of recent attempts to integrate organizational research with management theory (see Ouchi, 1980, on organizational form; Miner, 1980, on organizational control; Perrow, 1970, on technology; Lawrence and Lorsch, 1967a, on coordination; and Mitroff and Mason, 1982, on policy formation). Quinn believes that there is an understructure common to many of the extant theories of organization that essentially follows the theory of functions developed by Jung (Hall and Lindzey, 1970).

Quinn and Rohrbaugh (1983) also offer evidence that three basic value dimensions underlie much previous theory construction: (1) control versus flexibility, (2) internal versus external focus, and (3) means (processes) versus ends (outcomes). These three competing dimensions imply that a common set of value orientations pervades much organizational work. Furthermore, each axis itself defines a key opposition or tension. For example, a balance is often seen to exist between the degree of organizational control needed to operate efficiently and the amount of flexibility needed to develop new products and services.

These fundamental organizational tensions seem to have a parallel in Jung's theory about polar tendencies within individual personalities (Jung, 1968). These tensions are not necessarily detrimental or destructive to human behavior; indeed, they can constitute the essence of life itself. Figure 19.1 provides a summary diagram of this competing values model.

Each of the four quadrants created by the vertical and horizontal axes reflects a value area that is likely to influence or create a managerial bias toward engaging in the associated means and ends activities. For example, a manager for whom rational considerations were highly salient (quad 1) would be likely to encourage goal-setting and planning activities in an attempt to achieve production efficiency. In contrast, a manager whose world view places a particularly high value on human commitment (quad 4) is likely to encourage activities designed to enhance cohesion, morale, and the development of human skills.

As a framework for analyzing culture the quadrant scheme has certain advantages. For one, this approach is holistic. The model starts with an entire universe, which it then breaks down into complementary,

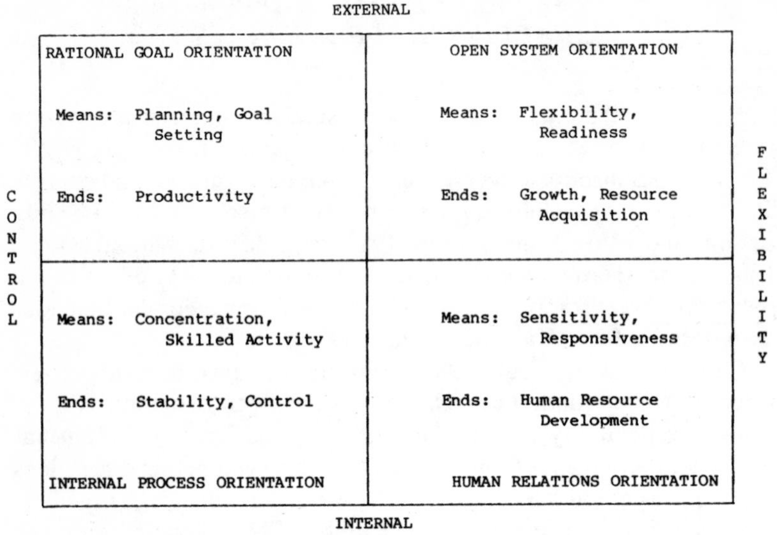

EXTERNAL

	RATIONAL GOAL ORIENTATION	OPEN SYSTEM ORIENTATION	
	Means: Planning, Goal Setting	Means: Flexibility, Readiness	F L E X I B I L I T Y
C O N T R O L	Ends: Productivity	Ends: Growth, Resource Acquisition	
	Means: Concentration, Skilled Activity	Means: Sensitivity, Responsiveness	
	Ends: Stability, Control	Ends: Human Resource Development	
	INTERNAL PROCESS ORIENTATION	HUMAN RELATIONS ORIENTATION	

INTERNAL

SOURCE: Quinn and Rohrbaugh(1983).

Figure 19.1 The Competing Values Model

counterbalanced subcomponents. It requires a structural style of analysis (Maranda and Maranda, 1971). Instead of building up or listing an unlimited number of possible elements, this approach defines an entire universe and then constituent elements that are either X or not X by nature. Furthermore, such an overview displays its sets of opposites in a combined fashion. Hence the pull of two different axes leads to the separate characterization of each quadrant. This lends the analysis an element of dynamism and energy not present in simpler, bipolar schemes. Nevertheless, the model is simple enough for the human mind to grasp easily. Adding further dimensions would add more confusion rather than clarify the processes and patterns involved.

The above model has been described in detail by Quinn and McGrath in Chapter 18 of this book. What we do in this chapter is to modify and apply this four-quadrant model of the domain of culture. Culture, as a set of attitudes, values, and related popular symbols, can also be mapped in terms of competing polar concepts. The construction of a competing values model using cultural labels is shown in Figure 19.2. For example, the dimension Quinn has called control versus flexibility can now be depicted as a tension present between deliberate, human-made features of social organization (human-controlled or -created) and a "natural" surrounding of environmental features (given and envi-

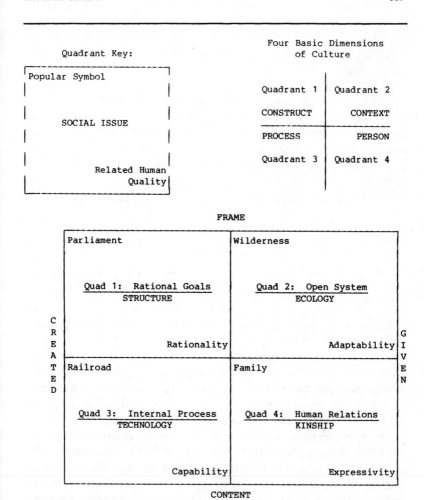

Quadrant Key:

```
┌ ─ ─ ─ ─ ─ ─ ─ ─ ─ ─ ─ ─ ─ ┐
│ Popular Symbol           │
│                          │
│                          │
│        SOCIAL ISSUE      │
│                          │
│                          │
│            Related Human │
│                  Quality │
└──────────────────────────┘
```

Four Basic Dimensions
of Culture

Quadrant 1	Quadrant 2
CONSTRUCT	CONTEXT
PROCESS	PERSON
Quadrant 3	Quadrant 4

FRAME

	Parliament	Wilderness
C R E A T E D	Quad 1: Rational Goals STRUCTURE Rationality	Quad 2: Open System ECOLOGY Adaptability
	Railroad	Family
	Quad 3: Internal Process TECHNOLOGY Capability	Quad 4: Human Relations KINSHIP Expressivity

G I V E N

CONTENT

Figure 19.2   General Matrix for an Analysis of Culture and an Organizing Sketch for Basic Themes in Canadian Popular Culture

ronmentally adaptive). The first creates the political or institutional "frames" inside which we live. The second constitutes those God-given aspects of our surrounding: our ecological environment, our biological makeup, and (from a personal perspective) our early family life. On another axis, that which Quinn calls the "external" will be referred to here as the "framing" aspects of culture (metacharacteristics or tenets of society). What Quinn labels "internal," we define in cultural terms as the contents of day-to-day social life (elements of organizational interaction). If these new axes are laid out in a fourfold table, one obtains a general matrix for an analysis of culture such as that shown in Figure 19.2.

In each quadrant of the matrix, one key Canadian symbol has been noted, along with a salient social issue and a highly valued human quality. These have been selected for illustrative purposes. Many other attributes of Canadian culture can be identified and located on the matrix as well. By identifying dominant patterns or themes at several levels in a broad cultural milieu, pattern congruencies (or anomalies) can then be further explored.

ANALYSIS

In order to add flesh to the bare bones of this new cultural matrix, we shall now tap a variety of sources. At the broadest level, national symbols can be found in such facets of society as folk art, political history, economic ideology, music, geographic patterns, demographic trends, literature, journalistic accounts, and even everyday language. Thus it will always be impossible to completely describe or understand all aspects of a given culture. Instead, the anthropologists concentrates on identifying those cultural attributes that seem to have particular relevance for explaining human attitudes and behaviors, generally by using a process of induction. Convergent evidence about the nature of a particular cultural phenomenon, when provided by two or more information sources, adds strength to any propositions that emerge. Eventually, like a jigsaw puzzle, an overall pattern of images begins to appear. These can then be compared or contrasted with other cultural patterns.

Our investigation of Canadian culture has been multifaceted and is ongoing. We have examined materials ranging from folk art and poetry to music, used statistical analyses of demographic trends, and even studied Canadian royal commission reports. The linkages reported in this chapter have been arrived at primarily on the basis of induction; that is, we have identified a number of specific themes and have defined several general patterns that emerged from our data. Our intent is to set out a number of tentative cultural linkages that may provide the groundwork for more precise exploration at a later stage.

At the level of organizational culture, our analysis is based on findings derived from the ongoing investigation of managerial style in five of Canada's national banks plus one regional bank. Within these corporations, we have specifically looked at branch managers. These major Canadian corporations form an appropriate base in which to conduct a study of organizational culture. The major Canadian banks constitute an oligarchic financial elite. The five largest banks are characterized by strong similarities in size, technology, organizational structure, and customer service goals (Stewart, 1982). Their functions, furthermore, have been uniformly defined by the Canada Bank Act. Their base lending rates and currency transfer procedures are similarly regulated by the Bank of Canada (Canadian Bankers' Association, 1983). Finally, these same banks constitute a fundamental and indispensable institution in contemporary Canadian society.

We developed an interview format containing seven critical incidents in our attempt to identify the attitudes, beliefs, and other social constructions that influence behavior for the 68 male branch managers we studied.[1] Situations and problems actually encountered by the managers were carefully represented by this decision set. Each critical incident was designed with the advice and help of a panel of six highly experienced bankers.

A number of possible behavioral responses were proposed to interviewees in connection with each incident. The respondent was first asked to indicate how a "typical" manager might react, reflecting on the spectrum of managers with whom he had worked throughout his career. Each participant was then requested to select a metaphor most representative of that typical branch manager, making specific reference to the problem just encountered. Each metaphor choice had to be explained. These answers were then coded and analyzed to reveal the rich background role-related imagery associated with each prior response (Deetz, 1983).

Additional metaphor sets were used to explore more abstract concepts associated with banking culture such as structural shape, power configurations, and business environment. A mail-in questionnaire obtained data on each respondent's personal values; person-thing orientations; attitudes about superiors, peers, and subordinates; responses to social situations; and various other attitudinal characteristics plus demographic data (see Appendix).

Overall, we collected information about cultural imagery at three levels: (1) the broad cultural context, (2) the specific organizational milieu, and (3) local managerial culture. This information enabled us to explore key multilevel linkages. To illustrate our work, some dominant themes identified as existing at all three levels in the competing values model will be examined for only one of the model's four quadrants. Quadrant 1, concerning an orientation to rational goals, has been selected for discussion here. Our more complete analysis includes the other three quadrants shown in Figure 19.2.

Rational Goal Orientation

Societal Level

Canada's political identity finds expression in a beautiful carpet woven for the country's centennial in 1967. The carpet was designed to recognize Canada's legitimate nationhood. The structure of this legal whole is visually portrayed by the use of shields, one for each of the ten great provinces and two territories. A delicate relationship between Canada as a unified, centralized entity and these twelve semiautonomous pieces holds the key to Canadian attitudes toward power.

Canada was gradually settled by European immigrants, and its ties to mercantile interests in Britain and France have always remained strong. There were few great nation building events to focus on in Canadian history. Instead, Canada's evolution has been characterized by a process of gradual, orderly development in rather stark contrast to that of the United States, which emerged out of the decision to face a major cultural crisis head-on—a civil war. Canadians rejected the American Revolution, and many American loyalists fled north for protection. Even today Canadians feel a certain "colonial loyalty" to the English crown. In Canada there is a trust in and reverence for royalty that serves to distinguish its population from that in the United States. Indeed, it is only very recently that the constitution of Canada has been fully and symbolically freed from British control.

This history of seeking direction from a centralized and distant power source is clearly reflected in Canada's current banking structures. These institutions grew from mercantile organizations that originated in England. The men of Fleet Street, furthermore, fostered in Canadians a strong sense of respect for authority and defined roles. The powers that ran the banks in Canada continued to want monopolistic control. They favored large-scale bureaucratic organizations that could be directed from a central point. To this day, banking in Canada reflects this history, and the results remain one of the truly distinctive institutional features of this country. Canadian banks are centralized and highly symbolic of the national character as a whole. The banks have been largely responsible for Canada's population dispersion, and for orderly, evolutionary regional economic development. These corporations remain central to political decision making in Canada today. Further-more, these major banks have remained Canadian, resisting U.S. take-over more effectively than any other key sector of business activity in this country.

Organizational Level

The centralization of the Canadian banking system thus reflects important historical trends in this country generally. It is not surprising that attitudes about status in the banking environment should reflect these major themes. When asked to describe the organizational system of a branch bank metaphorically, most managers responded with images expressive of centralization. Furthermore, their sense that branch bank operations resemble the life of a family was often mentioned. This too corresponds to a feeling for family values that is alive and strong in Canada today (Blishen and Atkinson, 1982).

Here are some typical responses bank managers made to a query about the banks' internal status structure. The favorite metaphoric image selected was "family," and banker explanations of this choice clearly reflect their confidence in order, hierarchy, and unity (other metaphors in the set are listed in the Appendix, Section 2).[2]

> The manager is a father/mother figure and so on down the line. Every member of the staff feels part of the family on an equal basis. There is leadership plus a family unit at the same time.

> Ideally, a branch is like a family. The manager sees that the rest of his unit works for him. There is a need for someone in charge.

Other frequently chosen metaphors were the sun and planets, a beehive, and a staircase, with explanations again focused on centrality, benevolent authority, and hierarchy.

> There is one central unit, the manager, around which the rest of the office revolves. It is not like a string of beads; not everyone can be located on a straight line.

> The branch has a queen bee, drones and workers. Everybody has his position. Sort of an autonomous organization, getting policy from above. And the manager is benevolent.

> People generally start at the bottom and hope to go to the top. Sometimes they fall down, but if they are energetic they can jump a few steps at a time. The branch is also on a staircase. If it gains more accounts it can improve its image.

When asked to discuss the internal climate in the bank, the metaphors that bankers selected most frequently were water, wine, and milk. Here, their explanations emphasized neutrality, stability, and quality.

> Water is neutral. You should have a fairly even internal climate, not one that is acidic or bubbly.

> Water is stable and there is no shortage of it.

> Wine gets better with age. We have so many people with experience, and the aging process with wine denotes experience. We have a very low turnover rate. Wine is also smooth, like a smoothly running office.

> Milk is settling. It is usually cold and steadying. It has more taste than water and blends in. It is not domineering.

The above responses show a general acceptance of hierarchy by bank managers and indicate their clear respect for authority and well-defined roles. These attitudes, furthermore, are found to be coupled with a sense of orderly conduct and civility. Canada had no "Wild West" era. Instead, the RCMP provided Canada with a ubiquitous symbol of governmental or crown authority. These men were seen to stand for law, morality, and civilized behavior, exemplifying a general Canadian respect for the powers that be. Canadians similarly expect the crown and their members of Parliament to perform in a reasonable, even genteel, manner. These assumptions reflect a popular concern for conformity with tradition, for stability, and for calm, predictable surroundings generally.

Canadian culture has traditionally been described as having high levels of system confidence and low levels of personal assertiveness (Governor General, 1983: 3). Banks and bank managers in Canada seem to be well in tune with these wider values. Related to the sense of social compromise, so strong in Canada, is an emphasis put on balancing the need for a central authority with a tolerance for local diversity. This issue is significant in banking because of the varying financial needs of various provinces and of various subpopulations. Similarly, each bank manager also needs to have a modicum of individual authority for local credit judgments. With the present rapid computerization of branch office information, this individuality of the local manager is being severely challenged and has become a significant banking issue.

Managerial Level

As previously mentioned, we used critical incidents so that the typical branch manager's role-related beliefs, values, and behaviors could be described and explored in relation to specific scenarios. Related metaphor sets were used to further explore image patterns. In Quadrant 1 the major emphasis rests on the company's shape or design and on formal arrangements with customers, the public, competitors, and employees.

Our analysis of the responses to critical incidents concerned with Quadrant 1 issues highlights the extent to which Canadian managerial imagery is focused on hierarchy and formality. In one incident, the branch manager was losing customers and staff because of intolerably overcrowded physical conditions. The text of the incident was as follows:

> Over the past several years the volume of customer traffic in a small, well located branch has greatly increased. A number of floor layout changes have been tried, but conditions in the customer area and the work area are overcrowded. During the past three years, staff turnover has been much higher than average, and the head office has recently pointed this out by letter. Enlarging the physical space would include acquiring an adjacent building.

Here are some typical responses:

> In making a complaint or suggestion it must be put in writing and go to the top. If the matter is discussed informally it gets put on the bottom.

> Formalization in banking has gotten to the point that anything done on an informal basis doesn't succeed.

> Until the district manager sees the problems the branch manager is facing, nothing will happen. The branch manager is the only one who can really take things up with higher levels. A continual nagging process. The staff must be informed but made to realize that these things take time.

The metaphor responses associated with Quadrant 1 issues also point to themes like growth and improvement or facilitation. For example, for the overcrowded conditions incident, the two most frequently chosen metaphors were sunshine and oil. Here are some characteristic responses:

> The manager is trying to solve client problems and improve working conditions, i.e., bring sunshine into their lives and those of the staff too. Give light to something. Being a source of enlightenment, guidance and information to improve the entire staff operation.

> The manager keeps the parts of the operation moving, as oil is a lubricant.

In sum, the competing values model has been used as a framework for analysis. We have identified and compared dominant imagery themes that characterize all three levels of culture as they are found embedded within each quadrant. In this way it becomes possible to trace the congruence and linkages across levels. In Quadrant 1, a concern with hierarchy and order, deference to authority, and acceptance of centralization appears to permeate the culture at large, the organizational milieu, and local management traditions. Figure 19.3 summarizes the dominant image patterns we identified at each of these levels.

Branch managers hold beliefs about their operating units that are quite consistent with a more generalized set of values common to Canada as a nation. As mentioned earlier, our analysis has been extended to the other three quadrants of organizational culture as well. In general, our preliminary data indicate that in each of the four quadrants, the dominant cultural themes defined at the broader cultural level are repeated in segmented and modified form at the organizational and managerial levels.

DOMINANT IMAGERY OF CANADIAN BANK MANAGERS

Our analysis of coded incident and metaphor responses led us to identify twelve role categories: figurehead, leader, coordinator, reward allocator, implementor, monitor, disseminator, communicator, decision maker, goal setter, disturbance handler, and resource allocator. These twelve are similar but not identical to a list of ten roles previously described by Mintzberg (1973). Our changes relate to certain task features unique to branch banks. The coded responses we obtained were also subjected to smallest-space analysis (Gutman, 1968), a procedure that revealed a structure underlying the twelve role categories and that helped us to relate them to a four-quadrant model. The twelve role categories could be effectively partitioned with only 21 percent error in a four-quadrant space (Moore and Beck, 1984). Further, the twelve role categories tend to be located within the framework according to the competing values model. However, eight of the twelve roles are found on the left side of the model.[3]

The dominant role pattern or style of the typical branch manager is revealed by examining the relative percentage of times each role appeared in the coded responses to the seven incidents. In Figure 19.4 these percentages are plotted and connected to allow a composite analysis. The relative locations of the twelve roles are shown as radials.

In general, Quadrant 1, which contains rational elements concerned with the advancement of well-being of the company as a whole, received

Quadrant One — RATIONAL GOAL ORIENTATION

LEVEL OF CANADIAN CULTURE — the national identity

Dominant Social Issue — structure

Themes
unified centralized identity
colonial loyalty
conformity with tradition
legitimacy of authority
evolutionary, orderly development

LEVEL OF ORGANIZATIONAL CULTURE — the banking system

Dominant Organizational Issue — rational goals

Themes
hierarchical and orderly expansion of operating networks
defined roles
deference to authority
importance of quality
compromise
image of stability, strength, conservatism
high system confidence

LEVEL OF MANAGERIAL IMAGERY

Dominant Managerial Issue — the company

Value themes
materialism
ambition
comfortable life

Belief themes
hierarchy
ultimate responsibility
formal authority
adherance to procedures

Role themes
initiate action
exercise control
mediate

Figure 19.3   Quadrant 1 Themes Identified in Canadian Bank Culture

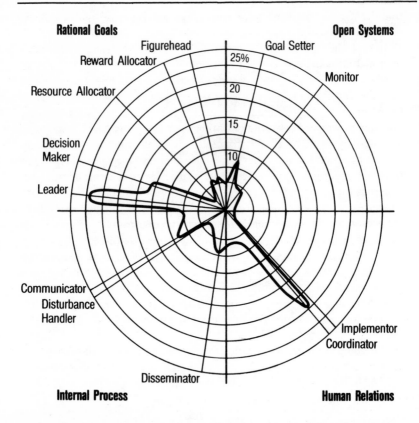

NOTE: The twelve role vectors were established using smallest space analysis on responses from the representative sample (N = 77).

Figure 19.4   Relative Importance of Twelve Managerial Roles for the Typical Male Branch Bank Manager

the strongest emphasis in imagery. The leader role could be identified more than any other, occurring in 22 percent of all incident and metaphor explanations. The leader role was defined as "directing, inspiring, coaching, telling, and shaping others; working through others." One can clearly see the up-front, direct, goal-oriented Quadrant 1 quality of this role. The decision-maker role was also identified in a relatively large percentage of the explanations (13 percent).

The strong appearance of the coordinator role attests to the frequent mention of the branch manager's intermediate position necessitating careful and wise liaison between customers, staff, and the head office. This role is characterized by temporary and changing alliances requiring that the effective manager have empathy and adaptability and that he be able to provide much support to his staff.

In sum, the typical male branch manager is characterized by a fundamental duality in his response to the demands of his office. On one hand he shows a strong, direct, efficiency-oriented approach quite consistent with the traditional image of a manager in a large hierarchy. This relates to the principles of ultimate responsibility, top-level decision making, one-way downward communication of rules and procedures, impersonal reward systems, unity of command, and dedication to the company and its product. On the other hand, the average manager, much more than his superiors, experiences role demands from another quarter. Whereas those managers in regional or head office positions are more concerned with paper and information flows, the branch manager is also the person on the firing line. He must face the irate customer whose loan application was disapproved, and he must provide suitable explanations to his staff concerning policy changes that may disrupt established routines or even eliminate or restructure their jobs. Hence the coordinating or liaison role, in the human relations quadrant, provides the manager with the means of softening, pragmatizing, and humanizing the often impersonal and autocratic operating decisions passed down from above.

We asked respondents to tell us which of all the metaphors they had considered would best characterize the typical manager. Overwhelmingly, the choice was that of "coach." Here are some examples:

> The manager has to be able to get the very best work out of his employees. If he doesn't have adequate staff, he goes out and gets them. Ultimately he is responsible for the performance of the branch.

> The employees are here to do the work. The manager is on the sidelines most of the time. He is just there to give guidance on how to do the job better, and basically to see that everything runs smoothly.

> The good manager brings those less competent along; he has an understanding of everyone's capabilities.

> The manager tries to get the best out of the staff without breaking the game rules. On the customer side, this means being able to find out their needs and solve them with the right services.

> The branch manager tries to get employees working together as a team. The employees need to fill in for each other, work together, and help each other out.

> The branch manager has several departments that ultimately report to him. He can't run the branch himself. He can only fulfill his role through the involvement of other people. He has to coach these people so they are best able to function properly and thereby achieve the results.

As coach, the branch manager has the responsibility to oversee training
and development of subordinates and running the whole business.

Thus, the coach metaphor, an image quite consistent with Canadian
tradition, furnishes an excellent summary of the role-related elements of
the typical male branch manager's style. Of first importance is the sense
that he must be in charge, exercise authority and control, and solve problems. He is more likely to use influence and diplomacy than to give direct
orders. He gives guidance, information, and direction as a professional
advisor and recognizes the importance of earning the respect of his staff
and customers. Seeing himself as a professional, he provides training
and instruction to members of his staff. As one manager stated, "One
measure of how well a branch is managed is how well it runs when the
manager is not there." The manager gives support in terms of empathy,
understanding, and responsiveness when individual employees have
needs. He also seeks to enhance order, peace, harmony, and stability in
the institution as a whole.

Is the coach metaphor laden with managerial culture implications
unique to Canada? Exploratory samples of bank managers in Australia,
France, Germany, and Japan provided more varied and widely distributed responses when respondents were asked for a "best" metaphor. We
anticipate that further work with larger samples will enable us to begin
to define culture-linked differences in management styles in order to
determine what is or is not uniquely Canadian.

CONCLUSION

In looking at these diverse pieces of imagery, we believe we have
gained insight into everyday Canadian managerial work life and also
into the attitudes of the popular culture at large. What is most striking,
perhaps, is the degree to which the branch bank atmosphere gets described in the same terms that Canadians use to describe their own
national character. For example, a strong belief in a unified, centralized
identity is mirrored at the level of the organization as the hierarchical
and orderly expansion of operating networks, defined roles, and deference to authority. In turn, this theme is evident at the managerial level as
hierarchy, formed authority, and adherence to procedures. The managerial role is to initiate action and exercise control.

Furthermore, although sometimes there are contrasting themes
contained in the metaphor responses, the dominant themes stand out
quite strongly. To what degree these themes would be found in other

Canadian industries or regions is a matter for future study. Thus we regard the identification of cultual linkages within the banking industry as a first step in developing a set of propositions about the cultural assumptions and beliefs that may form the skeletal underpinning of doing business in Canada. Our planned future efforts will also include studies of the contrasts between the Canadian cultural milieu and that of other societal cultures, and how these contrasting cultures may be translated into differences in business strategy, operations, and performance.

APPENDIX

Seven critical incidents were written especially for the situational demands of branch bank management. A number of possible behavioral responses were proposed to interviewees in connection with each incident. The interviewee was asked to indicate how the "typical" manager would respond. A specific metaphor set followed every behavioral decision set, and each manager was asked to choose the metaphor most representative of the typical branch manager (with reference to the problem just encountered) and to explain the choice. This metaphor-based explanation was designed to reveal the rich imagery associated with the behavior response. Additional metaphor sets were subsequently used to explore more abstract concepts, such as structural shape, bank power, and business environment. Finally, the mail-in questionnaire obtained measures of personal values, person-thing orientations, attitudes about superiors, peers and subordinates, responses to social situations, other attitudinal characteristics, and demographic data.

The Interview Format

Section 1:
Critical Role Incidents and Associated Metaphors

CRITICAL INCIDENT	METAPHOR SET
(1) Promotion of a good teller	flower, twig, branch, trunk, root, seed, leaf
(2) Improper transaction	hand, brain, eye and ear, teeth, tongue, breast, leg

CRITICAL INCIDENT	METAPHOR SET
(3) Two incompetent tellers	brush, level, pliers, saw, clip, hammer, file
(4) Overcrowded conditions	fire, water, stone, oil, wind, ice, sunshine
(5) Offensive odors	mother, father, brother, sister, uncle, cousin, spouse
(6) Technological change	owl, snake, dog, lion, horse, parrot, elephant
(7) Teller competition	doctor, lawyer, coach, professor, prime minister, farmer, engineer
(8) Elements of commonality across seven chosen metaphors (above incidents)	
(9) Best metaphor? Why?	
(10) Free-form metaphor proposal. Why?	

Section 2:
Metaphors Relating to the
Branch Bank as an Organization

ORGANIZATIONAL ELEMENT	METAPHOR SET
(1) Structural form	family, sport team, church, deacons, temple management, fire department, drama troupe, orchestra, musical group, medical clinic
(2) Production, service type	steel-rolling mill, auto assembly line, fruit cannery, filling station, dentist's office, supermarket, bakery
(3) Power	school of fish, dam water, generator, lock and key, spider/fly, doctor/patient, king/subjects, tennis game
(4) Status system	sponge, string of beads, hammer and nail, sun and planets, staircase, beehive, family
(5) Communication flow	canal system, waterfall, bubbling spring, watering can, grapevine, leaky faucet, drought
(6) Internal climate	coffee, milk, wine, whiskey, water, Coca-Cola, vinegar

ORGANIZATIONAL ELEMENT	METAPHOR SET
(7) Business environment	fire, rain, stone, oil, wind, cloud, sunshine
(8) Company image	cotton, clay, gasoline, chewing gum, steel, glass, egg shell
(9) The banking system	mouth, heart, brain, lungs, phallus, womb, intestines

Section 3:
The Take-Home Questionnaire

(1) Manager's perception of superiors, peers, and subordinates. Three 26-item adjective scales.

(2-4) Free-form metaphor elicitation (maximum 10 each) describing
   a. the typical B.C. manager
   b. the typical Ontario manager
   c. the typical Canadian manager

(5) Critical social incident response differences based on position in banking milieu.
   a. invitation to wedding; honeymoon trip
   b. son's auto accident involving questionable conduct

(6) Metaphors for branch bank personnel—forced-choice selection using four sets: body, family, zoo, and natural setting

(7) Personal attitudes
   a. person/thing orientation (Barnowe et al., 1979)
   b. self-description inventory—subscales include supervisory ability, intelligence, initiative, self-assurance, decisiveness, masculinity/femininity, maturity, working-class affinity, achievement motivation, self-actualization, need for power, need for high financial reward, need for security (Ghiselli, 1971)
   c. value survey—terminal and instrumental value profiles (Rokeach, 1967)

NOTES

1. The original representative sample of 77 included both male and female managers; however, the female subgroup constituted only 11 percent of the whole. A subsequent study of the entire population of female managers in these banks (N = 41) revealed a number of important differences; hence the female portion of our sample was dropped for present purposes. The male portion is a 10 percent random sample of branch managers in the five largest nationally chartered Canadian banks in British Columbia, plus The Bank of B.C., a regional bank.

2. Notice that the metaphor choices only serve to stimulate the formation of imagery about the focal subject. The image descriptions must be interpreted for their underlying themes. Two independent coders were used. The coders achieved 68 percent perfect agreement, and any disagreement was resolved by discussion and consensus.

3. This is not surprising, since branch bankers are not near the top of the organization hierarchy, and thus the environmental/organizational interface is of concern not from a policymaking standpoint but rather from an execution standpoint. On the other hand, it is important to monitor the environment on behalf of the bank and to set branch-level goals accordingly. A second reason that the left side of the model is loaded more heavily with the role categories that resulted from our coding process is that the incidents themselves are strongly task related.

20

A CULTURAL PERSPECTIVE ON THE STUDY OF INDUSTRIAL RELATIONS

Robert J. Davies

New York University

Nan Weiner

University of Toronto

Trade unions are an important part of the operating environment of most work organizations. Their impact in unionized environments is obvious. Less obvious, though no less real, is their impact on the behavior of organizations that are seeking to remain union-free. Surprisingly, however, the field of organizational behavior and the emerging organizational culture literature has largely ignored unions. This appears true whether unions are considered as focal organizations worthy of study in their own right or as subcultures influencing the culture of an employing organization.

A second, more widely recognized weakness in the literature has been its tendency to ignore the influence of the broader external or societal culture on organizational culture (Salaman, 1981; Jelinek et al., 1983). This chapter seeks to address both of these omissions. The primary focus is on trade unions. Particular attention is paid to how the structure, goals, and behavior of unions in different countries have been influenced by their external environment and to the influence they have had on the development of corporate culture.

Figure 20.1 illustrates in greater detail the relationship that will be examined in the course of this chapter. In this highly simplified scheme, both union culture and corporate culture are set within a broader societal culture. Union culture, as Figure 20.1 illustrates, is influenced by the broader culture directly as well as indirectly through its interaction with corporate culture. A parallel argument applies to corpora-

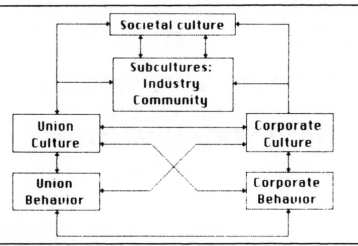

Figure 20.1   Organizational Culture and the Broader Cultural Context

tions. The figure also indicates that there is not one external culture, but many. The union and the corporation represent points of convergence for a variety of external cultural influences. These include the local community culture, the industry culture, and, depending on the heterogeneity of the wider society, possibly a variety of ethnic and religious cultures. An important issue to be addressed below is the degree of congruence among these cultures, and between them and prevailing union and corporate cultures.

The relationship between external culture and union culture is explored in the first section of the chapter. An international perspective is adopted in seeking an answer to the question, To what extent can differences in the character of trade unions in different countries be explained by differences in the social values and culture of the broader society? Drawing upon examples from the industrial relations literature, the section also explores the impact of community and industrial cultures on union culture.

In the first section the canvas of union culture is painted with broad brush strokes. In terms of finer detail, however, the culture or subculture of any given union environment can be linked on a more immediate level to the corporate culture that dominates its operating environment. But just as union culture depends on the immediate corporate culture, so the reverse is true. One means of modeling this complex process of interaction, which draws upon a transactions cost perspective, is presented in the second section. An alternative approach, based on the degree of congruence between the union as subculture and the dominant corporate culture, is discussed in the third section. Here the aim is to use the concept of culture to shed light on the nature and form of labor-management relations. Once again, the approach is broadly comparative in scope, enabling the argument to be cast in sharper relief. Finally, the chapter's conclusions are presented in the fourth section.

UNION CULTURE, INDUSTRIAL RELATIONS, AND THE WIDER SOCIETY

Unions and Societal Culture

Lipset (1962a, 1962b) applies the notion of broad societal culture to explain differences in the characteristics of trade unionism among countries. His particular concern is with the explanation of "American exceptionalism." Compared with the nations of northwestern Europe and Australasia, American unions are seen as ideologically more conservative, lacking in their sense of class solidarity and inclined to pursue more narrowly self-interested economistic strategies. They are also more militant, and often violent, in their tactics. In addition, American unions have adopted a structure and a pattern of collective bargaining that is highy decentralized. Though similar to Canada and the private sector in Britain, this stands in marked contrast to the pattern in Germany and Scandinavia, where bargaining is much more centralized. As further contrasts, American unions rely more heavily on full-time salaried officials than do their European counterparts. They have also shown a much higher propensity to engage in corrupt practices.

Taken together, Lipset argues, these characteristics can be seen as reflecting the basic cultural values of American society. Foremost among these is the strong emphasis on individual achievement and equality. This philosophy has bred a highly competitive culture, and one that emphasizes ends—especially pecuniary ends—over means.

These values contrast sharply with those prevalent in more traditional ascriptive societies, where motives are often more important than results and where more weight is placed on behavior appropriate to one's station. In these societies, stress on general achievement regardless of background is more limited, while failure is perceived as less of a reflection of personal worth than of structural impediments in society. Overcoming these impediments requires a collectivist form of action. Against this threat, privileged groups are likely to encourage the development of beliefs that justify their right to high status and power. One example, common but by no means confined to societies with historic roots in feudalism, is the propagation of a submissive or deferential culture as a mechanism of social control. The effect will be a more prevalent form of class consciousness and, again, a much weaker sense of personal failure. Where they are motivated to seek change, deprived individuals are very likely to attempt to improve their situation collectively, through mass unionism and class-based political parties whose aim is to change the overall structure of society rather than to marginally alter the prevailing distribution of income. Unions, in other words, are likely to become a social and political force as well as simply an economic force.

Such arguments have important implications for the level of union membership observed in different countries. As Lipset notes, American unions have had great difficulty organizing new segments of the employed population. They have also recruited a smaller proportion of the available labor force than unions in other industrialized countries. One reason is that American unions have been handicapped by their slightly illegitimate position relative to the American value system (Lipset, 1962a: 82). In particular, American unions are often seen as opportunistically pursuing policies of narrow self-interest, securing as much as possible even at the expense of less privileged or less organized groups. Studies of wage structure by economists, for example, point to the impact of unions in raising their own wages at the expense of workers in the non-union sector. Moreover, American union leaders are often viewed as simply using the labor movement as an avenue for individual advancement and personal gain.

Unions and External Subcultures

Below the broad societal level, union behavior and the general pattern of industrial relations may also be influenced by a strong community-based subculture. An early and forceful illustration is provided in Lloyd Warner's classic "Yankee City" studies, particularly *The Social System of the Modern Factory* (Warner and Low, 1947).[1] These studies, located in the northeastern United States, painted an overall picture of industrial harmony and community integration among workers in the local shoe industry. However, this harmony was shattered by a major strike that occurred against a background of high unemployment and long-run economic and technological change. As Rose (1975: 143) summarizes it:

> The previously deferential, unorganizable shoeworkers struck spontaneously against further wage cuts and redundancies. Solidarity was virtually total, crossing previous ethnic, religious, sex and skill divisions. Within a month the strikers had joined, and become the most active group in an industrial union; and the employers had capitulated.

Two points are forcefully illustrated by this example. The first is the contribution of a "deferential culture" to the process of workplace control and to the suppression of industrial conflict. The second is the extreme fragility of this control in the face of rapid economic and technological change. This should not be confused with simple economic or technological determinism. Culture itself influences the evolution of economic and technological forces, and disentangling their interplay calls for careful historical analysis.

A further example of the importance of external culture, this time of an *industrial* subculture, is provided by Blauner in his classic, *Alienation and Freedom* (1964). As part of his study of the technological determinants of alienation, Blauner discovered something of a paradox among his sample of machine-minding textile workers. Objectively, their work appeared to be alienating, being characterized by minimal control over highly repetitive, monotonous, and grueling tasks. Workers were also subject to autocratic supervision and restricted social contact during work. Nevertheless, in terms of subjective experience, they appeared relatively satisfied with their work.

Ironically, since it is hardly consistent with the technological determinist tone of the rest of his analysis, Blauner's explanation is based on the mediating effect of out-plant attachments.[2] His sample was drawn from textile mills in small, tightly knit rural communities in the southern United States—ingredients adding up to a strong external culture dominated by notions of submissiveness and fatalism that has been described as a form of "industrial caste." Objective alienation generated by technology can, in other words, be partly neutralized by an appropriately submissive out-plant culture. From a Marxist perspective, the existence of such a culture is a clear indication of false consciousness and a measure of the true alienation of these workers. It is also a measure of the potential instability of their industrial relations.

As a final illustration, it is useful to consider a case in which potentially distinct external cultures actually coalesce, mutually reinforcing their impact on union culture and union behavior. A classic example is to be found in the comparative research on strike activity. On the basis of an analysis of strike records from eleven countries, Kerr and Siegel (1954) identify certain groups of workers as consistently strike-prone, even within societies that more generally deprecate overt industrial conflict. One common characteristic of these workers, in addition to their industry attachment, is that they tend to inhabit isolated communities.

> The miners, the sailors, the longshoremen, the loggers, and, to a much lesser extent the textile workers form isolated masses, almost a "race apart." They live in their own separate communities. These communities have their own codes, myths, heroes and social standards. There are few neutrals in them to mediate the conflicts and dilute the mass. All people have their grievances, but what is important is that all members of each of these groups have the same grievance [Kerr and Siegel, 1954: 191-192].

Here the coalescence of industrial and community cultures based on geographical isolation, and hence the absence of cultural alternatives, supports a strong antimanagement union culture. Attempts to create a more favorable, promanagement culture as a means of reducing industrial conflict would be difficult, to say the least, and would likely be doomed to failure.

UNION CULTURE AND CORPORATE CULTURE: A TRANSACTION COST PERSPECTIVE

Union culture and union behavior reflect the broader cultural values of the community, industry, and society. Unions thus act as one agent through which external influences are brought to bear on the internal organization of a firm. The direction of influence is not, however, only one-way. Union culture and corporate culture are also influenced by a mutually reinforcing process of day-to-day interaction. The transaction cost framework offers one means of analyzing this interaction (Ouchi, 1980; Wilkins and Ouchi, 1983; G. R. Jones, 1983).

Transaction Cost and the Firm

Transaction costs may be defined as the costs of negotiating, monitoring, and enforcing exchanges between individuals to ensure that the value given and received is in accord with their expectations (Ouchi,

1980). From a transaction cost perspective, organizations are viewed as systems of patterned exchanges, and the form of culture that emerges is the result of an attempt to economize on the transaction costs associated with any given method of production (G. R. Jones, 1983). In general, these costs will be increased if for any reason an individual's contribution to production is difficult to determine, especially if the contracting parties behave in a self-interested or opportunistic manner. Thus the greater the ambiguity that surrounds the exchange of effort for reward within the organization (the effort-reward bargain) and the lower the degree of trust between the parties, the greater will be the transaction costs.

Applying this analysis, it has been argued that different types of production processes are characterized by different degrees of ambiguity over the effort-reward bargain. From the point of view of management, capital-intensive production, combined with the extreme division of labor and work standardization—the classic assembly line—provides considerable control over the production process. Such arrangements also make employee behavior relatively easy and cheap to monitor. Ambiguity over the effort-reward bargain in these circumstance will be low. Where trust is also low, thus increasing the chances of opportunistic behavior, minimally acceptable standards of effort and performance can be achieved relatively cheaply through worker supervision. Coercion, including the threat of dismissal, can be used to avoid shirking or absenteeism. This type of machine-paced "production culture" (G. R. Jones, 1983) is vividly described by a number of authors (e.g., Beynon, 1973; Kamata, 1982).[3]

More process-oriented forms of technology, or more labour-intensive forms of production based on interdependent specialist skills, clearly make the task of identifying the contribution of individual workers more difficult. Ambiguity over the effort-reward bargain from the point of view of management is increased accordingly. In the absence of trust—itself something of a cultural trait—the costs of monitoring and enforcement can rise substantially. Under such circumstances, it is argued, transaction costs can be more effectively minimized by a bureaucratic form of organizational culture. Rules and procedures, often in the form of negotiated employment contracts, supplant direct supervision, and rights and obligations are made more explicit. Arbitration by third parties may also be built into the system to resolve differences. Such measures serve to provide legitimacy, both to management authority and to the rules governing the production process, thus creating a higher level of trust.

As ambiguity over the effort-reward bargain increases still further, because of nonroutine tasks and the exercise of very high levels of skill, even the bureaucratic form may become inefficient. This occurs because the nature of the employment relationship becomes too complex to specify and regulate in any detail. The work of professionals and specialized research and development personnel is an obvious example. In such cases, a "clan" culture is seen as the most appropriate governing mechanism (Ouchi, 1980; Wilkins and Ouchi, 1983).

Within the clan organization, members remain self-interested, but they are selected and socialized in such a way that their natural inclination is to do what is best for the clan, without the need for close supervision. The clan represents a high trust environment in which generalized acceptance of a dominant culture paradigm allows for more discretionary and more decentralized decision making. Recent literature has also associated the clan form with high performance and greater efficiency (Deal and Kennedy, 1982; Peters and Waterman, 1982).

One implication of the transaction cost approach, however, is that the clan form is not always the most efficient organizational choice. The clan requires a much greater degree of social understanding specific to the enterprise than either a production or bureaucratic culture. Given this specificity, new members are unlikely to bring clan values with them from their background culture. This implies selection, training, and socialization costs that may be quite substantial. Moreover, these costs must be incurred in the short term for an uncertain long-term return. In this sense, the choice of a clan culture can be seen as somewhat akin to a long-term investment decision with an uncertain payoff, since even if shared understandings are generated, there is no guarantee that they will necessarily enhance corporate performance.

If a clan culture is not universally appropriate, it is useful to make explicit those circumstances under which an investment in this type of "thick" culture is likely to be worthwhile. Obviously, clans are more likely to be efficient for small groups with common, well-defined skills (professionals) and within relatively small organizations. A closely knit clan is also more likely where a group shares a long history and has a stable membership.[4] This creates a more secure socializing environment and provides more scope for the generation of shared values and organizational myths and legends. Extensive interaction among individuals on or off the job will, in turn, increase the likelihood that these will be passed on. Finally, the absence of institutional alternatives to the clan's proposed value system is also important. The more the members of an organization are exposed to cultural alternatives, particularly where these are inconsistent with clan values, the more difficult and costly it will be to generate a clan. The earlier reference to strike-prone cultures located in an "isolated mass" made clear, however, that the culture that emerges under these circumstances will not necessarily be pro-management.

Transaction Costs, Organizational Culture, and Union-Firm Interaction

This brief review usefully highlights two important weaknesses of the transaction costs approach. First, it is assumed that a firm's decision to economize on transaction costs is a simple management optimizing decision made without regard to the possibility of a response by a trade union. Second, the argument comes dangerously close to technological determinism. Indeed, the close link postulated between the production system (or production function) and organizational culture (G. R. Jones, 1983: 465) is reminiscent of earlier work on the technological determinants of industrial organization (Woodward, 1965). Explicit recognition of possible union responses to a firm's attempts to economize on transaction costs provides a useful corrective on both counts.

To illustrate, consider the perspective of the individual worker in the context of his or her effort-reward bargain with a firm. Where workers do not know the extent of value of their individual contribution to production, and where the ability to exercise discretion over individual effort is low, there will be an incentive to hire the policing services of a union. These circumstances are most likely where work is fragmented by the extreme division of labor, is machine-paced, or is closely supervised. This incentive to hire a union may, however, be offset if trust between the worker and employer is high—that is, where there is a belief in the firm's adherence to the principle of a fair day's work for a fair day's pay—or where external cultural influences are supportive of a deferential or submissive value system. Even here, however, we have noted the instability of such values in the face of a sustained challenge to the worker's material prosperity. Alienation as an instrument of production only appears tolerable if workers are placated as instruments of consumption. Once the latter condition is challenged, the legitimacy of the system is undermined. In general, then, unionization is likely to be a natural outgrowth of a low trust production culture. Its formation and operation wil then represent one significant element of the transaction costs that must be factored into the firm's decision about the appropriate cost-minimizing organizational form for the long run.

At the other end of the spectrum, where individual worker discretion over the effort-reward bargain is high—perhaps because of highly specialized skills, considerable task variety, and so on—the demand for union policing services will be low. Trust is also less likely to be an issue between employer and employee. The firm clearly has no incentive to engage in short-run opportunistic behavior or to raise doubts about its long-run commitment to equity. To do so would simply undermine its own position. All in all, this implies that high trust professional cultures (G. R. Jones, 1983) or clan cultures (Ouchi, 1980) are likely to be union-free.

Implicit in this brief discussion is an extremely important principle about transaction costs which needs to be made more explicit. It is that within an employment relationship, the contracting parties' experience of transaction costs tends to be *asymmetric*. Stated more simply, a high degree of control over the effort-reward bargain for the firm, based for example on standardized machine-paced production, actually implies minimal control for the individual worker. Conversely, high discretion for the individual implies a loss of control for the firm. Recognition of the existence of this asymmetry in the experience of transaction costs introduces an important dynamic element into the determination of organizational culture and offers one explanation for the process of cultural change. It also highlights the dangers of economic and techno-logical determinism inherent in a static, short-run analysis of transaction costs.

To illustrate, consider a firm's choice of a low trust environment in which control over the production process is exercised through the extreme division of labor, the fragmentation of skills, and machine-paced work. While this represents one means of economizing on the costs of monitoring and enforcing the effort-reward bargain, it is achieved simply by shifting the costs onto the worker. Unionization represents one way of shifting them back. Through collective pressure, backed up by strike action—an obvious transaction cost—workers seek to regain control over their work tasks via the negotiation of substantive and procedural rules (explicit contracts) and the creation of independent monitors (third-party arbitration). Rules and procedures thus begin to replace direct supervision as a means of enforcing property rights. In short, a more bureaucratic culture emerges.

The more effective the union is in shifting transaction costs back onto the firm—that is, the more restrictive the rules and the more frequent and costly the strikes—the greater the incentive for the firm to seek an alternative organizational form capable of avoiding some of these "unanticipated costs of bureaucracy." The clan is one such form. It is, however, a form resting on a relatively high degree of trust. Thus, where early corporate history can be traced to a low trust protection culture, modified through the medium of sustained union pressure, attempts to generate a clan culture are, to say the least, likely to be highly suspect. They will also be vehemently opposed by the union, since such moves challenge its very organizational survival. The development of a corporate clan culture from a bureaucratic culture, though not impossible, is therefore unlikely in the absence of some fundamental external shock to the nature of the relationship. This might involve the threat of bankruptcy, fierce foreign competition, a national economic crisis, or even some more dramatic event, such as the declaration of war.[5]

The implication is that where the clan form exists, it is likely to have emerged as the initial organizational form. Depending on the nature of the external culture, this may have involved substantial investments in screening and socialization. Nissan's efforts to create a clan culture at its new U.S. truck assembly plant in Tennessee provide a good example. While on the union side prevailing industry culture was hostile to such efforts, the immediate community culture was more supportive and largely non-union.[6] The benefits of this clan strategy for the firm lie in the fact that, unlike alternative organizational forms, the clan does not economize on transaction costs in the short run simply by shifting them onto workers. It is therefore less likely to give rise to a long-run reactive response from workers in the form of union organization. Moreover, the clan also offers the prospect of efficiency gains through a more highly motivated labor force.

This argument suggests that the emergence of different types of culture within an organization is likely to be a much more complex process than suggested in the transaction cost literature. More specifically, what appears optimal for the firm in the short run may prove suboptimal in the longer run, when the emergence of a union is factored into the calculation. Minimizing transaction costs thus becomes a problem of joint operation.

The game theoretic nature of the problem is illustrated in Figure 20.2. The figure illustrates the expected payoff for the firm and the union given different corporate transaction cost decisions and union/worker responses. Suppose the firm is initially in row one, operating a non-union plant and faced with a choice between investing in a high trust clan culture or a low trust, closely supervised, production culture. Other things being equal, the high initial costs of the clan (witness Nissan's investment in Tennessee) suggests a pay off of 40—lower than under the production culture, where the short-run return is 50. With the latter choice, however, the return to the workers is minimized. Their response is the formation of a dissonant or countercultural union. This improves

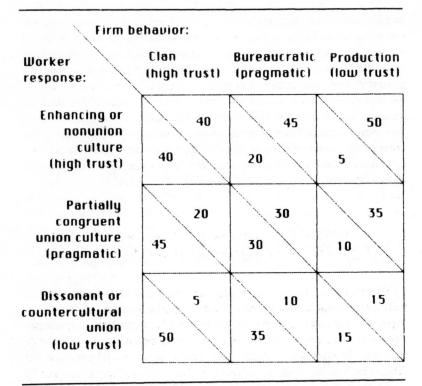

Figure 20.2 Cultural Payoff Matrix

their payoff relative to that under the non-union production culture from 5 to 15, but only at the expense of a substantial reduction in the payoff to the firm.

The final outcome leaves everyone worse off, with antagonistic labor relations, low trust, and the lowest possible joint payoff. If the parties recognize this, they may seek to establish a higher trust convention and a more bureaucratic culture. As the figure illustrates, however, neither party has an incentive to act alone. Unilateral action by either party in the lower right-hand cell will only worsen their own position. The unfortunate lesson is that low productivity cultures can be both stable and individually rational. Moreover, as the figure also indicates, even the bureaucratic/collective bargaining outcome (30/30) is potentially vulnerable to opportunistic behavior, particularly if the firm believes that it can break the union.[7]

Should the firm therefore anticipate this and invest in the development of a clan culture? Much will depend on the firm's assessment of the likelihood of a union being formed. This decision must also depend on the congruence between the desired values of the clan and those of relevant external cultures—societal, community and industrial—as well as on such factors as organization size, membership stability, and the availability of institutional alternatives. Reaching any a priori assessment of these issues is impossible. Meaningful judgment is more appropriately left to detailed case studies. One fact that does seem clear, however, is that a dynamic analysis of transaction costs appears to be more supportive of the choice of a clan type of organizational form than does a static analysis that concentrates solely on the short-run interests of management.

UNION AND CORPORATE CULTURE AND THE PATTERN OF LABOR-MANAGEMENT RELATIONS

This section examines union and corporate culture in the context of different international patterns of labor-management relations. Three aspects of the cultural context are of particular relevance for this task. First is the degree of congruence between the union culture or subculture and the corporate culture. The second aspect may be termed the "thickness" of the relevant cultures, with a thick culture being one in which there is a strong sharing of values. Third is the coercive power of the union culture or subculture, in the sense of the resources it could bring to bear in challenging the dominant corporate culture.

Starting with the degree of congruence between union and corporate cultures, it is possible to conceive of a broad continuum ranging from fully congruent or enhancing at one extreme to dissonant or countercultural at the other. To use industrial relations terminology, full congruence between union and corporate goals implies a "unitary" frame of reference. It implies one source of fully legitimate authority, one focus of loyalty, and it is suggestive of team analogies, with all members of the organization striving toward a common corporate objective (Fox, 1966).

Japan's enterprise unions are often considered in this light, though there is some suggestion that this reflects more how Japanese business would like to be perceived than how it actually is (Hanami, 1981). Strikes, for example, are far from uncommon in Japan, though their short and frequently symbolic character makes them much less damaging than the protracted trials of strength typical of disputes in North

America. Collective bargaining, the accepted device for reconciling conflicting interests, is also common, suggesting some diversity of goals.

All this, however, is a matter of degree At the limit of full goal congruence, there would presumably be no need for the reactive presence of a union subculture at all. Indeed, the obvious North American examples of fully congruent or unitary cultures are non-union firms such as IBM, Hewlett-Packard, and 3M (Peters and Waterman, 1982). Within these organizations the pattern of labor-management relations appears to be broadly harmonious. Open conflict, especially collective conflict, is rare.

At the other end of the continuum, dissonant or countercultural union values fundamentally question the legitimacy of the dominant corporate values. Conflict is ongoing and inevitable; moreover, it is so deeply embedded in the structure of the situation that any form of durable compromise is ruled out. In industrial relations terms, this pattern is consistent with a "radical" frame of reference within the enterprise. Conflict from this perspective is closely linked with "the operation of contradictory tendencies within the capitalist system" (Hyman, 1972: 31). Ultimately it is irreconcilable in the absence of a total transformation of the whole structure of control in society.

An approximation to this extreme is to be found in the historic pattern of French industrial relations. The traditional role of the French unions has been to heighten class consciousness by emphasizing the extent of worker alienation within the capitalist system in the hope of precipitating revolutionary change (Gallie, 1978). One ironic consequence of this stance, however, has been that it has evoked a highly authoritarian management response under which decisions are imposed by fiat and a tight system of overt control is exercized over work. That this situation has gone largely unchallenged—that a more bureaucratic pattern of labor-management relations has not developed—is explained by the fact that the unions' primary emphasis on ideological warfare while encouraging a highly distinct counterculture has also served to generate fierce internal ideological conflicts. Though firmly held by union activists, countercultural values are fragmented. Workers have thus become fickle in their support, depriving the unions of the strength necessary to stage a sustained attack on management prerogatives. From a mangement point of view, the cost and consequences of employee ill will associated with this authoritarian strategy have been seen as significantly less than those associated with establishing a more participatory system.

The pattern of labor-management relations in France reflects this relatively important countercultural union presence. Relationships are generally antagonistic, and strikes, though frequent, are short, reflecting the weakness of the unions in sustained combat. They are also often politically motivated, aimed at precipitating government intervention rather than simply pressuring management. Collective bargaining is poorly developed, leaving a great deal to local management prerogatives. Put simply, the development of mediating institutions requires both a meaningful amount of ideological common ground between the dominant culture and subcultures and sufficient power in the hands of the latter to pose a realistic threat.

Between the extremes of fully congruent and countercultural values lies a broad continuum of partial congruence. Conflicts between dominant corporate and subcultural values exist, but they are a matter of degree and are typically set against a broader background of mutual acceptance. The operation of this pluralist value system (Fox, 1966) within the corporation implies an approximate balance of power between the union subculture and management, and a willingness to engage in negotiation aimed at the achievement of a workable compromise. The ritual of collective bargaining is an obvious example.

Collective bargaining relationships show a diversity of forms, however, ranging from highly adversarial to broadly consensual. International examples again allow the point to be made forcefully. Thus American, British, and Canadian union-management relations have all been placed toward the adversarial end of the spectrum. They are also all relatively "high" strike countries where outcomes are determined more by overt displays of power than by covert consultative mechanisms. At the more consensual end of the spectrum, the industrial relations systems of Scandinavia are characterized by low strike rates and the much more extensive use of nonadversarial consultative mechanisms to resolve conflicts. However, this has not always been the case. During the interwar period (1914-1939), conflict levels were among the highest in the world. Both unions and management possessed sufficient group soldarity and coercive power to inflict enormous damage on one another and on the national economy. Recognition of this fact led to the development of a mutually acceptable institutional framework for resolving differences and achieving an ideological compromise.

The implication of this discussion is that the concepts of cultural thickness and coercive power may be seen as qualifiers on the impact of the union culture on industrial relations. As our French example makes clear, a thick counterculture may be organizationally fragmented, thereby diffusing its threat to the dominant culture. Indeed, this diffusion may be actively fostered through a corporate policy of divide and rule. In the French case, it also seems to have emerged as a consequence of "the high level of ideological explicitness and systemization through which (the unions) sought to insulate the workplace from the dominant cultural beliefs of society" (Gallie, 1978: 314). Put simply, French unions have attempted to create a clan culture that is too distinct from that of its environment. In addition to fragmentation among countercultural unions, a radical unofficial subculture may also emerge within a union in response to a dominant culture that is perceived to be too congruent with that of management. Such radical elements are to be found in many of Japan's enterprise unions.

Paradoxically, some countercultural elements may actually serve to bolster the legitimacy of a dominant culture. Like the fool or jester in the medieval court who gently parodies and ridicules the king, a weak counterculture may serve as a useful safety valve, providing a harmless focus for discontent. For the radical scholar of industrial relations, of course, this is the tragedy of trade union incorporation, which integrates the working class into capitalist society and serves as a mechanism of social control by diverting union energies from the "real" task of fundamental societal change (Hyman, 1972).

Some Caveats

While the interaction of corporate and union cultures provides an intuitively appealing way of viewing labor-management relationships, the approach does have serious pitfalls. First, the importance of culture relative to other factors, such as technology or organizational and market constraints, should not be overplayed. Cultural determinism is just as reprehensible as technological or economic determinism. A more realistic approach is to view culture as an intermediate variable mediating the influence of other structural factors. Second, cultural explanations can easily slip into tautology. The existence of a thick counterculture, for example, is used to explain a strike-prone, adversarial labor-management relationship, while the existence of a counterculture is in turn deduced from the existence of a high level of labor-management conflict. To avoid such pitfalls, it is necessary to provide an independent explanation for the emergence of culture. Why do countercultures emerge in some contexts and harmonious subcultures in others? Why are some cultures "thick" and others "thin," some powerful and some weak? How and why do cultures change?

The answers to such questions are to be found in careful historical analysis. As one illustration, Eldridge (1968) seeks to disentangle the interaction of cultural, economic, and organizational factors in explaining contrasting conflict patterns between different plants within the British steel industry. Given the structural similarity of these plants, culture emerges as a key variable. The explanation of the marked differences in culture between the plants, according to Eldridge, is rooted in the "principle of cumulation," based on the juxtaposition of a series of mutually reinforcing historical accidents or events. Understanding this historical process of cumulation involves a movement beyond the analysis of culture as a single independent variable.

CONCLUSIONS

The purpose in this chapter has been largely exploratory and illustrative. In particular, an attempt has been made to highlight two important omissions in the emerging corporate culture literature—namely, the inadequate treatment of the impact of external culture(s) on corporate culture, and the neglect of trade unions, both as organizations in their own right and as subcultures within work organizations.

The first part of the chapter explored the impact of external culture—societal, community, and industrial—on union culture. The conclusion was that culture represents a crucially important and multifaceted mediating variable, the analysis of which serves as an important corrective to the excesses of economic and technological determinism. The discussion also highlighted the need for congruence between cultural values and the technological and economic experience of workers if stability in the industrial relationships is to be maintained.

Stability also emerged as an important issue in the analysis of transaction costs in the second section, which concluded that the omission of trade unions has resulted in a failure to capture the dynamic nature of the interaction between corporate and union subcultures at the workplace. Once unions are introduced, outcomes take on a game theoretic character. While the cultural payoff matrix presented is usefully illustrative, the values chosen for the various payoffs for participants were arbitrary. Establishing their value more precisely represents an intriguing empirical opportunity.

Attention in the final section of the chapter was focused on the pattern of labor-management relations. The degree of congruence between corporate and union subcultures, their relative thickness, and their coercive power were identified as important variables. The interaction between them, both in the workplace and with the external cultural environment, clearly highlighted the potential complexity and richness of the analysis of corporate culture. This complexity, together with the factors that contribute to the development of culture and cultural differences, as well as of cultural change, can only be understood historically and contextually. Detailed case studies of unionized environments should therefore occupy an important position on the corporate culture research agenda.

NOTES

1. This is a useful illustration of the fact that the application of the concept of culture, and of the techniques of cultural anthropology, to an industrial setting is not a new phenomenon.

2. For a recent empirical assessment and critique of Blauner's thesis, see Gallie (1978).

3. Beynon's book is based on observations in a British auto factory, while Kamata's are from Japan. Elements of a production culture can thus be found within the context of very different societal cultures.

4. Societal culture may be of considerable significance here. Competitive individualism and emphasis on personal advancement through career mobility will be generally less conducive to clan formation than a strong group identity and a lifetime attachment to firms such as that found in Japan.

5. Postwar cooperation between labor and management in several European countries has been traced to the needs of reconstruction following the devastation of World War II.

6. Tennessee is, of course, a "right to work" state.

7. Again, broader values are likely to be of relevance. Corporate willingness to engage in union busting is likely to be strongly influenced by how socially acceptable such activities are. They are, for example, likely to be more acceptable in the United States than in Canada.

21

CULTURE AS CULTURE

Mavor Moore

University of Victoria

It is an axiom of art that what has been left out is as important as what has been kept in. By that criterion, the picture of culture that we have been given is seriously distorted.

The word "culture" has, of course, different meanings in various contexts—which was presumably why this distinguished group of researchers came to an early agreement not to settle on a definition: There might have been more difference than conference. But for each speaker to play Humpty Dumpty ("When *I* use a word, it means just what I choose it to mean, neither more nor less") would have led straight to anarchy, and there seemed to be a general inclination to defer to the sociological sense of "lifestyle."

I don't wish here to insist on my own meaning, but rather to point out that the word has another common meaning, somewhat more precise. In government, for example, a minister (or whatever) of culture is usually the one in charge of the arts, letters, and communications—and sometimes also of theoretical science, recreation, and religious and educational matters. I would venture to suggest that unless and until the language changes, that (still very general) meaning of culture is the most widely held.

If one were to ask for a list of organizations having to do with culture, most people would surely think of libraries, publishers, film festivals, theatres, orchestras, artists' unions, galleries, museums, architectural firms, arts councils, fine arts faculties, and the like—all the way up to the United Nations Educational and Cultural Organization. Yet I have not heard mentioned, in the past three days, a single organization of this kind, despite the fact that they cry for analysis (even if only from a sociological viewpoint) and that UNESCO is at this moment a storm center.

A second sense in which "organizational culture" might be understood is the management of major institutions with what can be considered a cultural function, such as religious denominations, universities, school systems, broadcasting networks, and newspaper chains. It was, for example, from the Roman Catholic church that we got the word "propaganda" ("de propaganda fide"), which basically meant selling an official line and keeping the sellers in line. This sense is much closer to the one that those from the fields of commerce have been using, but unless I missed it, reference was never made to such institutions.

In the religious sense, incidentally, organizational culture is obviously alive and well in places such as Northern Ireland, South Africa, Iran, Tibet, Argentina—even among the Inuit of Canada—and would benefit greatly from academic study. This conference has not seen fit to include these ancient examples either, although plenty of room has been found for modern creeds such as "productivity improvement."

And yet "cultural exchange," in the usual sense of international give and take of the arts and letters, communications software, scholarship, and the like, may well be more important to our future than the business affairs that have been absorbing our attention. Two years ago I was invited to China to discuss exchanges of artistic personnel and materials between our two countries. Near the end of my visit, I was summoned to meet Vice-Premier Bo Yi-bo, a onetime economist who had previously visited Canada. I was asked by the Canadian Embassy to put to the Vice-Premier certain questions about the Chinese economy, since the commercial attaché had been unable previously to get an audience for the purpose. Since the subjects were not unconnected, I agreed.

After we had discussed the urgent need for our peoples to get to know each other—through books, films, theatre, painting, music, dance, and so on—I told Bo Yi-bo that Canada was in a recession and that, important as these things were, we were concerned about the cost to the economy. I wondered whether China had similar priorities. The Vice-Premier replied: "The economy is a very important matter, a very difficult matter just now—but nothing is important enough to stand in the way of cultural exchange." As I left Beijing, I asked Canada's commercial attaché if he had any messages for me to take back. He said: "Yes. Please try to convince them in Ottawa that cultural exchange comes before trade and commerce, not after it. They have to get to know you *before* they do business with you." Yet in Beijing, where two universities have departments of Canadian studies, there is only one library of Canadian books. It is in the embassy, which is in a compound where Chinese may not go.

If I am at some pains to suggest that we are working with the wrong priorities, it is because these priorites can be the real stumbling blocks in getting to know each other. It is precisely the mind set of each of us, raised in our cultural context, that can impede our understanding of the mind set of others—whether in another country or working beside us in firm or factory. We have talked here a great deal about "values." Not all values are cultural (unless, that is, you wish to define culture as the field of value setting), but all values have their cultural aspect. Our perceptions of the relative importance of creative achievement and commercial power, like our differing valuations of time, provide each of us with a set of assumptions—most of them unconscious—that can prove to be expensively wrong in another context. We are betrayed by our biases.

Take the notion of networking, or bonding. An individual, in any society, is a nexus of intersecting relationships. We must take into consideration not only cultures, but subcultures and countercultures; each person is usually a combination of these, not simply a unit of one relational organization. An audience is more than a collection of "asses in the seats"—in fact, the various arts (including collective ones) are most often ways of *escaping* membership in a herd. It is this proliferating function of art that curses all those who try to pin it down. Art resists both classification and stability, and it is this that keeps the critics busy and the establishment nervous. Those who try to regulate art most often end up looking foolish.

This makes the organization of culture a very dicey operation for those who imagine that it can be used for political ends or commercial gain. Whenever a formula is found in art, it eventually kills the happenstance that is its lifeblood. "We rightly associate creativity," said leading British psychiatrist Anthony Storr, "with spontaneity, freedom, and an absence of fixed preconception." Put art in a harness and its efficacy vanishes. To mix the metaphor, it's a great social oil but a poor glue; and mercury is useless for building frameworks.

Anyone who would use the arts or entertainment as instruments of homogenization must face their tendency to do just the opposite: to stimulate variety and individuality. They are better at inter- than intra-relationships, but unpredictable in either capacity. I can do no better than to repeat the warning given by Frost and Krefting in their abstract:

> Recent evidence indicates the importance of strong cultures in successful organizations. However, the complexity of organizational culture, including its origins in the unconscious and the existence of multiple cultures within organizations, make outcomes of efforts to manage culture difficult to predict or tightly control.

Even this is a careful understatement. What is something so difficult to predict or control doing in the garb of a social science?

Experience has shown us, if we are willing to learn, that the arts as culture perform a different function altogether, but one that is no less important. They teach us to make capital out of our differences, not to iron them out. We have heard much talk about controlling the lifestyles of company employees—not expanding their interests or activities, but channeling them—in order to increase productivity, lubricate the gears of mergers and takeovers, and in general accommodate the corporation. I find this strangely analogous to the "socialist realism" of the Marxist governments that see art, science, and scholarship as servants of the state. Here we have private industry instead of the state, but in a like master-servant relationship with culture.

In the real world—which politicians and advertisers often regard as their private possession—civilization is not the instrument of government and commerce, but vice versa. And people know this. A government seal of approval on a meat carcass may establish its purity, but a government seal on a work of art only establishes its impurity. Likewise, the imprimatur of a commercial sponsor invites skepticism of the vested interest involved. Governments genuinely concerned to develop cultural activity in a community do not reduce culture to the function of a propaganda machine. Likewise, corporations genuinely interested in encouraging their employees to enrich their lives through cultural involvement do not debase the coinage by using it to buy corporate compliance. Their own, far more intelligent, concern is with the long-range future of civilization, both their own and others'.

I cannot help feeling, when I consider what has been left out of our discussions, that our social scientists, or at least too many of them, have sold their souls to Mammon. With the organization of culture, or the role of culture in organization or organizations, as our subject matter, why do we seem to be discussing almost exclusively the use of culture as a tool of business? To put it another way, what are the unexamined assumptions that pay so little heed to other, and surely more important, aspects of our topic? What are the prevailing unconscious biases? We have heard a lot about "deep meaning" here; perhaps we should look at some of the deeper meanings of the attitudes expressed.

To a European, as Luigi Barzini recently pointed out, some of the presuppositions of commerce today seem peculiarly North American— and to a Canadian, some of these seem especially American. For Americans, Barzini generalizes, every day begins with a problem to be solved before sundown. I guess Canadians feel even *more* guilty about sins of omission, but a Canadian may be forgiven for remarking on the U.S. belief that every problem can be solved by some sort of organized attack on it. To those of us outside the famous melting pot, there is something endearing in the American idea of persuasion as the main function of social groups in a democracy. We Canadians tend to leave each other alone. The British go further and often don't speak to each other. Americans, however, like to set up an organization and evangelize all comers.

There was a time when I wondered if the American appetite for culture (shamelessly buying up European art and artists) didn't represent some sort of conscience pang, a compensatory urge for the dehumanizing effects of ruthless capitalism; but I examined my own assumption and came to the conclusion I was merely envious. Yet I still think that probably the American proclivity for neologisms of every sort (I'll cherish "Janusian" and "cogifact" from this meeting) is related more to a compulsive neo-Elizabethan explosion of language than to any need for terminological exactitude. Their love of change is not unrelated, I would hazard, to the attempts we have heard described to make corporations over, including the lives of their employees. By contrast, in this country we're strong on laissez-faire, or letting George do it his way.

Of course, there are also some Canadian biases at work here, since this is an international conference, and we must not slide over the relevant ones. In this country we keep a sharp eye out for systematizers. We don't trust them. We are all separatists at heart, and the systematizers want to homogenize us. We're all regionalists, and they want to centralize us. Our main problems are not those of organization but of communication—how to keep in touch though separated by rivers, ice, tundra, prairies, and Rocky Mountains. Canadians seldom go to meetings—it's impractical—so they use the telephone more than any other people. When I heard Joanne Martin's "surfing analogy," referring to the useful American principle of waiting for the wave before riding it, I couldn't help thinking that the homily is useless in Canada; here we have to make our own waves.

These are some of the differences in our cultures. They may suggest to you, and I hope they do, that there is validity to pluralism. That if we were all the same, civilization would be poorer, and that all attempts to narow the cultural focus or channel it in certain directions are in fact anticultural and seriously antisocial. What we share are not the same or even similar forms of cultural activity, but rather the impulse to create. The organization that encourages that impulse and gives it opportunity, instead of harnessing it for political or commercial ends, will in the long run achieve more than the organization that tries to find and impose a formula.

No government, no industry, no kind of social organization whatever can produce what may come to be known as art, or guarantee its adoption inside the group or outside it. What it can do is remove restraints of right or access, provide a climate in which creativity can occur, and encourage it with financial support. But facilitators, sponsors, distributors, or governors cannot sit down and say, "Now we will create art!" The truth seems to be that art works best when unregulated, since in many cases culture is what people do when they are *not* working. My culture is my individuality, and ain't no company store gonna take that away from me. So far as I can see, organizational culture as it is understood today has far more to do with a lust for organization than with a passion for cultivation.

PART V

DOES ORGANIZATIONAL CULTURE HAVE A FUTURE?

PETER J. FROST

The answer is "yes" or "no" depending on the interpretation.
(Albert Einstein, in Scientific American, April 1950)

We do not presume to have a definitive answer to the question we pose here. Interest and research in this topic has waxed and waned in the past. We are now in a second wave of attention to organizational culture. The chapters in this volume provide considerable evidence that the wave still has plenty of impetus. They detail some of the ground covered thus far, as well as some of the issues and concerns that remain as scholars pursue various facets of the topic.

Important questions remain, however, about the utility of the concept. Have we perhaps said all there is to say about organizational culture? (One noted scholar who has worked with the concept is reputed to have stated, at a recent conference on organizational culture, that it is already overworked and ought to be set aside for the time being.) How does it relate to other major organizational concepts currently of interest to scholars in our field? Is the concept of any use to researchers who grapple with methodological issues in the study of organizations and organizing? Does it provide any assistance to those in our field who are searching for ways to bridge the variety of perspectives that characterize organizational science? In general, does organizational culture have qualities and characteristics that will attract and encourage current and future scholars in our field to devote their intellectual energies to its study over a prolonged period of time?

Karl Weick, in his chapter, provides an insightful affirmation that there ought to be a future for organizational culture. His thoughtful analysis of the concept suggests ways in which working with organizational culture may help us to solve old puzzles about organizations and organizing, as well as to identify new puzzles to be investigated. As he works and plays with the concept of organizational culture, Weick challenges the reader to think about the concept in new and illuminating ways.

Weick's chapter and those that precede it in this volume provide several concrete leads for further work on organizational culture. It is up to those of us who are interested to commit ourselves to serious, caring, sustained, and creative study based on this intriguing concept.

22

THE SIGNIFICANCE OF CORPORATE CULTURE

Karl E. Weick

University of Texas at Austin

> Culture is a blank space, a highly respected, empty pigeonhole. Economists call it "tastes" and leave it severely alone. Most philosophers ignore it—to their own loss. Marxists treat it obliquely as ideology or superstructure. Psychologists avoid it, by concentrating on child subjects. Historians bend it any way they like. Most believe it matters, especially travel agents.
>
> *(Douglas, 1982a: 183)*

The preceding chapters represent a serious effort to insert some substance into the blank space that Douglas describes. The substance that is proposed, however, has an unusual property when it is examined in the context of existing scholarship on organizations. To see this property firsthand, take the following test.

Listed below are four statements extracted verbatim from published articles. The first word in each statement has been deleted. The reader is asked to decide whether the first word in each statement should be "strategy" or "culture."

- _____ evolves from inside the organization—not from its future environment.
- _____ is a deeply ingrained and continuing pattern of management behavior that gives direction to the organization—not a manipulable and controllable mechanism that can be easily changed from one year to the next.
- _____ is a nonrational concept stemming from the informal values, traditions, and norms of behavior held by the firm's managers and employees—not a rational, formal, logical, conscious, and predetermined thought process engaged in by top executives.
- _____ emerges out of the cumulative effect of many informed actions and decisions taken daily and over years by many employees—not a

"one-shot" statement developed exclusively by top management for distribution to the organization.

While each of these four statements is paraphrased several times in the preceding chapters, suggesting that these are four descriptions of culture, in fact all four statements come from a single article, titled "Senior Executives as Strategic Actors" (Greiner, 1983: 13), and the missing word in all four sentences is "strategy."

What I find striking is the plausibility of either term in each sentence. It is as if there were a common set of issues in organizations that some of us choose to call culture and others choose to call strategy.

Consider two definitions of culture that I have paraphrased from Douglas (1982a) and Keesing (1974):

(1) Culture consists of internally consistent patterns of affirmations, restrictions, and permissions that guide people to behave in sanctioned ways, and that enable people to judge others and justify themselves to others.
(2) Culture consists of a person's theory of what his fellows know, believe, and mean, a theory of what code they are following. It is this theory to which the actor refers when interpreting the unfamiliar and creating sensible events.

With those two definitions in mind, now consider Burgelman's (1983: 66-67) description of corporate strategy:

The concept of corporate strategy represents the more or less explicit articulation of the firm's theory about its past concrete achievements. This theory defines the identity of the firm at any moment in time. It provides a basis for the maintenance of this identity and for the continuity in strategic activity. It induces further strategic initiative in line with it. Corporate level managers in large, diversified major firms tend to rise through the ranks, having earned their reputation as head of one or more of the operating divisions. By the time they reach the top management level they have developed a highly reliable frame of reference to evaluate business strategies and resource allocation proposals pertaining to the business of the corporation. Top managers, basically, are strategies-in-action whose fundamental strategic premises are unlikely to change.

Common properties shared by the referents of these three definitions are as follows:

(1) Their objects are theories rather than facts.
(2) They guide both expression and interpretation.
(3) They are retrospective, summarizing patterns in past decisions and actions.
(4) They are embodied in actions of judging, creating, justifying, affirming, and sanctioning.

(5) They summarize past achievements and practices that work.
(6) They provide continuity, identity, and a consistent way of ordering the world (i.e., they resemble a code or cosmology).
(7) They are social, summarizing what is necessary to mesh one's own actions with those of others.
(8) They are often neither completely explicit nor completely articulated, which means that expressions of culture and strategy may vary in specifics.
(9) Their substance is seen most clearly when people confront unfamiliar situations where the routine application of existing understanding is not possible.
(10) They are tenacious understandings that resist change and that are unlikely to change.

Given these points of correspondence, several implications follow. First, strategy and culture may be substitutable for one another.

> If values, beliefs, and exemplars are widely shared, formal symbolic generalizations [strategic plans] can be parsimonious. In effect, a well developed organizational culture directs and coordinates activities. By contrast, if an organization is characterized by many different and conflicting values, beliefs, and exemplars, those whose authority dominates the organization cannot expect that their preferences for action will be carried out voluntarily and automatically. Instead, considerable direction and coordination will be required, resulting in symbolic generalizations formalized in plans, procedures, programs, budgets, and so on [Bresser and Bishop, 1983: 590-591].

If beliefs, values, and exemplars diverge and become more idiosyncratic, there is a greater necessity for detailed planning. But there is also a greater probability that the detailed plans will not be implemented as intended, because they will be interpreted in diverse ways and lead to divergent actions. Thus the substitutability of culture for strategic plans may be asymmetrical. Culture can substitute for plans more effectively than plans can substitute for culture.

Second, there is the intriguing question of whether strategy is an outgrowth of culture, or vice versa. High-tech companies that start as spinoffs manned by a handful of like-minded people may gain their initial coherence either from shared culture or from shared strategy. Shared strategies usually consist of agreements on means (here's what we can do better than others), whereas shared cultures consist of agreements on ends (here's what we believe more fervently than others). Each form of sharing can represent a fundamentally different starting point for new organizations, with different implications for adaptation and adaptability.

Lest it be thought that we are making much ado about nothing, simply because we have omitted structure, it should be noted that structures are patterns that develop along lines of communication. Both strategy and culture can generate structure.

Robert Modrow,[1] in discussions at the UBC culture conference, noted that developmental sequences often start with a set of constraints and contingencies that people treat as a problem. To manage the problem, people act and justify their actions with a focused set of reasons. As activities, justifications, and objects become shared, a routine is established and a structure comes into being.

An example of this sequence seems to be evident in field medical facilities or MASH units. One problem for these units is that they have to treat the enemy as well as allies. This makes it hard to justify what they do by scapegoating the enemy. Instead, they scapegoat the military. They solve problems imposed by constraints through a view of the world in which the military bureaucracy is hopeless and silly. Once this set of beliefs and values is shared, then a workable structure of authority, deference, allocation of resources, and division of labor forms and medical care is reliably delivered. The point is that culture is not a by-product of structure. If anything is a by-product, it is the patterns of communication that stabilize once people agree on what they're doing and why.

A third implication of the apparent similarity between culture and strategy is that both may serve a common function. That function is imposing coherence, order, and meaning. Strategy and culture resemble one another because they both gather bits and pieces of action and find coherence in them. Both assign action to well-justified categories, categories that are outgrowths of interaction. As Douglas (1982b: xx) portrays the process, "There is no form of social life which is not announced, justified and criticised or otherwise made to fit conceptual categories. . . . This work of fitting actions to ideas in the course of negotiations and of bargaining about categories is actually the essential part of social life." Both the concept of strategy and the concept of culture are attempts to capture this categorizing process and its products. Categorizing is done to create meaning, and the ongoing argument over the nature of categories and the assignment of particulars to these categories constitutes the bulk of the action from which cultures and strategies are inferred. Threats, opportunities, problems, and solutions are general categories within which specific events assume meaning. These categories are implied by the theories associated with strategy and culture. Even though a culture or a strategy can create meaning, it is important to remember that neither one is understood or described in its entirety by any single individual.

Having defined culture as "learned ways of coping with experience," Gregory (1983: 364), for example, emphasizes that people act as if they shared culture: "Through trial and error, sometimes through conversation and negotiation, they confirm whether or not their meanings are similar enough to get through social interactions appropriately. Sometimes their expectations are confirmed; at other times they break down, leading to further negotiation or even conflict."

Individuals neither share precisely the same theory nor do they understand equally well different sectors of the culture. Thus, any cultural description is an abstracted composite that will never be contained entirely in one person's account.

While this incomplete representation may seem unfortunate, it can be viewed as a source of adaptive strength (Keesing, 1974: 88). If there is diversity in individual versions of "common" culture, people will respond to slightly different environmental inputs and will preserve slightly different capacities and justifications. This diversity acts as cultural insurance that enables people to respond effectively to shifts in environmental demands.

While strategy and culture may be valued because they provide coherence and meaning, a fourth implication is that this very coherence may be a liability. A coherent statement of who we are makes it harder for us to become something else. Strong cultures are tenacious cultures. Because a tenacious culture can be a rigid culture that is slow to detect changes in opportunities and slow to change once opportunities are sensed, strong cultures can be backward, conservative instruments of adaptation.

Strong cultures may be slower to respond to external change, but because of their coherence, they may also be more forceful actors and better able to create the environments they want. Strong cultures may exhibit action rationality (Brunson, 1982) and be able to bypass the laborious deliberations that are necessary to achieve decision rationality. Strong cultures may be slow, but they may also be powerful. Because they are successful at proaction, they could suffer less from their inherent tendency to be slow to react.

Whether strength is an asset or a liability is likely to depend on variables such as nature of industry, size of organization, and "grain" of environment (Hannan and Freeman, 1983). It is clear that even the strongest cultures can determine their environments for only limited periods of time. As environments change, flexibility becomes a better predictor of effectiveness than does coherence. During these transitions, resilience is severely tested because people alter a known system of meaning with consequences that are unknowable.

A fifth implication amplifies an earlier suggestion (point 9) that people may be most likely to notice culture when their daily routine breaks down and they encounter something that is strange, unfamiliar, or ambiguous. Just as people seem to think before they act only if they're not sure what to do (Thorngate, 1976), they also seem to notice culture only when routine breaks down (Walter, this volume, is sensitive to this issue).

If awareness of culture covaries with the presence of novelty, this could affect what we think organizational culture consists of. If we ask people about their culture in routine times, they should provide cliché-ridden, socially acceptable, brief descriptions ("we want to be the best," "we are a team," "excellence matters").

People who work in organizations that encounter few crises should provide relatively superficial descriptions of culture, since they have few occasions where they are forced to become self-conscious about their assumptions. Bureaucracies, for example, are often said to epitomize routine, which suggests that they have fewer occasions to discover the content of their culture that might tempt both participants and observers to conclude that bureaucracies have no culture (e.g., Wilkins and Ouchi, 1983). Bureaucracies may have just as much culture as other settings, but they have fewer occasions to be made conscious of it. Public bureaucracies would seem to have the most elaborated cultures when their members are interviewed coincident with a change in administration, budget negotiations, changes in funding, or revision of mission. People learn how they have always done things when someone tells them to do things differently.

A problem with accounts collected during times of puzzlement is that puzzles are arousing, and arousal tends to simplify cognition (Holsti, 1971). While people are most conscious of their culture during times of novelty, they may also be least able to detect nuance and complexity. Thus reports collected during times of novelty may be no more complete than accounts collected during times of placidity. If culture is studied during times of change, then observers might learn more if they make respondents feel more secure and less aroused.

A sixth implication derives from the odd mixture of levels found in each of the three definitions. Each definition talks about theories of justification, expression, interpretation, and judging, all of which are individual variables. Yet the processes being described are clearly also social, and in the case of Burgelman refer to sets of organizations.

Part of the value of a concept like culture or strategy is that it enables people to attribute an individual level variable, "meaning," to interdependent collectivities. Investigators basically add up individual stories and discover macro constraints and opportunities. The process by which this occurs is straightforward. If you solicit several stories from several people in the same organization and lay these stories side by side, you will see overlap, similarity, and redundancy among the stories. Overlap can be treated as a first approximation of culture.

The development of overlap might be charted in the following way. If you sort the stories of newcomers to an organization, you would expect to find as many piles as there are stories. Even individuals are not always consistent within themselves, so you would expect to find more stories than people. As newcomers become socialized, you would expect as many piles of similar organizational stories as there are newcomers. Each person begins to have repetitious experiences unique to that person, so the stories generated by each individual hang together, although each person sees and hears about a slightly different organization. As socialization progresses still further, individuals have similar experiences and become substitutable for one another. We would now expect to see fewer piles of stories than there are people who report the stories. There is now orderliness across people, time, and space, thereby representing a true macro-level process (Collins, 1983).

Thus when investigators impose the metaphor of culture, they avoid reification, identify a phenomenon that can be observed in individuals, and preserve their ability to aggregate individual reports into higher-level determinants, constraint that are not evident in any single account. That is a basic form of explanation toward which organizational scholars work but that they find hard to achieve (Knorr-Cetina and Cicourel, 1981).

A seventh implication of working with the concept of culture is that it shows clearly the limitations of a preoccupation with rationality. Rationality is one (and only one) theory about how to express oneself clearly and interpret what others are doing. Rationality is not indigenous to organizations; rather, it is a choice about what to affirm, restrict, and permit. Other choices are possible.

Interestingly, the concept of culture whittles the concept of rationality down to size, not because culture accepts rather than dismisses the reality of symbols, rituals, and ceremonies, but because culture treats the social character of organizations as axiomatic.

Keesing's definition is distinctly social in the sense that culture is not defined by what I do but by what I presume *others* know, believe, and mean when *they* do what *they* do. I act as if they know what they are doing, and I continually test this understanding by acting "in kind." Most of the time I'm successful, but that is for them to judge, as well as me. They judge the appropriateness of my actions just as I specify and sanction the appropriateness of their actions.

Organizations are a form of social life, even though many theories (e.g., rational choice theory) treat rational individuals as if they were nonsocial beings. Individualist models of organizational behavior neglect such variables as social influences on the selection of facts, the negotiation of categories for judgments and choices, and social limits to belief and curiosity. This neglect of social life is evident in the debate over whether organizations "have" culture or "are" cultures. If it is believed that most organizational outcomes can be explained by an individual model, then culture is simply one more constraint, or one more set of premises, that can mislead rational individuals. If organizational actions are seen as inherently social, then action is never separate from culture.

CONCLUSION

The clue to the importance of these essays lies in the second half of the title of the conference that preceded this book: "Organizational Culture and the Meaning of Life in the Workplace." What I have tried to suggest is that the unity found in the preceding chapters lies less in the fact that all of them are about culture than in the fact that all of them are about *meaning*. These chapters could just as well have been about strategy, because both concepts describe ways in which people understand what is happening. Both strategy and culture contain premises, axioms, and first principles that define the nature of appropriate action. Since organizational activity is lived in nine-minute bursts (Mintzberg, 1973), people seldom have time to reflect on what the bursts mean. When culture and strategy are intact, they don't have to. But when cultures rupture, the bursts lose their meaning. That is when we realize that "good managers make meanings for people, as well as money" (Peters and Waterman, 1982: 29). There is no shortage of attention to money. Unfortunately, the same cannot be said for meaning. That is why the concept of culture is significant.

NOTE

1. Robert Modrow is director of the Health Services Planning Program at the University of British Columbia.

References

Abrahamsson, B. (1977) Bureaucracy or Participation: The Logic of Organization. Beverly Hills, CA: Sage.

Abravanel, H. (1983) "Mediatory myths in the service of organizational ideology," in L. R. Pondy et al. (eds.) Organizational Symbolism. Greenwich, CT: JAI.

Ackoff, R. L. (1979) "Obstructions to corporate development," in C. A. Bromlette and M. Mescon (eds.) The Individual and the Future of Organizations. Atlanta: Georgia State University Press.

Adams, G. B. and V. H. Ingersoll (1983) "Managerial metamyths: bridges to organizational boundary crossing." Presented at the invitational conference on Myth, Symbols and Folklore: Expanding the Analysis of Organizations, University of California, Los Angeles.

Adorno, T. and M. Horkheimer (1972) Dialectic of Enlightenment. New York: Herder & Herder.

Alcock, L. (1971) Arthur's Britain: History and Archaeology. Middlesex, England: Penguin.

Alderfer, C. (1968) "Organizational diagnosis from initial reactions to a researcher." Human Organizations 27: 260-265.

Alinsky, S. (1971) Rules for Radicals. New York: Random House.

American Heritage Dictionary (1976) Boston: Houghton Mifflin.

American Psychological Association (1973) Ethical Principles in the Conduct of Research with Human Participants. Washington, DC: Author.

Apel, K. P. (1980) Towards a Transformation of Philosophy (Adey and Frisby, trans.). London: Routledge & Kegan Paul.

Argyris, C. (1952) "Diagnosing defenses against the outsider." Journal of Social Issues 8: 24-34.

———(1957) Personality and Organization. New York: Harper & Row.

———(1961) "Explorations in consulting-client relationships." Human Organization 20: 121-133.

———(1970) Intervention Theory and Method. Reading, MA: Addison-Wesley.

———and D. A. Schon (1978) Organizational Learning: A Theory of Action Perspective. Reading, MA: Addison-Wesley.

Arnold, D. (1970) "A process model of subcultures," pp. 112-118 in D. O. Arnold (ed). The Sociology of Subcultures. Berkeley, CA: Glendessary.

Ashe, G. (1983) A Guidebook to Arthurian Britain. Wellingborough, Northhamptonshire: Aquarian.

Asplund, J. (1970) Om undran infor samhaellet. Stockholm: Argus.

Astley, W. and P. Sachdeva (1984) "Structural sources of intraorganizational power." Academy of Management Review 9: 104-113.

Bailyn, L. (1980) Living with Technology. Cambridge: MIT Press.

———(1983) "Resolving contradictions in technical careers: or what if I like being an engineer." Technology Review 85: 40-47.

Baker, E. (1980) "Managing organizational culture." McKinsey Quarterly (Autumn): 51-61.

Baker, R. L. (1978) "The study of folklore in American colleges and universities." Journal of American Folklore 91: 792-807.

Bandura, A. (1969) Principles of Behavior Modification. New York: Holt, Rinehart & Winston.

Barley, S. R. (1983) "Semiotics and the study of occupational and organizational cultures." Administrative Science Quarterly 28: 393-413.

———(1984) "The professional, the semi-professional, and the machine: the social ramifications of computer based imaging in radiology." Ph.D. dissertation, MIT, Sloan School of Management.

Barnard, C. (1938) The Functions of the Executive. Cambridge, MA: Harvard University Press.

Barnowe, J. T., P. J. Frost, and M. Jamal (1979) "When personality meets organization: exploring influences on choice of business major." Journal of Occupational Psychology 52: 1-10.

Barthes, R. (1967) Elements of Semiology. Boston: Beacon.

Bass, B. M. (1981) Stogdill's Handbook of Leadership. New York: Free Press.

Bateson, G. (1979) Mind and Nature: A Necessary Unity. New York: Dulton.

Bausinger, H. (1969) "Folklorismus in Europa: eine umfrage . . . mit Beitraegen aus Polen, Ungarn, Jugoslawien, Schweiz, Portugal; and Richard M. Dorson, 'Fakelore.' " Zeitschrift fuer Volkskunde 65: 1-64.

Bazgoz, I. (1972) "Folklore studies and nationalism in Turkey." Journal of the Folklore Institute 9: 162-176.

Beck, B. and L. Moore (1984) "Sharing images: metaphor use and business." Presented at the First International Conference on Organizational Symbolism, Lund, Sweden.

Becker, H. S. (1982) "Culture: a sociological view." Yale Review 71: 513-527.

———and B. Geer (1960) Latent culture." Administrative Science Quarterly 5: 303-313.

———(1970) "Participant observation and interviewing: a comparison, pp. 133-142 in W. J. Filstead (ed.) Qualitative Methodology. Chicago: Rand McNally.

Beckhard, R. (1969) Organization Development: Strategies and Models. Reading, MA: Addison-Wesley.

———and R. T. Harris (1977) Organizational Transitions: Managing Complex Change. Reading, MA: Addison-Wesley.

Bednar, D. A. and J. Hineline (1982) "The management of meaning through metaphors." Presented at the annual meeting of the Academy of Management, New York.

Beer, M. (1980) Organization Change and Development. Santa Monica, CA: Goodyear.

Bell, M. J. (1976) "Tending bar at Brown's: occupational role as artistic performance." Western Folklore 35: 93-107.

———(1981) "Making art work." Presented at the Conference on Aesthetic Expressions in the City: Art, Folk Art, and Popular Culture, UCLA, February.

Benne, K. D. (1959) "Some ethical problems in group and organizational consultation." Journal of Social Issues 15: 60-67.

Bennis, W. (1985) Taking Charge. New York: Harper & Row.

Benson, J. K. (1973) "The analysis of bureaucratic-professional conflict: functional versus dialectical approaches." Sociological Quarterly 15: 376-394.

Beres, M. E. and J. D. Porterwood (1979) "Explaining cultural differences in perceived role of work: an international cross-cultural study," in G. England et al. (eds.) Organizational Functioning in a Cross-Cultural Perspective. Kent, OH: Kent State University Press.

Berg, D. N. (1980) "Developing clinical field skills: an apprenticeship model," in C. L. Cooper and C. P. Alderfer (eds.) Advances in Experiential Social Processes. New York: John Wiley.

Berg, P. O. (1983a) "Corporate culture development: the strategic integration of identity, profile and image." Presented at the meeting between the Nordic Schools of Business Administration, Copenhagen, August 24-27.

———(1983b) "Rites, rituals and ceremonies as symbolic operations." Presented at the Organizational Folklore Conference, Santa Monica, CA, March.

———and C. Faucheux (1982) "Symbolic management of organization cultures." INSEAD. (unpublished)

Berger, P. L. and T. Luckmann (1966) The Social Construction of Reality. Garden City, NY: Doubleday.

Bernstein, R. (1983) Beyond Objectivism and Relativism: Science, Hermeneutics, and Praxis. Philadelphia: University of Pennsylvania Press.

Beynon, H. (1973) Working for Ford. Harmondsworth, England: Penguin.

Black, M. (1962) Models and Metaphors. Ithaca, NY: Cornell University Press.

Blau, P. (1955) The Dynamics of Bureaucracy. New York: John Wiley.

———(1967) Exchange and Power in Social Life. New York: John Wiley.

———and W. R. Scott (1962) Formal Organizations. San Francisco: Chandler.

Blauner, R. (1964) Alienation and Freedom: The Factory Worker and His Industry. Chicago: University of Chicago Press.

Blishen, B. and T. Atkinson (1982) Regional and Status Differences in Canadian Values. Toronto: York University, Institute for Behavioral Research.

Bohr, N. (1950) "On the notion of causality and complementarity." Science 11: 54-55.

Boje, D. M., B. Fedor, and M. Rowland (1982) "Myth making: a qualitative step in OD interventions." Journal of Applied Behavioral Science 18(1): 17-28.

Bougon, M., K. E. Weick, and D. Binkhorst (1977) "Cognition in organizations: an analysis of the Utrecht Jazz Orchestra." Administrative Science Quarterly 22: 606-639.

Boulding, K. E. (1956) The Image. Ann Arbor: University of Michigan Press.

Boyd, R. (1979) "Metaphor and theory change: what is 'metaphor' a metaphor for?" in A. Ortony (ed.) Metaphor and Thought. Cambridge: Cambridge University Press.

Bradley, G. W. (1978) "Self-serving biases in the attribution process: a re-examination of the fact or fiction question." Journal of Personality and Social Psychology 36: 56-71.

Braverman, H. (1974) Labor and Monopoly Capital. New York: Monthly Review Press.

Breckenridge, A. C. (1970) The Right to Privacy. Lincoln: University of Nebraska Press.

Bresser, R. K. and R. C. Bishop (1983) "Dysfunctional effects of formal planning: two theoretical explanations." Academy of Management Review 8: 588-599.

Broms, H. and H. Gahmberg (1979) "Myths and language in business strategy." Presented at the Seminar on Strategic Management Practices in Business: Myths, Norms and Reality, St. Maximin Abbey, France, June.

Bronner, S. [ed.] (1982) "Special section: historical methodology in folkloristics." Western Folklore 41: 28-61.

Brown, L. D. and R. Kaplan (1981) "Participative research in the factory," pp. 303-314 in P. Reason and J. Rowan (eds.) Human Inquiry. New York: John Wiley.

Brown, J. D. and R. Tandon (1983) "Ideology and political economy in inquiry: action research and participatory research." Journal of Applied Behavioral Science 19: 277-294.

Brown, R. H. (1973) "Bureaucracy as praxis: toward a political phenomenology of formal organizations." Administrative Science Quarterly 23: 365-382.

———(1976) "Social theory as metaphor: on the logic of discovery for the sciences of conduct." Theory and Society 3: 169-197.

———(1977) A Poetic for Sociology. Cambridge: Cambridge University Press.

Brunsson, N. (1982) "The irrationality of action and action rationality: decisions, ideologies, and organizational actions." Journal of Management Studies 19: 29-44.

Buber, M. (1970) I and Thou. New York: Scribner.

Burawoy, M. (1979) Manufacturing Consent: Changes in the Labor Process Under Monopoly Capitalism. Chicago: University of Chicago Press.

Burgelman, R. A. (1983) "A model of the interaction of strategic behavior, corporate context, and the concept of strategy." Academy of Management Review 8: 61-70.

Burgeois, L. J. and D. B. Jemison (1982) "Analysing corporate culture in its strategic context." Exchange 7: 2.

Burke, W. W. (1982) Organizational Development: Principles and Practices. Boston: Little, Brown.

Burns, T., L. Karlsson, and V. Rus [eds.] (1979) Work and Power: The Liberation of Work and the Control of Political Power. Beverly Hills, CA: Sage.

Burrell, G. and G. Morgan (1979) Sociological Paradigms and Organizational Analysis. London: Heinemann.

Business Week (1980) "Corporate culture: the hard to change values that spell success or failure." Vol. 148, No. 160.

Cafferata, G. L. (1982) "The building of democratic organizations: an embryological metaphor." Administrative Science Quarterly 27: 280-303.

Cameron, K. and D. Whetten (1981) "Perceptions of organization effectiveness across organization life cycles." Administrative Science Quarterly 26: 525-544.

———(1983) "Organizational effectiveness: one model or several?" pp. 1-24 in K. Cameron and D. Whetten (eds.) Organizational Effectiveness: A Comparison of Multiple Models. New York: Academic.

Cammann, C., E. Lawler, G. Ledford, and S. Seashore (1984) Management-Labor Cooperation in Quality of Worklife Experiments: Comparative Analysis of Eight Cases. U.S. Department of Labor, Technical Report 21-26-80-18. Washington, DC: Government Printing Office.

Camp, C. (1977) "State folklorist and folklife programs: a second look." Folklore Forum 10: 26-29.

Canadian Bankers' Association (1983) Bank Facts: The Chartered Banks of Canada, 1983. Toronto: Author.

Carey, G. (1976) "State folklorists and state arts councils: the Maryland pilot." Folklore Forum 9: 1-8.

Carpenter, C. H. (1975) "Many voices: a study of folklore activities in Canada and their role in Canadian culture." Ph.D. dissertation, University of Pennsylvania.

———(1978) "Folklore and government in Canada," pp. 53-68 in K. S. Goldstein (ed.) Canadian Folklore Perspectives. St. John's: Memorial University of Newfoundland.

Cassirer, E. (1944) An Essay on Man. New Haven, CT: Yale University Press.

Chandler, A. D. (1962) Strategy and Structure. Cambridge: MIT Press.

Charlton, W. (1975) "Living and dead metaphors." British Journal of Aesthetics 15(2): 172-178.

Chayes, A. H., B. C. Greenwald, and M. P. Winig (1983) "Managing your lawyers." Harvard Business Review 61: 84-91.

Chinn, J. (1983) "The problem of the polyester quilt: defining folk arts in the field." Presented at the annual meeting of the American Folklore Society, Nashville, October.

Clark, B. (1970) The Distinctive College: Antioch, Reed and Swarthmore. Chicago: Aldine.

———(1972) "The organizational saga in higher education." Administrative Science Quarterly 17: 178-184.

Clegg, S. (1979) The Theory of Power and Organization. Boston: Routledge & Kegan Paul.

———and D. Dunkerly (1980) Organization, Class and Control. Boston: Routledge & Kegan Paul.

Cohen, A. (1976) Two-Dimensional Man. Berkeley: University of California Press.

Collins, C. (1978) "Twenty-four to the dozen: occupational folklore in a hosiery mill." Ph.D. dissertation, Indiana University.

Collins, R. (1983) "Micromethods as a basis for macrosociology." Urban Life 12: 184-202.

Conference Board (1978) Organization Development: A Reconnaissance. New York: Author.

Conklin, H. C. (1955) "Hanunoo color categories." Southwestern Journal of Anthropology 11: 339-344.

Connolly, T., E. Conlon, and S. Deutsch (1980) "Organizational effectiveness: a multiple-constituency approach." Academy of Management Review 5: 211-217.

Conrad, C. (1983) "Organizational power: faces and symbolic forms," pp. 173-194 in L. L. Putnam and M. E. Pacanowsky (eds.) Communication and Organizations. Beverly Hills, CA: Sage.

Crane, D. (1972) Invisible Colleges. Chicago: University of Chicago Press.

Crozier, M. (1964) The Bureaucratic Phenomenon. London: Tavistock.

Cummings, L. L. (1984) "Compensation, culture, and motivation: a systems perspective." Organizational Dynamics (Winter): 33-44.

Daft, R. and J. Wiginton (1979) "Language and organization. Academy of Management Review 4: 179-192.

Dahrendorf, R. (1959) Class and Class Conflict in Industrial Society. Stanford, CA: Stanford University Press.

Dalton, M. (1959) Men Who Manage. New York: John Wiley.

Dandridge, T. C. (1983) "Ceremony as an integration of work and play: the example of Mattel." Presented at the Organizational Folklore Conference, Santa Monica, CA, March.

———I. I. Mitroff, and W. F. Joyce (1980) "Organizational symbolism: a topic to expand organizational analysis." Academy of Management Review 5: 77-82.

Danielson, L. (1972) "The ethnic festival and cultural revivalism in a small midwestern town." Ph.D. dissertation, Indiana University.

Davis, S. D. (1984) Personal communication.

Deal, T. E. and A. A. Kennedy (1982) Corporate Cultures. Reading, MA: Addison-Wesley.

Dearborn, D. C. and H. A. Simon (1958) "Selective perception: a note on the departmental identifications of executives." Sociometry 21: 140-144.

DeBoard, R. (1978) The Psychoanalysis of Organizations. London: Tavistock.

Deetz, S. (1979) "Social well-being and the development of an appropriate organizational response to de-institutionalization and legitimation crisis." Journal of Applied Communication Research 7: 45-54.

———(1982) "Critical-interpretive research in organizational communication." Western Journal of Speech Communication 46: 131-149.

————(1983a) "Keeping the conversation going: the principle of dialectic ethics." Communication 7: 263-288.

————(1983b) "Metaphors and the discursive production and reproduction of organization." Working paper, Southern Illinois University.

————and A. Kersten (1983) "Critical models of interpretive research," pp. 147-171 in L. Putnam and M. Pacanowsky (eds.) Communication and Organizations. Beverly Hills, CA: Sage.

Deetz, S. and D. Mumby (1984) "Metaphor, information, and power." Information and Behavior 1.

Degh, L. (1977-1978) "Grape-harvest festival of strawberry farmers: folklore or fake?" Ethnologica Europaea 10: 114-131.

DeMarco, W. (1984) "Unlocking the meaning of a multi-billion dollar corporation's culture to affect strategic change: a case study." Presented at the First International Conference on Organizational Symbolism, Lund, Sweden.

Denby, P. (1971) "Folklore in the mass media." Folklore Forum 4: 113-125.

Denhardt, R. B. (1981) In the Shadow of Organization. Lawrence, KS: Regents Press.

Devereux, J. (1967) From Anxiety to Method in the Behavioral Sciences. Paris: Mouton.

Dewhurst, C. K. (1983) "Artist-workers in foundaries and factories: esteem and community through symbolic behavior." Presented at the Organizational Folklore Conference, Santa Monica, CA, March.

Dimaggio, P. J. and W. W. Powell (1983) "The iron cage revisited: institutional isomorphism and collective rationality in organizational fields." American Sociological Review 48: 147-160.

Ditton, J. (1977) "Perks, pilerage and the fiddle: the historical structure of invisible wages." Theory and Society 4: 39-71.

Dorson, R. M. (1950a) "Folklore and fake lore." American Mercury 70: 335-343.

————(1950b) "The growth of folklore courses." Journal of American Folklore 63: 345-359.

————(1956) "Paul Bunyan in the news, 1939-1941." Western Folklore 15: 26-29, 179-193, 247-261.

————(1962) "Folklore and the National Defense Education Act." Journal of American Folklore 75: 160-164.

————(1968) The British Folklorists: A History. Chicago: University of Chicago Press.

————(1971) "Applied folklore," pp. 40-42 in D. Sweterlitsch (ed.) Papers on Applied Folklore. Bloomington, IN: Folklore Forum.

————(1972) "Introduction: concepts of folklore and folklife studies," pp. 1-50 in R. M. Dorson (ed.) Folklore and Folklife: An Introduction. Chicago: University of Chicago Press.

————(1978) "Editorial comment: boosterism in American folklore." Journal of the Folklore Institute 15: 181-182.

Douglas, M. (1975) Implicit Meanings: Essays in Anthropology. London: Routledge & Kegan Paul.

————(1982a) "Cultural bias," pp. 183-254 in M. Douglas (ed.) In the Active Voice. London: Routledge & Kegan Paul.

————(1982b) Natural Symbols: Explorations in Cosmology. New York: Pantheon.

Driver, M. J. and A. J. Rowe (1979) "Decision-making styles: a new approach to management decision making," pp. 141-182 in C. Cooper (ed.) Behavioral Problems in Organizations. Englewood Cliffs, NJ: Prentice-Hall.

Dundes, A. (1965) "What is folklore?" pp. 1-3 in A. Dundes (ed.) The Study of Folklore. Englewood Cliffs, NJ: Prentice-Hall.

————(1966) "The American concept of folklore." Journal of the Folklore Institute 3: 226-249.

Dyer, W. G., Jr. (1982) Patterns and Assumptions: The Keys to Understanding Organizational Culture. Office of Naval Research, Technical Report TR-ONR-7.

——(1984) "Tracking cultural evolution in organizations: an historical approach." Working paper, MIT, Sloan School of Management.

Eco, U. (1976) A Theory of Semiotics. Bloomington: University of Indiana Press.

Edelman, M. (1977) Political Language. New York: Academic Press.

Edwards, R. (1979) Contested Terrain: The Transformation of the Workplace in the Twentieth Century. New York: Basic Books.

Elden, M. (1983) "The limits of socio-technical systems as a political change strategy." Working paper, University of Southern California, Center for Effective Organizations.

Eldridge, J.E.T. (1968) Industrial Disputes. London: Routledge & Kegan Paul.

Eminov, S. (1975) "Folklore and nationalism in modern China." Journal of the Folklore Institute 12: 257-277.

Etzioni, A. (1961) A Comparative Analysis of Complex Organizations. New York: Free Press.

Falassi, A. and G. Kligman (1976) Folk-wagen: folklore and the Volkswagen ads." New York Folklore 2: 73-96.

Faulds, S. Selene (1981) " 'The spaces in which we live': the role of folkloristics in the urban design process." Folklore and Mythology Studies, 5: 48-59.

Filley, A. C., R. J. House, and S. Kerr (1976) Managerial Process and Organizational Behavior. Glenview, IL: Scott, Foresman.

Fine, G. A. (1979) "Small groups and culture creation." American Sociological Review 44: 733-745.

——(1983) "Letting off steam? redefining the work environment." Presented at the Organizational Folklore Conference, Santa Monica, CA, March.

——and S. Kleinman (1979) "Rethinking subculture: an interactionist analysis." American Journal of Sociology 85: 1-20.

Firestone, S. (1971) A Dialectic of Sex. New York: Bantam.

Forgus, R. and B. H. Shulman (1979) Personality: A Cognitive View. Englewood Cliffs, NJ: Prentice-Hall.

Fortune (1983) "The corporate culture vultures." Fortune Magazine (October 17): 66-72.

Fox, A. (1966) Industrial Sociology and Industrial relations. London: HMSO, research paper 3.

Fox, R. S., R. Lippit, and E. Schindler-Rainman (1973) Towards a Humane Society. Fairfax, VA: NTL Learning Resources.

Frake, C. O. (1961) "The diagnosis of disease among the Subanum of Mindanao." American Anthropologist 63: 113-132.

Frankl, V. E. (1966) "Logo therapy and existential analysis—a review." American Journal of Psychotherapy 20: 252-260.

Freilich, M. (1970) Marginal Natives: Anthropologists at Work. New York: Harper & Row.

Frost, P. (1980) "Toward a radical framework for practicing organizational science." Academy of Management Review 5: 501-508.

——and L. Krefting (1983) "Multiple metaphors: breaking out of the psychic prisons of organizational life." Presented at the Organizational Folklore Conference, Santa Monica, CA, March.

Gadamer, H.-G. (1975) Truth and Method (G. Barden and J. Cumming, trans.). New York: Seabury.

Gallie, D. (1978) In Search of the New Working Class. Cambridge: Cambridge University Press.

Geertz, C. (1973) The Interpretation of Cultures. New York: Basic Books.

———(1983) Local Knowledge: Further Essays in Interpretive Anthropology. New York: Basic Books.

Georges, R. A. (1969) "Toward an understanding of storytelling events." Journal of American Folklore 82: 313-328.

———(1983) "Folklore," pp. 134-146 in D. Lance (ed.) Sound Archives: A Guide to Their Establishment and Development. International Association of Sound Archives, Special Publication No. 4.

———and M. O. Jones (1980) People Studying People: The Human Element in Fieldwork. Berkeley: University of California Press.

Gephart, R. (1978) "Status degradation and organizational succession: an ethnomethodological approach." Administrative Science Quarterly 23: 553-581.

Geyer, F. R. and D. Schweifzer (1981) Alienation: Problems of Meaning, Theory and Methods. London: Routledge & Kegan Paul.

Ghiselli, E. E. (1971) Explorations in Mangerial Talent. Pacific Palisades, CA: Goodyear.

Giddens, A. (1979) Central Problems in Social Theory. Berkeley: University of California Press.

Gilligan, C. (1982) In a Different Voice: Psychological Theory and Women's Development. Cambridge, MA: Harvard University Press.

Goldman, P. and D. van Houten (1977) "Managerial strategies and the worker," in J. K. Benson (ed.) Organizational Analysis. Beverly Hills, CA: Sage.

Goldner, F. H. and R. R. Ritti (1967) "Professionalization as career immobility." American Journal of Sociology 72: 489-502.

Goodenough, W. W. (1971) Culture, Language and Society. Reading, MA: Addison-Wesley.

———(1981) Culture, Language and Society. Menlo Park, CA: Benjamin Cummings.

Goodman, P. S., M. Bazerman, and E. Colon (1980) "Institutionalization of planned organizational change," in B. Staw and L. L. Cummings (eds.) Research in Organizational Behavior, Vol. 2. Greenwich, CT: JAI.

Gordon, D. (1978) Therapeutic Metaphors. Cupertino, CA: Meta.

Gouldner, A. (1954) Patterns of Industrial Bureaucracy. New York: Free Press.

Governor General (1983) Report on Canadian Mentality Entering 1983, Ottawa.

Green, J. R. (1980) The World of the Worker: Labor in Twentieth-Century America. New York: Hill & Wang.

Greenway, J. (1968) "Folklore and the big money," pp. 283-291 in T. P. Coffin (ed.) Our Living Traditions: An Introduction to American Folklore: New York: Basic Books.

Gregory, K. L. (1983) "Native-view paradigms: multiple cultures and culture conflicts in organizations." Administrative Science Quarterly 28: 359-376.

Greiner, L. E. (1972) "Evolution and revolution as organizations grow." Harvard Business Review (July/August): 37-46.

———(1983) "Senior executives as strategic actors." New Management 1(2): 11-15.

Grinder, J. and R. Bandler (1976) The Structure of Magic. Palo Alto, CA: Science and Behavior Books.

Guerreiro-Ramos, A. (1980) "A substantive approach to organizations," pp. 140-168 in C. Bellone (ed.) Organizational Theory and the New Public Administration. Boston: Allyn & Bacon.

Guskin, A. E. and M. A. Chesler (1973) "Partisan diagnosis of social problems," in G. Zaltman (ed.) Processes and Phenomena of Social Change. New York: John Wiley.

Gutman, H. G. (1977) Work, Culture and Society in Industrializing America. New York: Vintage.

Gutowski, J. A. (1978) "The protofestival: local guide to American folk behavior." Journal of the Folklore Institute 15: 113-132.

Guttman, L. (1968) "A general nonmetric technique for finding the smallest coordinate space for a configuration of points." Psychometrica 33: 469-506.

Habermas, J. (1972) Knowledge and Human Interests (J. Shapiro, trans.). Boston: Beacon.

———(1975) Legitimation Crises (T. McCarthy, trans.). Boston: Beacon.

———(1979) Communication and the Evolution of Society (T. McCarthy, trans.). Boston: Beacon.

Hall, C. S. and G. Lindzey (1970) Theories of Personality. New York: John Wiley.

Hall, R. (1980) "Effectiveness theory and organizational effectiveness." Journal of Applied Behavioral Science 16: 536-545.

Hallowell, A. I. (1955) Culture and Experience. Philadelphia: University of Pennsylvania Press.

Hammer, T. and R. Stern (1984) "Labor representation on company boards of directors effective worker participation." Working paper, Cornell University, New York School of Industrial and Labor Relations.

Hampden-Turner, C. (1981) Maps of the Mind. New York: Macmillan.

Hanami, T. (1981) Labour Relations in Japan Today. Tokyo: Kodansha International.

Hannan, M. T. and J. Freeman (1983) "The population ecology of organizations." American Journal of Sociology 88: 1116-1145.

Haque, A.S.Z. (1975) "The uses of folklore in nationalistic movements and liberation struggles: a case study of Bangladesh." Journal of the Folklore Institute 12: 211-240.

Harris, M. (1981) Cultural Materialism. New York: Crowell.

Hartland, E. S. (1981) "Folklore: What is it and what is the good of it?" in R. M. Dorson (ed.) Peasant Customs and Savage Myths: Selections from the British Folklorists, V. Chicago: University of Chicago Press.

Haug, M. (1975) "The deprofessionalization of everyone." Social Forces 8: 197-213.

———(1977) "Computer technology and the obsolescence of the concept of profession," in M. Haug and J. Dofny (eds.) Work and Technology. Beverly Hills, Ca: Sage.

Hawkes, T. (1977) Structuralism and Semiotics. Berkeley: University of California Press.

Hebdige, D. (1979) Subculture: The Meaning of Style. London: Methuen.

Heidegger, M. (1977) The Question Concerning Technology, and Other Essays. New York: Harper & Row.

Henderson, M. C. (1973) "Folklore scholarship and the sociopolitical milieu in Canada." Journal of the Folklore Institute 10: 97-107.

Herskovits, M. J. (1948) Man and His Works. New York: Knopf.

Heydebrand, W. (1977) "Organizational contradiction in public bureaucracies, pp. 85-109 in T. Benson (ed.) Organizational Analysis: Critique and Innovation. Beverly Hills, CA: Sage.

Hickson, D. J., C. R. Hinings, C. A. Lee, R. A. Schneck, and J. M. Pennings (1971) "A strategic contingency theory of interorganizational power." Administrative Science Quarterly 16: 216-229.

Hirsch, P. (1980) "Ambushes, shootouts, and knights of the round table: the language of corporate takeovers." Presented at the annual meeting of the Academy of Management, Detroit.

———and J. A. Andrews (1984) "Ambushes, shootouts, and knights of the round table: the languages of corporate takeovers," pp. 145-156 in L. R. Pondy et al. (eds.) Organizational Symbolism. Greenwich, CT: JAI.

Holsti, O. R. (1971) "Crisis, stress, and decision making." International Social Science 23: 53-67.

Horney, K. (1945) Our Inner Conflicts. New York: W. W. Norton.

Hrebiniak, L. G. (1981) "The organizational environmental research program: an overview and critique," pp. 338-346 in A. H. Van de Ven and W. F. Joyce (eds.) Perspectives on Organization Design and Behavior. New York: John Wiley.

Hull, F. M., N. S. Friedman, and T. F. Rogers (1982) "The effects of technology on alienation from work." Work and Occupations 9: 31-57.

Humphrey, L. T. (1979) "Small group festive gatherings." Journal of the Folklore Institute 16: 190-201.

Hyman, R. (1972) Strikes. London: Fontana/Collins.

Ingersoll, V. H. and G. B. Adams (1983) "The child is 'father' to the manager: images of organizational behavior in children's literature." Presented at the First International Imagery Conference, Queenstown, New Zealand.

Ingham, G. (1974) Strikes and Industrial Conflict: Britain and Scandinavia. London: Macmillan.

Ivey, S. K. (1977) "Ascribed ethnicity and the ethnic display event: the Melungeons of Hancock County, Tennessee." Western Folklore 36: 85-107.

Janis, I. L. (1972) Victims of Groupthink. Boston: Houghton Mifflin.

Jastrow, R. (1980) God and the Astronomers. New York: Warner.

Jelinek, M., L. Smircich, and P. Hirsch (1983) "Introduction: a code of many colors." Administrative Science Quarterly 28: 331-338.

Jensen, M. C. and R. S. Ruback (1983) "The market for corporate control: the scientific evidence." Journal of Financial Economics 11(1-4): 5-50.

Jones, G. R. (1983) "Transaction costs, property rights, and organizational culture: an exchange perspective." Administrative Science Quarterly 28(3): 454-467.

Jones, M. O. (1975) The Hand Made Object and Its Maker. Berkeley: University of California Press.

———(1980a) "A feeling for form as illustrated by people at work," pp. 260-269 in C. Lindahl and N. Burlakoff (eds.) Folklore on Two Continents: Essays in Honor of Linda Degh. Bloomington, IN: Trickster.

———(1980b) "L.A. add-ons and re-dos: renovation in folk art and architectural design," pp. 325-363 in I.M.G. Quimby and S. T. Swank (eds.) Perspectives on American Folk Art. New York: W. W. Norton.

———(1981) "Introduction: folkloristics and the private and public sectors." Presented at the annual meeting of the California Folklore Society, UCLA, April.

———(1982a) "Another America: toward a behavioral history based on folkloristics." Western Folklore 41: 43-51.

———(1982b) "A strange rocking chair . . . the need to express, the urge to create." Folklore and Mythology 2(1): 4-7.

———(1983) "Interpreting narratives and understanding narrating: ramifications for organizational development." Working paper, University of California, Los Angeles, Folklore and Mythology Program.

———(1984) "Is ethics the issue?" Presented at the Organizational Culture and the Meaning of Life in Workplace Conference, University of British Columbia, Vancouver.

———D. M. Boje, T. Wolfe, M. Moore, R. Krell, S. Gordon, and D. Christensen (1983) "Dealing with symbolic expression in organizations." Presented at the OD Network Conference, Pasadena, CA, October.

Jones, W. T. (1961) The Romantic Syndrome: Towards a New Method in Cultural Anthropology and the History of Ideas. The Hague: Martinus Nijhoff.

Jönsson, S. A. and R. A. Lundin (1977) "Myths and wishful thinking as management tools," in P. C. Nystrom and W. H. Starbuck (eds.) Prescriptive Models of Organizations. Amsterdam: North Holland.

Jung, C. G. (1958) The Undiscovered Self. New York: Atlantic Monthly Press.

———(1959) Archetypes and the Collective Unconscious. Princeton, NJ: Princeton University Press.

———(1965) Memories, Dreams, and Reflections. New York: Vintage.

———(1968) Analytical Psychology. New York: Pantheon.

———(1971) Psychological Types (R.F.C. Hall, trans.). Princeton, NJ: Princeton University Press.

Kamata, S. (1982) Japan in the Passing Lane. New York: Pantheon.

Kanter, R. M. (1977) Men and Women of the Corporation. New York: Basic Books.

Karlsson, A. (1984) "On the symbolic legitimation of strategic change." Presented at the First International Conference on Organizational Symbolism, Lund, Sweden.

Keeley, M. (1984) "Impartiality and participant-interest theories of organizational effectiveness." Administrative Science Quarterly 29: 1-25.

Keesing, R. M. (1974) "Theories of culture." Annual Review of Anthropology 3: 73-97.

Kelman, H. C. (1979) "The types of ethical issues that confront different social science methods." Presented at the Conference on Ethical Issues in Social Science Research, Georgetown University, Washington, DC.

———and D. P. Warwick (1978) "The ethics of social intervention: goals, means, and consequences," in G. Bermant et al., (eds.) The Ethics of Social Intervention. Washington, DC: Hemisphere.

Kerr, C. and A. Siegel (1954) "The inter-industry propensity to strike," in A. Kornhauser et al. (eds.) Industrial Conflict. New York: McGraw-Hill.

Kets de Vries, M.F.R. (1984) The Invisible Hand: Hidden Forces in Organizations. San Francisco: Jossey-Bass.

Kidder, T. (1981) The Soul of a New Machine. Boston: Little, Brown.

Kilmann, R. H. (1982) "Getting control of the corporate culture." Managing 2: 11-17.

———(1983) "A typology of organization typologies: toward parsimony and integration." Human Relations 36: 523-548.

———and M. J. Saxton (1982) "Organization cultures: their assessment and change." (unpublished)

Kimberly, J. (1979) "Issues in the creation of organizations: initiation, innovation, and institutionalization." Academy of Management Journal 22: 437-457.

———and R. H. Miles (1981) The Organizational Life Cycle. San Francisco: Jossey-Bass.

Kitching, J. (1967) "Why do mergers miscarry?" Harvard Business Review (November/December): 84-101.

Klein, B., R. Crawford, and A. A. Alchian (1978) "Vertical integration, appropriable rents, and the competitive contracting process." Journal of Law and Economics 21: 297-326.

Klymasz, R. B. (1975) "Folklore politics in the Soviet Ukraine: perspectives on some recent trends and developments." Journal of the Folklore Institute 12: 177-188.

Knorr-Cetina, K. and A. V. Cicourel [eds.] (1981) Advances in Social Theory and Methodology: Toward an Integration of Micro- and Macro-Sociologies. London: Routledge & Kegan Paul.

Krackhart, D. and R. Stern (1984) "Crisis management and social networks." Working paper, Cornell University, Graduate School of Management.

Krefting, L. A. and P. J. Frost (1984) "The implications of alternative game metaphors for organizational success." Presented at the First International Conference on Organizational Symbolism and Corporate Culture, Lund, Sweden, June.

Krefting, L. A., B. R. Baliga, P. J. Frost, and W. R. Nord (1983) "Failures and successes in managerial interventions: the impact of organizational games." (unpublished)

Kroeber, A. L. and C. Kluckhohn (1952) Culture: A Critical Review of Concepts and Definitions. Harvard University, Papers of the Peabody Museum of American Archaeology and Ethnology, Vol. 47.

———(1963) Culture: A Critical Review of Concepts and Definitions. New York: Vintage.

Kroeber, A. L. and T. Parsons (1958) "The concept of culture and of social systems." American Sociological Review 23: 582-583.

Kuhn, T. (1970) The Structure of Scientific Revolutions. Chicago: University of Chicago Press.

Kunda, G. (1983) "The cultural context of occupational ideology and identity: the case of probation officers." MIT, Sloan School of Management. (unpublished)

Lakoff, G. and M. Johnson (1980) Metaphors We Live By. Chicago: University of Chicago Press.

Langer, S. K. (1953) Feeling and Form. New York: Scribner's.

Larson, M. S. (1977) The Rise of Professionalism. Berkeley: University of California Press.

———(1979) "Professionalism: rise and fall." International Journal of Health Services 9: 607-627.

Laue, J. and G. Cormick (1979) "The ethics of intervention in community disputes," in G. Bermant et al. (eds.) The Ethics of Social Intervention. Washington, DC: Hemisphere.

Lawrence, P. R. (1981) "The Harvard organization and environment research program," pp. 311-337 in A. H. Van de Ven and W. F. Joyce (eds.) Perspectives on Organization Design and Behavior. New York: John Wiley.

———and J. W. Lorsch (1967a) "Differentiation and integration in complex organizations." Administrative Science Quarterly 12: 1-47.

———(1967b) Organization and Environment. Cambridge, MA: Harvard University Press.

Leach, E. (1976) Culture and Communication. Cambridge University Press.

Legman, G. (1962) "Who owns folklore?" Western Folklore 21: 1-11.

Levi-Straus, C. (1964) Structural Anthropology. New York: Basic.

Levy, R. (1980) "Legends of business." Dunns Review: 92-98.

Lewin, K. (1951) Field Theory in Social Science. New York: Harper & Row.

Lippit, R., J. Watson, and B. Westly (1958) The Dynamics of Planned Change. New York: Harcourt Brace Jovanovich.

Lipset, S. M. (1962a) "Trade unions and social structure: I." Industrial Relations 1 (October): 75-89.

———(1962b) "Trade unions and social structure: II." Industrial Relations 1 (February): 98-110.

Litwin, G. H. and R. Stringer (1964) "The influence of organizational climate on human motivation." Presented at a conference on organizational climate, Foundation for Research on Human Behavior, Ann Arbor, MI, March.

Lockwood, Y. (1981) "'Homers': the joy of labor." Presented at the Aesthetic Expressions in the City: Art, Folk Art, and Popular Culture Conference, UCLA, February.

Lodahl, T. M. and S. M. Mitchell (1980) "Drift in the development of innovative organizations, pp. 184-207 in J. R. Kimberly and R. H. Miles, (eds.) The Organization Life Cycle. San Francisco: Jossey-Bass.

Louis, M. R. (1980a) "Organizations as culture-bearing milieux," in L. R. Pondy et al. (eds.) Organizational Symbolism. Greenwich, CT: JAI.

———(1980b) "Surprise and sense-making: what newcomers experience in entering unfamiliar organizational settings." Administrative Science Quarterly 25: 226-251.

———(1981a) "A cultural perspective on organizations: the need for and consequences of viewing organizations as culture-bearing milieux." Human Systems Management 2: 246-258.

———(1981b) " 'The emperor has no clothes': the effect of newcomers on work group culture." Presented at the annual meeting of the Western Academy of Management, Monterey, CA, April.

———(1983) "Culture: yes; organization: no!" Presented at the annual meeting of the Academy of Management, Dallas.

Luhmann, N. (1979) Trust and Power. Chichester, England: John Wiley.

Lundberg, C. C. (1980) "On organization development interventions: a general systems cybernetic perspective," pp. 247-270 in T. Cummings (eds.) Systems Theory for Organization Development. New York: John Wiley.

———(1981) "Characterizing an organization: a metaphor techinque for initial assessment." Journal of Experiential Learning and Simulation 3: 53-56.

Lundberg, C. C. (1984a) "On the feasibility of cultural interventions in organizations." Presented at the Conference on Organizational Culture and the Meaning of Life in the Workplace, University of British Columbia, Vancouver.

———(1984b) "Strategies for organizational transitioning," in R. E. Quinn and J. R. Kimberly (eds.) New Futures: Managing Organizational Transitions. New York: Dow Jones-Irwin.

———and M. Finey (1984) "Emerging models of consultancy," in T. L. Maris (ed.) Managerial Consultation: A Handbook for Students and Practitioners. New York: Reston.

Maccoby, M. (1976) The Gamesman: The New Corporate Leaders. New York: Simon & Schuster.

Manning, P. K. (1979) "Metaphors of the field." Administrative Science Quarterly 24: 660-671.

Maranda, P. and E. K. Maranda (1971) Structural Analysis of Oral Tradition. Philadelphia: University of Pennsylvania Press.

March, J. G. (1980) "How we talk and how we act." David D. Henry Lecture, University of Illinois, Urbana, September 25.

———(1981) "Footnotes to organizational change." Administrative Science Quarterly 26(4): 563-577.

———and H. Simon (1958) Organizations. New York: John Wiley.

Martin, J. (1982a) "Can organizational culture be managed?" Presented at the annual meeting of the Academy of Management, New York.

———(1982b) "Stories and scripts in organizational settings," in A. Hastorf and A. Isen (eds.) Cognitive Social Psychology. New York: Elsevier-North Holland.

———M. S. Feldman, M. J. Hatch, and S. B. Sitkin (1983) "The uniqueness paradox in organizational stories." Administrative Science Quarterly 28: 438-453.

Martin, J. and M. E. Powers (1982) "Truth or corporate propaganda: the value of a good war story," in L. R. Pondy et al. (eds.) Organizational Symbolism. Greenwich, CT: JAI.

Martin, J. and C. Siehl (1983) "Organizational culture and counter culture: an uneasy symbiosis." Organizational Dynamics (Autumn): 52-64.

Martin, J., S. B. Sitkin, and M. Boehm (1983) "Riding the wave: the culture creation process." Research paper no. 730, Stanford University, Graduate School of Business.

———(1984) "Founders and the elusiveness of a cultural legacy." Presented at the Conference on Organizational Culture and the Meaning of Life in the Workplace, University of British Columbia, Vancouver.

Maruyama, M. (1963) "The second cybernetics: deviation-amplifying mutual causal processes." American Scientist 51: 152-179.

Mason, R. and I. Mitroff (1981) Challenging Strategic Planning Assumptions New York: John Wiley.

Mason, R. (1982) Participation and Workplace Democracy. Carbondale: Southern Illinois University Press.

McCannell, D. and J. F. McCannell (1982) The Time of the Sign: A Semiotic Interpretation of Modern Culture. Bloomington: Indiana University Press.

McClelland, D. C. (1961) The Achieving Society. Princeton, NJ: Van Nostrand.

McLuhan, M. (1960) "Myth and mass media," in H. A. Murray (ed.) Myth and Mythmaking. Boston: Beacon.

Meadows, P. (1967) "The metaphors of order: toward a taxonomy of organization theory," pp. 77-103 in L. Gross (ed.) Sociological Theory: Inquiries and Paradigms. New York: Harper & Row.

Merton, R. K. (1957) Social Theory and Social Structure. New York: Free Press.

Meyer, J. W. and B. Rowan (1977) "Institutionalized organizations: formal structure as myth and ceremony." American Journal of Sociology 83: 340-363.

Michael, D. N. and P. H. Mirvis (1977) "Changing, erring, and learning," in P. H. Mirvis and D. N. Berg (eds.) Failures in Organization Development and Change. New York: John Wiley.

Mieder, W. (1982) "Proverbs in Nazi Germany: the promulgation of anti-Semitism and stereotypes through folklore." Journal of American Folklore 95: 435-464.

Mieder, B. and W. Mieder (1977) "Tradition and innovation: proverbs in advertising." Journal of Popular Culture 11: 308-319.

Miles, R. E. and C. C. Snow (1978) Organizational Strategy, Structure, and Process. New York: McGraw-Hill.

Miles, R. H. (1980a) "Findings and implications of organizational life cycles research: a commencement," in J. R. Kimberly and R. H. Miles (eds.) The Organizational Life Cycle. San Francisco: Jossey-Bass.

———(1980b) Macro-Organizational Behavior. Santa Monica, CA: Goodyear.

Miller, D. T. and M. Ross (1975) "Self-serving biases in the attribution of causality: fact or fiction?" Psychological Bulletin 82: 213-255.

Miller, E. J. (1959) " Technology, territory, and time: internal differentiation of complex production systems." Human Relations 12: 245-272.

Miller, W. B. (1965) "Two concepts of authority, " pp. 766-775 in P. Lawrence and J. A. Seiler (eds.) Organizational Behavior and Administration. Homewood, IL: Dorsey.

Miner, J. B. (1980) "Limited domain theories of organizational energy." in C. C. Pinder and L. F. Moore (eds.) Middle Range Theory and the Study of Organizations. Leiden, Netherlands: Martinus Nijhoff.

Mintzberg, H. (1973) The Nature of Managerial Work. New York: Harper & Row.

————(1979) The Structuring of Organizations. Englewood Cliffs, NJ: Prentice-Hall.

Mirvis, P. H. (1982) "Know thyself and what thou art doing." American Behavioral Scientist 26: 177-197.

————(1984a) "Longitudinal study of a takeover target." Working Paper, Boston University.

————(1984b) "Managing research whilst researching managers: being ethical crossing cultural boundaries." Presented at the Organizational Culture and the Meaning of Life in the Workplace Conference, University of British Columbia, Vancouver.

————(1984c) "Negotiations after the sale: the roots and ramifications of conflict in an acquisition." Journal of Occupational Behavior.

————and D. N. Berg (1977) Failures in Organization Development and Change. New York: John Wiley.

Mirvis, P. H. and E. E. Lawler (1984) "Accounting for the quality of work life in a U.S. corporation." Journal of Occupational Behavior 5: 197-212.

Mirvis, P. H. and M. R. Louis (1985) "Self-full research: working through the self as instrument in organizational research," in D. N. Berg and K. K. Smith (eds.) Exploring Clinical Methods for Social Research. Beverly Hills, CA: Sage.

Mirvis, P. H. and S. E. Seashore (1979) "Being ethical in organizational research." American Psychologist 34: 766-780.

Mitroff, I. I. (1974) The Subjective Side of Science. New York: Elsevier.

————(1983a) "Archetypal social systems analysis: on the deeper structure of human system." Academy of Management Review 8: 387-397.

————(1983b) Stakeholders of the Organizational Mind. San Francisco: Jossey-Bass.

————(1984) "Mutual projection in performance and criticism of work in the social sciences: reply to Obert." Academy of Management Review 9: 763-764.

————and R. O. Mason (1982) "Business policy and metaphysics: some philosophical considerations." Academy of Management Review 7: 361-370.

Moe, J. F. (1977) "Folk festivals and community consciousness." Folklore Forum 10: 33-40.

Mohrman, A. M., Jr., and E. Lawler (1983) "The diffusion of QWL as a paradigm shift." Working Paper G81-13(18), University of Southern California, Center for Effective Organizations.

Montagna, P. D. (1968) "Professionalization and bureaucratization in large professional organizations." American Journal of Sociology 74: 138-145.

Moore, L. F. and B.E.F. Beck (1984) "An empirical investigation of the competing values theory of organization and management using smallest space analysis." Working paper, University of British Columbia.

Moore, M. D. (1983) "Old People's Day: drama, celebration, and aging." Unpublished Ph.D. dissertation, University of California at Los Angeles.

Morgan, G. (1980) "Paradigms, metaphors, and puzzle solving in organization theory." Administrative Science Quarterly 25: 605-622.

————(1982) "Cybernetics and organization theory: epistemology or technique?" Human Relations 35: 521-537.

————(1983) "More on metaphor: why we cannot control tropes in administrative science." Administrative Science Quarterly 28: 601-608.

————and L. Smircich (1980) "The case for qualitative research." Academy of Management Review 5(4): 491-500.

Mouzelis, N. (1967) Organization and Bureaucracy. Chicago: Aldine.

Munch, R. (1981) "Talcott Parsons and the theory of action, I: The structure of the Kantian cove." American Journal of Sociology 86: 709-739.

————(1982) "Talcott Parsons and the theory of action, II: The continuity of development." American Journal of Sociology 87: 771-826.

Nickerson, B. (1976) "Industrial lore: a study of an urban factory. Ph.D. dissertation, Indiana University.

Nisbett, R. and L. Ross (1980) Human Inference: Strategies and Shortcomings of Social Judgment. Englewood Cliffs, NJ: Prentice-Hall.

Noble, D. F. (1979) "Social choice in machine design: the case of automatically controlled machine tools," in A. Zimbalist (ed.) Case Studies in the Labor Process. New York: Monthly Review Press.

Nord, W. (1968) "Individual and organizational conflict in an industrial merger: an exploratory study." Proceedings of the Academy of Management, pp. 50-65.

————(1978) "Dreams of humanization and the realities of power." Academy of Management Review 3: 674-679.

————(1984) Personal communication.

Nystrom, P. and W. H. Starbuck (1984) "To avoid organizational crises, unlearn." Organizational Dynamics 12(3): 53-65.

Obert, S. L. (1984) "Archetypal social systems analysis: a reply to Mitroff." Academy of Management Review 9: 757-762.

O'Day, R. (1974) "Intimidation rituals: reactions to reform." Journal of Applied Behavioral Science 10(3): 373-386.

Oinas, F. J. (1975) "The political uses and themes of folklore in the Soviet Union." Journal of the Folklore Institute 12: 157-176.

O'Rourke, P. J. (1982) "How to get a job." Rolling Stone (September 30).

Orthe, C. (1963) Social Structure and Learning Climate: The First Year at the Harvard Business School. Boston: Harvard University Business School, Division of Research.

Ortony, A. (1975) "Why metaphors are necessary and not just nice." Educational Theory 25: 45-53.

Ortutay, G. (1955) "The science of folklore in Hungary between the two World Wars and during the period subsequent to the liberation." Acta Ethnographica 4: 6-89.

Osgood, C., G. J. Suci, and P. Tannenbaum (1957) The Measurement of Meaning. Urbana: University of Illinois Press.

Ouchi, W. G. (1980) "Markets, bureaucracies, and clans." Administrative Science Quarterly 25: 129-141.

————(1981) Theory Z. Reading, MA: Addison-Wesley.

Pascale, R. T. and A. G. Athos (1982) The Art of Japanese Management: Applications for American Executives. New York: Warner.

Perkins, D.N.T., V. F. Nieva, and E. E. Lawler III (1983) Managing Creation. New York: John Wiley.

Perrow, C. (1970) Organizational Analysis: A Sociological View. Belmont, CA: Wadsworth.

Peters, T. (1978) "Symbols, patterns, and settings: an optimistic case for getting things done." Organizational Dynamics 9: 3-23.

————and R. H. Waterman (1982) In Search of Excellence. New York: Harper & Row.

Peterson, R. A. (1979) "Revitalizing the culture concept." Annual Review of Sociology 15: 137-166.

Petrie, H. G. (1979) "Metaphor and learning," in A. Ortony (ed.) Metaphor and Thought. Cambridge: Cambridge University Press.

Pettigrew. A. (1979) "On studying organizational cultures." Administrative Science Quarterly 24(4): 570-581.

Pfeffer, J. (1981a) "Management as symbolic action: the creation and maintenance of organizational paradigms," in L. Cummings and B. Staw (eds.) Research in Organizational Behavior, Vol. 3. Greenwich, CT: JAI Press.

———(1981b) Power in Organizations. Marshfield, MA: Pittman.

———and G. R. Salancik (1978) The External Control of Organization: A resource dependence perspective. New York: Harper & Row.

Piggott, S. (1974) The Druids. Middlesex, England: Penguin.

Pinder, C. C. and V. W. Bourgeois (1982) "Controlling tropes in administrative science." Administrative Science Quarterly 27: 641-652.

Pinkard, T. P. (1979) "What constitutes an invasion of privacy and confidentiality in social science research?" Presented at the Conference on Ethical Issues in Social Science Research, Georgetown University, Washington, DC.

Pondy, L. R. (1982) "The role of metaphors and myths in organization and the facilitation of change," pp. 157-166 in L. R. Pondy et al. (eds.) Organizational Symbolism. Greenwich, CT: JAI.

Putman, L. and M. Pacanowsky (1983) Communication and Organizations. Beverly Hills, CA: Sage.

Quinn, R. E. (1984) "Applying the competing values approach to leadership: towards an integrative framework," in J. G. Hunt et al. (eds.) Managerial Work and Leadership: International Perspectives. New York: Pergamon.

———and D. Anderson (1984) "Formalization as crisis: a transition planning program for young organizations," in J. R. Kimberly and R. E. Quinn (eds.) New Futures: The Challenge of Transition Management. New York: Dow Jones-Irwin.

Quinn, R. E. and K. Cameron (1983) "Organizational life cycles and shifting criteria of effectiveness: some preliminary evidence." Management Science 29: 33-51.

Quinn, R. E. and R. H. Hall (1983) "Environments, organizations, and policy makers: towards an integrative framework," in R. H. Hall and R. E. Quinn (eds.) Organization Theory and Public Policy. Beverly Hills, CA: Sage.

Quinn, R. E. and Kimberly J. R. (1984) "The management of transitions," in J. R. Kimberly and R. E. Quinn (eds.) New Futures: The Challenge of Transition Management. New York: Dow Jones-Irwin.

Quinn, R. E. and J. Rohrbaugh (1983) "A spatial model of effectiveness criteria: towards a competing values approach to organizational effectiveness." Management Science 29: 363-377.

Radcliffe-Brown, A. (1952) Structure and Function in Primitive Society. London: Cohen & West.

Reuss, R. A. and J. Lund [eds.] (1975) Roads into Folklore: Festschrift in Honor of Richard M. Dorson. Bloomington, IN: Folklore Forum.

Richards, I. A. (1936) The Philosophy of Rhetoric. London: Oxford University Press.

Ricoeur, P. (1971) "The model of the text: meaningful action considered as a text." Social Research 39: 529-562.

———(1977) The Rule of Metaphor. Toronto: University of Toronto Press.

Riley, P. (1983) "A structurationist account of political cultures." Administrative Science Quarterly 28: 414-437.

Rinn, J. L. (1965) "Structure of phenomenal domains." Psychological Review 72: 445-466.

Roethlisberger, F. J. and W. J. Dickson (1939) Management and the Worker. Cambridge, Harvard University Press.

Rogers, C. (1961) On Becoming a Person. Boston: Houghton Mifflin.

Rokeach, M. (1968) Beliefs, Attitudes, and Values. San Francisco: Jossey-Bass.

————(1973) The Nature of Human Values. New York: Free Press.

Rorty, R. (1982) Consequences of Pragmatism. Minneapolis: University of Minnesota Press.

Rose, M. (1975) Industrial Behaviour: Theoretical Developments Since Taylor. Harmondsworth: Penguin.

Rothenberg, A. (1979) The Emerging Goddess: The Creative Process in Art, Science and Other Fields. Chicago: University of Chicago Press.

Runcie, J. F. (1983) " 'Deviant behavior': achieving autonomy in a machine-paced environment." Presented at the Organizational Folklore Conference, Santa Monica, CA, March.

Sahlins, M. (1976) Culture and Practical Reason. Chicago: University of Chicago Press.

Salaman, G. (1981) Class and the Corporation. London: Fontana.

Sales, A. L. and P. H. Mirvis (1984) "When cultures collide: issues in acquisition," in J. R. Kimberly and R. E. Quinn (eds.) Managing Organizational Transitions. Homewood, IL: Richard D. Irwin.

Salmans, S. (1983) "New vogue: corporate culture." New York Times (January 7).

Sarason, S. B. (1972) The Creation of Settings and the Future Societies. San Francisco: Jossey-Bass.

Sathe, V. (1983) "Some action implications of corporate culture: a manager's guide to action." Organizational Dynamics (Winter): 4-23.

Sathe, V. (1982) "Managerial action and corporate culture." Harvard Business School. (unpublished)

Savage, G. T. (1982) "Organizations as conflicting small group cultures." Presented at the annual meeting of the Speech Communication Association, Louisville, KY, November.

Schein, E. H. (1981) "Does Japanese management style have a message for American managers? Sloan Management Review 23(1): 55-68.

————(1983a) "On organizational culture." Presented at the Academy of Management Convention, Dallas, TX.

————(1983b) "The role of the founder in creating organizational culture." Organizational Dynamics (Summer): 13-28.

————(1985) Organizational Culture. San Francisco: Jossey-Bass.

Scholz, C. (1984) "The dualism between strategic fit and corporate culture." Presented at the First International Conference on Organizational Symbolism, Lund, Sweden.

Schon, D. A. (1979) "Generative metaphor: a perspective on problem-setting in social policy," in A. Ortony (ed.) Metaphor and Thought. Cambridge: Cambridge University Press.

————(1982) "Organizational learning: a research perspective." Working paper, MIT.

————(1983) The Reflective Practitioner. New York: Basic Books.

Schrank, R. (1978) Ten Thousand Working Days. Cambridge: MIT Press.

Schroyer, T. H. (1973) The Critique of Domination: The Origin and Development of Critical Theory. Boston: Beacon.

Schutz, A. (1967) The Problem of Social Reality. The Hague: Martinus Nijhoff.

Schwartz, G. (1972) Youth Culture. Reading, MA: Addison-Wesley.

————and D. Merten (1968) "Social identity and expressive symbols: the meaning of an initiation ritual." American Anthropologist 70: 1117-1131.

Schwartz, H. and S. Davis (1981) "Matching corporate culture and business strategy." Organizational Dynamics (Summer): 30-48.

Seashore, S. E. (1976) "The design of action research," in A. W. Clark (ed.) Experimenting with Organization Life: The Action Research Approach. New York: Plenum.

Seeger, C. (1962) "Who owns folklore? A rejoinder." Western Folklore 21: 93-100.

Selznick, P. (1949) TVA and the Grass Roots. Berkeley: University of California Press.

——(1957) Leadership and Administration. Evanston, IL: Row Peterson.

Shepard, J. M. (1971) Automation and Alienation. Cambridge, MA: MIT Press.

Siehl, C. (1984) "After the founder: a potential opportunity to manage culture." Presented at the Conference on Organizational Culture and the Meaning of Work Life, Vancouver.

——and J. Martin (1982) "The management of culture: the need for consistency and redundancy among cultural components." Presented at the annual meeting of the Academy of Management, Boston.

——(1983) "Measuring organizational culture. Working paper, Stanford University, Graduate School of Business.

Silverman, D. (1970) The Theory of Organizations. New York: Basic Books.

Silverzweig, S. and R. F. Allen (1976) "Changing the corporate culture." Sloan Management Review (Spring): 33-49.

Smircich, L. (1983a) "Concepts of culture and organizational analysis." Administrative Science Quarterly 28(3): 339-358.

——(1983b) "Organizations as shared meanings," in L. R. Pondy et al. (eds.) Organizational Symbolism. Greenwich, CT: JAI.

——(1983c) "Studying organizations as cultures," in G. Morgan (ed.) Beyond Method: Social Research Strategies. Beverly Hills, CA: Sage.

——(1984) "Is the concept of culture a paradigm for understanding organizations and ourselves?" Presented at the Conference on Organizational Culture and the Meaning of Work Life, University of British Columbia, Vancouver.

——and C. I. Stubbart (1983) "Strategic management in an enacted world." University of Massachusetts, Amherst. (unpublished)

Smith, K. (1984) "Rabbits, lynxes, and organization transitions," in J. R. Kimberly and R. E. Quinn (eds.) New Futures: The Challenge of Transition Management. New York: Dow Jones-Irwin.

——and V. M. Simmons (1983) "A Rumpelstiltskin organization: metaphors on metaphors in filed research." Administrative Science Quarterly 28: 377-392.

Snow, L. F. (1979) "Mail order magic: the commerical exploitation of folk belief." Journal of the Folklore Institute 16: 44-74.

Snyder, L. L. (1951) "Nationalistic aspects of the Grimm brothers' fairy tales." Journal of Social Psychology 33: 209-223.

Spender, J. C. (1983) "Executive myth-making: industry-level responses to uncertainty." University of California, Los Angeles. (unpublished)

Sproull, L. S. (1979) "Beliefs in organizations," in P. Nystrom and W. H. Starbuck (eds.) Handbook of Organizational Design. New York: Oxford University Press.

Starbuck, W. H. (1976) "Organizations and their environment," in M. P. Dunkette (ed.) Handbook of Industrial and Organizational Psychology. Chicago: Rand McNally.

Starr, P. (1983) The Social Transformation of American Medicine. New York: Basic Books.

Steiner, G. (1975) After Babel: Aspects of Language and Translations. Oxford: Oxford University Press.

Stekert, E. (1966) "Cents and nonsense in the urban folksong movement: 1930-1966," pp. 153-168 in B. Jackson (ed.) Folklore and Society: Essays in Honor of Benjamin A. Botkin. Hatboro, PA: Folklore Associates.

Stevrin, P. (1983) Samhaellelig Problemlosning—en metforisk Aktivitet. Greenwich, CT: JAI.

Stewart, W. (1982) Towers of Gold, Feet of Clay: The Canadian Banks. Toronto: Collins.

Stonich, P. J. (1984) "The performance measurement and reward system: critical to strategic management." Organizational Dynamics (Winter): 45-57.

Sullenberger, T. E. (1974) "Ajax meets the Jolly Green Giant." Journal of American Folklore 84: 53-65.

Susman, G. and R. Evered (1978) "An assessment of the scientific merits of action research." Administrative Science Quarterly 23: 582-603.

Swanson, C. (1978) "Joking at the office: coffee-break humor." Folklore Forum 11: 42-47.

Tavris, C. (1983) "Edward T. Hall: a social scientist with a gift for solving human problems" [interview]." Geo (March): 10-16.

Terkel, S. (1974) Working. New York: Pantheon.

Teske, R. T. (1977) "On the making of bobonieres and marturia in Greek-Philadelphia: commercialism in folk religion." Journal of the Folklore Institute 14: 151-158.

Thompson, J. D. (1967) Organizations in Action. New York: McGraw-Hill.

Thorngate, W. (1976) "Must we always think before we act?" Personality and Social Psychology Bulletin 2: 31-35.

Tichy, N. M. (1982a) "Corporate culture as a strategic variable." Presented at the annual meeting of the Academy of Management, New York.

———(1982b) "Managing change strategically: the technical, political, and cultural keys." Organizational Dynamics (Autumn): 59-80.

Tolbert, P. and L. Zucker (1983) "Institutional sources of change in organizational structure: the diffusion of civil service reform, 1880-1930." Administrative Science Quarterly 28: 22-39.

Trice, H. M. and J. M. Beyer (1983) "Studying organizational cultures through rites and ceremonials." Working paper no. 557, Cornell University, School of Industrial and Labor Relations.

Trist, E. L. and K. W. Bamforth (1951) "Some social and psychological consequences of the longwall method of coal-getting." Human Relations 4: 1-38.

Turner, B. A. (1972) Exploring the Industrial Subculture. New York: Herder & Herder.

Turnstall, W. B. (1983) "Cultural transition at AT&T." Sloan Management Review 25(1): 1-12.

Tyler, S. (1969) Cognitive Anthropology. New York: Holt, Rinehart & Winston.

Van de Ven, A. (1983) Book review. Administrative Science Quarterly 28: 621-624.

Van Maanen, J. (1979) "The self, the situation, and the rules of interpersonal relations," in W. Bennis et al. (eds.) Essays in Interpersonal Relations. Homewood, IL: Dorsey.

———and S. R. Barley (1984) "Occupational communities: culture and control in organizations," in B. M. Staw and L. L. Cummings (eds.) Research in Organizational Behavior, Vol. 6. Greenwich, CT: JAI.

Vickers, G. (1978) "Rationality and intuition" pp. 143-164 in J. Wechsler (ed.) On Aesthetics in Science. Cambridge: MIT Press.

Vinton, K. (1983a) "Humor in the workplace: it's more than telling jokes." Presented at the annual meeting of the Western Academy of Management, Santa Barbara, CA, March.

———(1983b) "The small, family-owned business: a unique organizational culture." Ph.D. dissertation, University of Utah, Graduate School of Business.

Wallace, M. and A. L. Kallenberg (1982) "Industrial transformation and the decline of craft." American Sociological Review 47: 307-324.

Walter, G. A. (1982) "The morning after: symposium on mergers and acquisitions." Cornell Executive (Summer): 15-19.

———(1984) "Organizational development and individual rights: symposium on ethics." Journal of Applied Behavioral Science 20(4).

Walton, R. E. and D. P. Warwick (1973) "The ethics of organization development." Journal of Applied Behavioral Science 9: 681-698.

Wang, B. (1935) "Folksongs as regulators of politics." Sociology and Social Research 20: 161-166.

Warner, W. L. and J. Low (1947) The Social System of the Modern Factory. New Haven, CT: Yale University Press.

Warwick, D. P. (1975) A Theory of Public Bureaucracy. Cambridge, MA: Harvard University Press.

Watzlawick, P., J. H. Weaklund, and R. Fisch (1974) Change: Principles and Problem Formulation. New York: W. W. Norton.

Weber, M. (1968) Economy and Society (G. Roth and C. Wittach, trans.). Berkeley: University of California Press.

Weick, K. (1979) The Social Psychology of Organizing. Reading, MA: Addison-Wesley.

———(1983) Letters to the editor. Fortune (October 17): 27.

Weiner, B., I. Frieze, A. Kulka, L. Reed, S. Rest, and R. M. Rosenbaum (1971) Perceiving the Causes of Success and Failure. Morristown, NJ: General Learning Press.

Wexler, M. N. (1983) "Pragmatism, interactionism and dramatism: interpreting the symbol in organizations," pp. 237-253 in L. R. Pondy et al. (eds.) Organizational Symbolism. Greenwich, CT: JAI.

White, O. F. and C. J. McSwain (1983) "Transformational theory and organizational analysis," pp. 292-305 in G. Morgan (ed.) Beyond Method: Strategies for Social Research. Beverly Hills, CA: Sage.

Whorf, B. L. (1956) Language, Thought and Reality. Cambridge: MIT Press.

Whyte, W. H. (1956) The Organization Man. New York: Simon & Schuster.

Wilkins, A. L. (1978) "Organizational stories as an expression of management philosophy: implications for social control in organizations." Ph.D. dissertation, Stanford University.

———(1983a) "The culture audit: a tool for understanding organizations." Organizational Dynamics (Autumn): 24-38.

———(1983b) "Organizational stories as symbols which control the organization," in L. Pondy et al. (eds.) Organizational Symbolism. Greenwich, CT: JAI.

———and W. G. Ouchi (1983) "Efficient cultures: exploring the relationship between culture and organizational performance." Administrative Science Quarterly 28: 468-481.

Williamson, O. E. (1975) Markets and Hierarchies. New York: Free Press.

———(1981) "The economics of organization: the transaction cost approach." American Journal of Sociology 87: 548-577.

Willis, P. (1977) Learning to Labor. New York: Columbia University Press.

Wilson, W. A. (1976) Folklore and Nationalism in Modern Finland. Bloomington: Indiana University Press.

Winer, B. J. (1962) Statistical Principles in Experimental Design. New York: McGraw-Hill.

Witkin, W. R. and P. O. Berg (1984) "Organization symbolism: towards a theory of action in organizations." Presented at the First International Conference on Organization Symbolism, Lund, Sweden.

Woodward, J. (1965) Industrial Organization: Theory and Practice. Oxford: Oxford Universtiy Press.

Wynn, E. H. (1976) "Office conversation as an information medium." Xerox Palo Alto Research Center, December.

Yen, A. C. (1964) "Red China's use of folklore." Literature East & West 8: 72-87.
Yoder, D. (1963) "The folklife studies movement." Pennsylvania Folklife 13: 43-56.
———[ed.] (1976) American Folklife. Austin: University of Texas Press.
Zemljanova, L. (1964) "The struggle between the reactionary and the progressive in comparative American folkloristics." Journal of the Folklore Institute 1: 130-144.

About the Authors

Guy B. Adams is a member of the faculty in the Graduate Program in Public Administration at Evergreen State College, Olympia, Washington. His current research focuses on symbolism and mythology in organization studies. He completed his Ph.D. in public administration at George Washington University.

Anthony G. Athos, formerly Jessie Isidor Straus Professor of Business Administration at Harvard Business School, is now an independent consultant, lecturer, and writer based in Gloucester, Massachusetts. Coauthor of the bestselling *The Art of Japanese Management,* he is now at work on his next book, tentatively titled *Decision, Choice, Change, and Transformation.*

Stephen R. Barley is an Assistant Professor of Organizational Behavior in the School of Industrial and Labor Relations at Cornell University, Ithaca, New York. His research centers on the study of how new technologies influence the social organization of work and occupations. He recently completed an ethnographic study of computerized medical imaging technologies used by radiology departments in community hospitals and is pursuing the application of linguistic techniques to the study of organizational life. He received his Ph.D. in organization studies from MIT.

Brenda E.F. Beck is Professor of Anthropology at the University of British Columbia. Her interest in work cultures is international. In addition to her current focus on bank managers in Canada, she has spent much time doing research in India. She holds a D.Phil. from Oxford University.

Per-Olof Berg is Associate Professor in the Department of Business Administration, University of Lund, Sweden. His research interests include the analysis of methods for corporate identity development and organizational diagnosis. He is the author of "Emotional Structures in Organizations."

Michael Boehm is a doctoral student in organizational behavior at the Stanford Graduate School of Business. His research interests include corporate culture, the relationship between structure and socially constructed reality, and myths of rationality in organizations. His background includes research on cognition and a B.A. in anthropology, both at Northwestern University.

Charles Butcher is owner and Chairman of the Board of the Butcher Polish Company, manufacturers of chemical specialties used in the cleaning and maintenance of buildings. He is also owner and President of the Lazy Eight, a research and development company. For some time, he has been interested in how business leaders affect the ethical behavior of the companies they run.

Thomas C. Dandridge is an Associate Professor with joint appointments in the School of Business and the Rockefeller College of Public Affairs and Policy at the State University of New York at Albany. He obtained his Ph.D. from UCLA; his dissertation was on organizational symbolism. He has since continued to write on that topic and publishes an informal newsletter on organizational symbolism and culture.

Robert J. Davies is a Visiting Associate Professor in the Department of Management, the Graduate School of Business New York University. His current research interests include the comparative analysis of industrial relations institutions and economic performance, and the human resource/industrial relations implications of different corporate competitive strategies. He received his Ph.D. from Warwick University, England.

Stanley Deetz is an Associate Professor of Communication at Rutgers University. His research interests include symbols and their relation to systems of domination and participatory skill development. His is the author of *Managing Interpersonal Interaction* and has written several articles on communication and organizations.

Peter J. Frost is an Associate Professor in the Faculty of Commerce and Business Administration at the University of British Columbia. He has published numerous studies on organizational effectiveness, goal setting, and political behavior. He has also coauthored books on organizational stories (*Organizational Reality*) and on symbolism (*Organizational Symbolism*). He recently completed a book with L. L. Cummings entitled *Publishing in the Organizational Sciences*. He is interested in the implications for meaning in organizational life of symbolism, particularly as revealed through the investigation of myths, metaphors, power, and charisma. He is currently concentrating his research efforts in those areas. An avowed fan of British comedy and an avid movie watcher, he received his Ph.D. in industrial relations at the University of Minnesota.

Virginia Hill Ingersoll is a member of the faculty in the Graduate Program in Public administration at Evergreen State College, Olympia, Washington. Her current research interest is the relationship between information technology and organizational culture. She received her Ph.D. in communications and organizational psychology from the University of Illinois.

Michael Owen Jones is a Professor of History and Folklore at UCLA. Formerly vice-chair and acting chair of the teaching program in folklore and mythology, he is now Director of the Center for the Study of Comparative Folklore and Mythology, an organized research unit with an extensive library and several archives. He is perhaps best known for his many works on folk art and aesthetics and occupational folklore. His current research interests concern symbolic behavior in organizations, particularly rituals, celebrations, narratives, and artistic expression as these relate to such expectations of organizational life as larger purpose, fellowship, and personal satisfaction.

Linda A. Krefting is an Associate Professor in the area of management at Texas Tech University. After earning a Ph.D. in industrial relations from the University of Minnesota, she taught at the University of Kentucky and served as a faculty fellow in the Office of the Secretary of the Interior in Washington, D.C. In addition to the use of metaphors in understanding organizational culture, her research has addressed such issues as the sex typing of jobs and the meaningfulness of pay increases.

Meryl Reis Louis is an Associate Professor in the School of Management and Center for Applied Social Science at Boston University. Her research interests concern the sociology of social science, sense making in work settings, career transitions, workplace cultures, and the implementation of management information systems. For the past eight years she has been studying "life after MBA school" with a panel of graduates from several universities. One of her current interests is in identifying organizational forms that facilitate a sense of empowerment. The notion of responsible membership is central to this work.

Craig C. Lundberg is a Professor of Management and Organization in the Graduate School of Business Administration, University of Southern California. He has authored numerous articles on organizational change and managerial behavior, and consults frequently on organizational design, development, and strategy. He is the Editor of the *Organizational Behavior Teaching Review* and serves on the editorial boards of *New Management* and *Organizational Dynamics*.

Joanne Martin is an Associate Professor of Organizational Behavior and Sociology at the Graduate School of Business, Stanford University. Her research interests include inequality and distributive injustice, organizational cultures, and methodological orthodoxes. She received her Ph.D. in social psychology from Harvard University.

Michael R. McGrath is an Assistant Professor of Management and Organization in the School of Business Administration at the University of Southern California. His research interests focus on issues of organizational effectiveness and managerial decision making. He is currently collaborating on a book with Thomas Cummings on enhancing the effectiveness of transorganizational systems. He received his Ph.D. from the Rockefeller College of Public Affairs and Policy at SUNY, Albany.

Philip H. Mirvis is an Associate Professor in the School of Management and Center for Applied Social Science, Boston University. His research interests concern research ethics, field relationships, and the use of the self as a research instrument. The substantive areas of his current studies include the quality of work life, work in the nonprofit sector, the human impact of new technology, and human issues in mergers and acquisitions. His most recent publication is a map and guidebook to *Work in the 20th Century.* His current consulting work is concerned with human and economic development in the Third World.

Larry F. Moore is an Associate Professor and the Director of Ph.D. and M.Sc. programs in the Faculty of Commerce and Business Administration at the University of British Columbia, Vancouver. His research interests focus on occupational attitudes of people at work, organizational theory building, human resource planning, and management style. He received his DBA and MBA from the University of Colorado.

Mavor Moore, former chair (1979-1983) of the Canada Council for the Arts, has had a distinguished career in theatre, radio, television, and journalism as playwright, performer, director, producer, executive, and critic. He has been active on the boards of many organizations, including the Center for Inter-American Relations in New York. Professor Emeritus of York University in Toronto and now Adjunct Professor of Fine Arts at the University of Victoria, British Columbia, he chaired the 1984 world conference on the "The Arts and International Communication" at Banff, Alberta.

Walter R. Nord is a Professor of Organizational Psychology in the School of Business, Washington University. His current research interests include critical theory and organization analysis, behavior modification in organizations, work values, and innovation. He received his M.S. from Cornell University and his Ph.D. in psychology from Washington University.

Robert E. Quinn is Executive Director of the Institute for Government and Policy Studies at Rockefeller College, SUNY, Albany. His research interests center on organizational change and effectiveness. He and his colleagues have played a major role in developing the Competing Values Research Program at Albany.

Caren Siehl is an Assistant Professor of Management and Organization at the University of Southern California. Her research interests focus on organizational culture, including the management of culture and the transmission of cultural values by first-line and upper-level managers. She is currently exploring the relationship between customer service and culture. She received her Ph.D. from Stanford University.

Sim B. Sitkin is a Ph.D. candidate in organizational behavior at the Graduate School of Business, Stanford University. His research interests center on the interaction between formal organizational policies and structures and individual behavior and beliefs. His specific research activities have concerned secrecy in organizations, organizational culture, mergers and acquisitions, and structural relations in organizations. He received his M.A. in educational administration from the Graduate School of Education, Harvard University.

Linda Smircich is making a meaningful life as a faculty member at the School of Management, University of Massachusetts, Amherst. In her teaching and scholarly writing she has the aim of expanding the ways people think about organizations and their possibilities. She is particularly interested in developing interpretive and radical humanist perspectives on organizational and management theory issues. Her interests in assumptions, epistemology, and symbolism are expressed in her research on leadership and strategic management, organizational change, culture, and the nature of inquity.

John Van Maanen is Professor of Organization Studies in the Sloan School of Management at MIT. He spent one year (1983-1984) on sabbatical in England as a Fulbright Senior Research Fellow in the Department of Sociology, University of Surrey. He has published a number of books and articles in the general area of occupational sociology. Cultural descriptions figure prominently in his studies of the work worlds of patrol officers on city streets in the United States, fishermen of the northeastern Atlantic, and, most recently, police detectives and their "guv'nors" in London.

Gordon A. Walter is an Associate Professor of Organization and Management at the University of British Columbia. He received his Ph.D. in business from the University of California at Berkeley. His research interests include psychoanalytic applications to organizational behavior, individual change, ethics, organizational change, leadership, strategy implementation, and mergers and acquisitions.

Karl E. Weick, who holds the Harkins & Company Centennial Chair in Business Administration at the University of Texas at Austin, is also Editor of the *Administrative Science Quarterly.* He was trained in psychology at Ohio State University, where he received his Ph.D. Since graduating, he has been associated with faculties at Purdue University, the University of Minnesota, and Cornell University. He studies such topics as how people make sense of confusing events, the effects of stress on thinking and imagination, techniques for observing complicated events, self-fulfilling prophecies, the consequences of indeterminacy in social systems, and substitutes for rationality.

Nan Weiner is a Visiting Assistant Professor with the University of Toronto's Faculty of Management Studies. Her research interests include managerial succession, organizational reward systems, and culture. She received her Ph.D. from the University of Minnesota in industrial relations.